Loyola's Greater Narrative

aus
american university studies

Series II
Romance Languages and Literature

Vol. 229

PETER LANG
New York • Washington, D.C./Baltimore • Bern
Frankfurt am Main • Berlin • Brussels • Vienna • Oxford

Frédéric Conrod

Loyola's Greater Narrative

The Architecture of the *Spiritual Exercises* in Golden Age and Enlightenment Literature

PETER LANG
New York • Washington, D.C./Baltimore • Bern
Frankfurt am Main • Berlin • Brussels • Vienna • Oxford

Library of Congress Cataloging-in-Publication Data

Conrod, Frédéric.
Loyola's greater narrative: the architecture of the spiritual exercises
in golden age and Enlightenment literature / Frédéric Conrod.
p. cm. — (American university studies. Series II:
Romance languages and literature; vol. 229)
Includes bibliographical references and index.
1. Ignatius, of Loyola, Saint, 1491–1556. Exercitia spiritualia.
2. Ignatius, of Loyola, Saint, 1491—1556—Influence. 3. Spiritual exercises.
4. Spiritual direction. 5. Spiritual life—Catholic Church.
6. European literature—History and criticism. I. Title.
BX2179.L8 C64   271'.53—dc22   2008006201
ISBN 978-1-4331-0249-3 (hardcover)
ISBN 978-1-4331-0497-8. (paperback)
ISSN 0740-9257

Bibliographic information published by **Die Deutsche Bibliothek**.
Die Deutsche Bibliothek lists this publication in the "Deutsche
Nationalbibliografie"; detailed bibliographic data is available
on the Internet at http://dnb.ddb.de/.

Cover design by Clear Point Designs

Cover art "Vision at La Storta" from Pedro Ribadeneira's First Latin
Edition of the *Vita*, (1610)/Church of Il Gesù (Rome).
Courtesy of I Gesuiti della Chiesa dil Gesu di Roma

The paper in this book meets the guidelines for permanence and durability
of the Committee on Production Guidelines for Book Longevity
of the Council of Library Resources.

© 2008 Peter Lang Publishing, Inc., New York
29 Broadway, 18th floor, New York, NY 10006
www.peterlang.com

All rights reserved.
Reprint or reproduction, even partially, in all forms such as microfilm,
xerography, microfiche, microcard, and offset strictly prohibited.

Printed in the United States of America

Contents

Figures vii
Foreword ix

Chapter I: Baroque Orders of Corruption 1

Chapter II: The *Spiritual Exercises*, or the Formation of Mental
Territories and Orders of Corruption 15
    Totalitarian Structures and Orders of Corruption 17
    The Formation of an Image Reservoir 27
    Imitatio Christi and Baroque Inversions 43

Chapter III: "Ego Vobis Romae Propitius Ero": Diffusion
of the *Spiritual Exercises* in Rome (1550–1650) 54
    The First Mission of a New Apostle 54
    An Image Reservoir in the Multiple-Layer Urban Fabric 61
    Corresponding Dynamics? 67
    Roman Churches after the *Spiritual Exercises* 73
    The Mother Church of Il Gesù and Sant'Andrea Al Quirinale 77
    The *Roma Ignaziana* 88

Chapter IV: Transformation of the Visual Dynamics of the *Spiritual Exercises* in the Late Works of Miguel de Cervantes 94
    Cervantes, Corruption, the Urban, and the Company 97
    Don Quixote, an Excessive Projection in a Greater Narrative 104
    The Last Pilgrimage: Cervantes' Representation of Rome
        in *Los Trabajos de Persiles y Sigismunda* 121
    Conclusion 131

Chapter V: Transforming the Orders of Corruption in *El Criticón*: The Case of Baltasar Gracián, a Jesuit Preparing the Way for the Enlightenment 133
    Pre-Enlightenment Coming Out of the *Exercises?* 133
    The Exercise of Decoding Monstrosity 143
    Contemplating Eternal Arts beyond the *Roma Ignaziana* 151
    The Enigmatic Parallel Writing of *El Comulgatorio* 161
    Conclusion 164

Chapter VI: From Loyolan Imagination to Sadean Enlightenment: Parodistic Inversions of the *Spiritual Exercises* in the Novels of the Marquis de Sade 168
    Philosophical Criticism of the Loyolan System in Early
        Enlightenment France, from Descartes to Voltaire 168
    Sadean Inversions of the *Spiritual Exercises* 184
        Collecting the *Tableaux* in the *Cent Vingt Journées* 189
        Melting Down the Concept of Spiritual Direction 193
        Forcing the Exercitant to Desire the Opposite 195
        Revisiting the *Roma Ignaziana* in *Juliette* 199
        Conclusion 206

Afterword 209
Notes 215
Works Cited 245
Index 251

Figures

Figure 1: "Vision at La Storta" from Pedro Ribadeneira's First Latin
Edition of the *Vita*, (1610)/ Church of Il Gesù (Rome)......................60

Figure 2: Matthaüs Greuter "Ignatius at La Storta"
from Richedôme La Peinture Spirituelle, (1611) 66

Figure 3: Façade of the church of Il Gesù,
Rome (Photograph by Frédéric Conrod) 82

Figure 4: Chapel and Altar of Saint Ignatius, Gesù, Rome......................85

Figure 5: Façade of Sant'Andrea al Quirinale
(Photograph by Conrod)..86

Figure 6: "Roma Ignaziana" also from Ribadaneira's in the 1610
edition of the *Vita* (Church of Il Gesù) 90

Foreword

Luis Avilés,
University of California at Irvine

In Loyola's Greater Narrative, Frédéric Conrod confronts us with the sort of historical narrative that is not afraid of risks and, at the same time, surprises us with new readings of canonical writers such as Cervantes, Gracián and Sade. The book identifies the Baroque as a transitional period between the Renaissance and the culture of the Enlightenment. At first glance, this may not seem to constitute a new and radical assessment of the historical periods involved. However, Conrod tackles this transition by focusing on the reactions that one single author (Ignatius of Loyola), and one single book (the Spiritual Exercises) had on the overall Roman Catholic culture, in particular the countries comprised by southwestern Europe (mainly Spain, France, and Italy). Loyola's Spiritual Exercises becomes the center of an intense response to the Protestant Reform based on an intensification of the institutional control over the economy of salvation. Loyola's book confronts us with a total structure designed to exert control over the relationship between director and exercitant by means of what Conrod calls orders of corruption (following closely De Certeau's phrase). Baroque artifacts appropriate corruption through an interplay of images designed to confront subjects with the intensity of decay, disintegration, mortality, death, and an overall absence of the divine. This strong negativity is designed to open the possibility of salvation by means of a confrontation and eventual conquering of evil. The Spiritual Exercises becomes a locus of intense cultural energy that is appropriated and refracted by authors such as Cervantes, Gracián and Sade. Conrod postulates that these authors use images as a response to Loyola's scopic regime, producing in their works a crisis of the total structure imposed by the Jesuit order. Although such a reaction still depends on the Baroque's need to saturate culture with images, nevertheless it opens up new deviations of the original purposes of the visual by reconfiguring the relationship to religion and divinity. Images now do not tell a coherent story of the "greater narrative" of Catholicism, but instead propose new eschatological, highly secular alternatives that effectively transform French and Spanish culture. Conrod has produced what should be considered a solid interdisciplinary and comparative approach to a very complex cultural period. By concentrating on the deep influence of the Spiritual Exercises written by Loyola, and by working on the rich dialogues between the Jesuit order and major artists at the time, Conrod is able to propose new, compelling and sometimes controversial readings that will certainly attract the attention of scholars in the Humanities.

CHAPTER I

Baroque Orders of Corruption

In an invisible contemplation or meditation—as here on the Sins—the composition will be to see with the sight of the imagination and consider that my soul is imprisoned in this corruptible body, and all the compound in this valley, as exiled among brute beasts: I say all the compound of soul and body.

Ignatius of Loyola, Spiritual Exercises (1548)

Vese ser esto así claramente, porque si bien consideramos, hallaremos que Ignacio se convirtió de la vanidad del mundo a servir Dios y a su Iglesia al mismo tiempo que el desventurado Martín Lutero públicamente se desvergonzó contra la religión católica.

Pedro de Ribadeneira, Vida de San Ignacio (1610)

The history of Roman Catholicism is a part of a longer and more complex story. It recognizes this dimension as the *Magisterium*, the institution's own "greater narrative." From its inception to its development and to its attempts to stabilize itself in spite of antagonistic historical parameters, the Church of Rome has insisted on the continuity between the Gospel and its own history. Every episode in its history has therefore to be placed in this greater narrative. Catholicism has always followed a 'greater narrative' in which the Gospels are recognized not only as the crucial moment when divine truth was revealed, but also as the starting point. This 'greater narrative' contains the history of the Church itself which unfolds as the logical continuation of the Gospels, an everlasting Book of Acts, followed by the lives and writings of various recognized actors of Christianity such as Augustine of Hippo, Dominic of Guzman, Francis of Assisi or Thomas Aquinas. This linear and ongoing perception of Christianity defines Rome as its epicenter since the crucifixion of Peter. The institution that claims to hold the legacy of Peter the apostle has gone through various phases of dogmatic reformulation and reaffirmation of its religious practices, but has never reformed its fundamental belief in a linear conception of time. In defense of its rituals, Roman Catholicism has stood against various waves of theological challenge and criticism. The political circumstances in Western Europe from the fall of the Roman Empire on and scientific discoveries often challenged these dogmas, and threaten the very essence of the ideological pillars of the Church and the narrative on which it is based.

In the history of this religious institution, two moments on the eve of Modernity are worth noting being particularly relevant to the narrative of Rome's efforts to assert and detend its doctrinal core: first, the Protestant Reformation and its artistic connections to the Renaissance, and second, the French Revolution following the age of Enlightenment. Of all crises in its history, these two proved most difficult to overcome in order to reaffirm the continuity of Christianity and Rome as its center. These two transitional moments—the Reformation and the French Revolution—are also significant landmarks in the history of the West since they correspond to the opening and the closing of the period of powerful artistic revolution that we commonly call the 'Baroque,' originally found in religious art directly associated with the Roman Church of the Counter-Reformation. It is an age of reformulation *par excellence*, since the Baroque echoes the anxiety to reconcile the contradictory natures of the rising Modernity and the Roman Catholic faith; it is also an age marked by great religious conflicts.

Let us look closer at these two transitions. First, the Reformation finds its roots and inspiration in Humanism and in medieval criticism of Catholic observances and attempts to reduce the role of the institution in individuals' religious practices. As we know, Martin Luther's propositions negate the role of the hierarchy and the institution of Rome in what he considers to be a decadent era of Catholicism, far removed from the simplicity of Apostolic times. This German Catholic priest places more importance on Scripture than on the "greater narrative" that follows it; he accuses Rome of placing more importance on its own history than on the actual texts that founded it. According to Luther, the texts contain a divine message that is revealed to the Christian through individual readings and not through interpretations added by the Church: "The profoundest mysteries of the supreme Majesty are no more hidden away, but are now brought out of doors and displayed to the public view. Christ has opened our understanding, that we might understand the Scriptures, and the Gospel is preached to every creature" (*Bondage of the Will*, 72).[1] His is a vision of transparency in which, after centuries of obscurantism, a personal reading of Scripture and an economy of salvation through divine grace alone would liberate the faithful from medieval dogma. The mental territory in which these new concepts are directly applied—and for which they are designed—is the individual human conscience. Only in individual conscience can authentic change take place. Moreover, faith is an atemporal perspective that stands outside all historical continuity, a moment of direct divine revelation. From his point of view, the revelation has already been made in its entirety and no longer narrative is needed.

In a polemical series of writings, Luther tries to prove to Erasmus that the will is not a free entity but only an instrument by which the divine operates directly on the believer. Erasmus is already suggesting the freedom of will, a concept that will be extremely controversial in the future disputes of the next century. Luther represents a threat to the institution he attacks primarily because his intention is to draw attention to a single narrative layer: that of the Gospels. As we know, Luther points to the deformation of the original message of the Gospels; he blames it the priority Roman Catholicism places on the interpretation of religious history, that is, the "greater narrative."

In response to Luther, the Roman Church of the Counter-Reformation reaffirms its determination to build structures of ecclesiastical guidance, both doctrinal and institutional, around the life of the Christian believer so that s/he can be, in turn, included in the 'greater narrative.' This process of reaffirmation would not be possible without the strategic help of Southern European nations that reject the Lutheran Reformation. In the era of Absolutism, Rome's position is secured within a total political structure in which there is no room for heresies. Nevertheless, the Roman religion changes drastically in the sixteenth and seventeenth centuries as it organizes its crusades against Protestantism and the scientific revolution. Catholicism responds with more visual representations and images, the doctrine of justification by works, an insistence on free will within the economy of salvation, the development of a spirit of competition between artists, and unfailing support of Absolutist regimes.

Until the Revolution, the Holy See in Rome constantly needs to re-define and re-affirm its 'divine legacy.' The position it had acquired throughout the first fifteen centuries of Christianity, before the Reformation, is rendered fragile by the evolution and transformation of religious practices and beliefs throughout Northern Europe, especially in the Netherlands, Germany and Switzerland. Southwestern Europe however remains under its control and participates almost completely in the spirit of the Counter-Reformation. For instance, the political systems of Spain, Portugal and Italy are still in close relation to the Vatican and do not permit the Protestant presence the way the French state and its Protestant-friendly king Henri IV do with the publication of the Edict of Nantes in 1598. In territories such as France, England and Germany, the tensions are greater between the two systems of beliefs since both live in close if tense proximity. But these tensions are also felt greatly in the rest of Western Europe. The experience of the wars of religion and the famous Saint-Barthélemy massacre on August 24th, 1572 in France increases the fear of expanding such cohabitations, as it might also weaken political systems often depending on the religious cohesion of the population. As a result, many regimes evolve toward the Absolutist model (France and Spain), a type of totalitarian monarchy whose role is also to protect Catholic dogma within political life through the delegation of power to the person of the king. The Baroque is therefore an age also associated with this political system and the affirmation of the divine right of kings. The Vatican reinforces its links with monarchs willing to cooperate in the protection of the Roman faith. The theoretical power of these partnerships is exalted in courtly practices as well as in the arts that develop at the turn of the seventeenth century. This is why the Baroque can also be perceived as defining the period between the Reformation and the Revolution, that is, a moment of doctrinal retrenchment and certitude in desperate need of supporting visual representations.

The French Revolution—the other transition that declares the death of the Baroque age after several decades of philosophical Enlightenment—marks the end of political involvement of the Roman Church in traditionally Catholic states; the separation of Rome and France in particular is felt like the 'treason of the first daughter of the Church.' In a way, the Revolution is also a consequence of the Counter-Reformation that echoes the Lutheran Reformation: its primary goal is to erase a regime in which religion justifies political power through a constant renewal of its 'greater narrative:' Absolutism appoints the king a role in the ongoing divine revelation. The philosophers of the Enlightenment, as well as some libertine writers, formulate direct attacks against Rome and its Church; they preach the superiority of Reason over an organized religion built on narrative anticipations. They seek to deconstruct the "greater narrative" of Rome but also realize how deeply it is embedded in the historical and social composition of France and Spain. So their denunciations echo the Enlightenment's determination to undermine the Roman

Catholic spirituality and, particularly, the form that it has taken since the Counter-Reformation. They particularly admire and attack the importance Roman Catholicism places on visual art as a means of persuading believers to enter into the greater narrative and thus participate in the continuity of Catholic Christianity.

In order to bridge these two transitional periods at the advent of Modernity, I propose a re-exploration of this age through the analysis of one of its fundamental dimensions: the representation of corruption in spirituality, art and literature as a means of recovering the essence of Roman Catholicism, that is, its "greater narrative," know in theology as *Magisterium*. Truly we do not read these anxieties any better than in the Roman works of art produced between 1550 and 1750. The term 'Baroque' which corresponds to this era is generally associated with and attached to the field of Art History but it can be extended to the study of literature and spirituality as well since they all work in close relation during this period. There is, of course, a great deal of approximation in defining this rather enigmatic age. The Baroque inaugurates various aspects of modernity, such as the imperialism of the visual effect and the dominion of the artificial over the natural. It is an age characterized by the anxiety following the Copernican revolution, when Europeans lose progressively the enthusiasm for human beauty acquired during the Renaissance. The representation of the human body itself works through new parameters, including the emphasis on its violent nature and its progressive decomposition. The thirst for eternity so typical of the Renaissance is replaced by a fascination with the ephemeral, the mortal and the corruptible nature of the body. Generally speaking, Baroque art is a constant reminder of the passing of time—a *memento mori*—and a threatening acceptance of our mortal condition and coming bodily corruption. As Michel Foucault points out in *Les mots et les choses*, we can consider that the whole spirit of representation of the Baroque age is somehow contained in the physical character of Cervantes' Don Quixote, since the old hidalgo represents this decomposition of the early sixteenth-century and its humanist ideals, a sharp criticism for an age of anxiety and disillusion, that is, a negative print of the world of the Renaissance (47). In a way, the knight-errant is a body already in corruption[2] when the story begins, and his story a slow progression towards death. His is also a function of *memento mori*, of physical and mental decay. Don Quixote is, in this sense, a representation of the visual *order of corruption* in which the Baroque subject is precipitated, epistemologically speaking.

What is understood by the term 'corruption' here is, from a theological point of view, the absence of divine presence and the imminence of death. Its primary definition applies to the body and its disintegration after death. But the Baroque age relates the principle of corruption to far more than the human body. It also perceives and represents this corruption in civilization, in architecture and in politics, and it reflects it then back on the body. The principle of corruption, that is, of disintegration, becomes a systematic element of the *esprit de siècle* that we will discuss here. Very briefly and in accordance with principles that are commonly accepted, we could distinguish the Renaissance from the Baroque in the following manner. The Renaissance emphasizes the eternal beauty of the human, human civilization and the human power to control the world and overcome time, in imitation of ancient Roman culture, in an effort to create a sense of continuity and cohesion. By contrast, the Baroque adopts a more apocalyptic spirit in which the eternal and the divine can only be perceived through an organized contrast with corruption, its metaphysical opposite and temporal counterpart. The constant confrontation with corrupted elements in order to emphasize what is incorruptible is typical of the Catholic Baroque the related techniques of representation in the arts, such as *chiaroscuro* in painting. Several art historians, since Heinrich Wöfflin's classic definition of Baroque art, have attempted to identify a set of parameters and characteristics that distinguish the Baroque from the Renaissance. This work of distinction has also been carried out from a great many different points of view, and the term 'Baroque' has been applied to a wide variety of artistic forms outside of its primary temporal and spatial location in post-Renaissance southern Europe. But the difference goes far beyond the guidelines given in the theoretical foundations of Art History.

As a term, it encompasses more concepts than can be discussed here. That is why we will narrow down our discussion to the definitions of 'Baroque' that make a direct connection between the evolution of the Roman Catholic Church and the perception of the human body through the spirituality the Church redefines in the sixteenth century. We will therefore confine the investigation exclusively to Catholic Baroque forms.[3] The fascination with the corrupted dimensions and capacities of this world is not a new phenomenon coming with the Baroque age. But it is deeply revived by the Counter-Reformation and its aesthetics: never before had relics been so venerated, never before had the suffering of Christ on the cross been so emphasized. The emphasis is placed on the mortality and bleeding of the body as never before in the history of Christianity. Within a century after the magnificent enthusiasm for the comprehension of the cosmos coming out the Florentine Renaissance,[4] the Baroque age depicts Nature as the evil component of the universe, an enemy that the believer needs to overcome after getting familiar with the illusions it produces. Yet the various forms of evil should be heavily represented in and conquered by the visual arts in order to familiarize the believer's gaze with the atrocity of sin with other horrific visions of divine retribution on sinners. The condition of human existence was rendered negative, hopeless, and fundamentally violent in this representational process. On the one hand, the Catholic Baroque as an aesthetical movement almost encourages a backlash against emergent modernity in favor of medieval beliefs and practices. It stands as a space of confrontation with the abundance of scientific discoveries in the sixteenth and seventeenth centuries. On the other hand, it cultivates the optical illusion of incorruptible bodies, it depicts the kingdom of heaven as an extremely sensual place, and it stimulates the believer to follow the highly decorated path of salvation in which the new technologies are often involved. In summary, it creates through these two extremes a tension in which the believer's mind is forced to evolve.

Of course, the question of representing physical and spiritual corruption in the Baroque age is a complex and a large one. There are many different views that one can have on the rise and fall of the Catholic Baroque and its representation of corruption. Jesuit philosopher Michel de Certeau envisions this projection as '*ordre corrompu*,' and it seems to be the definition that applies the best to the analysis of Catholic Baroque forms since it connects the *communication with the divine* directly with the exposure to *physical disintegration*. From now on, we will refer to this central notion as '*order of corruption*.' It points to the Counter-Reformation mystical need for visualizing sin, horror and decay in their starkest form in order to be granted access to virtue, beauty and resurrection. Luther's propositions were about letting the representational spaces exist only in the conscience of the believer and in the private exercise of reading the Holy Scriptures; Rome responded by an explosion of collective spaces of representation where access to the Scriptures would continue to be restricted, but where images were multiplied in order to satisfy the believer's need for illustration.

When describing this process, very few scholars of this period can avoid mentioning the Society of Jesus, or, in other words, the 'heroes' of this highly representational Roman Counter-Reformation. For instance, Gauvin Alexander Bailey points out in *Between Renaissance and Baroque* (2004) that "[scholars] continue to maintain that as the vanguard of the "Counter-Reformation" the Jesuits played a leading role in bringing about the demise of the Renaissance" (3). There is a lot of value in describing the Jesuits as a vanguard, if one considers vanguard to be an experimental phase in artistic development in which the observer finds emergent new genres and narrative traditions. The Jesuits, with Ignatius of Loyola as their founder, develop this rather Modern capacity to assemble elements belonging to various trends in order to present a quite totalitarian space of representation in which believers will contemplate the contest between the divine and omnipresent corruption. As a result, the perspective I have chosen for this investigation is centered around the development of this religious order in its first century of existence and the consequences it has on the representation of various kinds of corruption throughout the age of the Enlightenment. It is impossible indeed to approach the Counter-Reformed Roman Church without considering the intervention of the Jesuits.

However, critics are divided on the matter. Some minimize the importance of the Jesuit influence on the whole Baroque question. For instance, Rudolph Wittkower analyses this problematic in *Baroque Art: The Jesuit Contribution* (1972) and includes the Jesuits and their rhetorics in the greater picture, but denies the original nature of their influence on seventeenth-century art and architecture. He also seeks to challenge and limit the use of the nineteenth-century term *Jesuitenstil*, often poorly adapted to the description of Baroque art. In opposition to this rather mild and neutral approach, more recent works, such as Evonne Levy's *Propaganda and the Jesuit Baroque* (2004), propose daring associations and see in Jesuit representations the rise of modern propagandistic tactics as well as a source of inspiration for Nazi architecture. The debate around the Jesuits is complicated because it often conflicts with or, on the contrary, adheres to political and religious agendas. In the same fashion that "Catholic Baroque" is a problematic term, so is the term "Jesuit Baroque." Again, what is defined by it? Is it a form of spirituality, a set of stylistic characteristics developing in Jesuit circles, or a combination of both? When it comes to the Jesuit perception and representation of earthly corruption in the Baroque age, our present investigation needs to be narrowed down once again and focused. If it represents a fundamental characteristic of the Baroque fascination discussed above, it is due to the direction and spiritual guidance given by the founder of the Society, Ignatius of Loyola.

The life of this Spanish knight—who converts to *Imitatio Christi*, travels through Europe with the manuscript of his *Spiritual Exercices* until he reaches Rome, and ultimately becomes one of the most important actors of the Counter-Reformation before dying and being canonized as one of the most venerated saints of the Roman Church—is truly fascinating. Not only is it an inspiring story for mocking authors such as Cervantes or Cyrano de Bergerac, but it also illustrates a fundamental evolution that needs to be studied more closely in order to comprehend the problematic of represented corruption discussed above. Loyola represents a crucial revolution in perception and representation in the Baroque period. His *Spiritual Exercises* (1547) contributed to the ongoing artistic revolution in both their acceptance and their rejection, and this is the central problematic of this investigation. Loyola's method of spiritual conversion contains a pattern for the forms of representation later on adopted by the Church. It combines elements coming from various traditions;[5] it constantly projects the gaze into a forced contemplation of corruption; it offers a total structure—with an exterior and its independent interior—in which the gaze is forced to identify various layers of interpretation; it confirms the necessity of institutional intercession in the economy of salvation and reinforces the need for a 'greater narrative.' All in all, it provides the Counter-Reformation with a total strategy. In this sense, the *Spiritual Exercises* guide us through the re-exploration of Baroque culture—corruption and its 'omnipresent representation'—conducted in this analysis.

This project of investigation partially originates from my reading of Roland Barthes' *Sade, Fourier, Loyola* (1971), a structuralist approach to three thinkers who have in common a similar obsession with the kind of structures that he calls the "total occupation of the mental territory" of their readers (54) by the text they produce. In his essay on Ignatius of Loyola, Barthes talks about a "linguistic vacuum necessary for the elaboration and the triumph of a new language", and immediately adds that: "it is in this negative, repellent sense that the Ignatian imagination must be interpreted" (49). Even though his discussion does not lead us so much toward the question of representing corruption, this rather intriguing image is in close relation to it since the techniques typical of the *Spiritual Exercises* are reproduced in the arts in general, and in literature particularly: by saturating his readers with images derived from various narrative traditions, Loyola forces their imagination into a constant confrontation with corruption and progressively injects doses of imitative techniques which he considers to be of the very essence of Christianity and of the true mission of the Church of Rome.

More than a method of meditation, the *Spiritual Exercises* become a practice of perception and representation based on an image reservoir, whose consequences go far beyond the historical boundaries of the Society of Jesus. We can therefore identify four phases in the study of the *Exercises*: their *formation* during the errantry of their author, their *diffusion* through the institutional structures of the Roman Church which supports them, their *transformation* through the codification operated by writers such as Miguel de Cervantes and Baltasar Gracián—two Spanish authors both familiar with the life of Loyola and the content of his *Exercises*-, and eventually their deconstructive *negation* in the age of Enlightenment by philosophers educated in their tradition such as Diderot and Sade. This is, of course, one way to envision the connection between the Reformation and the Revolution. The following comparative approach does not pretend to be exhaustive or comprehensive in any way, but to follow a theoretical path and offer a different and hopefully complementary mapping of the problematics concerned.

The development of the questions raised will be divided in the five following chapters. The initial question of image formation will be developed in the second chapter where we will consider the personal conversion experience of the saint, its consequences for the composition of his text and the role given to "orders of corruption" in the spiritual evolution of the Catholic believer. In discussing these "orders of corruption," we shall attempt to understand the narrative mechanisms of the *Spiritual Exercises*. Particular attention will be paid at this point to the structure of the text in the light of Barthes's observation, as well as those of other scholars. But we will use this great piece of scholarship only as a starting point, since Barthes limits his reading of Loyola to a strict structuralist approach and does not consider the formation of the images that he describes. As Paul de Man wrote: "Despite the proliferation of a technical vocabulary primarily derived from structural linguistics (structure, code, sign, text), the actual innovations introduced by Roland Barthes in the *analytic study of literary texts* are relatively slight" (178). I propose, however, to revisit the Barthean notion of 'totalitarian structure' that coexists with the images devoted to corruption, and to add to it several other parameters in connection with Loyola's historical context in order to return to an analytical perspective. This second chapter will therefore be dedicated primarily to the narrative traditions that inspire Loyola in the making of his conversion method, such as Humanist literature, novels of Chivalry, hagiographies, and the greater Christian narrative present in the Gospels. Eventually, this will lead our discussion to an exploration of the practice of *imitatio Christi*, an originally medieval practice weakened by Renaissance Humanism that Loyola resuscitates and implements in his exercises in order to reintegrate himself and other believers within the Christian narrative.

The third chapter will follow up this question by shifting the focus outside literary analysis and bringing it to the realm of the fine arts, focusing on the role played by Rome as both institution and city in the diffusion of Loyola's method. Ignatius of Loyola does not get to publish his *Exercises* widely until his arrival in Rome by the mid- sixteenth century. His life prior to this date is a long series of rejections from all the places where he tries to plant the seeds of his spiritual method for conversion. The reception of his method in Salamanca, Alcalá de Henares and Paris is largely negative and gets him in conflicts with ecclesiastical authorities. Finally, Rome and the Holy See give him an opportunity to exercise his inclination for visual effects in various spheres. There are several dimensions to the analysis of the development Loyola's *Exercises* in the Roman context. First of all, why is Rome such a propitious place for the development of Ignatian spirituality and why is this method so readily adapted to the needs of the Counter-Reformation? The association of the Holy See with the Society of Jesus is highly cordial from the start. Their agreement on questions regarding the uses of representations is almost total. Nonetheless, Rome has a certain predisposition for the reception of Loyola's method, due to its past, its structure, and its political needs as an institution. In summary, the Holy City had all the advantages for the staging of theatrical performances—in other words, the *dramatic mode*—that would make the experience of the exercises worthwhile for the believer: the "orders of corruption" were present, the division between the standards of Heaven and those of Hell were recognizable, and the city itself was part of the "greater Christian narrative" in which the exercitant was placed, since Peter and Paul had come to the capital of the decaying Empire in order to preach before meeting their death there. The crisis of Christendom needed resolution and the *Spiritual Exercises* gave the Church the new impulse it had been lacking since the sack of Rome. The first Jesuits not only find their Jerusalem in the city of the Holy See, but they get to participate as lead actors in the ongoing and most needed revolution in the arts. Their agenda for the reformation of representation is established through their belief in the omnipresence of images, and—as I wish to point out—through a desire to reproduce the dynamics of the *Spiritual Exercises* in the production of religious images.

As Gauvin Bailey points out: "Art historians for the past century have linked the *Exercises* with an emphasis on sensuality in the work of Baroque artists from Gianlorenzo Bernini (1598–1680) to Caravaggio (1573–1610), with varying degrees of success" (8). This analysis will be extended to Jesuit church architecture and the inclusion of elements taken from the exercises. The model offered by Rome at the turn of the seventeenth century for the design of churches has a very close connection with the highly mental structure in which the exercitant is guided. Jesuit-friendly Cardinal Charles Borromeo writes his *Instructiones Fabricae et Supellectilis Ecclesiasticae* in the 17th century, and this architectural treatise becomes a reference for the building of Baroque churches. In many ways, architecture applies the concept of *total occupation of the mental territory* to the work of art before literature does. Roman Baroque architecture makes the sacred aspects of the Christian narrative literally explode in the eyes of its spectator, and requires the believer to involve his/her senses in the contemplation of the work of art. The Mother Church of the Jesuits is a great example of this phenomenon that will be analyzed. Some of the most important artists working in Rome in the remodeling and construction of churches are actually close friends of the newly established Society of Jesus and have practiced the exercises. Although not primarily concerned with literary analysis, this second part will be fundamental since the three following chapters will analyze how Cervantes, Gracián, and Sade use the city of Rome as a critical catalyst where their characters will experience an initiation to the visual dynamics of Loyola's text.

In a fourth chapter, we will parallel this diffusion of the *Spiritual Exercises* through Roman Baroque architecture to the new structures found in literary genres in 17th-century Spain. While Loyola is conquering the institutional territory in Rome, he receives the support of influential Spanish figures such as Dr. Pedro Ortiz, emissary of Charles V. It is particularly significant that Spain—Europe's wealthiest and most powerful state—would place Rome under its protective wing and help in the development of Counter-Reformation aesthetics throughout the Catholic South. Unlike Naples, Rome is not officially a Spanish territory, but Rome's influence on the political, cultural, and religious movements in Spain is enormous. The aesthetics of the Roman Baroque will serve the agenda of the Spanish Crown of Felipe II and his successors. It is in this context of symbiosis and constant exchange that Cervantes is going to get acquainted with Rome, his late compatriot Ignatius of Loyola, and the visual imperialism deriving from his works. The author of Don Quixote was in contact with the first generations of Jesuits at many points in his life, and is therefore familiar with the functioning of the spiritual exercises. As pointed out in my first chapter, many authors such as Miguel de Unamuno have drawn parallels between Ignatius of Loyola and the mad hidalgo of La Mancha. Some more recent works even suggest a very strong inspiration and a encoded re-writing of the life of Loyola in *Don Quixote*. Even though this is not the position of this analysis, it is interesting to consider this perspective in the general process of *transformation* on which this chapter is centered.

The literary production of the Spanish Golden Age in general reflects the Modern desire to bend the rules around genres, and the merging of narrative traditions for the economy of representation contributes to the birth of the novel. One might consider Modernity to be a superimposition of narratives and a combining of several of their respective components with the purpose of producing a monstrous outcome. As a matter of fact, the first modern novels share with the *Spiritual Exercises* this palimpsestic character. This is a purely structural approach however, and will be rendered explicit in comparisons between Loyola's conversion method and Cervantes' *Don Quixote* as well as Gracián's *Criticón*. Of these latter, both works have the capacity to reformulate and implement the anxieties of the Counter-Reformation through a re-exploration of the director/exercitant relationship. For instance, it has been underlined that Sancho was an exercitant walking in the steps of Don Quixote, his director.[6] However, this quite logical approach has drawn attention away from the real director/exercitant dynamics presented in the novel: Don Quixote is not a director for Sancho, although he builds a total structure in order to prepare the path for an exercitant. The parallel mental peregrinations of the hidalgo and his squire are crucial in order to understand the transformation operated by Cervantes in his masterpiece: the director and the exercitant have come to coexist within the same decrepit physical body.

We will pursue the analysis of these questions in the fifth chapter by envisioning Baltasar Gracián as a precursor of the Enlightenment. His Jesuit identity, combined with the heavily critical nature of his works toward Jesuit visual education, makes his work a unique place to stop and contemplate the correspondences between the Reformation with the Revolution. In the footsteps of Cervantes, Gracián represents human corruption come to its maximal point of monstrosity. His *Criticón* is an initiation in the perversion of the Catholic South in which the human body has been overexposed to corruption and has finally become entirely corrupt. The body is now allegorically monstrous, and it is granted a specular function designed to exhibit this fact. One could consider Gracián's works as a territory in which the over-representing of a monstrous and corrupted reality conceals epistemological anxieties. Gracián is educated in the tradition of the *Exercises* and simultaneously generates the most Baroque forms of prose recognized to this day. Gracián deals with the simulation of the orders of corruption as a potentially dangerous device for the human mind, which both contradicts and confirms its importance in the salvation of souls. In many ways, this Jesuit author wants to reverse the power and preserve the elitist nature of salvation. His negative reaction to the development of mass-media cultural events and forms of entertainment parallels his rejection of the *Spiritual Exercises*. For this reason Gracián has finally to abandon the Jesuits and write under the protection of influential political figures. In the voyage of initiation that his texts propose, the imagination of corruption becomes an instrument that only a few people should master, since its nature is essentially oracular (since the sign is incomplete and inscrutable), and leads the exercitant to visions of monstrosity.

The sixth chapter will open on a short history of various French literary figures that carry on Gracián's critical project in literature. Among them we will find Descartes, Pascal, and Voltaire. Their continued critique of the Loyolan imaginative system proves that it is often the ex-students of the Jesuits who come up with the harshest criticism of their old masters. By the turn of the eighteenth century, France offers a relative flexibility in literary production that Spain has entirely lost after Gracián, when the Inquisition reinforces its censorship on literary output. Simultaneously, the works of Cervantes and Gracián are widely translated, published, and read in France in the second half of the seventeenth century and the beginning of the eighteenth. We will therefore dedicate the first part of this final chapter to the analysis of these transitions. But the purpose of this overview is mostly to prepare us for the final analytical part dedicated to the novels of the marquis de

Sade. The libertine author develops the capacity in his novels to make characters and readers progress toward the highest forms of anti-Catholic representation. At the same time, Sade offers a comprehensive look at the Counter-Reformation as a whole and warns his reader against the dangers of the invincible capacities of Rome: the French Revolution might be another obstacle for the Church, but the Church has overcome many worse obstacles that the marquis brings back to the memory of his readers.

As an ex-student of the Jesuits, a devoted reader of Cervantes and the Enlightenment philosophers, and an admirer of Baroque art and architecture, Sade offers in his novels a quite exhaustive perspective on the disintegration of Loyolan imagination under the philosophical action of the Enlightenment. We will pay particular attention in this final chapter to the notion of 'parody' and 'inversion,' since it is through these two processes that Sade operates most of his deconstructive *negation* of the *Spiritual Exercises* in his extremely repetitive narratives. Of all the writers analyzed here, Sade appears to be the most aware of the functions and consequences of the 'greater narrative of Christianity' on which the Roman Church has based its entire belief system. It is only through a reproduction of the greater narrative that one can overcome its powers. Eventually, the *orders of corruption* are developed to such extent in the novels of Sade that they progressively lose their capacity to configure the believer's mental territory. Through this mapping, I pretend to make only *one* analytical connection between Loyola and Sade out of the many possible connections suggested in Barthes's work. But above all, I intend to offer a reading of the Baroque period, from the perspective of comparative literature, in which the *Spiritual Exercises* can be envisioned as a major text of influence not only on the politics of the period but also on the rise of Modern literature, through the formation, diffusion, transformation, and negation of Counter-Reformation visual dynamics.

CHAPTER II

The *Spiritual Exercises,* or the Formation of Mental Territories and Orders of Corruption

L'infirmité de la méthode dramatique est qu'elle force d'aller toujours au delà de ce qui est senti naturellement. Mais l'infirmité est moins celle de la méthode que la nôtre.
Georges Bataille, *L'expérience intérieure*

And yet if there has ever been on earth a real stupendous miracle, it took place on that day, on the day of the three temptations.
Fyodor Dostoevsky, *The Grand Inquisitor*

The *Spiritual Exercises* written by Ignatius of Loyola in Manresa, Spain, as a result of his conversion experience, and published for the first time in 1548, were never an object of study for literary criticism before the twentieth century. They were simply considered to be the founding text of the Jesuits, the written form of a religious practice that would later on characterize the spirit of the Counter-Reformation. The Spanish saint had conceived them in order to help the believer in the experience of divine intervention on a personal level. They exposed step by step the method of imitation of Christian soldiers, saints, and ultimately Christ in the form of preparatory prayers, meditations, and colloquies. Their minimalist and rather dry nature had them classified in a category of texts that would apparently never be read for pleasure or even for philosophical interest, since they could not possibly fall in any of the established genres of Western literature.[1] Only a few curious scholars in theology would venture inside them in order to understand the spiritual and political essence of the Society of Jesus.

Jesuit historian John W. O'Malley comes to the conclusion in *The First Jesuits*: "One of the world's most famous book, the *Exercises* are (. . .) one of the least read and least well understood (. . .) the *Exercises* were never meant to be read" (37). This argument is not necessarily counter-attacked by anti-Jesuit sentiment. Manfred Barthel, whose book *The Jesuits* gives a rather negative image of Ignatius of Loyola and his Society, writes: "anyone who reads it straight through will probably be disappointed, and anyone who reads it carefully will certainly be confused" (71). It seems that this text has no intended literary angle, and no intention to please whatsoever. The basic function of the *Exercises* as a text has been considered to be a guide for a four-week spiritual practice given to a Jesuit director for the guidance of an exercitant; unlike other contemporary meditation methods, they were not even intended to be read directly by the repentant pilgrim. Therefore, the text is directed to a reader that has already undergone the process of the spiritual exercises and has the shape that it requires to guide another soul through them. This is the reason why the style has almost no particular rhetoric to it, since there is no need to preach to a converted soul. As a consequence of this phenomenon, penetrating the world of the exercises without any previous initiation to them is a rather difficult task.

In 1971 however, Roland Barthes decides to break with this tradition when he publishes a series of four essays entitled *Sade, Fourier, Loyola*.[2] One of these essays is dedicated to a close-reading analysis of the *Spiritual Exercises*. In this article, he recommends to consider the spiritual method of conversion with the eyes of the cultural observer. His structuralist approach is based on the identification of systems existing within the texts of these authors. At the same time, it reintegrates Loyola's text in a tradition to which it has never really belonged. Barthes justifies this oblivion and blames it on the Jesuits themselves: "ce prestige de la littérature, qu'ils ont aidé à former, les jésuites le refusent facilement au livre de leur fondateur" (*Sade*, 43). He denounces with this initial sentence a legacy that has been lost to Western scholarship and points to a form of appreciation that was unexpected. He invites the reader to go back to this specific root of Modernity in order to identify the mechanisms that have a legacy in other texts, in history, or in culture itself. As a matter of fact, one can find in this text not only a method for conversion in times of Christian reformation, but also a complete structure for propaganda made of different religious and secular narratives. In the meantime, Barthes isolates Loyola from the rest of the Christian tradition in order to compare his work to non-Christian religious practices, such as the hindu *mantra*. In the 1970s, the interest in contemplative practices—whether they belong to the Judeo-Christian tradition or not—was very active.

Totalitarian Structures and Orders of Corruption

Let us start with a brief recapitulation and visit the most essential concepts surrounding this critical work. Not only does Barthes' essay place the *Exercises* in a continuity of texts that can be read for pleasure, but it also deliberately juxtaposes them to the libertine novels of the marquis de Sade and the writings of the Socialist Fourier. This work is a great example of the possibilities of comparative literature in an age of multiculturalism. Needless to say, there was also a certain desire in 1971 to '*épater le bourgeois*' by placing a respected Catholic figure between two icons essentially studied by and associated with the French Left of the 1970s. The concept behind this work is the following: the structures of sex, politics, and religion might have more in common than it is usually accepted and we need to re-explore and compare them. Sade himself had been a lost figure to the world of literature and undergoes a critical resurrection by Maurice Blanchot, Pierre Klossowski, and Simone de Beauvoir.[3] No one really reads the works of the marquis in a critical perspective before their time. However, just as we cannot ignore the political agenda these authors had in mind when writing about the marquis, we can perceive a similar initiative in Barthes' interest in writing about Loyola. The intellectual bourgeois reader would want to know what the first Jesuit saint could have in common with Sade or Fourier; the attraction lays in the 'blasphemous' nature of the book's title. At first sight, nothing seems to connect the literary production of these three authors. One could very well read each essay separately as an *exemplum* of literary system—or structure—designed by the French theorist in order to illustrate a critical tendency.

Most of the time indeed, scholars use *Sade, Fourier, Loyola* as three independent units. According to Barthes' introduction to the first edition however, these three thinkers have in common more than space for structure recognition. Barthes claims in his short introduction to the collection that: "Aucun des trois n'est *respirable*" (7). What he means by *respirable*,[4] in a text, is the space that an author decides to leave for imagination in the text s/he conceives. That is, the space that a reader is free to fill with personal experience, thoughts, images, or emotions. Indeed, Barthes often compares literature to a form of pleasure comparable to sexual pleasure,[5] and it is in this sense that we should interpret the notion of breath that he applies to Loyola's *Exercises*. Indeed, *pleasure* is the key word for French critic Roland Barthes. The constant insistence on the use of the five senses in the meditation process awakens the interest of those who study the history of sensuality. In the 1960s and 1970s, sensuality was actually the center of studies of a whole generation of critics, such as Barthes, Michel de Certeau, Gilles Deleuze and Michel Foucault. Their common objective is to retrospectively grant these writings through theoretical analysis the pleasure they contain. There is apparently no such thing as pleasure in the writings of the Spanish saint, the Libertine marquis, and the Socialist utopian. They communicate their vision in an almost totalitarian way, refusing the contributing *breath* of the reader; they impose their perspectives and invade the dialogistic territory that bridges author and reader. But the absence of pleasure might be its most obvious manifestation: this absence is part of the mechanism on which these texts are based. In the *Spiritual Exercises*, pleasure is never mentioned but it is still present and associated with sin, it is part of the process of encounter with the 'orders of corruption,' that is, the spaces of confrontation with evil.

Barthes envisions and baptizes Loyola, Sade, and Fourier as *logothètes*. These thinkers all share views derived from a central structure that admits no failure whatsoever as an effect of the language they create. Their vision is exposed in their text as unilateral and irrevocable. Barthes was fascinated by total mechanisms that could be formed in texts, i.e., mechanisms that do not omit any aspect of existence. They prepare their reader/spectator/believer for an undivided perception of the surrounding creation. The French structuralist had conceptualized an encyclopedic project where he would classify all kinds of *logothètes*.[6] Obviously, the philosophical, religious, and political consequences of these texts have made them unique and different from their contemporaries. Their worldview tries to be complete and to cover every aspect of human existence, in an almost obsessive fashion. They have all succeeded, up to a certain point, in turning their theoretical structure into a practice. The *Spiritual Exercises* became the pillar of the Jesuit order, the novels of Sade reflected and gave materialistic guidelines in times of political apocalypse, and Fourier's socialist visions were a source of great inspiration, although never truly practiced by a society or a congregation. Their often utopian nature and their idealization of a system seem to have condemned them to failure, but not to critical oblivion.

The attraction for the study of these texts—ours and Barthes'—also lies in their limits, in what they fail to cover. Indeed, the practices they have engendered all relatively died out. As history has often shown, a totalitarian structure based on a utopia—textual or political—is eventually turned upside down. This is what makes Loyola, Sade, and Fourier attractive authors in post-1968 French intellectual circles. They all offer examples of structures that have failed to survive socially the atemporality they had once claimed. It is essentially in this cultural-studies perspective that French criticism envisions Loyola. However, as we will try to demonstrate in the following chapter, the structure as such might fail at what it is trying to achieve (in the case of Loyola, the conversion of Christian believer to the ideals of Counter-reformed Catholicism with potential enrollment in the Society of Jesus), but it does not necessarily fail in the various influences and consequences that come out the practice of this structure. In other words, they are often recovered by other cultural and artistic practices.

As Jonathan Culler perfectly sums up: "Barthes's example encouraged the reading of the connotations of cultural images and analysis of the social functioning of the strange constructions of culture" (42). Indeed, one of the aspects of the *Exercises* that most fascinates the critic is their insistence on controlling imagination, "selon une sorte d'économie totalitaire" as Barthes underlines (55). Totalitarian imagination—as we could name it and such as the French structuralist encounters it in the *Exercises*—is a great matter for criticism and deconstruction. The *logothète*'s obsession with unconditional control over his reader's mind becomes the first failure of his text, as will be underlined later on. Many other scholars of Western literature before Barthes have looked at several writing from the saint. For example, the German art historian Arnold Hauser had observed in his *Social History of Art* (1957) that "nothing [was] more typical of the change in the general affairs than the foundation of the Jesuit order, which was to become a model of dogmatic strictness and ecclesiastical discipline, and which became the first embodiment of the totalitarian idea" (118). It is true that, of all the religious figures that have influenced the tradition, Loyola remains an extremely enigmatic figure owing to his capacity to transform the spirit of the Renaissance, in which he evolves, into a totalitarian structure.

In the 20th century the field opens up to a new form of secular criticism that is going to look at mystical writings from a much more theoretical point of view precisely to explore their socio-political dimensions and implications. Saint Augustine, Saint Ignatius of Loyola, Saint Teresa of Avila, and Saint John of the Cross are among these most famous new literary figures from the Catholic tradition, associated with an institution that acknowledges the literary quality of their work. While one can easily understand the literary quality of Augustine's theological vision, enjoy the mysticism of Teresa's autobiography, and surely savor the lyricism of

John's poetry, it seems radically more difficult to find a similar pleasurable dimension in the rather dry works of Ignatius of Loyola.

The problem when approaching the *Spiritual Exercises* is twofold: first of all, the writings of Loyola were never *intended* to become canonical works of literature. In many ways, these guidelines given by the founder of the Jesuit order could present a negative impression of the common conception of the act of writing: the style is plain, flat, authoritarian, and commanding, never lyrical and certainly not metaphorical. The second dimension of the problem is the notion of *exercise*[7] itself contained in the title, for it reveals at once all the secrets that a text may contain; it reveals its writing process in the same fashion that some minimalist works do. There again, it seems that 'less is more.' This is precisely what Barthes admires in Loyola: the capacity of the author to control all of the possible textual dimensions, in a very extreme way. It is a problematic that he had already explored in the *Degré zéro de l'écriture* (1954), when he attempts a genealogy of bourgeois *écriture*. His first step in the essay on Loyola, however, is to counterattack the common belief that one cannot be a Catholic saint and an author of literature at the same time. The founding text of the Jesuits has often been recognized as the simplest form of transmission of a mental experience, which is precisely why it should be accepted and honored as an object of literary criticism. According to Barthes, 'simple' means extremely complex and this attitude follows the critical pattern of Michel de Certeau and Georges Bataille in many ways. The criticism found in the works of these two latter combines close-reading analysis with historical context and philosophical reflection.

Certeau, in *La Fable Mystique* (1982), acknowledges a certain continuity between Loyola and Teresa de Avila, that is, a common attraction for an imagined *order of corruption*, the notion that most concerns us in this analysis: "Ignace de Loyola, Thérèse d'Avila, bien d'autres ont desiré entrer dans *un Ordre "corrompu"*. Non qu'ils sympathisent avec la décadence. Mais ces lieux défaits, quasi déshérités représentent la situation effective du christianisme contemporain" (43). This term defines the spaces of trial for mystics: the deserts where the monks would confront evil spirits, the spaces of abjection, places where salvation is absent. This *order of corruption* is in mysticism a mental or physical place associated with the body and its capacities because, in opposition to the soul, the body is corruptible. Loyola indicates the necessity to discover these places through the power of imagination, and even though he does it in a very plain textual form, this is precisely where the complexity of his writing begins. He preaches the necessity to engage in a voluntary encounter with abjection in order to fully understand its importance in creation and to be able to recognize it when choices are made. Only this capacity to come close to temptation will enable the believer to get familiar with the ways of salvation through good works. The *order of corruption* is an absence of grace and defines in the meantime everything that it opposes; it is an attractive literary place to explore in a century generally fascinated with the birth of the modern literary space. Spanish surrealists, for instance, recognize the mystical "orders of corruption" in their poetry.[8] We will see in the second part of this chapter how the notion of *order of corruption* helps us understand the relationship between the *Exercises* and the narrative traditions from which Loyola often draws his inspiration.

Georges Bataille, in his *Expérience intérieure* (1954), had already discussed notions central to Spanish mysticism and the analysis of the spaces that it presents: he starts his argument with the elimination of the problematic word *mystique* that he soon replaces by *intérieure* to make it more universal and inter-religious. It is fundamental indeed to conceptualize the orders of corruption presented in the *Exercises* as interior and internalized spaces; they become virtual theaters for the economy of salvation. In order to present his argument in this perspective, Bataille wants to separate Loyola's exercises from the common conception that they are based on a *discursive* mode: « A ce sujet, c'est une erreur classique d'assigner les *Exercices* de saint Ignace à la méthode discursive : ils s'en remettent au discours qui règle tout mais sur le mode dramatique » (26). On the contrary, according to him, this text is a great example of a *dramatic* method that forces the disciple to represent places and people in his/her imagination, and to become part of this drama. The saint's writings are in that sense almost *theatrical*, and already show the Jesuit inclination for this latter form of representation, announcing their contribution to its development in the seventeenth century. Numerous studies can be found on the Jesuit influence in the seventeenth-century theater of France, Germany, and Spain.[9] The *theatrical* dimension that Bataille identifies in the *Exercises* does not mean, however, that theater as a genre and a literary tradition has any direct influence on the creation and the dynamics of the mental stage on which Ignatius is going to guide his exercitants.

Barthes launched the debate on the *Exercises* by elaborating on the observations of Bataille, and Certeau continued to work in this direction. As a follow-up of the recognition of theatrical dynamics in Loyola's text, his first own breakthrough is the notion of a *multiple text* that he develops at the beginning of the essay, in order to set the tone for the rest of his analysis. His structuralist interpretation invites us to distinguish four layers of textual exchange in Loyola's writing: the first one (literal) from the saint himself to the spiritual director (true recipient of the book), the second connection (semantic) happens therefore between the director and the person receiving the guidelines to perform the exercises. The saint explains it in the following fashion: "The person who gives to another the method and procedure for meditating or contemplation should accurately *narrate* the history contained in the contemplation or meditation, going over the points with only a brief or summary explanation" (*Exercises*, 121). As a matter of fact, this narration is made up of several layers drawn from previous narrative traditions, superimposed in a multiple text. In its introductory guidelines, it imitates the mechanisms of many other texts of pedagogy: short and concise, with an obvious concern for the student-exercitant. But Loyola's text passes on to a third and a fourth textual exchange: the third happens allegorically between the person receiving the method and the divinity in the mode of meditation, and the fourth is the reply of the divinity to this person in a mode of contemplation (anagogic relation). The most interesting factor in this structure is the opposition between Ignatius (beginning of the chain) and the 'one receiving the Exercises', as the two ends of a same spectrum of textual communication, given that he writes in the *Spiritual Diary* how often he would himself assume all of the positions except the one of the divinity. The hero of the Counter-Reformation is therefore capable of being author, director, disciple and recipient of divine language, because he is separated from the imperfection of language.

In the 1540s, Loyola has established a system that is going to characterize the whole spirit of the seventeenth century, what we like to call the Baroque. The concept of a *multiple text* identified here by Barthes might be at times a bit reductive, but overall it does identify appropriate levels in the text. Its complexity voluntarily reflects the complexity of and the precise preparation for communication with the divinity; it emphasizes implicitly that the Reformation is wrong when it defines a direct relationship of the believer with the divinity through faith alone. At the same time, it corresponds to the Society's agenda itself, that is, to reduce the enthusiasm of Renaissance Humanism to forms of authority and control. The complexity of the economy of salvation needs to be recuperated by the Roman Church, and furthermore, needs to obey common aesthetic laws. In this sense, the *Exercises* represent the first step that the Counter-Reformed institution makes in that direction. The four-level structure of interpretation—originally a medieval structure promoted by Thomas of Aquinas—stands as a pillar of these High Renaissance aesthetics. Anthony Raspa writes in *The Emotive Image* that: "in baroque writings generally, anagogy was a term applied to the whole of the four-level way of thinking and to the fourth of its levels of meaning" (20), and later on in the discussion makes the connection with the methodology of the *Exercises*: "The peculiar retreat from the world into the self represented by *Exercises* excluded the Renaissance ideal of the civil man as someone versed in public polity" (46). In this sense, the *Exercises* announce the model of the Baroque world view and its detachment from the ideals of the Renaissance, its anxiety about a West now divided by the Reformation and its desire to return to scholastic models.

The method of isolation and self-reflection given in the text is extremely strict, as if there were only a totalitarian answer to the religious crisis of the sixteenth century, the answer to a corresponding need in the public—and often urban—sphere. There is a rule for each particular situation of the exercises. Indeed, the reader does not enter in the actual division of the four-week spiritual diet right away, but only after spending time in the anti-chamber of twenty *explanations*. The time dedicated to preparation is greater than the time spent in meditation. The numbering itself is quite interesting: Barthes emphasizes that there is a reason for the division of the exercises into four weeks instead of the more logical/traditional separation into three[18] that one could expect. The number four forces us to remain in a binary figure (2+2); therefore the middle of the exercises is just a turning point and is not stable; it does not give an opportunity to rest, to breathe. It negates the possibility of a gray area such as purgatory. It is designed that way in order to force the person undergoing the exercise to enter a linguistic void and accept it: sin is the absence of virtue and evil is the void of good. In this sense it is a totalitarian text that requires from its applicant a great passivity and acceptance of this radical cosmic division. In the words of Barthes, the mind is a territory and it needs to be *entirely occupied*: "cette variété de distinctions (dont le modèle est évidemment scolastique) provient, comme on l'a vu, de la nécessité d'occuper la totalité du territoire mental" (57). This is the kind of typically structuralist observation we obtain when reading Barthes. The notion underlined here will be crucial in order to understand the perspective taken in this analysis. However, it is also necessary to step away from Barthes and his perceptions in order to turn more to the historical and epistemological parameters of the analysis.

Previously, we have identified the notion of 'totalitarian imagination' in the text on which the Ignatian exercises are based. Let us now take a look at this capacity of the mind and how it also falls under the control of the text. The structuralist essay suggests that, as critical readers of the *Exercises*, we need to make a clear distinction between the imaginary and the imagination. The imaginary has been defined and redefined by Bachelard and Lacan as a capital of internal representations unknown to the subject because of a separation operated by the symbol. Since the imaginary of Loyola's text is extremely flat and the style is fairly poor, the imaginary of the disciple should be, like language, the same way. This is probably why Loyola spends so much time laying down his long list of requisites in the form of preparatory rites before one slowly progresses toward the actual exercises. He prepares the structure and, in the meantime, reduces his 'points' to a minimalist structure. The text is supposed to take the place of this imaginary, instead of building up on the symbolical experience of the subject. On the contrary, the text does not allow the exercitant to reflect on his/her personal experience or even to get an existential dilemma involved in the structural development of the practice. The exercise consists in giving an image to contemplate to a soul that does not possess any. The believer is then forced to accept an imaginative structure and adapt to it. Again, the believer's access to 'respiration' is denied.

The creation of extremely explicit images will become the Jesuit's favorite tool to take control of the disciple's mental territory and, by the same token, the aesthetic credo of Baroque church architecture.[11] The Loyolan imaginary reservoir,[12] as we could designate it according to the definition we find of it in Barthes' essay, is a new language that totally replaces a previous one, and whose linguistic method is based on imitation of the divine image, generally present in saints, martyrs, Loyola himself, Christ and the Holy Trinity. It is hard to disagree with this last point given the number of times that the text insists on the act of reproducing and imitating Christ. The image must penetrate through sensual experiences the vacant imaginary of the sinner. Barthes admires the Spanish saint for his capacity to fill, in a totalitarian fashion, the disciple with these images through all of the five senses. The spirit of the imitated object must take total control of the exercitant, and by the same token, negates all voluntary acts of contemplation in the practice. A great example of this totalitarian process is found in the first meditation on Hell:

66. **First Point.** This will be to see in imagination the vast fires, and the souls enclosed, as it were, in bodies of fire.
67. **Second Point.** To hear the wailing, the howling, cries, and blasphemies against Christ our Lord and against His saints.
68. **Third Point.** With the sense of smell to perceive the smoke, the sulphur, the filth, and corruption.
69. **Fourth Point.** To taste the bitterness of tears, sadness, and remorse of conscience.
70. **Fifth Point.** With the sense of touch to feel the flames which envelop and burn the souls (32–3).

Nonetheless, it is sight that prevails in Loyola's hierarchy of the senses, and this is going to be a crucial element of the aesthetics of the Counter-Reformation, that is, Jesuit imagery in the Baroque. Barthes affirms that: "l'oeil devient l'organe majeur de la perception (le baroque en témoignerait, qui est art de la chose vue)" (68). This consideration does not include the importance that music is going to have in later Baroque aesthetics, as an essential tool of sensorial stimulation. But it is true, however, that, at the rise of Modernity, the importance of visual art is going to increase in Counter-Reformed cultures. Furthermore, the disciple of the *Exercises* is constantly asked to visualize a scene whose geometry systematically places him/her at/as the central point: "Upon awakening, I will imagine myself as a great sinner, deserving death, and brought in chains before the eternal judge" (142). Loyola has a clear tendency to always place the divinity at the center of its worldview and the believer as a gravitating dot around it whose chances to get close to the center are limited. In this sense, the position of the believer in relation to salvation is not contrary to that exposed by Luther. It places believers in a position which forces them to perceive their centrality and uniqueness. Christine Buci-Glucksman in *La Raison baroque* sees in Ignatius of Loyola the thinker responsible for the "apologie post-tridentine des images et de l'*impérialisme visuel*" (97). If we accept this position, this would make Loyola one of the founding *logothètes* of the modern obsession with the gaze. After the Council of Trent the Jesuits will enjoy the artistic freedom to develop this form of art. The second half of the sixteenth century will be marked by these revolutions in architecture, paintings, and literature, and will continue throughout the seventeenth century.

The believer's gaze toward images is a key concept for spiritual guidance since it reflects the very space of confrontation between Lutherans who reject them and soldiers of the Counter-Reformation who adopt them: the human conscience, the mental territory that can be modified. Barthes makes an interesting—and inevitable—parallel between Ignatius's method of forcing the image reservoir into virtual corrupted orders with modern psychology and calls the saint "un psychothérapeute qui cherche à injecter à tout prix des images dans l'esprit mat, sec et vide de l'exercitant, à introduire en lui la culture du fantasme, (. . .) [à] 'névroser' le retraitant" (72). What is the purpose of such a discipline? It is probably a form of self-control of the subject; it prepares a machine that will sustain itself automatically, "une machine qui s'entretient toute seule" (73), echoing here the words of Gilles Deleuze when discussing the schizophrenia of the modern subject in the *Anti-Oedipe* as a "machine désirante". Barthes adds that Loyola begins the therapy of the disciple but never ends it, and leaves him in a place (the outcome of the exercises) where problems are far from being resolved.[13] Nonetheless, it is important to underline that this could be the problematic of Baroque aesthetics in general: they never propose stability, but force dramatically the subject into the worst forms of neurosis, similar to the mystical *order of corruption* described by Michel de Certeau. It is a place of lack and absence, even when it is saturated with images, and only through this void can salvation be sought and obtained.

Saturation with images, as a Baroque artifice, begins with the *Spiritual Exercises*. Barthes goes back to Roman Jakobson's image of the tree (which is actually

Saussure's) to explain the totalitarian structure of the exercises, a figure that he includes in his essay (60). The mind of the exercitant is saturated with narrative images. Each week is divided into days, and then divided into exercises; each exercise is divided into several steps, and each step into different sensorial experiences, contemplations of sins, Christian capacities to develop, prayers to recite, etc. From this point of view, it is easy to conceptualize the branching that Barthes mentions in his essay, and how it resembles not only a tree but also a brain with all of its ramifications.[14] These images are useful in order to understand how important it is for Loyola to spread images through the totality of the human mind as if it were, again, a territory to conquer. But such a structure is inevitably going to involve a great deal of repetition, which is probably why this text resists so much our literary appreciation at times, since it forces our senses to engage in the same acts several times.

These few considerations regarding his essays are indeed the starting point of a large discussion on theoretical concepts that can also be useful for the critical study of Loyola's *Exercises*. We can still wonder, after reading Barthes's essay, why Loyola happens to be psycho-analyzed by the theorist of textual pleasure. On the contrary, the saint's text has the capacity to become a true torture for the modern reader, for it does not breathe at all; it blows its air into the reader. Very little space is left for contemplation since Ignatius takes care of all the transitory moments. Nonetheless, the model of "total occupation of the mental territory" that it offers has had imitations, parodies, admirers, and detractors. Barthes's key point in this essay still remains in the very first line: the Jesuits have contributed to the formation of Western canonical literature. In the same fashion, the *Exercises* have served as a pillar of Western artistic development and cannot be dissociated from the transition observed between Renaissance and Baroque.

Unlike other studies that have looked at the *Spiritual Exercises* within their historical context only, I wish to explore the legacy of this intriguing text and its 'totalitarian' methodology in the secular sphere through the transition from the Baroque to the Enlightenment. This question will be revisited several times in coming chapters and the analysis of similar artistic structures will be pursued. In the rest of this chapter, however, particular attention will be given to the circumstances surrounding the creation of *The Spiritual Exercises*. In order to begin this discussion of a particular system for orienting the imagination, I intend to demonstrate that Loyola combines dramatic and narrative elements gathered in anterior textual forms and narrative traditions, chooses deliberately to modify the modes of perception of the world and establishes a system that uses imagination (a human capacity that he traditionally associates with evil and sin) to give priority to representation over perception. That is why one should not envision the text of the exercises as a totalitarian structure that invents the necessary confrontation with the corrupted orders. Rather, it should be considered as a confluence of various narratives that already had a preference for images of these orders.

The Formation of an Image Reservoir

First, I would like to situate Loyola as a reader of novels of chivalry and a soldier. This first parameter of his personal formation in Spanish letters will show how there is already a variety of genres in Renaissance Spain that have a direct influence on Loyola's construction of an image reservoir. Like Teresa of Avila before him, Ignatius is a reader of *Amadis de Gaula*. The war strategist also speaks through the spiritual director of the *Exercises* and I intend to demonstrate that this text voluntarily puts exercitants at the imaginary center of a cosmological war and invites them to engage direct contact with the order of corruption. In parallel, Loyola's conversion experience originates from his reading of the *Lives of the Saints*, an older genre in prose still extremely popular in Renaissance Spain. Also, as a religious man, he demonstrates a great knowledge of Scripture: the *Exercises* offer a strategy to guide the exercitant through a narrative, by pointing to passages in the Gospels. I would like to discuss here the interaction of these different narrative parameters in Loyola's text, and the importance they each have in the making of an imaginary system such as the one we encounter in this spiritual guide.

Ignatius, like Luther and Calvin, is a product of the skeptical crisis unleashed by the Reformation and Humanism that characterizes the turn of the sixteenth century. It is indeed difficult to find a definition of 'Renaissance' that easily suits the phenomenon in all the countries where it happens and that adapts to the analysis of Loyola's work at the same time. Arnold Hauser proposes several parameters in his *Social History of Art II*, and here is what we could particularly underline in relation to the focus of this work: "the more society and economic life emancipate themselves from the fetters of ecclesiastical dogma, the more freely does art turn to the consideration of immediate reality" (5). This might be the case in Italy, but it does not necessarily mean that such a definition applies to all countries. In this sense, Hauser's view is a highly traditional one that will not by itself take our analysis very far. However, Loyola grows up precisely in such a time of emancipation and relative freedom, and these circumstances are going to help his cause. If we turn in complement to Julia Reinhard Lupton's definition of this rebirth, we find that "the Renaissance presents the model as well as the object of the historian's cultural inquiry, not only because its artifacts coalesce into the unity of a distinct period and way of life, but because they do so by themselves *recreating an earlier's epoch universe* of form and meaning" (8). This angle seems to have a more universal take on the phenomenon. It is in that sense that Loyola's *Exercises* are essentially a product of the Renaissance; his fascination with bringing the mental subject into a recreated dimension whose elements belong to other periods is easy to identify. The Renaissance is not only a rebirth of classical culture out of Christianity, but also a time of re-creation, that is, of re-ordering natural orders through observation, experience, and the fusion of genres on all levels: political, cultural, artistic and also religious. Loyola with his *Spiritual Exercises* participates fully in this movement of image recycling.

The Renaissance in Spain, as it is in many other countries in Western Europe, is without a doubt a period of experimentation in which we observe the development of this naturalistic interest in the human subject. It is not, however, a period of emancipation from Catholic doctrine. But it is a time of exploration of the representation of the world. The sudden liberty that the artist is granted not only applies to sculpture, painting, and architecture, but also reaches the spheres of the literary work. Genres are intertwined, mocked, and suddenly associated in spite of their contrary natures. For instance, the turn of the century itself is marked by the publication of Spain's first and most famous tragic-comedy, *La Celestina* (1501). This work by Fernando de Rojas is in itself a transgression of the established genres for it seeks to combine tragedy and comedy, and at the same time, this emancipation from Aristotelian principles is also emancipation from ecclesiastical dogma. For instance, its heroine is a witch and proves to be in control of the feelings and actions of the other characters around her, therefore stilling the position of the divine. The publication of this tragicomedy (which is also a sort of novel) marks a turning point between medieval literature and the Golden Age. But transgression of older models does not limit itself to the work of art. In the meantime, the Reformation appears as another transgression of an established order for Catholic Southern Europe. Ignatius grows up in a world marked by experimental transgressions in which the dramatic modes are often in conflict with narrative modes, and even though he will stand as a defender of rather medieval values, his own production stands at the crossroads of several narrative genres.

The attitude of experimentation typical of the Renaissance can also be found and reflected on other levels and in other disciplines. Again, what first appears to be a transgression will turn out to be a successful artistic doctrine. On the philosophical level, for instance, the turn of the century is an extremely rich period for Europe since most of medieval theology suddenly transforms into a great enthusiasm and rediscovery of pre-Christian art and philosophical treatises. Pagan texts are rediscovered and praised, beauty is associated with the human body, and spirituality tends toward models of relative independence from institutionalized religion. Between the years 1514 and 1517, Spain sees the publication of its first *Biblia políglota complutense*, the first edition of Scriptures in Castilian. The advent of the Humanist movement quickly followed by the Lutheran Reformation around the year 1517 provokes a great questioning of religious hierarchy and philosophy is no longer reserved for the elite of the Catholic orders. Once again, this represents all together another transgression of medieval principles that Spain will try to resist more than France or England, because of the latter's relative acceptance of Protestant ideas at the beginning of the century. On the political level, Spanish borders and ethnic composition have been altered; a new kingdom has formed a single nation imposing a single language and a single religion. It is definitely not in a time of political unification that a Christian Reformation would be welcome. The Spanish sixteenth century becomes a theater where all doors to the outside are progressively closing and prepares for the autharcy of its interior. By 1559, it is prohibited for a Spaniard to go abroad to study in a foreign university such as La Sorbonne, Oxford, and Bologna. Ignatius of Loyola will be one of the last Spanish students to have the opportunity to do so and to spend some years as a student in Paris, before the law passes.[15]

On the economic level, Spain is starting to benefit greatly from the conquest of South America and now stands as a dominating port of entry for its gold. The turn of the century is a prosperous time and the Holy Roman Emperor Charles V can finance his wars against French opponent King François I. However, it is still far from being a united nation. Northern Spain, where Ignatius was born and raised,[16] still claims pride in having resisted the Muslim invasion, and its inhabitants call themselves '*cristianos viejos*,' in opposition to Southern Spain[17] wich has only recently been re-conquered by Catholic Castile. Even though funds are available and foreign artists are starting to join the Spanish court, Renaissance Spain does not have the artistic flexibility of Italy or France, but on the contrary seeks to secure its border and its politics. A certain paranoia hovers over the importation of foreign models. Most of all, Habsburg Spain wants to think of itself as the fortress in which Roman Catholic values are being preserved from the Reformation. The emperor himself entertains a pre-absolutist idea of divine right in his person: "Charles believed that God had called him to a position of preeminence, shortly to be sanctified by the imperial dignity, so that he might defend Christianity from the Turks and preserve the internal unity of Europe from heresy" (Lovett 41). For this reason, Spain enters a state of cultural and religious isolation.

It is essential to recapitulate these few factors in order to fully comprehend the particular climate in which Ignatius will undergo his conversion and write his masterpiece. In his youth, for instance, he is formed to be a soldier in the army of the Emperor, to fight against the French. This 'other' Catholic nation is not resisting as efficiently as Spain does the cultural changes of the times and, particularly, the Protestant Reformation and the influence of humanist writers. As many soldiers have done before and after him—Cervantes being the most flagrant case—Loyola is going to turn to Spanish literature for military inspiration. Soldiers are often motivated by literary images of conditions of combat. The importation of genres and the political circumstances around the diffusion of knightly romances will play a great role in the composition of this defender of Catholic values. His eyes are exposed to four major genres: Humanist essays, the novels of Chivalry, the lives of saints, and the Scriptures. Each of these represents a specific parameter in which we ought to analyze his literary production. We should also restore Loyola's *Exercises* to this phase of literary experimentation[18] that Spain hosts in this period. But first we need to take a brief look at the some of these major 'degenerative genres' and the potential influence—be it negative or positive—they might have had on the writing of the saint. Let us not forget that Barthes admires Loyola for his image reservoir,[19] although he does not care to investigate its sources very closely.

Let us first take a look at the conflictive and controversial influence that the Humanist movement might have had on the writing of the founder of the Jesuits. What he surely inherits from his reading of Erasmus is an interest in knowledge of the Creation. Loyola is aware that no soldier in the army of the Christian lord is efficient without a direct contact with the social and geographical parameters that define it. Father Pedro Ribadeneira, author of the *Vida de San Ignacio de Loyola*, writes a few years after the saint's death, at a time when Loyola has proven his authority in Rome: "es cosa muy probada y manifiesta en todo el mundo el fruto que ha traído por todas partes el uso de estos sagrados ejercicios a la república cristiana" (42).[20] In this meta-hagiography,[21] the Jesuit father justifies the existence of the exercises as sacred writings and attributes it to divine inspiration. But indeed it is right: the *Spiritual Exercises* starts circulating in Europe during Loyola's lifetime and are re-edited several times before his death. They become the manifesto of the Counter-Reformation *par excellence*. They reach the four corners of the world in a very short time, given the Jesuit interest in missionary work. This outreach to non-Christian civilizations could be interpreted as an expansion of Humanist ideals. One could easily compare the influence of the *Spiritual Exercises* and their circulation in that era to that of Erasmus' *De Milite Christiano*, written in France under the reign of François I around 1505. Both works have in common the metaphor of the 'Christian soldier' but do not share the same application of it.[22] In many ways, Erasmus is a controversial figure in Spain, since most see in him the instigator of the Lutheran revolution.[23] Ribadeneira himself indicates that Loyola was a critical reader of his work. In the following passage he gives us a detailed account of the saint's experience in reading Erasmus:

> Prosiguiendo pues en los ejercicios de sus letras, aconsejáronle algunos hombres letrados y píos que para aprender bien la lengua Latina, y juntamente tratar de cosas devotas y espirituales, que leyese el libro *De Milite Christiano* (que quiere decir de un caballero cristiano), que compuso en latín Erasmo Roterodamo, el cual en aquel tiempo tenía grande fama de hombre docto y elegante en el decir. Y entre los otros que fueron de este parecer, también lo fue el confesor de Ignacio. Y así, tomando su consejo, comenzó con toda simplicidad a leer en él con mucho cuidado, y a notar sus frases y modo de hablar. Pero advirtió una cosa muy nueva y muy maravillosa, y es, que en tomando este libro (que digo) de Erasmo en las manos y comenzando a leer en él, juntamente se le comenzaba a entibiar su fervor y a *enfriársele* la devoción. Y cuanto más iba leyendo, iba más creciendo esta mudanza. De suerte que cuando acababa la lección, le parecía que se le había acabado y *helado* todo el ardor que antes tenía, y apagado su espíritu y trocado su corazón, y que no era el mismo después de la lección que antes de ella. Y como echase de ver esto algunas veces, a la fin echó el libro de sí, y cobró con él y con las demás obras de este autor tan grande ojeriza y aborrecimiento, que después jamás no quiso leerlas él, ni consintió que en nuestra Compañía se leyesen sino con mucho delecto y mucha cautela (60).[24]

It is crucial to see here the progression in Loyola's experience as described by Ribadeneira. Ignatius seems to have the same reaction to works from other genres. The act of reading Erasmus literally turns him cold; he starts losing his body temperature and even freezes. The warmth that represents religious fervor disappears progressively. Ignatius is forced to throw the book away as one who heroically resists temptation. Later on, Ignatius prohibits the reading of Erasmus to those who do not have the spiritual capacity to face this physical figure of evil. Obviously, the humanist tendency is the enemy that Loyola will be fighting on the benches of Renaissance universities Alcalá de Henares, Salamanca, and the Sorbonne in Paris. He is determined to participate in the most heated debates and, like a humanist student, will tour these schools of theology.

Rejecting violently a text could also mean that, simultaneously, the subject acknowledges his/her acceptance of it. The survival of Humanist writing in Renaissance Spain is often attributed to or associated with the Jesuits. As Alexander Parker reminds us: "[Ignacio de Loyola y] los jesuitas prolongaron gran parte del movimiento humanista dentro y más allá de la Contrarreforma" (Rico 67).[25] Ribadeneira's description also tells us that there is a genuine reaction to the act of reading Erasmus, followed by a repetitive progression. This hagiographic twist here in this account is Loyola's exposure to the *order of corruption* contained in the essay of the Dutch thinker. It almost invites its reader to the experience, and to follow the bravery of Ignatius, but with extreme care. He particularly stresses the fact that Erasmus' text is potent since it acts physically on the body of its reader. We know the effect Erasmus' writings had on Martin Luther and how they became the rhetorical enemy of both Reformation and Counter-Reformation. As a matter of fact, the effect that Erasmus' work has on Loyola and his companions is undeniable as a consequence on the already existing opposition between Erasmus and Luther:

> The humanist movement had a palpable effect on the Society (...) Even the members of the original band of ten in varying degrees experienced its influence *well before* they entered Italy in 1537. Although they and many of their first recruits were more deeply imbued with the scholastic tradition of the Middle Age, they had all learned how to speak and write Latin in a humanist style and were not unaffected by humanist criticism (O'Malley 14–5).

So much for trying to keep the Companions safe from the 'heresies' of the father of Humanism. It is difficult to envision how Loyola could reconcile Humanist ideals with the practice of the *Exercises*, but we certainly cannot blame the first Jesuits for ignoring their enemy. On the contrary, getting familiar with its weapons and exposing oneself to the order of corruption has always been a critical and controversial Jesuit characteristic since the writing of its founding text. What Pedro Ribadeneira describes in the passage above is a reaction of corruption on the body of the saint in the activity of reading. The question concerning the Humanist influence on Loyola is controversial since he rejects Erasmus and promotes him at the same time. But the given reason was not because the ideas found in his books, which were used in schools, contained anything harmful or immoral, but he feared that once students became familiar with this author, they might become admirers of his style and go on to read other books of his and, perhaps, be enticed to look upon the Roman Church in the same manner as this author had done. As a result of this rejection, we might have a better understanding of the plain and dry style of Loyola's text. As we have commented earlier, no effort is made in it to adopt a Humanist rhetoric such as the one we encounter in Erasmus. On the contrary, the purpose of his minimalist structure, established around a practice, is to counter-attack the 'frozen intentions' of the father of Humanism, and to reject his style along with his ideas. For Loyola, the rhetoric has nothing to do with the eloquent style that one might have acquired through Erasmus' course of study, but rather with the dimension and the greater power of the images. From this angle, both Luther and Loyola react strongly to Erasmus' style. His work seeks to eliminate this purely Humanist persuasiveness and urbanity and simplify it to offer images.

This is probably how we should first envision Loyola's *Spiritual Exercises*, since they also have the pretension of conjugating a reading experience with physical reactions. In order to reintegrate them within a tradition, we could compare this reaction to that of another Spanish saint. Saint Teresa of Avila also describes the act of reading as an activity that involves bodily temperature. When talking about her first contact with literature during her adolescence, Teresa claims that: "Era aficionada a libros de caballerías (. . .) Yo comencé a quedarme en costumbre de leerlos, y aquella pequeña falta, que en ella ví, *me comenzó a enfriar los deseos*, y comenzar a faltar en los demás" (119).[26] Even though Teresa of Avila does not mention Erasmus in the account of her life, she admits that the novels of chivalry were a genre that she particularly enjoyed. Very early in her text however, she confesses that they were a source of temptation and that the vanity they contained was harmful to the Christian soul. Her conclusions are similar to that of Ribadeneira: she warns her reader against the potential of given texts circulating at the time. The text becomes a territory in which the soul comes to fight its enemy, i.e., an order of corruption. In the case of the novels of chivalry, both Loyola and Teresa of Avila have used the text to measure their human vanity.

In the first half of the sixteenth century, these novels were everywhere to be found in the new-born Spanish kingdom. As implied earlier, they often praised male values such as courage, resistance to temptation, adoration of a female object of desire, and military service to Christian kingdoms. Nonetheless, these virtues were in contradiction with some of the most intrinsic views of the Inquisition. But their publication and distribution were in complete accordance with the laws of the Catholic kingdom of Spain. Their depiction of the hero was, indeed, helpful propaganda for the ethnic cleansing that Spain had just undergone. Of all novels of chivalry, *Amadis de Gaula* (1508)[27] not only became the most famous story of a wandering knight but it also gave a pattern to the genre. We do not ignore the influence it had on Don Quixote who lived for the imitation of this knight. Ángel Rosenblat writes in his introduction to the modern translation of *Amadis* that: "Los leía con deleite en sus mocedades caballerescas Ignacio de Loyola" (x).[28] For a young knight such as the founder of the Jesuits before the conversion experience, Amadis represented the Christian soldier *par excellence*. Of all the readings, however, the novels of Chivalry had a great capacity to praise the vanities of this world. As Rosenblat points out again: "A pesar de las anatemas de autoridades seglares y eclesiásticas, la Inquisición no les prohibió nunca" (x).[29] They are an *order of corruption* that no one is able to condemn to the fire. Somehow, it is the same dilemma that Ignatius faces in his conversion experience with the novels of chivalry, the same conjunction of attraction and rejection. Father Camâra, another biographer of Ignatius of Loyola and author of the *Autobiography*,[30] gives us a clear account of the saint's experience in dealing with the vain imagination contained in these novels:

> As he read them over many times, he became rather fond of what he found written there. Putting his reading aside, he sometimes stopped to think about the things he had read and at other times about the things of the world that he used to think about before. Of the many vain things that presented themselves to him, one took such a hold on his heart that he was absorbed in thinking about it for two or three or four hours without realizing it: he imagined what he would do in the service of a certain lady, the means he would take so he could go to the country where she lived, the verses, the words he would say to her, the deeds of arms he would do in her service. He became so conceited with this that he did not consider how impossible it would be because the lady was not of the lower nobility nor a countess nor a duchess, but her station was higher than any of these (23).

Yes, Ignatius of Loyola also had his Dulcinea del Toboso to entertain his thoughts during his convalescence, right before the conversion. It is easy to imagine how Cervantes would have used the story of Ignatius for inspiration in the writing of his masterpiece. We can establish parallelisms between Amadís and Ignatius, but they are not as significant as the ones that could be established with Amadís' most pathetic imitation, that is, Don Quixote. If Loyola imitates the knights and adapts their morals to Counter-Reformed Christianity, his imitation itself is going to become a source of inspiration for Cervantes. We will further this comparison in the third chapter when dealing with the narrative dynamics of Cervantes' masterpiece.

Nonetheless it is important to mention this parallelism early enough in our analysis. Cervantes, who has found much inspiration in the story of Loyola, is very aware of the conflict surrounding novels of Chivalry and gives us an excellent bit of literary criticism in *Don Quixote*. He illustrates very well in his masterpiece the complexity of the status of these works in the sixteenth century in the episode when the curate and the barber decide to burn the books of Don Quixote in order to save his soul:

> Y el primero que maese Nicolás le dio en las manos fue *Los cuatro de Amadís de Gaula*, y dijo el cura: "Parece cosa de misterio ésta, porque, según he oído decire, este libro fue el primero de caballerías que se imprimió en España, y de todos los demás han tomado principio y origen de éste; y, así, me parece que, como a dogmatizador de una secta tan mala, le debemos sin excusa condenar al fuego" "No señor, dijo el barbero, que también he oído decir que es el mejor de todos los libros que de este género se han compuesto; y así, como a único en su arte, se debe perdonar" "Así es verdad, dijo el cura, y por esa razón se le otorga la vida por ahora." (61)[31]

In this passage, it is interesting to see that the curate and the barber present the same argument to condemn the book to the fire and, at the same time, to save it from it. As is well known, the novels of Chivalry are clearly designed as the origin of Don Quixote's madness. They are the fiction into which he wishes to transform his reality. Nonetheless, the values they contain turn him away from the Christian salvation of the soul.

The comparison between Loyola and the hidalgo of the Mancha has already been made. For instance, Spanish philosopher Miguel de Unamuno writes in 1904 in *Alma Vasca*: "Si hay algún hombre *representativo* de mi raza, es Iñigo de Loyola, el *hidalgo* guipuzcoano que fundó la Compañía de Jesús, el *caballero andante* de la Iglesia: el hijo de la tenacidad paciente" (Unamuno 4).[32] Unamuno is not the only one who dares to venture this comparison. Federico Ortés, in his *Triunfo de Don Quijote*, proposes the theory of a encoded message in Cervantes' masterpiece in which the reader is supposed to see a re-writing of the life of Ignatius of Loyola through the story of the hidalgo from La Mancha: "En el Quijote se demuestra sobradamente que Cervantes no solo leyó el Relato y la Vida, sino que prácticamente los conocía de memoria" (55).[33] This direct allusion to Don Quixote and the comparison established here between the founder of the Society of Jesus and the most famous madman of literary history points to an interesting factor: both men experience a conversion from the act of reading. O'Malley argues that "the essential elements of the *Spiritual Exercises* emerged and began to take form. The book was a kind of simplified distillation of *his own experience* framed in such a way as to be useful to others" (*First Jesuits*, 25). In other words, both characters reproduce a world in which they can practice their fantasy. For Loyola, it is the dramatic world of his exercises which he seeks to use as a conversion tool for a Counter-Reformed Catholicism.

Barthes has identified in the text a "culture du fantasme" (*Sade*, 72) that we could associate directly with the fantasy typical of novels of chivalry, as well as its parody in *Don Quixote*. For instance, the isolation from the world that the exercises[34] require does not mean that the Ignatian reform of Catholicism is based on a separation from earthly matters. On the contrary, this four-week withdrawal is considered to be a *sine qua non* preparation of the Christian who needs to structure his belief system around this series of practices in order to come back to the world, but better prepared strategically and, therefore, ready to fulfill his evangelical mission. This mandatory isolation reminds us of military practices in the times of medieval knighthood, in which the subject is forced to contemplate his/her position in the universe. But this practice has antecedents in Scripture, especially in the forty days that Jesus spends in the desert facing temptation. Therefore, the world according to the *Exercises* needs to be envisioned as an immanent structure where vice is in constant struggle with virtue. We can see in the following passage the mental theater created in the text and the dramatic mode built into its structure:

The Standard of Satan

140. **First Point**. Imagine you see the chief of all the enemies in the vast plain about Babylon, seated on a great throne of fire and smoke, his appearance inspiring horror and terror.
141. **Second Point**. Consider how he summons innumerable demons, and scatters them, some to one city and some to another, throughout the whole world, so that no province, no place, no state of life, no individual is overlooked.
142. **Third Point**. Consider the address he makes to them, how he goads them on to lay snares for men and bind them with chains. First they are to tempt them to covet riches (as Satan himself is accustomed to do in most cases) that they may the more easily attain the empty honors of this world, and then come to overweening pride.

The first step, then, will be riches, the second honor, the third pride. From these three steps the evil one leads to all other vices (155).

In this passage, we can see that the setting is almost *dantesque*. The space around the subject of contemplation is open and wide, in order to create a greater dramatic effect. It resembles the desert in which Jesus faces the temptation. René Girard studies the dynamics of these spaces in *Le bouc émissaire* (1982) and argues that: "on pourrait dire que Satan incarne le désir mimétique si ce désir n'était pas, par excellence, désincarnation. C'est lui qui vide tous les êtres, toutes les choses et tous les textes, de leur contenu" (235). In the *Exercises* the constant presence of the figure of Satan participates in the creation of the linguistic void defined by Barthes. Satan is placed in a central position from which he has control on all the other elements listed in this guided meditation.

Loyola insists on the omnipresence of evil elements, all departing from Babylon to associate them with corresponding elements of creation. We can see the *logothète* at work especially in the "Second Point" where he underlines that "no province, no place, no state of life, no individual is overlooked." The multitude of devils mirrors the proliferation of evil in humanity. Again, Girard points out: "Les démons sont à l'image du groupe humain, ils sont l'*imago* de ce groupe parce qu'ils en sont l'*imitatio*" (255). Satan himself is presented as a presence that occupies the totality of the cosmic territory and reaches the interior of the believer through the senses: "[the enemy] makes them imagine delights and pleasures of the senses" (Loyola 201). Consequently, Satan now occupies the totality of the exercitant's mental territory, during and after the practice of the exercises. The only possible way to fight the enemy is therefore to use the same method of penetration of the senses, but replace his presence by that of Christ. The Society of Jesus always believed in fighting evil with its own weapons.

The novels of chivalry already have a familiar structure for the confrontation with evil. They already contain their own corrupted orders. Again, we can quote Certeau on the matter when he affirms that Loyola and Teresa of Avila create a structure for these internal battles: "ces lieux défaits, quasi déshérités—lieux d'abjection, d'épreuve (. . .) et non lieux garantissant une identité ou un salut—représentent la situation effective du christianisme contemporain. Ils sont les théâtres des luttes présentes" (42–43). According to this observation, Counter-Reformed Christians are defined by their capacity to face the evil territory, and by the same token, to be able to enter a guided simulation of this order in the fiction of meditation that will prepare them for their own reality. Again, Ignatius is not the only promoter of these techniques. For instance, Teresa remembers in her childhood playing a game called 'the Moor and the Christian' with her brother after reading secretly a novel of chivalry or the life of a saint: "Concertábamos irnos a tierra de moros, pidiendo por amor de Dios, para que allá nos descabezasen" (117).[35] Both saints entertain a certain fantasy of struggle, of fight against the enemy and of a close encounter with death. Fiction becomes the space in which they can try and simulate their capacity to be saints against Satan and his agents.

In this sense, it is clear that Loyola has defined a method adapted to a *contemporary Christian*,[36] that is, a Christian who is able to recognize where the challenges are, is prepared to confront evil and sin on this own terms, and who refuses a secluded life whether in an enclosed space or in natural isolation. This preparation demands a precise familiarity with the *order of corruption*. During his stay at a hospital for the poor in Manresa, for example, Loyola turns to the lepers, the prostitutes, and the syphilitics and spends a great deal of his time preaching and working with them, since they are at the very locus of the cosmic struggle mentioned above, their bodies are literally in a state of physical corruption often associated with sin. We will see in the following chapter how he furthers and develops this enterprise in the city of Rome.

It is in the midst of this misery, next to the physical deterioration, that he has his first visions of Jesus: "While in this hospice it often happened that on a bright day he could see something in the air near him; because it was indeed very beautiful, it gave him great comfort" (Câmara 33). Christ appears to him more clearly when Ignatius is in a situation of contact with physical or spiritual corruption. The structure of the *Exercises* obeys the same principle: the divinity is provoked to appear through the confrontation with the order of corruption. Only in this case will it manifest its presence, as if it were a cosmic law. This example from his personal life illustrates the Jesuit obligation to be in constant contact with the misery of this world in order to find in the corruption signs from God.

Again, in these novels as well as in Dante's *Inferno* or in Homer's *Odyssey*, the hero needs to get familiar with the most atrocious place in creation: Hell.[37] This indispensable preparation of the victorious soul has always been part of the Western tradition, since Ancient Greece. The *Spiritual Exercises* just take the exercitant where every other hero is supposed to go and has gone before. But, in addition, these exercises are based on the sensual[38] experience of the *order of corruption* described above, since they direct the imagination toward interior visions of atrocity, sin, misery, and eternal pain in order to redirect the belief of the disciple and thereby give him a method that s/he can carry on in the outside world. The five senses are therefore participants in this descent into Hell which Loyola designs for the disciple. The director is supposed, at this point, to enhance this guided meditation with actual simulating tools, such as fire and odors that imitate the filth of the damned. One of the most obvious passages that illustrate this principle in the *Exercises*, is the second "Meditation on Hell"[39] where the believer is faced with a sensual simulacrum of divine retribution with the help of his director who guides him through this experience. Hell appears in all of its atrocity to the imagination of the exercitant. The following example demonstrates the implication of sensorial activity and the designated use of each of the five senses, this time through a sensual imaginary experience of the divinity, eventually encountered in the form of contemplation:

> 121. **The Fifth Contemplation.** *This will consist in applying the five senses to the matter of the first and second contemplations.*
> After the preparatory prayer and three preludes, it will be profitable with the aid of the imagination to apply the five senses to the subject matter of the First and Second Contemplation in the following manner:
> 122. **First Point.** This consists in seeing in imagination the persons, and in contemplating and meditating in detail the circumstances in which they are, and then in drawing some fruit from what has been seen.
> 123. **Second Point.** This is to hear what they are saying, or what they might say, and then by reflecting on oneself to draw some profit from what has been heard.
> 124. **Third Point.** This is to smell the infinite fragrance, and taste the infinite sweetness of the divinity. Likewise to apply these senses to the soul and its virtues, and to all according to the person we are contemplating, and to draw fruit from this.
> 125. **Fourth Point.** This is to apply the sense of touch, for example, by embracing and kissing the place where the persons stand or are seated, always taking care to draw some fruit from this (54–55).

The purpose of these exercises is to develop a capacity to apply sensual/sensorial experience to the imagination, as it appears clearly in this passage. It is a literal penetration of the image through the body of the believer to the soul s/he is willing to open up for this experience. François Ribadeau-Dumas defines this practice in the following terms:

> Il ordonne à ses disciples de voir, de toucher, d'adorer, de goûter les choses invisibles. Il veut que les sens soient exaltés dans l'oraison jusqu'à l'hallucination volontaire. Vous méditez sur un mystère de la foi, saint Ignace veut d'abord que vous construisiez un lieu, que vous le rêviez, que vous le voyiez, que vous le touchiez. Si c'est l'enfer, il vous donne à tâter des roches brûlantes, il vous fait nager dans des ténèbres épaisses comme de la poix, il vous met sur la langue du soufre liquide, il remplit vos narines d'une abominable puanteur ; il vous montre d'affreux supplices, il vous fait entendre des gémissements surhumains, il dit à votre volonté de créer cela par des exercices opiniâtres (216).

Following up on Barthes and his definition of a culture of fantasy in Loyola's text, this other reader of the *Exercises* has seen another dimension of the novels of chivalry present in the text, that is, witchcraft and esoteric Pagan practices. Loyola is accused by the Inquisition of practicing these heresies at various points in his life. This is a parameter of their founder's life with which the Jesuits will have to deal for centuries. We cannot forget that on several occasions, while trying to fit in one of the Spanish universities, Ignatius of Loyola had trouble with the Inquisition because of his early practice of the Exercises[40] on volunteering fellow students. Today, we would probably not define such a practice as witchcraft, but rather as self-hypnotism. But in those days, invocations and exorcisms in a state of ecstasy could be seen as occult activities. It seems that most of the accounts of these episodes in Loyola's life have disappeared from the biographies, or have never been sufficiently investigated.

They are definitely not described in these terms in the accounts of Ribadaneira or Camâra. However, François Ribadeau-Dumas has studied this chapter of the saint's life very well and explains that: "on remarqua que Loyola se livrait à des réunions spirites, dans lesquelles il entraînait de jeunes étudiants et de jeunes filles qu'il parvenait à hypnotiser, les mettant à genoux, les bras en croix, le visage ruisselant de pleurs, récitant à haute voix leur péchés" (214). Again, we can imagine why the practice of the *Exercises* in its beginning was probably seen as an occult ritual. This experience with the Inquisition obliged him to write down a structured text in which he could lay out the principles of his activity. Apparently, that was not enough for the Inquisition, and Ignatius was forced to leave Spain for France.[41]

This escape to the country of a former enemy did not improve his condition very much. Loyola would not find rest until the installation of the Society in Rome, under the Pope's protection.

From the perspective of the Reformation, these 'magical practices' would appear as a mere reinforcement of the darker sides of Catholicism. Whether one accepts or not to see such a dimension in his work, it is undeniable that the images used in the *Exercises* remind us of those often associated with the practice of witchcraft. First of all, the text is structured around a detailed preparation of the exercitant. Everything is calculated for him/her to enter a state of intense imagination of situations and sensations. Even though the founding text of the Jesuit order had to be reformulated in order to be accepted by the Inquisition, its final version still contains some of the original preparatory rites on which Loyola constantly insists. Nevertheless, we should only envision witchcraft and ritual preparation as part of the familiarization process with the order of corruption in which the exercitant is being immersed. As Ignatius once pointed out: "Let the beginning be as it may be, as long as the outcome is always ours" (Barthel 79). The structure that he establishes only serves the purpose of a conversion experience, the essential outcome. The method used in his text may resemble a recipe for enchantments indeed. He has never been afraid to recognize it.

Following this pattern, we will now turn to the next narrative tradition—or genre—that should be analyzed in order to comprehend the essence of the *Exercises*, that is, the *hagiographies*. With the invention of print and the control of the Inquisition on the publication of books, this genre becomes rapidly one of the fastest circulating.[42] As Camâra and Ribadaneira propose in their respective biographies, it is the genre from which Loyola's conversion originates without a doubt.[43] The Middle-Ages is a time of great production of these accounts of life of saints. Boccaccio himself parodies the hagiographies in his *Decameron* and draws his inspiration from these commonly encountered texts. Along with him, we can observe the same phenomenon in the works of Shakespeare, Vasari, and even Cervantes. They are all observers of this genre, whether they choose to ridicule it or not.[44] The hagiography is a genre that precedes the Reformation, and the interest in these stories is essentially cultivated in the Catholic countries during the Middles Ages and the Renaissance. As Julia Reinhard Lupton underlines in *Afterlives of the Saints*, it is a genre that is mostly associated with Roman Catholicism and can be seen as another form of idolatry by the Protestant Reformation: "Catholicism is not simply the necessary precondition and antithesis to the modern Protestant culture that subsumes and replaces it, but it exists beyond its resounding historical rejection in new forms of old memory (the Church of the Counter-Reformation and after)" (xxix). Similarly, as I pointed out earlier when mentioning Ribadeneira's *Vida de San Ignacio*, we should envision most attempts to write lives of saints after the Reformation as *meta-hagiographies*. In the High Renaissance, they have become an act of imitation based on an essentially medieval genre.

Loyola's choice to promote the reading of the lives of the saints could be envisioned—again, from an early-Protestant perspective—as a reinforcement of Roman Catholic dogma and as a rejection of beliefs about the worship of saints coming along with the Reformation. Moreover, these texts would never be granted by Protestants the capacity to replace the message of Scripture. On the contrary, they represent the Church's greatest asset, that is, its continuity since apostolic times. The Counter-Reformation reinforces the reading of hagiographies in its effort to return to a more Scholastic and medieval model for the Roman Church. A well-composed life of a saint, especially if written by the future saint him/herself, can be the reason why its writer achieves sainthood. For instance, we cannot ignore the importance of the *Libro de su Vida* (c.1560) in Teresa's process of canonization and her title of Doctor of the Church. Outside of the interest that we might have in the construction of the modern subject in these accounts, the hagiographies have a technical advantage that enables their wide circulation: they are written in Castilian and have a wider audience than the Scriptures themselves. They have the pretension to be more entertaining than the body of texts that compose the Bible and to present the intensity of religious beliefs through the perspective of the implemented 'greater narrative.' Their style is often in line with that of the novels of chivalry, that is, inspiring, lyrical, and, to a certain extent, entertaining.

Hagiographies and novels of chivalry are often placed in opposition, as if they were two competing genres. Santa Teresa, as we have seen before, rejects novels of chivalry at some point when she realizes the vanity they contain as well as their addictive nature: "Era tan en extremo lo que en esto me embebía, que si no tenía libro nuevo, no me parece tenía contento" (119).[45] In contrast, she depicts the reading of lives of the saints as the best source of inspiration, including for children: "entramos a leer vidas de santos, que era el que yo más quería; (...) y deseaba yo mucho morir ansí, no por amor que yo entendiese tenerle, sino por gozar tan en breve de los grandes bienes que leía haber en el cielo" (117).[46] Both saints place a higher value on hagiography as the acceptable genre for the Christian reader. In the same fashion, Pedro Ribadeneira depicts Loyola's relation to both genres during the conversion experience:

> Era en este tiempo muy curioso y amigo de leer libros profanos de caballería, y para pasar el tiempo, que, con la cama y la enfermedad, se le hacía largo y enfadoso, pidió que le trajesen algún libro de esta vanidad. Quiso Dios que no hubiese ninguno en

> casa, sino otros de cosas espirituales, que le ofrecieron; los cuales él aceptó, mas por entretenerse en ellos que no por gusto y devoción. Trajéronle dos libros, uno de la vida de Cristo, nuestro Señor, y otro de vidas de santos, que comúnmente llaman *Flos Sanctorum*. Comenzó a leer en ellos, al principio (como dije) por su pasatiempo, después poco a poco por afición y gusto. Porque esto tienen las cosas buenas, que cuanto más se tratan, más sabrosas son. Y no solamente comenzó a gustar, mas también a trocársele el corazón, y a querer imitar y obrar lo que quería (20).[47]

Ribadeneira explains very well here how the two genres stand in opposition. Nonetheless, we can easily observe the slip from one genre to the other through their common capacity to entertain. Ignatius reads to pass the time, not to get inspiration or become devout. The transition is described as perfectly smooth, as if divine will had planned for the sick reader to not realize the change. The reaction to the reading is similar to what we have observed previously in terms of the novels of chivalry: the immediate desire that the activity engenders is a desire for imitation.

The opposition described above can be explained by the various ideological parameters contained in each of the genres: novels of chivalry often pay attention to the vanity of the world, and the lives of saints call their reader to the ways of salvation. That would be the simple and fundamental difference on the surface. However, this difference should not be our major preoccupation here; on the contrary, I would rather point to what they have in common: a fascination with the orders of corruption. No saint can be a proven saint without a clear encounter with and demonstration of comprehension of the ways of Satan. This dimension which was already a great component of medieval hagiographies is often exaggerated or simply strongly underlined in sixteenth-century accounts of the lives of saints. Furthermore, it can be traced back in the Christian tradition to Augustine's *Confessions*, where the saint gives a clear account of his life as a sinner prior to his conversion experience. The equation is already clear in his life story: no sainthood is ever reached without prior exposure to the order of corruption. For Counter-Reformed Catholicism this remains a fundamental pillar of the economy of salvation.

Therefore, the only possible path that the Christian soldier is supposed to follow is that of imitation: imitation of Christ, imitation of the saints, imitation of famous knights, etc. Again, *Don Quixote* is a parody of this *mal du siècle* and this Loyolan obsession: imitation of older models is in the air and his hero is a negative print of this phenomenon. Cervantes, who was familiar with the life of Loyola and was a critical reader of Ribadeneira's work, is aware of this exaggeration of imitation in the hagiographies of the sixteenth century. We find the verb *imitar* repeated *ad infinitum* in both the *Spiritual Exercises* and Ribadeneira's *Vida de San Ignacio de*

Loyola. In the second chapter of this work, Ribadeneira uses it extensively, almost in a mantric fashion. In the following passage we can observe that he is not afraid of redundancy: "Y juntamente iba cobrando fuerzas y aliento para pelear y luchar de veras, y para *imitar* al buen Jesús, nuestro capitán y Señor, y a los otros santos, que por haberle *imitado* merecen ser *imitados* de nosotros" (21).[48] We cannot ignore that the biographer's effort here is to stress Ignatius's capacity to be a saint by imitating the works of Saint Francis or Saint Dominic. When Ribadeneira writes the autobiography, Loyola is not yet Saint Ignatius. As Evonne Levy points out in *Propaganda and the Jesuit Baroque*, "what was at stake in Ribadeneyra's biography of Ignatius was the hoped-for canonization" (127). It is important to envision this source as an advertisement for the imitation of Loyola. But even if this fact is ignored, the constant insistence on imitation of Christ and the saints becomes the mediator of each of Loyola's desires.[49]

Imitatio Christi and Baroque Inversions

Anthony J. Cascardi explains in his "Archeology of Desire" the dynamics of imitation in sixteenth-century Spanish literature: "During the European Renaissance, the concept and practice of imitation served as a stabilizing response to the problems generated by the increasing preoccupation with authority and desire in history (. . .) Taken at face value, imitation is designed to stabilize the play of desire" (El Saffar 49). In times of displacements of authority and theological disputes engendering wars, stability is a feeling that is surely needed among believers. The Renaissance itself is based on an imitation of Antiquity, and has revealed the benefits and the success of the mimetic act. The Counter-Reformed branch of the Christian Church adopts the same kind of dynamics, but not the same object of mimesis. Its purpose is not to stabilize the play of desire but, on the contrary, to develop authority and discipline around it, in an anti-Renaissance fashion.

The post-Reformation saints, such as Loyola and Teresa of Avila, are themselves imitators of other saints, who have in turn imitated the first generation of saints, direct imitators of Christ. After Loyola, the chain of imitation continues within the Jesuit pantheon of saints: Saint Francis Xavier, Saint Francis Borgia, Saint John Francis Regis are all imitators of Ignatius. One could argue that there is nothing special that distinguishes Loyola from other elements in this chain. Nonetheless, the condition of sainthood reaches a critical moment around the Renaissance, and the creation of the Society of Jesus and the conversion method established in the *Exercises* enhances the calling to canonization in the sixteenth and seventeenth centuries. To this day, the Society of Jesus counts 49 saints in the Catholic calendar, most of whom are from the second and third generations of Jesuits. Thomas James Dandelet recently came to the conclusion that "this is a dramatic sign of the transformation of Roman Catholicism during the Catholic Reformation to a Catholicism with a Spanish face" (12). The Spanish Jesuits have been the most productive branch of the Church in terms of sainthood. If we turn to the *Exercises*, its founding text, we find the same mimetic mechanism of projection into sainthood, but this time prescribed by the director to the exercitant. Not only is the mental territory transformed into a simulator of orders of corruption, but it also present the patterns of sainthood (withdrawal, temptation, suffering, martyrdom, sacrifice, etc.). The spiritual physician offers the remedy of the imitation of Christ in order to help the lost soul find its own particular way to salvation, and potentially to its highest form, sainthood.

The rejection of Humanist ideals can be seen in the chain of imitation defined above. Once again, the concept behind the *Exercises* is to reinforce the medieval ideals of Catholicism. As Christopher Braider points out: "The sources of perspective must then be sought not only in the socio-cultural developments with which Renaissance humanism is normally associated, but in what at one level looks like its antithesis, the medieval and more specifically Franciscan notion of the *imitatio Christi*" (28). Let us remember that Saint Francis of Assisi is one of the first models that Loyola seeks to imitate after reading from the *Flos Sanctorum* during his convalescence. Ignatius even tries to join the Franciscans during his first and only visit in Jerusalem in 1523, but they reject Loyola and urge him to go back to Spain because he was taking the imitation of Christ a little bit too seriously and was putting his own existence in danger.[58] From the conversion experience (1522) to his entering the Sorbonne (1528), Loyola lives as a beggar with the ambition to become a Franciscan friar. His rejection from the order for being too extreme in the ways of imitation will encourage him to formulate his own methodology.

The *Exercises* become the space in which he will be able to practice imitation on his own terms, and under his own direction, as if he needed to recover from the failure of joining the Franciscans. Not only is it a textual space that rejects most of the ideals of the Renaissance and tries to re-direct Christianity to its earlier forms, but it is also a structure that places the exercitant under the direct control of a mediator whose role is to recreate parameters in which the exercitant is going to be able to imitate Christ just as Ignatius imitates him in his youthful peregrinations, but with a much more secure structure around him/her. In that sense, Loyola brings an essential component to early-modern literature: the constant presence of a mediator in the mimetic act.⁵¹ Going back to the creation of a *linguistic vacuum* that Roland Barthes points out, a parallel can be drawn here with the role of mediation in the *Exercises*: the successful image reservoir that Loyola composes from different narrative traditions, such as the ones we have discussed above, guide the exercitant toward his/her mediator, that is, the saint himself. Once his authority as a holy man has been established, the value of his conversion method has been demonstrated.⁵² Anthony Raspa sums up this question very concisely:

> Ignatius founded in psychology a new world outside the context of public polity in which as a Spanish noble he paradoxically had been born to rule. The ideal Renaissance man in *Exercises* thus became a mediator on the self (. . .) Calling on man to approximate the divine, it encouraged him to imitate in his imagination God's creation of the universe by love (. . .) In *Exercises*, the world appeared to have fallen twice, first in Eden and now secondly in the sundering of the spirit of Christianity. Ignatius' work attempted to redeem the mediator from that impossible twice-fallen state (46–7).

It would be easy to conclude that Ignatius of Loyola systematically rejects Protestant theology and needs to create a system in which the indispensability of mediation between the believer and the divinity is reinforced. We have an indication in the text of the exercises that some of the earlier Protestant doctrines are refuted by Loyola's method; for instance, the saint declares in the fourth week, at the very end of the practice: "we ought not to fall in the habit of speaking much about predestination" (213). From his perspective, Erasmian Humanism and Protestantism both represent the second fall of man: as if it were a repetition of the original sin, the human claims that he can have access to his Creator without any mediation whatsoever. The soul loses its strength in this comforting Protestant idea that the divinity and the believer are directly linked without supervision, and the *Exercises* pretend to correct this worldview by creating a structure of extreme mediation. As we have seen before, the medieval models of orienting believers toward a mediator of their desire seem very appealing.⁵³ These structures have obviously failed and engendered the Reformation. Loyola's system of imitation is not a medieval structure: the association of mimetic desire through mediation with the control of the believer's imagination is, in that sense, a post-humanistic structure.

Eventually, this system has the advantage of turning the desiring subject into a mediator, just as saints have kept Christ the object of desire through their constant imitation. In turn, the exercitant who comes out of the *Exercises* will be a mediator in the world. The imitation of the Lord does not happen only during meditations and prayers but should constantly be an existential mode for the exercitant: "While one is eating, it is good to imagine Christ our Lord eating in company with his apostles, and observe how he eats, how he drinks, how he looks about, and how he converses, and then try to imitate him" (172). This act of mimesis prescribed by Loyola descends to gestures, facial expressions, and tone of voice, all imagined. This notion of an infinite chain of strict imitation whose origin is Christ Himself is not only attractive to the modern reader but becomes a characteristic of Modernity. This is, again, why we like to think that Cervantes takes Ignatius of Loyola as an inspiring figure for the construction of his Don Quixote, since the hidalgo will begin as a pathetic desiring subject obsessed by his mediator Amadís, but will eventually become in turn a mediator for Sancho and some of the other characters whom he meets on his journey. This progression could be seen as a parody of the Ignatian conversion method. It is, at least, the argument on which Federico Ortés has based his close-reading comparative study of the *Vida* and *Don Quixote*. We shall not pursue our analysis in this direction but re-orient it toward the ongoing debate around the role of Scripture in the economy of salvation.

In order to fully comprehend Loyola's indirect position in this controversy, let us now turn to the core of the structure laid out in the *Exercises*, that is, the reenactment of the various episodes of the Gospel, as coronation of the image reservoir. As we have just seen, Christ is recognized as the *logos* of the chain of imitation. The purpose of each spiritual exercise is to bring the exercitant back to his/her inherent mimetic capacities. One could roughly divide the four weeks according to Barthel's classification:

> **First week:** Sin and its eventual consequence, the torments of hell.
> **Second week:** The participant must now decide whether he or she wishes to follow the banner of Satan or to enlist in the company of Jesus Christ.
> **Third week:** The participant vicariously experiences, down to the smallest detail, the suffering and the ultimate sacrifice of Jesus Christ.
> **Fourth week:** The participant vicariously experiences Christ's Resurrection and is given a foretaste of the Christian's eternal reward (73).

In this simplified outline of the exercises, we can at least see the progression and the direction in which the participant is driven. Barthes, when describing the structure of the practice, asks the question: "Il s'agit donc d'une structure en relais, où chacun reçoit et transmet. Quelle est la fonction de cette structure dilatoire? C'est de disposer à chaque relais de l'interlocution deux incertitudes" (47). We can observe this phenomenon especially in the second week, when the participant is faced with a constant choice between the army of Satan and the one of Jesus. Logically, since it is a guided medi(t)ation, the choice will always reaffirm the decision to imitate Christ and to be a part of His army. Once the exercitant has overcome the trials of the two first weeks and has gone through the sensorial exercises of the several meditations on hell and its torments, he or she is ready to move on into the two last weeks of the *Exercises* where more images are going to be injected in his/her mental territory.

There is a certain instability in this structure, as Barthes points out. The fact that we are not dealing with a more classic scheme of three stages, such as what we have in the *Divine Comedy*, maintains instability and doubt (*incertitudes*) in the progress of the exercitant. The choice of a binary structure is, of course, not innocent. It goes along with the generally Manichean worldview of the *Exercises*. Earlier, we commented on the technical intention of the structure. Now, let us examine why the instability is a necessary condition in order to have the exercitant enter the second half of the exercises. The vocabulary of the saint becomes a lot more technical. By the time the reader reaches the Fourth Week, directions are given in an extremely minimalist style. For instance, the initial meditation of this concluding part begins as follows: "This is the history. Here it is how after Christ expired on the cross His body remained separated from the soul, but always united with divinity. His soul, likewise united with the divinity, descended into hell. There he sets free the soul of the just" (174). From then on, the tone is set: the rest of the meditation is going to be a precise walk in the footsteps of the Lord, verse by verse, always in a rather dry order. After the preparatory prayers that again force the exercitant to give up his/her mental territory, s/he eventually is granted access to Scripture and a meditation on short passages from each of the four Gospels.

If we follow up Barthes's notion of the *multiple text* once again, we realize that Scripture appears at the anagogic level of the *Exercises*, that is, the level of mystical interpretation above the literal, allegorical, and moral levels. It is only after three weeks of emotional training of the participant that the door is finally opened on the founding text of Christianity, as if no believer would have the capacity to approach the mystery of the Word without this special preparation. Needless to say, Loyola strikes another blow here at Protestant theology, with its insistence on divine communication through Scripture alone.[54] The spirit of the spiritual exercises opposes itself directly to such a belief in the human capacity to decipher the word of God. That is why Loyola purposefully places the verses of the Gospels in the final week: in order to resituate the mystery in its glorious position in the Church.[55] The expectation has been built and the vacuum created previously can be filled up with the images of the mysteries around the life of Christ. Loyola divides this final section in four major steps of the Savior's existence: the Infancy and Hidden Life, the Public Life, the Passion, the Risen Life. Again, we see the constant significance of the Ignatian 'tetralogical' structure.

However, the verses are included within the text of the *Exercises* instead of being quoted separately. As the saint explains to help the reader understand this unusual edition of the Gospels "in all the following mysteries, all the words enclosed in quotation marks are from the four Gospels, but not the other words" (183). As a result, we end up with a remarkable editorial work of 'cutting and pasting' in this final part. Not only is it easy to notice that Loyola merges his own text with the 'word of God,' but also that he composes his ideal gospel by compiling his favorite parts of the initial Gospels. In the original Spanish version, it is even more impressive to see how his literary style comes to match perfectly the style of Scripture in this section. Even in the more modern English translation, we can have a taste of it. In the following quote, for instance, only the words in italic characters are from the Gospel of Luke (2:21), and the rest is added by Loyola: "They circumcised the child Jesus. *His name was called Jesus, which was called by the angel before he was conceived in the womb.* They handed back the child to his mother, who felt compassion because of the blood that she had shed" (185). The compassion of Mary caused by the blood does not appear in any of the four Gospels, and Loyola adds his own narration to the initial story as it appears in the Scriptures. The Virgin Mary is given more importance in the writing of this ideal gospel for instance: with such additions he tries to adapt the Gospels to the need of the Church. Loyola initiates here a tradition, which is going to continue in Baroque art, of implementing the original story with such narrative ornaments. When confronted with the minimalist style of Scriptures, his own style turns into an artifice, a fictional decoration, and consequently a deviation from the original message. But deviations are necessary in order to bring back spiritual order.

Imitation goes very far in the reality of the Ignatian spiritual exercises, to the point where the writer imitates and implements an original text. This does not seem to be a problem for the first Jesuits, if we believe the words of Saint Francis Xavier, Loyola's most faithful disciple: "I would not believe in the Gospels were the Holy Church to forbid it" (Barthel 63). These words echo those of Loyola in the *Exercises* when he claims: "What I see as white, I will believe to be black if the hierarchical Church thus determines it" (213). The structure of the exercises always places the Church above all, including above the written Word. Scripture as an original word of divine inspiration is not their major preoccupation since the *Spiritual Exercises* have literally dissected the Gospels in order to form an improved version serving the needs of the Counter-Reformed Church. Yet the original word is *contained* there in the progression of the meditations on mysteries. The word of God is framed by the words of the spiritual mediator, as we have seen in the previous quote from the *Exercises*. As the Catholic mass prepares the audience for the central reading of the Gospel with framing rituals, the exercises lead the believer through the image reservoir that we have analyzed previously and turn each meditation on a mystery into a long moment of contemplation and imaginative activity. Loyola designs a literary frame around each quote from the Gospel in the same fashion as emblematic literature will frame its symbol in order to reinforce its centrality. The framing structure so typical of the fourth-week meditations is just sample of the general structure of the entire practice; Loyola presents the verses in the same fashion as he has presented the earlier meditations, by framing them between rituals. The Scriptures appear in a moment of revelation for the exercitant; in the perspective of Loyola's text, it is the only form of access to the divine message that a believer can be granted, and s/he has to earn it. After provoking the divine intervention through close contact with the imagined corrupted orders in which he or she has been immersed in the three previous weeks, the divinity manifests itself in the visualization of the Word.

By this time, the preparation has consisted of injecting images coming from the universe of the novels of chivalry, implemented by the desire of imitation drawn from the lives of the saints: the exercitant is then a soldier walking in the very steps of the Lord, exactly like Ignatius in Jerusalem. The anagogic revelation is the logical end of the personal narrative through which each participant is going to be guided. Whether we accept or not Barthes's notion of "total occupation of the mental territory," we cannot deny the fact that the Gospels occupy a very limited part of the territory of the exercises. Their position in the text is indeed relevant; they come at a climatic stage in the general process, but are constantly complemented by images that do not belong to their narrative tradition. They are literally contained by the dramatic ornaments that Loyola recuperates from the narrative traditions we discussed earlier. In that sense, Bataille makes a clear statement when he affirms that the dynamics that we observe in the *Exercises* are based on artifices: "l'artifice échoue (. . .) l'objet de contemplation qu'ils proposent est le drame sans doute, mais engage dans les catégories historiques du discours, loin du Dieu sans forme et sans mode des Carmes, plus que les Jésuites assoiffés d'expérience intérieure" (26). The ornaments are given more importance than the object at which it is supposed to point. The dramatic mode progressively comes to occupy more space than the actual message that it is supposed to emphasize. What comes to matter the most is the sensation that one experiences in this encounter with corruption through this obsessive imitation of familiar *dramatis personae*. Soon the exercise gives way to a frantic thirst for the interior experience, in which the ornament itself becomes the object of contemplation.

Art Historian Arnold Hauser dares to ask the question after meditating on these rather totalitarian tendencies in the *Exercises*: "And Ignatius Loyola, who would have crucified Christ a second time if the teachings of the Risen Lord had threatened the stability of the Church, as in Dostoevsky's story?"(119). Maybe one could answer, as French criticism from the 1970s does, that the stability of the Church could only be guaranteed by the emotional instability of believers. Loyola is, already in the nineteenth century, the subject of contemplation in Dostoevsky's *Grand Inquisitor*, a novella inserted in the *Brothers Kamarazov*. In this story about a Spanish inquisitor throwing Christ in jail during the Renaissance, it is easy to recognize a caricature of the founder of the Jesuits in the Inquisitor's constant, stubborn, and systematic reaffirmation of Roman dogmas over the very presence of Christ himself. The Russian author seems to identify in this philosophical tale the same phenomenon discussed by Barthes, Certeau, and Bataille: the believer-exercitant is constantly diverted from the direction in which s/he engaged initially, to the point where the only tangible circumstance that these authors recognize in the text is its reaffirmation of authority and discipline. The truth is that the four-week method of conversion is more about consolidating the Roman Church than guiding the exercitant through the steps of a modernized and systematic *imitatio Christi* in the line of the Franciscans.

Nonetheless, there is evidence in the text that Loyola is somehow aware of a potential lack of transparency. The methodology of the exercises during the Counter-Reformation is based on an agenda of unification of believers. Naturally, and in order to standardize the belief system of the Roman Catholic Church, the founder of the Jesuits comes up with a structure that guides believers toward the Gospels but makes them progress very slowly through various anti-chambers of practices and rituals in which the mental territory is conquered through the use of the senses. This structure creates expectations for the exercitant, but according to contemporary criticism, does not satisfy them during the course of the exercises and leaves them with a sense of void. An exercitant does not come out of the four-week training with a feeling of satisfaction. At the very end of the *Exercises*, Loyola writes about the 'desolation' that the exercitant experiences, as if it were a natural phenomenon, and seeks to excuse it:

> This is the counter-attack against the vexations which are being experienced. One should remember that after a while the consolation will return again, through the diligent efforts against the desolation which were indicated in the Sixth Rule. There are three main reasons for the desolation we experience. The first is that we ourselves are tepid, lazy, or negligent in our spiritual exercises. Thus the spiritual consolation leaves us because of our own faults. The second reason is that the desolation serves to test how much we are worth, that is, how far we will go in the service and praise of God, even without much compensation by way of consolations and increased graces.

> The third reason is to give us a true recognition and understanding, in order to make us perceive interiorly that we cannot by ourselves bring on or retain increased devotion (. . .) that all these gifts are a gift and grace from God our Lord (203).

The totality of the mental territory is effectively covered: even the post-exercise depression is recognized as part of the process. Loyola's observations about desolation in this passage might sound Calvinist at times in the justification by grace announced in the third reason: they nonetheless once again point to another stage, beyond the exercises, and to an infinite continuity of struggles with the order of corruption. It shows that the exercises are only a virtual space in which the lost soul is going in order to acquire techniques of meditation and strengthen the spiritual parameters that the contemporary Christian needs in order to return to the world and fight the army of the enemy. The subject has undergone a four-week training of meditation through sensorial decomposition, a process that can be compared to and that corresponds with our modern notion of 'neurosis' in psychology. It is an error to think that these exercises are based on voluntary choices coming from the believer's will only. At no point in the text are alternative paths offered. The structure is not only totalitarian in its interaction with the spirituality of the believers; it is also unilateral and unidirectional.

For Roland Barthes, there is no doubt: this methodology that promises an outcome in the evangelical message, but spends a much more important amount of time on the military-like training of the soul in an extremely repetitive manner, voluntarily engenders neurosis in the exercitant.[56] Now, we are defining here neurosis as a condition of defense in which the subject can only confront existential parameters through a personal decomposition (Barthes 72). For instance, one of the most revolutionary aspects of the *Exercises* is the role they give to the senses, as we have seen earlier. For this reason, Ignatius of Loyola has often been classified as one of the leading figures of Renaissance Spanish Mysticism. His exercises require a true decomposition of perception, and the senses are used one after the other in preparation for a simultaneous use of the five ways of perception in a climatic final moment: total participation of all these senses is required in the promise of a final dialogue with the divinity.

Of course, one could argue that this desire to provoke the divine intervention is a rather general phenomenon in Spanish Mysticism, but none of the other mystics come up with such a systematic approach—in other words, a discipline—to the divine. Mysticism is not therefore what best defines Loyola, since he modifies the humanistic relation to the world in which mysticism can relatively engage and, on the contrary, invites the exercitant to enter the confinement of an enclosed space in which a director is going to guide his/her every step and help in the process of decomposition. Other Spanish mystics do not necessarily adopt this attitude. In *La cultura del Barroco* (1975), José Antonio Maravall notes a clear difference between Loyola's method and the mysticism encountered in the rest of Spain during his lifetime:

> Los aspectos que caracterizan al misticismo, por lo menos tal como se dio en España—en santa Teresa, en san Juan de la Cruz–, son francamente diferentes de los del Barroco; son más bien antibarrocos, sin que obste a ello el fondo común de filosofía escolástica que en uno y otro lado se halla. Claro está, no incluimos aquí como místico a san Ignacio (43).[57]

Mysticism is clearly a religious stream that we can associate with the transition from the middle Ages to the Renaissance. But, as Maravall clearly points out here, it is not a belief system that reflects Baroque aesthetics. Nonetheless Loyola is often recognized as a pre-Baroque figure for his capacity to establish a total structure.[58]

In his text, the world becomes a representation prior to its perception, that is, a visual construction which is going to stimulate the senses of the exercitant. In this sense, Loyola's image reservoir, based on the multiplicity of the text and leading into the constant encounter with the corrupted order of the enemy, anticipates the latter fascination for perception in the visual arts, what we could identify as the '*Baroque inversion.*' The mimetic act no longer limits itself to an original object of desire; on the contrary the subject now follows a multiple mediation that becomes more important and takes more space in the practice of the exercices than the object of desire (the *imitatio Christi*). It is crucial to define this new dynamic of inversion, that is, of a representation that anticipates the perception, in order to understand the reception of the *Exercises* in the worlds of the arts, which will be the object of the following chapter. The spiritual method left by Ignatius of Loyola to his disciples already indicates the necessity for an inversion, for anticipated representations. But what makes this method original and fundamentally different from the medieval Catholic belief system?

Essentially, in a world that tries to define rationally and scientifically the natural existence of orders of corruption, medieval institutions have a tendency to fail automatically. In order to remedy this increase of belief in scientific explanations—which we will not discuss here—Loyola, and the Counter-Reformation in general, comes up with a new strategy: in the post-Renaissance worldview, the corrupted order is not necessarily a physical reality (such as the desert of the Temptation, the ruins of the Mysticism or even the subliminal spaces of the Romantics later on), but becomes an internalized mental reality in which the new Catholic believer is going to evolve from the fifth week on. The structure of the exercises creates an instability that can only be resolved beyond the practice itself, with the constant return to the image reservoir given during the four weeks. The subject will theoretically maintain these dynamics in the outer world, in the *real* order of corruption.

The *Spiritual Exercises* permitted the Society of Jesus to bring many novices into their army and has formed many students throughout the worldwide Jesuit scholar system. Their success goes beyond expectations during Loyola's lifetime and their practice spread out tremendously in the seventeenth century, a century of triumph for the Society. Nevertheless, the legacy of this method within the order is not going to be the object of this study in the next chapters. On the contrary, we will examine how the practice of the exercises influences the art of students of the Jesuits and how the mechanisms that we have just discussed (the occupation of the mental territory, the perception of the corrupted order through simulated representations, the mimetic guidance of believers through the *imitatio Christi*, and the taste for inversion that remains to be defined in the next chapter) have a repercussion in the secular sphere. It will inspire Baroque art in its foundations, but will go beyond the limits imposed by the Counter-Reformation. Loyola's minimalist style will soon be replaced by artistic forms that imitate the structure of the exercises, but mark their difference by an excess of signifiers. Progressively, the strict structure that we have visited will lose the unity of its strongest parameters. But each of them will remain separately a basic component of secular literary and artistic production in the seventeenth century through the Enlightenment. The *Spiritual Exercises* leave behind them a strategy for the conquest of this mental territory that the Reformation has declared private, personal, and beyond the reach of institutions. The simulation of the order of corruption, now an internalized reality in the believer which contains a part of the cosmological struggle within him/herself, will certainly become a characteristic of the Baroque art altogether until its decadence at the end of the eighteenth century. In the following chapter, we will analyze how this methodology has a direct effect on Catholic architecture, starting from Rome, the very heart of the Church, where Loyola and his followers emigrate in order to publish the *Exercises* and have them circulate throughout the entire world.

CHAPTER III

"Ego Vobis Romae Propitius Ero": Diffusion of the *Spiritual Exercises* in Rome (1550–1650)

> "We shall not have succeeded in demolishing everything unless we demolish the ruins as well. But the only way I can see of doing that is to use them to put up a lot of fine, well-designed buildings."
>
> Alfred Jarry

The First Mission of a New Apostle

Now that we have established that the *Spiritual Exercises* is a textual composition made of several narrative layers whose aim is to expand the 'greater narrative' of Christianity and to guide it progressively into a revolution of its representational modes, let us analyze the first reality that this text and its author will alter: the city of Rome. The traditionally perceived head of the world[1] can be envisioned as the first Jesuit mission. Almost naturally, the multiple text is going to form a symbiotic relation with the urban fabric on which Loyola and his followers will apply it. In this chapter, we will envision this problematic under the following interrogations: why did the *Exercises* need to be diffused from Rome and what do the city and the text share in their respective narrative dimensions? This will lead us to a complementary line of questioning due to the symbiotic nature of the analysis: how do the *Exercises*—and in what dimension—contribute to the transformation of sacred representation as we find it in Roman Baroque architecture?

Let us turn briefly to some preliminary circumstances around Loyola's decision to establish the Society in Rome. As we have underlined in the preceding chapter, Loyola is unsuccessful in the diffusion of the *Exercises* while in his own land, mysteriously expelled from the Holy Land by the Franciscans, harassed by the Inquisition in Spain, and persecuted by his masters of theology in Paris. Even though Loyola is not one of the usual targets of the Inquisition, he is deeply suspected and classified as a potential troublemaker, and is thrown in jail several times while studying at the universities of Álcala de Henares and Salamanca. In his constant effort to envision a reform of Catholicism—and a defense of Christianity in general—through the medieval inspirations of the *imitatio Christi*, Ignatius restlessly wanders around Western Europe and parts of the Middle East in order to find the place where his voice can be heard and his methods applied. He soon perceives that his exercises have greater chances to be diffused from an academic context. The universities had encouraged the works and the teaching of Erasmus, Luther, and Calvin, so Loyola was probably envisioning a similar personal itinerary and planned to use such means. In the sixteenth century however, the Spanish universities where he tries to find followers and recognition do not encourage unorthodox practices such as his spiritual exercises, and do not particularly appreciate the presence of *alumbrados*[2] in their ranks.

When forced into exile in France, Ignatius has to abandon the few faithful students he had gathered around the practice of the spiritual exercises. He will find in Paris a rather chaotic space, one of theological confrontation, at the time in an overpopulated and generally liberal campus.[3] The French capital stands on the borderline between a rising Protestant North and a still hesitant Catholic South. In the 1530s, the Sorbonne and its dependent colleges, such as Sainte-Barbe where both Loyola and Calvin are studying, are arenas for debate between the rising Reformation and the medieval scholastic model of the historic Church. There is already enough doctrinal material to be discussed and Loyola finds technical difficulties in integrating the practice of his exercises. Nonetheless, his rather charismatic personality appeals to some of the students at his *collège*, which will result in creating tension between Ignatius and his professors. As Pedro Ribadeneira recounts:

> Había persuadido Ignacio a muchos de sus condiscípulos que dejasen las malas compañías y las amistades fundadas más en sensuales deleites que en virtuosos ejercicios, y que se ocupasen los días de fiesta en santas obras, confesando y comulgando devota-

> mente. De donde venía que ellos en tales días, por acudir a estos devotos ejercicios que les aconsejaba Ignacio, faltaban algunas veces a los de las letras, que en París en los días de fiesta aun no se dejan del todo. Viendo el maestro de Ignacio que su escuela quedaba medio desamparada, faltándole los discípulos, tomólo pesadamente, y avisó a Ignacio que mirase por sí y no se entremetiese en vidas ajenas, y que no le desasosegase a los estudiantes si no quería tenerle por enemigo (83).[4]

Since Ribadeneira's account cannot be considered as offering an objective angle on the episodes of the saint's life, constantly aiming at a justification of his actions, we are forced to read between the lines. The biographer emphasizes the attraction of the students to the practice of the spiritual exercises. But the Humanist atmosphere in the Parisian university opposes practices that often remind them of medieval rules of asceticism, which is why the master in this passage seems to stand in radical opposition to the student Ignatius here. Nonetheless, Loyola succeeds progressively in gathering around him a group of Spanish students. They all believe in the authority of Rome and all receive the exercises directly from Ignatius.

Even though the Sorbonne is not receptive to the method of conversion he is still only in the process of designing,[5] Loyola still benefits greatly from this particular stage of his life; the companions willing to participate in his cause come from influential Spanish families[6] in close relation with the Roman hierarchy. These men are the first exercitants of the unpublished second draft of the future *Spiritual Exercises* brought to France. One evening, they secretly all walk up to the highest geographical point of the city and decide to join forces and take the vow to remain in contact and design a common plan of action for the salvation of the Church. The Oath of Montmartre, as it is called in Jesuit history, takes place on August 15th 1534. It is a preliminary celebration of the founding of the Society of Jesus: the companions promise to each other to remain united in a journey to the city of Jerusalem, and even if their project gets blocked, they will overcome technical difficulties and go to Rome instead.[7] It reveals the *transvaluation* process in the Jesuits' mind from the 'Holy City' of monotheism onto the Ancient capital of the Roman Empire.[8]

From then on, the spiritual and geographical direction of their new formation is indicated; it is around the throne of Peter that the Spanish companions are going to meet up once they have been ordained. Rome will become the focal point that gives a sense of direction to their quest. With this new sense of purpose, Loyola and his companions can envision each episode of their pilgrimage as part of a greater narrative. Outside of the fact that Rome is the city in which the Holy See is preserving the authority and proclaiming the supremacy of its Church over the rest of Christianity, there are many factors that make it the ideal place for the development of the Society and the diffusion of the exercises. It is important to make here a clear distinction here between the city of Rome and the still politically separated territory of the Vatican. That is why one could say that the ruined city is the first territory they will conquer, the first territory on which they will try the efficiency of their missionary works.

As we have commented earlier, every stage of Loyola's life since his conversion has been modeled around the imitation of a model in Christian history. His voyage to Rome also takes the form of an *imitatio Christi*, since Christ's journey also ends at the most significant religious point. Therefore Rome becomes the New Jerusalem that he will reach after performing various miracles, overcoming obstacles, and receiving the guidance of the Lord through visions. At this point, his most faithful companions have joined him in the fashion of faithful disciples, and follow his steps toward this 'new Jerusalem' whose most holy temple is in need of spiritual and architectural reconstruction.[9] On another level, the mission around the *Exercises* comes from a purely Pauline inspiration. Paul of Tarsus was another model in the greater narrative that Loyola was imitating. Like Paul and Augustine of Hippo long before him, Loyola accedes to sainthood after a conversion experience, coming out of a long exposure to 'corruption and sin.' According to Manfred Barthel, Loyola's life prior to the conversion is far from being a life of Christian virtue.[10] In his compelling biographical work titled *Ignatius of Loyola, the Psychology of a Saint* (1992), the Jesuit psychoanalyst W.W. Meissner analyzes this process and sees in these episodes more than a mere conversion experience; he makes an interesting connection between the imitation of Paul the Apostle in a radical conversion process, the change of identity that it requires, and the very nature of the *Exercises*:

> The physical trauma was a castration-like experience that shattered his image of himself as a dashing, gallant ladies'man and romantic knight and soldier. His dreams of glory and conquest, both sexual and aggressive, were dashed (366). In some profound sense, the transvaluation of identity that transformed Iñigo de Loyola into Ignatius was a process of evolution. (. . .) The identity of Iñigo was not destroyed; it was transformed (85). The reshaping of identity that the pilgrim sought in the cave of Manresa was distilled into the practices of the *Spiritual Exercises*. (. . .) The entire corpus of the *Exercises* is organized and directed to [a restructuring of the self] (108).

Logically, a sense of purpose is necessary in such a therapeutically driven quest: Rome or Jerusalem assumes this position in the 'transvaluation' process of Ignatius of Loyola, born as Iñigo. His need to change his name is as necessary as the change operated for both Peter (Simon, then Cephas) and Paul (Saul) in the New Testament. It is not necessary however to find evidence of temptation and sin in Ignatius's life prior or after the conversion; the reading of a few pages of his *Spiritual Journal* is more than enough to realize that the subject is psychologically tortured by the remembrance of his 'past sins.' From the perspective of psychoanalysis it seems, however, that the sin is the expression of a frustration: the physical reduction of his body becomes acceptable through the acceptance of its divine intention, through his willing subjection to divine will. This 'conversion' not only happens once in the castle of the Loyola family, it is constantly repeated and reaffirmed throughout his life.

The first generation of Christians inspires indeed his need for visions. Saul-transformed-into-Paul becomes Loyola's model of radical conversion: from being a persecutor of the first followers of Christ, he dies to this life of corrupted intentions after a vision of Christ while traveling, and then becomes the first and most respected theologian of Christianity, the one who makes Christianity comprehensible to the Greco-Roman world. The Pauline inspiration in Loyola[11] and the first Jesuits is obvious in graphic representations generally found in the various editions of the biographical accounts of Ribadeneira and Câmara, as well as on the walls of the first Jesuit novitiates. The forming Society of Jesus needs to affirm a fundamental connection with the leading Apostle of the first generation of Christians in these times of Reformation and theological 'deformations.' Paul is more than just a symbol of radical conversion, or an affirmation that corruption can be radically changed to saintly matter in the blink of an eye; he is also the first to suggest that the essence of Christianity lies in the mimetic capacities of the believer. Evonne Levy adds in her analysis of Jesuit propaganda that the Pauline persuasion stands as a model for Loyola and his followers:

> Hence Paul's idea of the unity of the believer with God in Christ, hence his famous statement that "we reflect as in a mirror the glory of the Lord, thus we are transfigured into his likeness" (2 Cor 3: 17–18). In more than one passage, Paul envisioned reconciliation with God as a matter of becoming His image. These are the roots of the *imitatio Christi*, a later mimetic practice of spiritual reform (116).

Moreover the messages from his vision need to be proclaimed and widely illustrated in order to replace Loyola's life in a 'clearer' hagiographic perspective for the future of the Society.

A great instance of this phenomenon is Loyola's most famous encounter with the divinity outside of the city of Rome, a few kilometers before his arrival. Christ and the Father descend from Heaven upon him to deliver him a message of confirmation. From the perspective of the hagiography, this marks another episode of conversion in the life of the saint. Christ speaks to him and utters the words:

'Ego vobis Romae propitius ero' [I shall be propitious to you in Rome] (Fig 1).[12] Ignatius, in his constant desire in imitation, assumes here the position of Paul, the Apostle chosen by Christ among his persecutors, when having a similar vision in his exile. By promising success to Loyola, the Holy Trinity acknowledges that his previous failures have been part of the divine plan for the saint. The analogy could not be clearer since, like Paul, Ignatius is given the chance to take control of the operations for the reestablishment of the true faith. Rome is therefore the final end of his peregrination, the place where his initiation eventually converts into works of teaching.

In order to see how crucial this epiphany is for the Jesuit election of Rome as its first mission ground, let us now analyze a first representation of this scene from the first half of the seventeenth century in order to read in it the apostolic function of the city in the intended development of the Society and the Exercises. In **Fig.1**, a great representation of this scene found in the *Vita Beati Patris Ignatii* of 1610 first Latin edition of Ribadeneyra's *Vida*, one can admire the representation of the city in the background behind Ignatius, in a perspective in which his companions are seen waiting for him in a circle.

His eyes are not looking at Christ bearing his cross, but at the Father whose hand directs the light of divine inspiration toward the face of Ignatius. God the Father is surrounded by small heads of angels coming out of the cloud on which he is sitting, a pattern that we also find in Roman churches built or restored in the first half of the seventeenth century. Christ's words are written on a white banderole coming out of his mouth and his position in front of Ignatius is almost a position of humility. A chapel appears on the left behind the Son and its rural aspect contrasts with the city in the right part of the picture: the observer can deduce that Ignatius will serve the same function in Rome as Christ serves in the entire world; it is the territory given to him.[13] Christ bears his cross symbolizes the march toward Jerusalem and Golgotha, and the fundamentally urban nature of His Passion. The image is generally balanced in a triangle where the three figures (Father, Son, and Ignatius) are represented in equal sizes. As René Girard once pointed out, "the purpose and limitations of this structural geometry may become clearer through a reference to 'structural models.' The triangle is a model of a sort, or rather a whole family of models" (Rikvin 226). The model here is that of the Trinity in which Loyola seems to be made a member: Christ and Loyola are at the same level in this representation. His human condition is only emphasized by his position: Ignatius is on his knees, his cane and his hat are on the ground; his hands are in a position recalling the *magnificat* of the Virgin.

Figure 1: "Vision at La Storta" from Pedro Ribadeneira's First Latin Edition of the *Vita*, (1610)/ Church of Il Gesù (Rome)

On the ground as well and in front of his bended knees, as if it were placed here in offering, a book is placed on the cane. It does not carry any inscription on its leather cover and seems to be his *cuaderno*, his writings all attached together. It represents the book in which Loyola had written the exercises and where he was also keeping his diary. In 1537, when he arrives in Rome for the second time, the exercises are still in a state of manuscript, a project in desperate need of publication. The saint has come to bring his 'method' to the city of Rome and Christ promises him the success of their diffusion through this episode. By promising success to Loyola, the Holy Trinity acknowledges that his previous failures have been part of the divine plan for the saint. The analogy could not be clearer since, like Paul, Ignatius is given the chance to take control of the operations for the reestablishment of the true faith. Rome is therefore the goal of his peregrination, the place where his initiation eventually converts into works of teaching. This apparition is not depicted in Jesuit seminaries only for its relation to the conversion of Paul; it also reaffirms the fundamental connection of Loyola's life with Rome and the institution of the Church. A reproduction of this image can be found in the *Casa Professa* in Rome, very near the rooms from which Ignatius directed the Society and where he died.

An Image Reservoir in the Multiple-Layer Urban Fabric

We would need to review first the circumstances around the urban *order of corruption* that the companions decide to conquer. This investigation will tell us why the city of Rome is a place in 1550s where Loyola and the *Spiritual Exercises* are going to meet success. In the middle of the sixteenth century, Rome is a quite unique urban fabric, composed of many layers of historical constructions. As if these layers were trying to cover the failures of previous regimes and civilizations, the city begins to rise symbolically as a monstrous territory. Rome is a dangerous combination of Babylon,[14] sumptuous symbol of corruption and contrasts—appearing various times as theater for the exercitant's mind in the exercises–, and a New Jerusalem that holds the most holy temple of Christianity in desperate need of reconstruction, financing, and defense. Yet, around the most sacred altar of Peter the Apostle, the pilgrim can find all kinds of agents of Satan blocking the way to the re-edification of an endangered Roman faith. The contrast between these two poles of attraction, like the contrast that we find in the *Spiritual Exercises* between the standards of Heaven and those of Satan, make Rome the ideal place for the development of the practice since the necessary mental images can be immediately drawn from the surrounding reality. The urban fabric becomes an illustration; it has exactly the kind of 'composition of place' that Loyola recreates in the mental territory of his method of conversion. According to his personal experience and the perceptions of the world presented in his text, God is most present in those territories of contrast: the divine can be felt where the most sacred engages in battle with the most wicked, that is, in the human spirit as much as in a urban territory such as Rome.

Moreover, the Humanist Renaissance and its intellectuals turn temporarily their back on the ancient city because of its general association with hierarchical corruption and its financial crises. For this reason, Rome offers more qualifications than any other place for the writer of the *Spiritual Exercises*: its physical decay and the economic circumstances around it make it a much poorer and a more chaotic city, and by the same token, a space in tension between opposing 'standards.' It is therefore propitious territory for a mission: it stands as a New Jerusalem that needs to be saved, a temple in ruins that needs to be destroyed and reconstructed differently, but with the same stones, in the same fashion as Christ performed in Jerusalem, that is, through his constant close contact with *orders of corruption*.[15] The progressive conquest of Rome by the first generation of Jesuits is another act of *imitatio*. The Eternal City is a place for the dramatic mode.

We should first understand that the city is charged with several accusations at the beginning of the sixteenth century. There is an 'image reservoir' that corresponds to the negative image that Rome projects throughout Europe.[16] We can contemplate it in many pre- and early-Modern texts. A simple walk through Dante's *Inferno* gives the reader an idea of how the author considers the Roman clergy and especially the popes; in a *bolgia*, their punishment is to push one another through a hole, with their head upside down, in an image that compares them to the excrement passing through the intestine. Dante's view of the popes is in this sense comparable to Florence's consideration of Rome. In the same line of thought, Giovanni Boccaccio writes in his *Decameron* (Day I, Story 2) the story of a Parisian Jew who converts to Catholicism after visiting Rome and enjoying its unlimited corruption: he is convinced that there is no other religion that permits such a great amount of corruption with a façade of holiness: "I believe that city is more of a forge for the Devil's work than for God's (. . .) in spite of all this your religion continuously grows and becomes brighter and more illustrious (. . .) it has the Holy Spirit as its foundations and support" (Boccaccio 42). Even though we can only appreciate the irony of this tale, it is still redolent of the aura that surrounds Rome by the end of the Middle-Ages. The Roman clergy is depicted in both Dante's *Divine Comedy* and Boccaccio's tales as the most corrupted hierarchy of the Western world.

In Spanish Golden Age literature, one can find a similar criticism of the Italian city, particularly in the common association between Rome and the Great Harlot of the Apocalypse. Contemporaries of Loyola often depict the *axis mundi* for Christendom as the "*Roma putana.*" In the seventeenth chapter of the book of Revelations, the city of Babylon is described as "the mother of the harlots and the abominations of the earth" (17:5). John the Evangelist invites the gaze of his reader to face the horror of his vision: "Come here. I will show you the judgment on the great harlot who lives near the many waters. The kings of the earth have had intercourse with her, and the inhabitants of the earth became drunk on the wine of her harlotry" (17:1–2). Anyone who has read or performed the *Spiritual Exercises* would be familiar with this rhetoric of forced horrific vision. The important factor here, however, is that the Christian image of the Great Harlot is applied to the city of Rome, the Holy City of Christendom. The image of Babylon not only indicates the ongoing prostitution in the Holy City, it also points to its economy and political circumstances in general. The image of the Great Harlot is not only heavily criticized in literature, it is also proclaimed out loud by religious figures such as the Dominican leader Girolamo Savonarola who saw the Apocalypse originating in Rome:

Savonarola identified the Rome of Alexander VI with the forces of Antichrist, whose downfall he predicted: "I saw in a vision a black cross above the Babylon that is Rome, upon which was written *Ira Domini* [the wrath of the Lord] . . . I say to you, the Church of God must be renewed, and it will be soon." Rome was a moral pig-sty, where everything, including the sacraments, was for sale (Duffy 197).

In 1520, Luther publishes an essay titled *On the Babylonian Captivity of the Church* that justifies theologically these visions and marks the official rupture with Rome. Such apocalyptic visions are projected in the literary production of Spanish authors that visit Rome before and after the sack. In his *Diálogo de las cosas ocurridas en Roma* (1527), Alfonso de Valdés defends the thesis that the sack of Rome was a divine punishment on a city that was marked by corruption around a papacy that had been encouraging it. Valdés was accused of Lutheranism for this essay, but was finally pardoned by Clement VII in mysterious circumstances. Francisco Delicado's representation of Rome before the sack, in his *Lozana Andaluza* (1524), is more grotesque. The young *lozana*[17] Aldonza comes to Rome and is shown the city by the vicious Rampín. While observing the downtown area, Aldonza asks Rampín why women who are not in the brothels are being paid by men in the streets. Rampín answers simply: "Pues por esso es la mayor parte de Roma burdel, y le dizen: 'Roma putana.'"(Delicado 9v).[18] Louis Imperiale underlines in *La Roma Clandestina de Francisco Delicado y Pietro Aretino* (1997) the geographic intentions of the author in a thematic designed as "prostitution-religion-syphilis":

> La famosa excursión de Lozana y Rampín por las calles y los diferentes lugares de la Urbe fue cuidadosamente pre-trazada por el autor, llevando a la pareja por los sitios cuyos topónimos ofrecían una *pluralidad de sentidos*, unas veces en español, otras en italiano. Sentidos que resultaban estrechamente vinculados al tema general de toda la novela dialogada: el sexo y su negocio (168).[19]

This perspective echoes a concept defined by Benjamin, that is, the *Spazierengehen*, the 'slow-walking' camera-like description of urban reality.[20] At the same time, the Spanish reader discovers through the *lozana*'s eyes that the Spanish presence in Rome is surprisingly enormous and has engaged both languages in the making of its own creole. Later on, the *lozana* is exposed to an entire 'catalog of whores' available in the city of Rome. The truth is that prostitution was not a small phenomenon in Rome in the first half of the sixteenth century. It would be hard to imagine that Valdés' *Diálogo* or Delicado's *Lozana* could be found in Loyola's portable library while traveling through Western Europe. Nonetheless, these two writings are circulating in Spain as much as in Italy. They reflect the commonly accepted representation of Rome in the Renaissance Spain of the last knights, the world from which the 'squire Iñigo'—that is, the personality that defines Loyola prior to the conversion experience—was coming.[21]

The setting for this literary production contemporary to Loyola is particularly interesting, since it combines the fantastic Babylonian aspects[22] with visible signs of past apocalypses, that is, the ruins of the Roman Empire. That is why Rome presents another mimetic advantage: it stands on the ruins of Caesar, still visible outside of the city walls, still witnesses to an age of great 'corruption' and violence. As we have seen in the preceding chapter, Michel de Certeau points out that ruins are the most acclaimed metaphor for the 'orders of corruption' in which the Jesuits engage their faith. It works as a reminder of the ephemeral qualities of human works, of the disintegration of each human attempt to create an artistic simulacrum of eternity. Of course, ruins are to be seen all over Europe in many other cities, but nothing compares to Rome when it comes to contemplating the remains of a pagan civilization that once dominated the world and exterminated the first generation of Christians. Modern criticism has often analyzed the role of ruins for the imagination[23] and has given them a great part of responsibility for the urban architectural fantasies of the Modern era. Ruins are, as a matter of fact, incomplete and, therefore, often require the imagination to fill out their shape. For Walter Benjamin, ruins are a theme in Baroque culture, which we can associate with its fascination for the ephemeral, the passing of time, and its function as a *memento mori*.[24] Nonetheless, the theme encompasses more than an association between fragments that are real and tangible and fragments that are imaginary; it forms textual layers on the urban space in which the mind is invited to represent a lost totality. The city stands as a text in which the inhabitant-exercitant can read the previous episodes of a narrative in which he is included. Rome even becomes a palimpsest in which several narrative traditions can be used and compiled together for the greater diffusion of the *Exercises*.

This is another power of the city that is going to awaken the interest of the Society of Jesus: the Holy See of the Church is built on a site of massacre, and therefore Rome symbolizes the triumph of Christianity over its persecuting Empire. Again, the urban fabric is a palimpsest in that the first churches are often built on the site of Pagan temples and one can identify several archeological layers of spirituality on a single site.[25] In this sense, Rome stands in opposition to Jerusalem; it is a place of massive conversion and therefore of confirmation since the beginnings of Christianity. The Church of the Counter-Reformation is in need of strong images like the ones usually associated with the first generations of Christians coming to Rome after the arrival of Peter. Just as Loyola needs to gather images coming from various narrative traditions in order to compose his *Spiritual Exercises*, the Church needs an image reservoir on which it will be able to base its reconstruction. This restores Rome to its vocation as *caput mundi* of miracles, divine intervention, and divine presence, where the same triumph could be repeated over the growing Protestant threat. The city offers this particular advantage since it can be associated with Babylon, Babel, Jerusalem, and Rome the Ancient. In other words, Rome already comes with an image reservoir included in her urban textuality and built, as I said above, as a palimpsest.

Let us now verify this position in a second depiction of the La Storta vision which illustrates perfectly how Rome is perceived and how its ruins are emphasized as a symbol of spiritual decay and thus of incipient regeneration. It is a representation by Matthaüs Greuter (**Fig.2**) found in *La Peinture Spirituelle*[26] that offers a different perspective on the vision at La Storta. This time Ignatius appears kneeling in prayer in the interior of a chapel, in front of an altar in ruins. The heavenly cloud carrying the Trinity comes through the fractured ceiling of the abandoned church. One of the pillars of the building is on the ground on the left of Ignatius.

The ground seems to open on the right side of the altar. Behind the saint in prayer contemplating the name of Christ, one can see a door opening directly on a landscape, and in its background a compact representation of the Vatican, the dome of Saint Peter, and the Castel Sant'Angelo, with the banner of the Holy See flying proudly at its top. The retroactive message of this representation could not be clearer: the chapel of La Storta, falling apart outside of the gates of the Holy Seat, represents the disintegration of the Roman Church in the outside world, also linked to its physical reduction after the sack of Rome in 1527. While the Vatican remains immaculate, triumphant, and invincible, the rest of the Catholic Church is fragile and in need of reconstruction. The city of Rome in ruins stands in contrast with the apparently indestructible Holy See. Ignatius' vision in such a disaffected place is significant since the Jesuits will inherit or acquire a great number of decaying church buildings in Rome, and then rebuild them. These two representations of the vision at La Storta complement each other since we can see two important factors: in the first representation, Rome appears as a territory given to Ignatius by divine order, and in the second, the divine order seems to be oriented more toward a most needed reconstruction of the decaying Church, in the allegorical form of ruins.[27]

Figure 2: Matthaüs Greuter "Ignatius at La Storta" from Richedôme La Peinture Spirituelle, (1611)

Rome might come with its own literary image reservoir, with its visible signs of 'cultural apocalypses,' and its ancient ruins. But when Loyola settles in the city, one can add another dimension to this multi-layered *order of corruption*: the fresh ruins of the sack of 1527 and its socio-psychological aftermath during Pope Clement's reign. After the beginning of the Reformation, the failure of conciliation marked by the Council of Trent has to be covered and disguised. The Church of Rome tries intransigently to reaffirm its doctrines and its liturgical practices in defiance of the growing Lutheranism. The importance of the sacred images for the comprehension of the Scriptures somehow became the basic ideology of the Counter-Reformation in second position after the theological debates around the economy of salvation as we find them earlier on in the century. The Roman clergy that felt the wake-up call of the sack of the city had seen the incredible rage of the Lutherans against paintings, sculptures, images of all kinds, and relics. In other words, the first Protestants had invaded Rome in order to destroy its most sacred products, an industry without which the city would not be able to survive financially.[28] It is the greatest blow Renaissance Catholicism received in the era of the Reformation. According to modern Catholic sources,[29] Lutherans enter Rome with violent intentions and destroy buildings, churches, palaces, ransom cardinals and bishops, and eventually rape the women like Barbarians. The sack of Rome might be, as a matter of fact, an unfortunate concourse of circumstances for the city, since both political and religious interests are at play in the physical reduction of the city. According to Judith Hook in *The Sack of Rome: 1527* (2004):

> No subsequent political event made such a deep impression as did the sack of Rome. The blow which the papacy had suffered was so severe that its effects were still being felt a hundred years later ... Many died in the sack or in its aftermath, many left the city and never returned. The artistic and literary circles, so characteristic of the High Renaissance, were completely destroyed. For Rome, at least, the sack was of the gravest consequence, a scar on her history which was long recalled in the popular and literary tradition of the city (280).

After the sack of 1527, the city has indeed a lot in common with Ignatius of Loyola, who had once seen, in 1523, the glory of Rome and the Church: it has been physically crippled like him after the battle in Pamplona. The city has lost its strength as well as its most recognized strategic capacities.[30] It is in a state of physical corruption as a result of political and religious turmoil. All in all, the Rome of the 1540s is a city contemplated for its ruins—recent and Ancient—, its past glory, and its more recent political abuses and disputes. A Rome attacked for its unorthodox adoration of the images, teeth, and bones of saints only had two options to reply: a submission to Lutheranism with no perspective of preserving the existing industry, or a grandiose *tour de force* on the Reformation in which the industry was going to find its rebound.

Corresponding Dynamics?

The Counter-Reformation gives the city the opportunity to re-establish an economy in which the creation of images is going to have a greater importance. Of course, Loyola's motivation for his establishment in decayed Rome is not the attraction of financial profit, but rather the restoration of the threatened image. Nevertheless, he was walking into a territory whose dynamics he had previously mastered and was educated enough to be aware of political turmoil and strategies.[31] For instance, in Ribadeneira's account, we find an Ignatius heavily concerned with the surrounding corruption which he immediately translates into *business*. In this passage, Loyola's awareness of circumstances and Ribadeneira's use of economic terms are rather surprising:

> Entrado en Roma, comenzó Ignacio a volver los ojos por todas partes y considerar

atentamente la grandeza del *negocio* que quería *emprender*, y apercibirse con oración y confianza en Dios, contra todos los encuentros y asechanzas del cruel enemigo; porque conoció y pronosticó que alguna grande tempestad de *trabajos* venía a *descargar* sobre ellos (107).[32]

The lexicon used here associates directly the economy of reconstruction with the presence of the Enemy: Rome is bathing in the presence of Satan, and Loyola envisions this directly in terms of economic activity. Unlike previous moves he had made in his life under the impulses of his youth and his faith, his arrival in Rome followed a much more elaborate calculation which involved the economic support of the Vatican. The 'companions of the Oath' had been encouraged to join the court of Paul III several months before the official arrival of Ignatius of Loyola in Rome. The Papacy needed ideological support, and when the newly-ordained Spanish priests come to Paul III on a Palm Sunday to ask his permission to bring their leader to Rome, the Pope does not hesitate in giving Loyola full financial support. Once more we can recognize a certain strategy informing the planned arrival of the author of the *Spiritual Exercises* in Rome, who had stayed in Venice while his companions prepared the way for him.[33]

Given the importance of both religious and secular Spanish communities in the city, Rome was filled with friends but also many enemies of his.[34] Ignatius of Loyola had a rather shy attitude in front of these important clerical figures who had earned a hierarchical status in Rome after leaving Spain. Most of them had heard about or read the *Spiritual Exercises* and, as a consequence, had developed admiration or animosity toward the crippled Spaniard and his on-going conversion method: after all, it was quite a complete structure of spiritual reformation, but had not been written by an appointed member of the Catholic hierarchy. Its value and its authority were heavily questioned, but it left no one indifferent. In this climate of competition, every new Spaniard coming close to the Vatican represented a threat to those already in place. Ignatius was just a recently ordained priest, not a recognized bishop. Going to Rome without making sure that such an inhospitable territory had already been prepared and modified for him in order to receive protection would have been equivalent to committing social, economic, and religious suicide. Let us remember that the story of his life had been to flee from his enemies, and most of these enemies were acquired along the way because of the nature of the *Exercises*. Since this conversion method had the pretension of conquering and re-configuring the spiritual territory of the believer, i.e. his/her very conscience, his opponents saw in it a potential danger to the Catholic values drawn from Humanism—a backlash, a return to the Medieval scholastic models. For some other enemies, it was perceived, on the contrary, as an overly liberal method that usurped the essential role of monastic life and adapted it to the outside world (Lucas 66–67).

The *Spiritual Exercises* were already famous among the Roman clergy of 1537, since Ignatius of Loyola had known some of its most significant representatives in Spain and in Paris during his peregrinations and his seven years of study. They were known, discussed, admired, or terribly dreaded. As Sabine Pavone recounts, the arrival of Loyola and his companions in the Holy City, in the months following the vision at La Storta, was rather triumphant; this glory was partially due to the expectations that the Curia had developed around Loyola's method of integration of the Christian narrative into the believer's mind:

> Ancora formalmente senza nome, nel 1540 questo gruppo ricevette da papa Paolo III l'approvazione ufficiale come ordine religioso con il nome di Compagnia di Gesù. L'agiografia gesuita ha sempre sottolineato l'importanza della "visione de La Storta" (1538) come momento chiave per la presa di conscienza di Ignazio che, in procinto di entrare a Roma, avrebbe visto il Signore che lo invitava a servirlo: di qui anche la scelta del nome di Compagnia di Gesù. Giunti nella capitale Ignazio e i suoi ricevettero subito segni di benevolenza da parte del papa, che affidò loro alcuni incarichi: Ignazio diede gli *Esercizi spirituali* al dottor Ortiz, conosciuto ai tempi di Salamanca e allora a Roma come inviato di Carlo V, a Lattanzio Tolomei (parente del cardinal Ghinucci) e al cardinale veneziano Gasparo Contarini; Fabre e Laínez insegnarono invece alla Sapienza, rispettivamente Sacra Scrittura e teologia. Conobbero anche Rodolfo Pio di Carpi che nel 1545 divenne—unico nella storia dell'ordine—cardinale protettore della Compagnia (7).[35]

As it seems, the whole process of installation went rather smoothly. Dr. Ortiz—a man who had strongly opposed Loyola in Paris (Ribadeneira 108)—was miraculously helping the companions in the financial realization of their project.[36] Now, beyond the *Exercises*, the small *compagnia* did not have much textual evidence of theological doctrines. Ignatius' first recognized occupation in Rome was to be 'director' of his own exercises, which he gives to the Pope's closest allies and, supposedly, under his order. Literally, according to Pavone's research, Loyola was put to work immediately as a spiritual director; his mission was to do nothing else but give the spiritual exercises, which were progressively to become the most crucial text of Counter-Reformation Rome. All in all, Loyola could not have chosen a more opportune moment in the history of Rome for the presentation of his fundamental notion of 'composition of place' which would find its resurgence in the rhetorics of Counter-Reformation church architecture.

In many ways, this text comes at a perfect time: the Roman Church is under attack for its lack of concern with the Holy Scriptures and it lacks unity in the face of her enemies. It is no coincidence that most of the higher clergy 'receives' the exercises in the months following Loyola's arrival, for there is a need for a text and a method that confirm the 'apostolic' mission of Rome over Christendom. As a matter of fact, the exercises are often presented as a divine revelation,[37] in the logic of the visions of Ignatius, gives it the dimension of 'ultimate textual authority' in the narrative of Christianity, beyond the Gospels and their problematic affinities with the Reformation. Let us not forget that the *Spiritual Exercises* is a text in which the author indicates to its supposed reader (the director) how to set the scene for a performance of episodes from the New Testament. Lutherans might believe in the solitary act of reading the Scriptures, but the Counter-Reformed Church prefers to adopt Loyola's total system of directed representation of evangelical highlights. The belief in the essential role of the clergy and its intercession in the economy of salvation are reaffirmed through the massive adoption of the exercises by the Roman Church of Paul III. The exercises reintegrate the use of the Scriptures in Catholic practice and, by the same token, combine this with the reaffirmed necessity of a spiritual hierarchy and direction.

So it is legitimate to ask the question: what are the dynamics contained in the *Spiritual Exercises* that could seduce the endangered Roman Church? It is commonly accepted throughout the abundant criticism on Loyola and the Jesuits that the method of the exercises *par excellence* solidifies the Counter-Reformation. Nonetheless, there seems to be little in common between this dry and minimalist text and the extravaganzas that typically mark the period that it opens. As we just mentioned, this text reaffirms the hierarchical structure through the basic relationship that it describes and *regulates* in a totalitarian fashion. The dynamic exercitant/director is widely accepted in Christendom because it means survival for the whole hierarchy of the Roman faith. Lutherans might question heavily the role of the clergy in the economy of salvation,[38] but the *Spiritual Exercises* reaffirm the links, the intermediates, and the intercession established between souls and their Creator.

Also, the *Spiritual Exercises* offers an interpretation of the purposes of history. Whereas the Reformation wants to stress the importance of a relation to the divinity outside of historical time, Medieval Catholicism has always looked at the historical continuity of the Church—the *Magisterium*—as a message in need for interpretation. Theologians usually watch out for sudden changes in the course of history, as much as in the course of one's life. The conversion experience (again, the experience common to Christ, Paul, Augustine, Loyola, etc.) is a theme of the 'mysteries of the faith.' The exercises work as a constant simulator of this essential experience, prepare the exercitant for it, project his/her desire in movements of anticipation, and finally place the subject of the exercise within the historical continuity. In other words, it prepares the soul to enter and participate in the 'greater narrative' of Christianity through its constant presentation of mental images.

This presentation of images follows a strict order and reflects a discipline. Unlike many other theological debates (whether spoken or written down) in the age of the Reformation, Loyola's *Exercises* almost obeys the laws of architecture, that is, their 'totalitarian' parts all come together to form a *physical place* of spiritual training. Most of the text functions as a map to guide the spiritual director through the labyrinth of opposing Standards, as well as through the exercitant's mind. First of all, there is an interior and an exterior to the text. *Outside* of the *Exercises*, one will find the 'introductory explanations' for the director, the preparation rites, and the prayers that should be said once inside. There is technical information that covers all areas of the simulated conversion experience, such as advice concerning food, sleep, age, etc. *Inside* the *Exercises*, the narrative voice adopts the "I" form in the future tense in order to direct the movements of the exercitant: for instance, "I will place before my mind a human king" (146). This speech form makes the mind progress from one image to the next. Nonetheless, there is a *constant correspondence between an outside and its inside*; they are both present and re-presented in one another. The critical reader can identify Loyola's logic in the order of the given images. For those reading the *Exercises*, this correspondence is visible and the artifice is revealed to them. For those doing the exercises, it should remain invisible; however, it should still produce an effect of guidance through an *architectural* structure whose secrets are not to be mastered. This is probably why Loyola first opposed the publication of his text and would refuse to give it away.[39] It could be dangerous for the sake of the text to circulate in some circles as a recognized *artifice* since it maps out the ideal conversion experience for the Counter-Reformation.

Unlike the Lutheran ideal mental space for the congregation,[40] the space of the *Exercises* is divided into *designated areas* for specific contemplations. This is at least what should be clearly understood by any potential director when Loyola specifies:

> I should read only about the mystery which I shall immediately contemplate. In this way I will avoid reading about a mystery foreign to my contemplation for that day and that hour. The purpose is to keep the consideration of one mystery from interfering with that about another (152).

The mental space designed in the *Exercises* is divided into specific *compartments*, smaller places of contemplation where the exercitant will concentrate on one particular aspect of his meditation or search for the divine. No connection is to be made between the several dimensions of the conversion experience. We are thus very far from a discipline of enlightenment whose dynamics provoke connections. On the contrary, each 'mystery' should be kept separated and isolated from the other. The exercitant's mind moves from one of those 'pockets' to the next as told.[41]

Even though the four-week adventure follows the linear (*horizontal*) logic of any narrative form, the moments of contemplation immobilize the exercitant in vertical perspectives. As we have discussed earlier, the *Exercises* require a complete projection into another sensorial sphere. This step-by-step progression through the designated pockets is implemented by 'special effects' that the director needs to engineer as well as he can. Colors, sounds, smells, touches, and tastes all participate in it. However, this participation obeys the laws of a strict scholastic perspective emphasized by the *verticality* of the simulated situations.[42] The vertical cosmology is, of course, typical of the middle Ages where the Church alludes to a three-level reality: paradise (heaven), earth (or its after-life correspondent, purgatory), and hell (underground). Ignatius seeks to reinforce this representation and to return the exercitant to his position of a vertical being contemplating a vertical relation to the divine. This is why, as analyzed in the preceding chapter, Roland Barthes sees four levels in the text in "Loyola" and Anthony Raspa insists on the anagogic nature of the contemplative act in the *Spiritual Exercises*.[43] These are particularly interesting dynamics for the Counter-Reformation since it reaffirms the leveling of the economy of salvation. The graduation and the passing of stages are essential to the construction of the Catholic faith. The hierarchy goes beyond the earthly organization of powers. Saints, virgins, angels, and demons are elements of the verticality in which the exercitant is supposed to find his/her correspondence, and—hopefully—to work his/her way up. Again, an *order of corruption* is a tension between the standards of Heaven and those of Hell and it takes vertical forms in the abundant images of the *Spiritual Exercises*.

We can in fact admit that there are corresponding dynamics between the text and the needs of the Church in its physical reconstruction. Nonetheless, we can only apply this comparison as long as we understand Loyola's text as *one* of the pillars of the architectural Counter-Reformation. It is very probable that Loyola would have not identified with the aesthetics of the Baroque architecture that revolutionized Rome after his death. His sensibility seemed to be other,[44] and anchored in medieval ideals. The *Spiritual Exercises* will follow a different path and participate in other movements of early-Modernity. This is probably why their author never wanted to have his name appear on the first editions (1548 and after); it might have been a way to give up the responsibility of these textual contents. According to the myth that the first generation of Jesuits was creating around the writing process of the exercises, the text had just gone through the mind of Loyola;

at no time did he perceive himself as the intended author of this method. This reality would give more flexibility to anyone who would want to interpret or represent the *Spiritual Exercises* in the artistic and religious realm.

Roman Churches after the *Spiritual Exercises*

Soon enough, the newly formed Society of Jesus would need a greater structure for the development of Loyola's *Spiritual Exercises*, their related teachings, and their diffusion in urban life, both secular and religious. Giving the exercises to the influential figures around the Pope was strategically admirable, but would soon get Ignatius in torments again if he did not protect himself from the envy of his enemies. Becoming the head of an official religious order gave him the authority to develop, but not the capacity to please everyone. In order to open up the capacities of his dramatic presentation of evangelical episodes in complete withdrawal, Loyola—not yet the General of his Army of Christ—needed to establish a visible Iñiguist presence in Rome. Logically, the Society could have proceeded as any other order: they should have built their headquarters as close to Saint Peter's as possible. But it did not turn out to be the case, since the object of their mission was precisely close contact with the orders of corruption and other places that would play a part in the valuation of the method.

So Ignatius and his companions looked at the more heteroclite parts of Rome, where there was a real need for ecclesiastical presence and ministry to the most 'corrupted' classes of Romans.[45] Gauvin Alexander Bailey—who has completed an extraordinary amount of research on this phenomenon and about the renovation of the small and technically abandoned church of S. Andrea al Quirinale—comments in his study:

> The Jesuits' taking over of S. Andrea fit a pattern we will see in many of their Roman foundations: they would acquire a decrepit church in a good neighborhood and restore it or rebuild it from the ground up, usually with funds provided by a generous private donor, and thereby insert themselves at minimal expense into a strategic neighborhood of the city (41).

Again, the Iñiguists could have built these churches on virgin ground at the same cost, but would prefer to superimpose their 'archi-text' on a ground that was already associated with the Christian narrative. The effect would be, again, one of palimpsest. This was altogether a revolutionary concept, since every precedent order of the Catholic Church had been structured around the monastic rule and had therefore chosen to avoid the corruption of the urban worl. The Jesuits would precisely settle where temptation existed, in 'orders of corruption' where salvation could be achieved through permanent confrontation with the enemy. Lucas confirms Loyola's attraction for these parts of the city: "Ignatius was the first founder of a major religious order in the history of the Church to locate his headquarters in Rome and the first to opt deliberately for complete insertion of a religious order's works and residences in the center of the urban fabric" (23). Indeed it was a central position if we consider the efforts that the Society puts into the acquisition of decrepit buildings of Rome.

Their first acquisition—and the most patent instance of this recycling of older churches buildings—was the chapel of the Madonna della Strada, located on the eastern edge of the central area, by the Piazza Venezia of today. This strategically placed building will become in 1544 the headquarters of the Society and will be later on replaced by their Mother Church of Il Gesù, one of Rome's most fascinating Baroque buildings, and a model for hundreds of churches across the world. The chapel of the Madonna came along with a house that Ignatius remodeled and enlarged (later on called the *casa professa*), where the Jesuits could establish their first community.[46] The closeness of the site to the ruins of Ancient Rome was extremely significant in the case of the Jesuits.

Ignatius of Loyola did not only have in mind a fundamentally urban ministry for the Church, but he also recognized the potential use of the images of Roman Antiquity. His church had to be built and his ministry had to be performed on a site that belongs to a greater narrative, as Bailey points out in his analysis of the first images of Jesuit art: "More important was the desire to link present-day Catholicism with the early Church; the frescoes were concerned with celebrating the role of Rome and the papacy as the legitimate centre of Catholicism, and the inheritor of the glory of Antiquity" (107). Just as the early Church had built the Romanesque churches on the ruins of Pagan temples, so would Loyola and his followers erect places of cult on the ruins of the medieval Church. But, as they started to construct their churches, they would paradoxically stress their connection with Pagan symbols of triumph, such as Corinthian columns and the triangular façades, in keeping with their fascination with Greek and Latin authors. The identification with a temporally remote spirituality—but spatially speaking, still present through its ruins—was part of the strategy for bringing the multitude into the dynamics of the exercises.[47] Progressively, elements of the ruins were included in the new art.

Since most of the churches had been destroyed or heavily vandalized during the month of the sack, there was no particular reason to restore these Roman buildings to their original glory of the early Renaissance. The sack had not only felt like a violent act on the city, but it also left behind a sense of rape in sacred spaces. As a consequence, these spaces needed to be re-conceptualized from the beginning in order to erase the traumatic experience. Even though the site of the temple would not evolve, its forms were invited to change radically, as if the memory of the Lutheran violations could be erased by the most triumphant artifices. Moreover, some major architectural projects were already conceptualized and presented before 1527, such as the renovation of the basilica of Saint Peter.[48] These projects, which were still impregnated with the spirit of the Renaissance, are suddenly void of sense in a city hurt by the Reformation. It is true that Rome had started, prior to the Reformation and its sack, to adhere to the ideals of Humanism.[49] But the city was now determined to reaffirm its fundamental nature as eternal *caput mundi*, even if this meant recognizing the pre-Christian disposition of the Empire. Under these circumstances, Humanism—and its fascination for with Pagan culture—was an influence to place under control, but also a source of energy to be used.

The Jesuit position in this matter was ambiguous in the same fashion. Indeed, contemporary Art historians have difficulties in coming to agreement when it comes to the intervention of the Society of Jesus in the evolution of Counter-Reformation Roman church architecture; it is a rather problematic question given the controversial nature of Jesuit history. Moreover, they have often promoted criticism against themselves, as if it were part of their methodic exposure to judgment and corruption.[50] As already mentioned in the introduction, one can identify two poles of attraction in this debate. As Evonne Levy reminds us: "In the mid-nineteenth century a public and politicized discourse on architecture and a hostile political debate over the survival of the Jesuit order converged in the concept of the Jesuit style. The Jesuit style has been challenged and declared dead since the beginning of the twentieth century" (11). It is undeniable that a false generalization is involved in using this term nowadays. But Levy's main point really is that we can still identify an intention if not a style: "Jesuit architecture specifically and Catholic Baroque in general have often been considered an art of propaganda" (2). For Rudolf Wittkower, the notion of *Jesuitenstil*, and that of *lo stile dei Gesuiti*[51] from which it derives, are to be handled carefully and in need of modification. That is why it is more commonly accepted to discuss—since the publication of Wittkower's works—the 'Jesuit *contribution*' to Baroque art. Whether or not the Jesuits are at the origins of Modern propaganda (Levy) or, on the contrary, their contribution to the artistic movement is innocent and inoffensive (Wittkower), we will not add here any fuel to the debate. However, it is impossible to doubt that the Society of Jesus, particularly given its insistence on creating a 'composition of place' in which corruption is emphasized, has played an important role in the development of Baroque architecture in Rome.

The *propaganda* factor was a phenomenon beyond Loyola's society, but always in close relation with them. For instance, non-Jesuit cardinal Charles Borromeo participates in the re-conceptualization of Counter-Reformation visual art. In 1577, Borromeo writes and publishes in Latin a manual of guidelines for the reformed church architecture of Catholicism. His *Instructiones Fabricae et Supellectis Ecclesiasticae* is another example of 'total occupation' since it covers every single aspect of church exteriors and interiors. This work analyzes the dynamics of church architecture from the past and comments on the efficiency of their various elements. At the same time, it also attempts to make churches more uniform and avoid extravagance in architecture. From his apparent concern about excess, we can deduce that Borromeo feared abuses of visual effects. Nonetheless, the importance of developing a highly sensual artistic form that combines several artistic and narrative traditions in order to make the triumph of the Catholic Church obvious to the entire world through its insertion in the urban fabric is highly emphasized in his treatise. James Ackerman, who studies this question in Wittkower's *Baroque Art: The Jesuit Contribution*, comments:

> The design and decoration of churches was the subject of Borromeo's third Provincial Council in 1573, and the regulations decided on at that time were the source of Borromeo's famous book of 1577, the *Instructionum Fabricae et Supellectilis Ecclesiasticae libri duo*. This book and its author have long been identified as a major stimulus to the creation of a Counter Reformation ecclesiastical style; but a close examination of the North Italian churches themselves proves that he was not the creator of a new style but the spokesman and codifier of a style already fully matured during the third quarter of the century (20).

The truth is that his book did not have to necessarily be an influence for Northern Italy only, as Ackerman seems to suggest intransigently here. Borromeo had spent five entire years in Rome studying the evolution of architectural trends. His reflections are directed toward Rome as much as Milan. But it is true indeed that Borromeo is more of a compiler than a creator in that sense. His friendship with the Iñiguists and his inclination for their spirituality is a more important factor. Charles Borromeo is responsible for the transformation of church sites into spaces dedicated to Ignatian spirituality. For instance, the Sacro Monte of Varallo[52] has a history that directly connects Borromeo with Loyolan visual mechanisms:

> First designed to be a surrogate Holy Land, the intention changed during the sixteenth century to one of Christological narrative. Following the dictates of the Council of Trent and the catalytic presence of St. Charles Borromeo (1538–84), archbishop

of Milan, the pilgrimage site metamorphosed into a physical manifestation of the *Spiritual Exercises* of St. Ignatius Loyola (1491–1556). Borromeo himself practiced the *Spiritual Exercises* on a regular basis, including a two-week practice at the mountain in 1584 (Gregg 49).

The Sacro Monte is an extremely obvious instance of 'physical manifestation' since the text is directly applied to an architectural construction as a clear purpose. With urban churches, however, we are dealing with much more restricted spaces where the verticality and the correspondences between exterior and interior can be better emphasized. Let us now turn to two instances of Roman churches in which we can contemplate some of these corresponding dynamics, as well as the reflection of the *Spiritual Exercises*, in order to judge whether we are dealing with a style that deserves its own epithet, or if we are indeed dealing with a form of propaganda, or possibly both.

The Mother Church of Il Gesú and Sant'Andrea Al Quirinale

The saint probably did not know that his project for a Mother Church could only be concretized through his death and the deriving cult of his person. Ignatius of Loyola gave his last breath in 1556 in the *casa professa* after a life of peregrinations and visions.[53] Immediately after his death, he became a venerated figure in Rome and throughout the entire Catholic world. The list of his achievements was long: author of the exercises, exemplary soldier for the papacy, founder and first 'General' of the Society of Jesus, and one of the most remarkable mystic figures in Rome in a long time, full of visions and often close to miracles. Practically he had given a sense of direction through his constant preaching of the *imitatio Christi*. Ignatius of Loyola was canonized sixty-six years after his death and, by then, his mission had been carried to great heights.

Pedro Ribadeneira's *Vida de San Ignacio*—a source that we have been using constantly here—started to circulate within months after his death and insisted on the continuity in the chain of imitation. Levy comments on the matter that: "it was Ribadeneyra who created a likeness of Ignatius to which he, in the spirit of the Society that he himself defined, could liken himself. [His] engravings enact the *imitatio Ignatio*: the Jesuits as an endless stream of likenesses of Ignatius" (127). All these factors lead to the necessity for a sanctuary in which the life of the saint and the contents of his works could be contemplated. Francisco Borgia[54] and Claudio Acquaviva, both generals of the Society in the second half of the sixteenth century, will dedicate a great part of their ministry to the cult of Ignatius of Loyola. They would supervise most of the construction of which the Jesuits would be in charge, especially the church of Il Gesù, the Novitiate of San Andrea al Quirinale, and the church of San Ignazio by the Colegio Romano. Naturally, the relics of Ignatius were adored and exposed for the multitude to see, but they had no 'composition of place' associated with them. The imitation of his person, supplemented by heavily illustrated hagiographies, was the only factor that could enhance a material progression. But the Jesuit mission needed an appropriate architectural agenda.

The Gesù was not begun until 1568, for lack of financial resources. Rome still counted several major temples, but none was dedicated to the '*imitatio Ignatio.*' The Mother Church was to become the most sacred place where the body of the saint would find its final rest. Loyola was not an architect, nor had he studied the laws of church construction, so he had not left any plans for the temple that was to be built. Nonetheless, those in charges of the project were in close connection with the Generals and understood very rapidly the concept of 'composition of place' so typical of the *Spiritual Exercises*. Moreover, as we have seen earlier in the commentary of Father Sanctis, Loyola's text was also engaged in its own process of 'canonization'—if such things exist for texts, after the Bible. They looked at it as a constant resource for inspiration now that Ignatius was no longer; the exercises were his most sacred relic. From missions to teaching to church buildings the text was consulted for guidance in every aspect of Jesuit life. Of course, such an architectural project as the Gesù did not escape this rule of consultation. As a work of art, this church can be read as a text through its many dimensions and through the lenses of modern critical theories. It would be extremely tempting to say that the Gesù is to architecture what the *Spiritual Exercises* are to Catholic literature, but such a statement would be too simplistic.[55] It would be more relevant to analyze what role the exercises played in the revolution of Roman church interiors. Indeed, one could wonder about the relation between, on the one hand, a text whose style is dry and minimalist and, on the other hand, a church that celebrates its triumphs, extremely charged with symbols and saturated with signs, from its façade to the very end of its nave. Indeed the church of Il Gesù is not a tangible adaptation of the Ignatian conversion method; there are more parameters to take into consideration for the analysis of such a complex work of art.

As an architect of the believers' mental territory, Loyola could have a rather clear idea of the powers of architecture; for Evonne Levy, there is no doubt, but it raises many questions:

> We can view a building in its representative function and evaluate its success by the work it does on the spectator. This is enormously difficult to measure. How would a Jesuit church increase one's spiritual ardor? How does a building form a subject? And how can we tell? First we must establish that architecture was seen as capable of doing this work, that it could contribute to subject formation (184).

Many commentators of the Gesù raise the same questions.[56] They all seem to consider the work of art as a unified piece. I would like to make an exception here and look at the Jesuit church as a bi-dimensional work of art with an *exterior* and an *interior*. Sixteenth-century artists needed to work as well on the creation of a 'composition of place': the exterior of the temple and its interior. These are two separate 'texts' that often stand in contradiction to each other, but also reveal each other's presence constantly. The exterior of Baroque buildings (churches but also palaces) invite the spectator to enter a rather rigid reality; it makes a promise of stability and symbolic balance. Once s/he has 'penetrated' this space, however, the spectator finds her/himself in another set of dynamics: the interior obeys other laws of 'composition.' Previous church architecture was not based on such discrepancies. The Romanesque style, followed by the Gothic and later on the often flamboyant Renaissance style, all had much more harmony between the exterior and the interior of buildings. Once a believer entered a Gothic cathedral, s/he would continue the same aesthetical process of observation than the one engaged on the outside of the building. There was no play on illusions such as the one we encounter in the Counter-Reformation churches of Rome. Jesuit-inspired buildings, however, do not follow the same logic. They would rather understand from a Loyolan viewpoint that the sacred interior is, like the corruptible body, "divided into interior and exterior. Interior penance is grieving for one's sins with a firm intention not to commit those or any other sins again. Exterior penance, a fruit of the former, is self-punishment for the sins one has committed" (Loyola 144). According to this principle, the dichotomy interior/exterior has to be emphasized.

Gilles Deleuze is one of the few observers of the Baroque who has pointed to this fundamental difference in his conclusions on Leibniz and his concepts of 'monads.'[57] Even though his investigation looks at more recent works of the Baroque period than the church of Il Gesù, it is undeniable that he establishes a pattern and identifies the dynamics of an architecture begun with the Mother church of the Jesuits. His allegory of the typical 'Baroque house' serves as a theoretical basis for the rise of Jesuit church art. I have isolated in the following passage some of the most convincing points:

> The Baroque does not refer to an essence, but rather to an operative function, to a

characteristic. It endlessly creates folds. It does not invent the thing: there are all the folds that come from the Orient—Greek, Roman, Romanesque, Gothic, classical folds . . . But it twists and turns the folds, takes them to infinity, fold upon fold, fold after fold (227). (. . .) In this respect, there is no need to refer to overly modern developments, except insofar as they aid in understanding what the Baroque enterprise already was. For a long time there have been places where what is on view is *inside*: the cell, the sacristy, the crypt, the church, the theater, the reading-room, or print collection. These are the places which the Baroque privileged in order to draw from them their power and glory. (. . .) It is impossible to understand the monad without relating them to Baroque architecture. (. . .) The monad is the autonomy of the *interior*, an *interior* without an *exterior*. Yet it has as a correlative the independence of the façade, an *exterior* without *interior* (232–33).

In a way, we find a similar structure in the *Spiritual Exercises*. There is a structure of the outside opposing a structure of the inside. Once again, once 'penetrated,' the reality *contained* in the four-week re-enactment of evangelical episodes is projected in an illusion of infinity. This illusion is kept secret behind the textual façade of the *Exercises*, which are the formal and more mathematical part of the text, that is, the Directions and the Twenty Explanations. In this opening part, Loyola underlines the importance of the exercises as a 'spiritual workout.' This preliminary structure in the text prepares the reader for a mathematical—or at least, physical—experience of the text, just as the façade of the Mother church promises an almost *avant la lettre* 'rational' experience of the divine. The inside of the text, truly beginning with a first week of intense image-injections, is in total disharmony with the expectations created by the outside. No mention of the techniques used around the conversion process is made on the outside of the text. In the same fashion, the Baroque façade makes promises it is not going to keep. In antecedent church architecture, these expectations were to be found on the altarpiece, in the deeper part of the interior. These '*retables*' were the most sacred textual form of the entire building. The illusion of the sacred interior is projected on the outside, although it is done in a quite fragmented way. The Baroque façade pretends to exhibit elements of the traditional altarpiece and brings it in its most extravagant forms on the outside of the building, on a plane and vertical format.

The façade of the Mother church of the Jesuits (**Fig. 3**) serves as an example for hundreds of churches throughout the world because it projects an extremely successful formula of balance and visual attraction. Any observer notices in it the pattern of the triangles above the windows, the main door, under the semi-circle, and at the very top of the plan. This image of mathematical perfection and the general symmetry of the entire pattern, all supported by imperial columns, evokes the universal stability of the religion this building pretends to contain. It truly combines—as the *Spiritual Exercises* do—several narratives on the same plane: the Greek motif of the triangle, the imperial base niches, the more Modern upper waves of support on the top of the plan (they actually serve no purpose but decoration), etc. As Levy points out, "the inventive reuse of past models is inextricable from early modern practice" (184). However, it is not always so systematic: the odd combination of elements is often a call for the believer's participation in the act of contemplation, but always under close guidance. Bailey underlines this more complex parameter in his reflections on the philosophy behind the Mother church and underlines the fragmented nature of the façade: "Ignatius's desire to allow the maximum flexibility compels readers to become *active participants* in the meditation, by *filling the blanks* and doing the mental sketching themselves" (8–9). This is quite a different approach to the dynamics of the *Exercises* previously observed in Roland Barthes' essay. Is the 'total occupation of the mental territory' compatible with the façade's invitation to 'fill the blanks' of its equations? Does the façade of this innovative church building follow specific rules that could be identified and laid down in a manual?[58] Well, for the sake of the 'composition of place' we could perfectly admit such compatibility between the vestibules of the spiritual exercises and the Baroque façade.

Indeed, this is precisely the function of the façade: it creates the illusion that the participant (the churchgoer in this case) is going to be given an active role, when in reality the interior of the building will force him/her to let the mental territory—the most sought-after conscience of the believer—accept the superiority of the images kept in the inside.

The interior of Il Gesù has been the object of many studies, among which one will find North American scholars mentioned previously, such as Blunt, Wittkower, Lucas, Bailey and Levy. Their studies have analyzed the dynamics of this most representative Baroque interior from the perspective of description. Usually, we get in this criticism a descriptive analysis of the space and its dynamics, and a focus on the interior only. Even though there is an obvious discrepancy between the promises of stability made by the exterior of the building and the disorienting and overwhelming decorative dispositions of the interior, the two dimensions maintain a symbiotic relation. One of the most innovative features of this overwhelming interior is its use of light. The inside diffuses the light only from the superior part of the building. No window is ever placed at the level of the human spectator so that s/he can have no direct visual access to exterior reality, therefore confirming Deleuze's theory of an 'independent interior.' The light is distributed in such a way that its origin is not perceivable to the human eye, only its effect and the way it is guided in the interior space toward the works of art. Also, one can speak of a unity of the exterior, but it would be very difficult to observe a similar phenomenon in the interior of the church: on the contrary the space is conceived in such a way that believers do not necessarily have to gather in a congregational center. For instance, the church offers spaces of private contemplation, of spiritual withdrawal. These 'side chapels' were already found in Gothic and Renaissance temples. In the dynamics of Il Gesù, however, they are transformed so that the contemplated image becomes their mathematical center. The verticality of the side chapels is reduced and contrasts with the central space under the dome of the church.[59] We observe an opposite phenomenon in Renaissance churches that are remodeled or implemented during the Counter-Reformation: for instance, the basilica of Santa Maria Maggiore is famous for the dramatic verticality of its two Baroque side chapels, especially its famous *capella sistina*. The Mother church of the Jesuits, however, is built in such a way that the same contrast is created between the smaller side chapels under the painted ceiling and the two major side chapels (the one on the left being the chapel of St. Ignatius) on each side of the central space under the dome.

**Figure 3: Façade of the church of Il Gesù, Rome
(Photograph by Frédéric Conrod)**

The emphasis on verticality and on the impossibility of access to the exterior reminds us of the structure of the exercises since the believer who penetrates that space enters a dimension whose totality is covered by images. Narratives are now presented along vertical lines of architecture instead of following the traditional linear patterns of previous church architecture. The pattern of the Counter-Reformation church is set in the Gesù so that the mind enters a total narrative with no visual contact with external reality.[60] As we concluded earlier, the verticality stresses the mystery of the relationship between the human and the divine; and the various layers of artifices that this verticality allows permits a greater understanding of the *order*[61] that has been placed between the human and the divine. It is in this sense that the verticality creates a composition similar to the four-level textual interpretation found in the practice of the exercises (literal, semantic, allegorical, and anagogic).

In the Mother church, it is precisely in the chapel of St. Ignatius that this Baroque verticality is truly emphasized. This is one of the most obvious illusions of infinite verticality that Wölfflin has identified in Baroque architecture: "the resurgence of Jesuit propaganda around Ignatius's cult culminates in the ceiling of the Church of Saint Ignatius and the Chapel of St. Ignatius in the Gesù, the most ambitious and cultically significant sites of their program" (Levy 118). Even though this is a later work by Jesuit artist Andrea Pozzo and was begun after the canonization of Loyola in 1622, it does recapitulate perfectly the characteristics of the church dynamics with the same level of interpretation for a vertical progressive gaze. The literal is the base (the casket where the body of the saint rests), followed by the semantic part of the chapel (the ornaments around the grave that tell the story of Ignatius by episodes and add a narrative dimension to the experience of the observer), followed by the allegorical level (the white statues on the side that incarnate both the diffusion of the true faith throughout the world and corruption as its enemy), all of it finally crowned by the anagogic (the ascension movement of the columns toward the Holy Trinity and the ceiling representation of Ignatius joining it).

This side chapel has become—along with the famous *trompe l'oeil* by Baccicio—the most sacred point of the interior space of Il Gesù. Interestingly enough, the actual mathematical center of the building—that is, the center of the Cross—is void of symbols: no altar, no statue, and no particular sign under the dome.'[62] The mathematical center of the church does not serve to stress the divine presence such as the one we encounter in Gothic churches; on the contrary its purpose is to indicate the position of the human element in the action of contemplation. This void forces the gaze into vertical movements. The *centers* that represent the divine are *de-centered* on purpose so that they can be contemplated from this empty mathematical center. The observer is therefore forced to discover the most central altar of the sacred space in which s/he is walking. Eventually, s/he is faced with the altar of St. Ignatius that was not visible from the entrance of the building. Through a vertical contemplation of this altar, the observer's gaze is oriented toward the most sacred image of the divine in the entire church, at the very top of the altar. The divine representations are therefore to be found on the margins of the sacred space, not in its middle. As a pilgrim, the observer is guided through a step-by-step process of visual integration. The effect that these dynamics seek to create is a sense of centrality from the observer's point of view that automatically associates him/her to the marginal presence of the divine in the work of art. Progressively, an exchange takes place between the observer and the divine: the observer assumes the position of the divine through inevitable contemplation, following the principles of the *Exercises*.

In order to fully comprehend this mechanism, let us continue with the example of a smaller scale Jesuit-designed church in Rome: Sant'Andrea al Quirinale (**Fig. 5**). As we have pointed out, this church is rebuilt on the site of a previous church, so its grounds are recognized as historically sacred: they belong to the greater narrative of the Church. From the outside, an observer can anticipate the dynamics of the interior. The façade of the temple once again follows the illusion of a vertical plan. Nonetheless, this verticality is broken by horizontal patterns that indicate the circular nature of the building, but without revealing it totally. Unlike the Mother church of Il Gesù, Sant'Andrea does not present itself as a congregational site of spiritual contemplation. On the contrary, its size announces from the street that the temple is designed for a religious community. It stands on a liminal space between the exterior urban reality and the interior spiritual reality of the novitiate. Sant'Andrea is the first complex of Jesuit formation. Today, most of the original complex has been destroyed or transformed, but the church has resisted this evolution.

The church of the novitiate, still open to this day, gives the observer a clear idea of the dynamics cultivated by the Jesuits in their architecture. As pointed out earlier, the church has a particularity also found in later Roman Baroque buildings of the seventeenth century (Santa Maria della Pace, Sant'Ivo alla Sapienza): it does not follow the traditional model of the cross but, on the contrary, works its visual effects around the figure of the oval.

Figure 4: Chapel and Altar of Saint Ignatius, Gesù, Rome

The novitiate is founded in 1566, but the church part of it will not be completed before 1661, after the architectural triumph of the Mother church. Nonetheless, it parallels in a smaller-scale, community-oriented way—rather than a congregation-oriented scale like the one we find in the Gesù—the dynamics of exterior/interior discrepancy. Marco Bussagli comments on this difference:

> La fachada externa incide en la forma del altar, coronado por un tímpano quebrado, y, análogamente a los elementos que decoran el tímpano de la parte saliente del portal, alberga la figura de San Andrés en éxtasis, obra de Antonio Raggi. La riquísima decoración interior, en mármol de múltiples tonalidades, está ribeteada por un entablamento, que crea un efecto de unidad en el espacio dotado de un ritmo casi pulsativo, debido al contraste de las aberturas de las capillas y del volumen de los muros (504).[63]

Figure 5: Façade of Sant'Andrea al Quirinale (Photograph by Conrod)

Of all Roman churches, its façade offers stability but very few ornaments, but its role is fundamental in order to prepare the observer for the experience of the interior, whose forms are already evoked on the external façade. Its interior on the other hand is an extremely complex interplay of symbols, colors, visual effects and sensorial teasers. Once in the interior, the effect of light control and verticality are formed on the Roman Baroque model. This oval building is a masterpiece by Gianlorenzo Bernini, an artist who had received the spiritual exercises from the aging first generation of Jesuits. As Vernon Minor underlines in *Baroque and Rococo* (1999):

> Having employed the finest marbles for the interior so as to create a sense of richness and other-worldliness, Bernini turned to a sculptor and a painter to help use the architectural space as the setting for a mystical event: the ascension of St. Andrew to Heaven. The portico-like frame of the altar, known as the *aedicula* or tabernacle, appears to have been affected by some miraculous event. As we know from studying the Jesuits' *Spiritual Exercises*, the religiously devout could be led into a visionary experience by employing their imagination in a vivid and sensuous fashion (86–7).

The movement of the gaze that leads the pilgrim/exercitant toward union with God is indicated by an inter-material continuum of symbols coming out of the altar and going toward the ceiling, in a vertical fashion similar to that encountered in the chapel of St. Ignatius. The suffering gaze of San Andrew on his cross points to the center of the dome, from which the light comes; it is the highest point in this temple and is adorned by angels' heads. Between this departure point (the gaze) and its corresponding point of arrival (the hole in the dome), a series of symbols mark the various stages of this visual peregrination, such as white doves symbolizing the Holy Spirit, and other angelic figures on the way.

Again we can contemplate in such a space the great variety of visual means and the superimposition of different narrative forms. Bailey has studied the disposition of the novitiate when it first opened and describes it in the following terms:

> A combination of biblical scenes, stories from the lives of the saints, images of Jesuit heroism past and present, tales of antiquity, allegories, geographical vistas, and visual pharmacopia, this tightly controlled and interrelated series was calibrated to allow the novices to meditate on their vocation and prepare for their works as professed Jesuits. It gave them hope in times of doubt, warned them against transgression, instructed them concerning their duties, provided recreation for their weary eyes, comforted or cured them when sick, and provided a *visual punctuation of their day*. More significantly, it was closely tied to the themes and sequences of Ignatius of Loyola's *Spiritual Exercises* with its emphasis on self-examination, personal choice, and step-by-step pilgrimage toward union with God (39).

As in the literary space projected in the *Spiritual Exercises*, the 'orders of corruption' that the believer's gaze is forced to confront are to be found in the independent interior of the building; Sant'Andrea al Quirinale is famous for its paintings of martyrs whose bodies are exposed to physical disintegration, while their souls are still alive and contemplate the divine presence upon them. The experience of martyrdom is, from a Jesuit point of view, the ultimate way to integrate the two standards in a common contemplation. The composition of place in Sant'Andrea is, in this sense, typical of Loyola's perceptions and recommendations. This building comes to replace a primary version—also dedicated to the martyrdom of St. Andrew—of a temple, that Bailey designates as a "chapel for those making the Exercises" (43). Even though the building is completed forty years after his canonization, the influence of Loyola, as a hero of the Counter-Reformation, is still omnipresent in this type of church architecture. Many churches, like Sant'Andrea, follow the same pattern in which corruption and divine presence face each other in dialectical visual interplay. Very often, however, almost a century goes by between the presentation of projects and the actual construction of the churches, so the architects and artists working on it do not live long enough to see the completion of the project. But the dynamics of 'composition of place' remain on the agenda of the entire community of artists. Obviously, the Mother church of Il Gesù and Sant'Andrea al Quirinale are two very significant examples of compositions of place that we encounter in church architecture as a result of the diffusion of the *Exercises*. Their parallel analysis offers an overview of the phenomenon, but not an exhaustive study of the phenomenon as a whole in the urban fabric of Counter-Reformation Rome. These buildings have the peculiarity of being directly affiliated with the Society of Jesus and conceptualized mostly during Loyola's lifetime. However, the diffusion of the *Spiritual Exercises* is not limited to these two examples of Roman Baroque architecture. It progressively 'contaminates' Rome at large.

The *Roma Ignaziana*

The not-so imaginary world of the *Exercises* projects itself into urban reality far beyond the sacred spaces. It becomes a group of codes that are used by the followers of Ignatius in the transformation of Rome and, more generally, in the evolution and re-definition of Christendom. As I mentioned earlier, it is Loyola's death and the beginning of a cult of both his person and his writings that inaugurate a whole century of artistic transformation in the city of Rome. Of course, it would be erroneous to forget the many other factors that throw the Eternal City into this revolution, such as the resolutions taken at the Council of Trent, the papacies of Paul III and Paul IV, the growing need for an economic resurrection through the arts in the city, the fear of another sack and the need for a stronger urban image. Moreover, Ignatius of Loyola is not the only recognizable emblematic figure of this ongoing transformation. Philip Neri, the founder of the Oratorians and a friend of the Jesuits and their founder, also has a great influence on the development of new dynamics within cult spaces. Along with the Jesuits and the Oratorians, the Theatines were another relatively recent order that wanted to remain close to the papacy, but that would live in tension with the Society of Ignatius.[64] Each of these orders wants to be highly represented in the city, and manifests its presence through the magnificence of their mother churches: the construction of Il Gesù begins in 1568; it is followed by the construction of Santa Maria in Vallicella, the Mother church of the Oratorians, in 1575; eventually the Theatines build their home temple, Sant'Andrea delle Valle, in 1591. The Oratorians and the Theatines, generally speaking, follow the guidelines established by the construction of the Jesuit Mother church.

The expansion of the architectural dynamics described above through non-Jesuit figures is very rapid, given the enormous success of Il Gesù for the Counter-Reformation. By the end of the sixteenth century, the style of the Mother Church has become the norm and the model for the great majority of the Catholic Church, and this institution understands that its preservation against the Protestant Reformation is now possible through the revival of previous narrative forms in combination with a constant exposition of the sacred images to the gaze of the observer. Whether this phenomenon can be qualified as propaganda or not is a different question and depends on the meaning that one grants to the word 'propaganda.'

However, if it is a meaning faithful to the Latin root *propagare* (to diffuse or to propagate), then yes, one can call *propaganda* what happens to church architecture in Rome between 1550 and 1650, since the purpose of the new form is to diffuse the use of sensorial experience in religious contemplation. After the construction of the Gesù, Rome blossoms with churches that imitated its style. Even the Jesuits sought to participate in this general movement of imitation with the construction of San Ignazio by the Colegio Romano, whose façade and interior ceiling are an *improved version* of the ones found in the Gesù.[65]

As Anthony Blunt notes: "The heroes of the Counter Reformation were canonized—Borromeo in 1610, Ignatius, Francis Xavier, Philip Neri, Teresa in 1622, Gaetano da Thiene in 1629—and these canonizations were the signal for the building of churches and chapels dedicated to the new saints" (10). This 'snow-ball' effect is comprehensible, given the crisis that the institution was facing. Barthes might have said that the totality of the urban territory needed to be covered exactly as the mental territory of believers needed to be conquered. It would have been a theoretical direction to follow. By the second quarter of the seventeenth century, one can envision the city of Rome as a territory that has been successfully conquered by the mission of the companions. By 1650, the glory has been doubled since, on the one hand, Rome counts a great quantity of Jesuit landmarks and, on the other hand, is now the re-conquered Jerusalem from which the Jesuits control all their other provinces where their Roman novitiates have established their mission. The totality is therefore *in* Rome and *from* Rome. Let us, for instance, take a look at an updated map of the city of Rome from the 1610 edition of Ribadeneira's *Vita*. This document is often referred to as the map of the *Roma Ignaziana*—perhaps in order to create a contrast with the *Roma Putana* described earlier and eventually 'overthrown by the holy powers' of Loyola. In this representation, the Jesuit churches, colleges, offices, and chapels are clearly emphasized. Once again, Pedro Ribadeneira stresses the glory of Ignatius of Loyola through his 'miraculous' accomplishments. The center of the city is clearly indicated here by the Gesù, whose size is, of course, extremely exaggerated in order to be highlighted on the map. One observes similar exaggeration in previous maps of the city, but never combined with a position of centrality such as the one given to the Mother church in this map.

90 LOYOLA'S GREATER NARRATIVE

Figure 6: "Roma Ignaziana" also from Ribadaneira's in the 1610 edition of the *Vita* (Church of Il Gesù)

The colleges (Romano, Germanicum) appear also emphasized to the left of Il Gesù. We can almost draw a horizontal axis of Jesuit buildings going through Rome, as if no one could go across the city without finding one on his/her path. It describes a web whose center (most holy temple) would be the Mother church, the resting place of the future saint. From the perspective of this cartographic masterpiece, a reader of the *Vita* could imagine Rome as the re-established center of religious activity that it once was thanks to the action of Ignatius and his followers. The most surprising element of this representation of the Jesuit web in Rome are the city limits that Ribadaneira determines. The amount of space east of the Gesù—that is, the upper part of the map—appears equal to the amount west of it—the lower half of the document. One can observe in this document how the urban fabric is once more considered as a palimpsest on which the followers of Ignatius have added their own layer. It stands on top of the Ancient and the Modern. The most active part of the city was located west of the Gesù, even though the Jesuits had the ambition to develop their action in the northeastern part of Rome as well.

It is surprising that Ribadeneira did not include Saint Peter's basilica and the city of the Vatican on this map. In this *Roma Ignaziana*, the Holy See is absent, or simply omitted. There are many ways in which the city could have been represented, but this artist chooses on purpose to adopt one of the few perspectives that cannot include the originally most holy temple of the city. It almost seems that the followers of Ignatius want to stress here their greater reverence to their re-constructed temple of the fallen Jerusalem, that is, Il Gesù. The same idea of centrality that we see developed in the architecture of the Counter-Reformation informs the drawing of such maps: clearly, the Gesù pretends to become the central temple of the central city of the most central religion. And for the sake of that perspective, the basilica of Saint Peter has to be gently erased from the greater picture. The most visible layer of the Roman palimpsest on this map remains essentially Ignatian. This map proves the totality of Jesuit occupation *in* Rome and declares it to be the center of spiritual activity, bypassing altogether the Vatican.

It turns out that the Jesuits—the first order that adds to its constitutions the vow of obedience to the Bishop of Rome—remove the architectural focus on the papacy traditionally associated with Rome, and substitutes it with the cult and the image of the author of the *Spiritual Exercises*. The period of expansion for Ignatian spirituality through Loyolan[66] visual methods (1550–1650) that we have just discussed parallels the renovation and construction of the new basilica above the grave of Peter the apostle. The Holy See of Paul III, who has contributed enormously to financing the church of Il Gesù,[67] needs to follow the architectural trends initiated outside its walls, in the city of Rome, and needs to find a harmony with it, a way to be integrated in the web of the *Roma Ignaziana*. Its principal temple, Saint Peter's basilica, had gone through various stages of political turmoil and was still not in a position, when Loyola died in 1566, to represent the glory of a Church that was in complete re-structuring.[68] For more than another century, Saint Peter's is going to be elevated in the spirit of the Counter-Reformation of the *Roma Ignaziana* and will try to regain the status of most sacred temple in Rome and in Christendom, above all the temples of Jerusalem.

Lucas comes to the following interesting conclusion in *Landmarking*:

> The romantic dream of the mission to Jerusalem gave way to the reality Ignatius and his companions encountered in their travels and their apostolic works in human cities. They had set out following a dream that offered the comfort of ancient landmarks. When that dream proved impracticable, they did not abandon dreaming. Rather, they were creative enough to reshape that dream, and daring enough to begin building new landmarks in the cities where they lived (164). Ignatius Loyola prodigally spent his treasure of hopes to build something new, a landmark on the landscape of the Catholic tradition. Wise builder that he was, he knew that where that landmark is placed makes all the difference (169).

'Placing the landmark' is indeed the right expression, although it makes it sound like a very innocent act. One could see more in the *Roma Ignaziana* than a landmarking; one could see a complete *reconfiguration* of the urban space. It is neither one nor the other: Rome remains Rome, but it has served as a laboratory for the former hidalgo. There he was able to experiment with the conquest of space through means other than wars and weapons. The dynamics found in the *Spiritual Exercises* and taken to the sacred spaces stimulate faith in the reconstruction of the city. Rome had been turned into a Babylon prior to Loyola's arrival; it was now elevated as the New Jerusalem. But this experiment revealed a fundamental truth about the Jesuit experience: it could be applied to every place on earth, especially urban territories, since any place had the potential to be Babylon and Jerusalem at once. The same phenomenon was going on in the human mind, always confronted by these two options, these two standards.

So the good news was that Jerusalem could be recreated anywhere. But it needed a 'direction,' or in other words, a *mise en scène* such as that prescribed in the *Spiritual Exercises*, a dramatic function equivalent to the Aristotelian *catharsis*. It is not long before the Jesuits naturally find their way to the sphere of drama and educate the most remarkable playwrights of the Baroque age (Calderón, Corneille for instance). But a question remains nonetheless: why is this *mise en scène* more important to them than the literal teaching of the Scriptures prescribed by the Reformation? Is there a need for more immediate answers? Why is there so much anxiety in keeping the narrative of Christianity going? Why are the spiritual practices of the Counter-Reformation based on reenactments and simulations? Maybe because it is already the sixteenth century of the Lord and the Lord hasn't returned yet. The *Spiritual Exercises* meet their full potential in the city of Rome because they receive, as a method, the means and the support necessary to develop. But their function, in return, is to provide an answer to this anxiety.

In the meantime, the spirit needs its workout, to simulate and anticipate the event to come. The trained spirit needs to encounter a tension that exists in its greatest intensity in the urban fabric. The city—Rome as well as any other city—has the required capacities. In the meantime, Christianity is moving on in a fundamentally urban society. The first Jesuits are aware of this new configuration and want to adapt their ministry to it. The city as a concept has been, and continues to be, part of the 'greater narrative' from the times of the Old Testament. Babel, Babylon, Sodom, Jerusalem, Rome are all *orders of corruption par excellence*. They all come together in one single text made of multiple layers of ruins. Rome functions as a Derridean *hors texte* for these preceding urban biblical figures (including the

Pagan Rome on which it stands). Jerusalem is no longer a biblical concept fixed in the temporal distance of the Scriptures; it becomes, thanks to the dynamics of the *Spiritual Exercises*, a reality that can be recreated and reenacted anywhere on the face of the earth. This is what the Ignatian Counter-Reformation wants to *rub in the face* of Lutheranism: spiritual emotion is the goal of the Christian message, and not the literal study of a text that relates it to remote epochs. The urban setting must understand this goal at all times and turn urban dwellers into exercitants, applying to them every artifice that their spirituality can accept. It anticipates the birth of aesthetics.

Naturally, this will be highly criticized in the following century, since it is a movement that contradicts the Humanist impulse for generic flexibility and imagination independent of religious thought. The systematic reenactment of a 'spiritual workout' can be taken to an extreme, and therefore recognized as a potentially dangerous system in early-Modernity. Moreover, the notion of 'urban fabric' to which it is associated undergoes a similar questioning. In many ways, the post-Loyolan Renaissance is condemned to transform reality into its negative prints. But the *Spiritual Exercises* do not seek to represent either reality or its opposite; they work as a principle on it and this principle can serve many other purposes outside the religious realm. Loyola must have been well aware of it.

CHAPTER IV

Transformation of the Visual Dynamics of the *Spiritual Exercises* in the Late Works of Miguel de Cervantes

> *The time in which Cervantes lived was the time in which one witnesses the last flourishing of a desperate grand mystique, the fanatical effort of a religion voluntarily sinking to get back to the surface with its own forces . . .*
>
> Georg Lukács, *Theory of the Novel*

The mental settings of the *Spiritual Exercises* will deeply influence the evolution of fiction at the turn of the seventeenth century, as much as they influence the world of architecture. Again, we need to isolate the text's principles and its dynamics in order to see that these are sometimes used to criticize the very purpose of the exercises, that is, the reunion with the Roman faith and a reaffirmation of its beliefs. As we have seen in both preceding chapters, European authors of fiction from Catholic countries are very attentive to the flaws of the Church and identify the age of Counter-Reformation as a period of transition and anxiety.[1] As a matter of fact, poetry, theater, and narrative fiction all participate in the changes of modes of representation. Literary production in Spain remains under the control of the Inquisition, so authors often need to develop encoded meanings in their texts, and this results in novels like *Don Quixote*, which supposedly inaugurates a new era in the writing of fiction. That is why I propose in this chapter to take a closer look at the relationship that one might identify between current trends of representation that derive from the *Spiritual Exercises* and the birth of the 'Modern novel.'

Georg Lukács analyzes this phenomenon in his *Theory of the Novel* (1916) and claims that the rise of the novel takes place at a moment of spiritual crisis related to the Counter-Reformation: in his terms, *Don Quixote* appears when the Christian God starts to abandon the world, when the human being turns into a solitary creature in search of new signifiers and interpretations of reality. The world needs another deity if God is no longer in it, and *Don Quixote* emphasizes this absence of divine presence (99). However, just as the Loyolan *theophany* motivates the entire process of the exercises, one could argue that literary *semiophany* generates the fundamental obsessions of the Modern character. Don Quixote is engaged in a search process, but he cannot connect the goal of his mission to external reality. From the angle of a more recent generation of criticism, Jean Starobinski takes this conclusion a step further when he writes in *L'Oeil Vivant* (1961) that :

> Le roman devient le champ tout profane d'un 'exercice spirituel' dont le bénéficiaire ne sera pas le Sauveur, mais l'humanité (124). Le lecteur s'approprie le monde du romancier comme l'étudiant s'approprie le savoir objectif d'un maître et la vision du monde qu'il en résulte. Il entre en possession du code interprétatif grâce auquel la réalité toute entière devient intelligible. Ainsi se produit une *éducation* du regard, comparable à celle que pratiquaient les jésuites dans leurs exercices spirituels (125).

In fact, the *Spiritual Exercises* appear right before the transition toward Modernity, as defined by Modern criticism defines it. Their dynamics and principles have a direct influence on the development of the novel as a genre of Modernity. It is a legitimate phenomenon if we consider that it is a text influenced by pre-Modern narrative forms. The term *code interprétatif* is particularly essential and interesting in Starobinski's conclusion since it bridges the gap between the nature of a spiritual exercise and the goals of the novel.

Let us remember that the still pre-Modern Loyola, after the conversion experience in Manresa, entertained a certain fear of and fascination with fiction as a whole. Narratives of all genres were a sphere that he would readily associate with sin and vanity, since they involved the use of the imaginative powers. Imagination, and the building of an image reservoir in general, was a human capacity that he also considered dangerous since it could lead to sin the same way it would lead to virtue, and was therefore a very delicate territory for the conscience.[2] This is also why the *Exercises* were based on a basic relationship of direction: the imagination would be established as a set of dynamics corresponding to a pair of pilgrims, the director and his exercitant. From the beginning of the manual, the tone was set: the director would have authority and control over the sinful dimensions of imagination that the exercitant would be lacking.

The *Spiritual Exercises* as a text was therefore intended to be read only by those who had the required training and the capacity to read about imagination and the possibilities to control and orient it. This position seems altogether anti-Modern enough. Whereas the Protestant Reformation would condemn the use of imagination for its same potential to lead a believer to sin, Loyola conceived it, once again, as an order of corruption, a territory where the soul could measure its power to resist temptation and sin, where it could virtually see the face of evil and would learn how to recognize it in the outside world. It was meant to be an exercise that would fortify the mental muscles on which the Christian God counted. Therefore imagination could not be ignored or discarded from the religious experience. Mark I. Wallace, in his analysis and introduction to Paul Ricoeur's *Figuring the Sacred*, underlines the close relationship between imagination and the experience of conversion from this particularly Catholic perspective:

> Earlier Ricoeur had written that the subject can construct a new identity through its commerce with self-generated figures of the imagination. The subject can experience "redemption through imagination" because in "imagining his possibilities, man can act as a prophet of his own existence" (Ricoeur 7).

In the case of the Loyolan practice, of course, the responsibility of image generation is left to the director. It is precisely in this equation that we observe a reflection of Loyola's *Exercises* in the works of Miguel de Cervantes. The author of *Don Quixote* entertains a great fascination with this same 'redemptive capacity' of the imagination identifiable in the practice of the exercises. After analyzing the *formation* and the *diffusion* of the exercises' dynamics, the problematic that we need to address here is their *transformation* with the rise of the Modern novel—a concept closer to *deformation* in this case. The literary spaces that I propose to explore as examplary instances of the phenomenon are Cervantes' masterpieces *Don Quixote de la Mancha*, as well as his less famous account of a pilgrimage to the Eternal City, *Los Trabajos de Persiles y Segismunda*.

Miguel de Cervantes entertains a close contact with the first generations of Jesuits, as well as their practice of the exercises, and he spends a great deal of time in the city of Rome where it flourishes. I wish to analyze here the ways in which Cervantes throws a bridge between the *Spiritual Exercises* and the emerging Modern novel in Spain. In order to do this, I will need to juxtapose here historical circumstances with literary analysis, since these two texts contain a great deal of specular representation and encoded criticism of institutional practices. It is this historicity of the texts, as well as the textuality of History itself, that needs to be considered here.[3] Moreover, there is reason to believe that they emphasize the potential of the mind-setting prescribed in the *Spiritual Exercises*. By the turn of the century, this celebrated text has become a reference all across Southwestern Europe, and readers often identify it as an *object* of Spanish pride. The kingdom of Spain needs such *objects* in order to build a political structure that echoes the triumphs of Rome, as well as building a Rome that reflects the glory of the Spanish Crown. Cervantes will respond to this diffusion of Spanish culture with a critical eye and a quite Modern impulse.

Cervantes, Corruption, the Urban, and the Company

The Rome that Cervantes will discover as a young artist is modified by the Jesuit presence. By the beginning of the seventeenth century, the author of the *Exercises* symbolizes the conquest of Rome by the Spaniards. Of the thousands of Spanish migrants who chose Rome as their home in the sixteenth century, no one will mark the history and the spiritual reshaping of the Eternal City the way Ignatius of Loyola did. Unlike many of his countrymen, Loyola chose to remain in Rome until his death and did not consider returning to Spain as an option for his missionary works. Since the most influential figures of Spanish Catholicism were most of the time in Rome, it was easier for him to distill the essence of his method from within the institution than to go back to his homeland and have to deal with the memories of his earlier trials with the Inquisition.[4] On March 13th, 1622, Loyola enters the Roman 'greater narrative' of Christianity when the Jesuits decorate Saint Peter's basilica to celebrate the canonization of their founder. A three-day festival of processions in the streets of Rome follows the ceremony. As Thomas James Dandelet points out, beyond the ceremonies, it is the inauguration of a new age for the Church:

> Combined with the canonization ceremony, the procession of March 13, 1622, possibly more than any other ceremony in the previous decades, constituted a synthesis of Spanish and Roman Catholic triumphalism that ritually claimed Rome for the Spaniards and left their heroes firmly ensconced in some of the central temples of the city (185).

Ignatius' posthumous triumph was not to have returned to Spain with the confirmation of a lifetime religious dedication but, on the contrary, to have Spain triumph along with him in Catholicism's most holy temple on this day of victory for the Counter-Reformation.

Even though Rome was never technically a Spanish territory like the kingdom of Naples, it had become after the sack of 1527 an obedient client of the Spanish crown. Many centuries after the conquest of Spain by Rome, it was the Spanish Crown that had colonized the Eternal City: the interests of both countries were once again working hand in hand in a configuration that one could call "Spanish Rome."[5] During the sixteenth century, the destiny of the papacy had been determined by Spain, in its moments of destruction as well as in its moments of reconstruction. Although it turns out to be a rather chaotic period on the political level, it is a time of enormous cultural exchange on all levels. Dandelet pursues his analysis of the Spanish conquest of Rome and explores its effects on the sphere of the arts, and especially literature:

> Spanish humanists began to devise a literary picture of the historical relationship between Spain and Rome. Renaissance Spain met Renaissance Rome more closely during these decades. Golden Age literature produced by a range of Spanish novelists, political satirists, historians, religious essayists, poets, playwrights, and pilgrims helped create a *distinctly Spanish idea of Rome*. [. . .] Powerful figures like Miguel de Cervantes made their way to Rome in search of a patron and perhaps inspiration (7, 10).

Rome represents a step in the artistic progression of many Golden Age figures from Spain: not only Cervantes, but also Spanish painters like Velázquez and Ribera.[6] They all participate in the early-modern revolution of representational techniques and practices. Many still perceive Rome as an indispensable step in any intellectual's personal evolution. Moreover, by the beginning of the seventeenth century, the city has recovered its financial capacity for patronage of the arts.

Cervantes, as a Humanist whose life is a succession of independent episodes, will follow this move and spend a good deal of time in the Eternal City in order to establish himself as a writer. Of course, this young man in search of inspiration does not possess yet the ironic maturity that characterizes the one-handed author of *Don Quixote*. But he witnesses Rome in its most glorious days of reform and urban renewal. We are inclined to believe that this is a quite comfortable episode in Cervantes' life, when he gets to pursue studies of history, philosophy, rhetoric, divinity, and astrology he had begun in Spain. Like many Spaniards who traveled to Rome, the young humanist writer hopes to find a patron who will give him shelter, food, and the opportunity to spend time on these studies. Young spirits like him had a purpose in the Rome of the Counter-Reformation since they helped to shape the image of the city, from a Spanish perspective; their perception of this unique urban reality would travel with them in their writings. The Society of Jesus is prepared to welcome to Rome and help any Spaniard with eclectic interests.

Eventually Miguel de Cervantes finds a quite comfortable position in the house of Cardinal Giulio Acquaviva. Armed with a blood purity certificate, the young Spanish author had come to Rome with the intention to serve this young Roman cardinal who had previously been to the court of Madrid in 1568. Cervantes' service as chamberlain starts in the winter of 1570. In other words, his first acquaintance with the city happens a few years after the death of Ignatius, at a time of enormous development for the Society of Jesus. Very little information is available about Cervantes' time in Rome, since none of his masterpieces correspond to this period of his life and the information doesn't exist. But the few indications available all confirm that he moved on to a position in the army as soon as he was given the chance. In his recent *Quixotic Frescoes* (2007), Frederick De Armas "argue[s] that Cervantes spent his life 'desiring Italy'–and that this desire is often represented in his literary texts through allusions to the art, architecture, and culture of the Italian peninsula" (4) During this short and almost insignificant episode in a life full of incidents, Cervantes is in close contact with the Church hierarchy and, particularly, the Jesuits. Giulio Acquaviva, the cardinal that he serves, is no less than the nephew of Claudio Acquaviva, disciple of Ignatius, and appointed third 'General of the Society of Jesus' a few months before Cervantes moves to Rome. The young cardinal Giulio is not officially a Jesuit, but as a close relative of the Father General, he lives in close contact with the Society and represents for Cervantes the new generation of clergy associated with Jesuit principles of education.[7] During this year of service, Cervantes has the flexibility to hear and participate in the life of the cardinal's palace. De Armas adds that "he came in contact with a papal court saturated with political subtexts whose laudatory thrust often stemmed from the authority of classical cultures" (5) His presence in such a 'privileged' circle and his service for a man who had worked closely with Ignatius of Loyola is enough to familiarize Cervantes with the practice and principles of the Ignatian exercises.[8]

Because of this particular experience, we are inclined to think that Cervantes always held the Society of Jesus in some kind of respect. His texts often emphasize the distinction he makes between the obviously corrupted hierarchies of the Roman institution on the one hand and, on the other hand, the Company of the Jesuits who seem to bring a new impulse with their eclectic approach to the acquisition of knowledge. However, by the end of his life, Cervantes entertains a cynical opinion of Counter-Reformation Rome and its effects on social behavior in general. There are possible autobiographical traces of this episode in his late works and, particularly, in the *Novelas Ejemplares* (1610). In the *Licienciado Vidriera*, for instance, the protagonist visits the city of Rome with the eye of a young Humanist observer. As we know, Vidriera travels the Southwestern European world with an unmatchable thirst for the acquisition of knowledge. He is, in other words, a caricature of the Early Modern Spanish student before the Inquisition prohibits the continuation of studies outside of Spain, later on in Cervantes' lifetime. His perception of reality is therefore influenced by the memory of a city ruled by extremely mechanical spiritual practices. One readily notices an ironic layer in the tone of the following passage:

> Visitó sus templos, adoró sus reliquias y admiró su grandeza; y así como por las uñas del león se viene en conocimiento de su grandeza y ferocidad, así él sacó la de Roma por sus despedazados mármoles, medias y enteras estatuas, por sus rotos arcos y derribadas termas, por sus magníficos pórticos y anfiteatros grandes, por su famoso y santo río, que siempre llena sus márgenes de agua y las beatifica con las infinitas reliquias de cuerpos de mártires que en ellas tuvieron sepultura; por sus puentes, que parece que se están mirando unas a otras, y por sus calles, que con sólo el nombre cobran autoridad sobre todas las de las otras ciudades del mundo (. . .). Notó también la autoridad del Colegio de Cardenales, la majestad del Sumo Pontífice, el concurso y variedad de gente y naciones. Y habiendo andando la estación de las siete iglesias, y confesádose con un penitenciario, y besado el pie de Su Santidad, lleno de *agnusdeis* y cuentas, determinó irse a Nápoles (49–50).[9]

The passage is marked by a rapid succession of preterite verbs and indicates a mechanical experience of the urban setting in which Vidriera is moving. There is no freedom of movement for the pilgrim in his progress through the urban space. On the contrary, the licienciado's perception of Rome develops through programmed sensorial contacts: vision, touch, and taste are all involved here and follow a pattern. Nonetheless, the objects of contemplation are all in a state of decomposition. It is particularly interesting here to note how the 'intellectually transparent' Vidriera sees Rome as a city composed of ruins and artifacts to be covered or recycled in new artistic forms. The city appears in this passage as a palimpsest of various historical periods whose corruption merges them all to form a unified territory: the bridges, for instance, look at each other as if comparing their respective state of decay.

Also, the analogy of Rome represented here as a lion emphasizes the evaluative nature of Vidriera's journey to Rome.[10] The City is compared to the 'king of animals' not only to emphasize its superiority to the rest of Christendom, but also to symbolize its often immobile, still but dangerous nature. Moreover, it is not the animal in itself that awakens the interest of the observer, but the quality of its claws: Vidriera is looking for small details or traces of weakness. His gaze underlines the fact that Rome is based on many artifacts and illusions, and a great deal of its political and spiritual power is based on the façades that have been raised all along its streets. De Armas comments that the Spanish observer "would have to learn how to clearly visualize the frescoes, statues, chapels and palaces. Visualization thus became a key to Cervantes' art" (9). Rome represents in that sense the Baroque illusion, that is, a fierce lion with unreliable claws. On his path, Vidriera encounters a lot of evidence of the masked weakness of a twice-fallen Empire.

Above all, this passage is interesting for its reference to the relics in the river; this image also underlines the fundamentally violent nature of Roman history and the relative veneration of violence in its spirituality. The City indicates to the eye of its observer that its History is a succession of massacres. In spite of its effort to cover up the past horror, the bodies of the innocent are still floating in the Tiber, and the Roman urban development evolves around this voluntary emphasis: the streets, the buildings, and the bridges all point to the contemplation of physical decomposition and encourage a fascination with it. This passage is full of vocabulary related to corruption as physical disintegration: *despedazados, medias estatuas, rotos, derribadas, reliquias, cuerpos, sepultura*. The City has no other choice but to reflect in its arts its own decomposition, since it has literally become a sepulchre. Even its most holy temple is constructed on the decaying body of Peter the Apostle. The relic as commodity for sale has become one of the main industries in Cervantes' time. Rome appears, therefore, in this passage as an order of corruption based on the systematic worship of hierarchical figures and bones in parallel with the accumulation of capital. Nonetheless, nothing in this passage appears as a direct attack on the Church. Vidriera's eye wanders through Rome as objectively as possible. There is no questioning of the spiritual practices in this passage, but on the contrary, an acknowledgment of the necessity for the City to project these images on the pilgrim. Cervantes underlines here the authenticity of the surrounding artifices for the eyes of a trained gazer. For this reason, the indicators of corruption cohabit with the positive energy that the place of pilgrimage creates: Cervantes mentions this dimension in the terms *grandeza, admiró, magníficos, grandes, famosos,* and stresses the city's Babel-like nature in the expression *variedad de gente y naciones*. Through Vidriera, he recognizes that the ruins and relics attract pilgrims around them and invite them to enter the 'greater narrative' of Christianity.

Now, we can surely juxtapose this passage with another one from the *Novelas Ejemplares* in order to see how Cervantes depicts the Company of Jesus as a new Humanist impulse within the old mechanical Roman Catholicism. There seem to be certain voices in his texts and places where Cervantes encourages the Jesuit presence in Spanish society, especially in spheres related to education. Literary critic Andres Trapiello seeks to emphasize in the tone of these voices a great affection for the new Catholic order which he directly relates to Cervantes' own admiration. According to him, this is due to the support he received from Jesuits at several points in his career.[11] Trapiello affirms that Cervantes "pasara luego al colegio recién fundado de la Compañía de Jesús, donde debió de estudiar dos cursos de Gramática. Cervantés escribió grandes elogios de estos padres jesuitas, y lo hizo con mucho afecto, años después, en el *Coloquio de los Perros*" (28).[12] This most interesting *novelas* evolves around the dialogue between two dogs that are in very close contact with corruption, since they are having their conversation in the Hospital de la Resurrección in Valladolid, next to a man in high fever. The *Coloquio* is one of the most intriguing *novelas* since it confronts two different experiences in the form of a single conversation. One of the two dogs, Berganza, recalls his experience while staying with the Jesuit fathers. One can indeed verify the connection between Cervantes and the Society at this point in the *Novelas Ejemplares* when the dog-narrator alludes to the remarkable experience he has had with the fathers:

> No sé qué tiene la virtud, que, con alcanzárseme a mí tan poco, o nada, della, luego recibí el gusto de *ver* el amor, el término, la solicitud y la industria con que aquellos benditos padres y maestros enseñaban a aquellos niños, enderezando las tiernas varas de su juventud, por que no torciersen ni tomasen mal siniestro en el camino de la virtud, que justamente con las letras les mostraban. Consideraba cómo los reñían con suavidad, los castigaban con misericordia, los animaban con ejemplos, los incitaban con premios y los sobrellevaban con cordura, y finalmente, *como les pintaban la fealdad y horror de los vicios y les dibujaban la hermosura de las virtudes*, para que, aborrecidos ellos y amadas ellas, consiguiesen el fin para que fueron criados (316).[13]

If we admit that the talking dog is not an instrument of irony in this passage, there seem to be three dimensions at the origin of Cervantes' admiration for the Jesuits. First of all, as I previously mentioned, the notion of *flexibility* and adaptation of educational principles to the intellectual configuration of the individual. Second, the *inclination toward literature* in Jesuit education and the function of fiction in their system since it simulates situations for the development of the imagination. Third, the efficiency of their *representational modes*, especially the capacity to "draw the vices and horror" of sins.

Of all three, the last is probably the most remarkable quality underlined by Berganza in this passage. There seems to be great admiration for the Jesuit capacity to *represent* on the part of Miguel de Cervantes. As we have seen in the previous passage, Vidriera points to the need to be exposed to representations of sin and vice in order to become familiar with their nature. Thomas Hanrahan underlines in this article on "Cervantes and the Moralists" this apparent continuity between the Humanist ideals of Cervantes and the pedagogy that the Jesuit fathers derive from the *Spiritual Exercises*: they both emphasize the essential function of familiarization with orders of corruption in human existence. Furthermore, there does not seem to be any contradiction between these ideals in terms of free will, the perception of desire and its sources, and the casuistry of the Jesuits. But Hanrahan also comes to the conclusion that it would be a mistake to force that connection and to go as far as to consider Cervantes a 'friend of the Society.' He argues that the recent Jesuit theology awakens his curiosity very much and, in consequence, is just part of "the wide intellectual interests of Cervantes and his eclectic approach to religious themes" (919). And indeed, *eclectic* characterizes the Modern impulse in the Spanish author.

We could challenge this interpretation given the one-dimensional nature of Cipión's response to Berganza's anecdote. The second dog not only confirms the appreciation in Berganza's argument, but also reinforces it with his own praises. His perspective on the Jesuit interest in public salvation nicely complements the previous passage:

> Porque yo he oído decir desa bendita gente que para repúblicos del mundo no los hay tan prudentes en todo él, y para guiadores y adalides del camino del cielo, pocos les llegan. Son espejos donde se mira la honestidad, la católica do[c]trina, la singular prudencia, y, finalmente, la humildad profunda, basa sobre quien se levanta todo el edificio de la bienaventuranza (316).[14]

The main difference that Cervantes stresses between the followers of Ignatius and the rest of the Church is their central function of *guiadores* (directors). Cipión seems to be fascinated by their capacity to move in the world with extreme 'prudence.' The acquisition of wisdom directly serves the purpose of mission and salvation, and their ministry is secular, urban and essentially intercultural, whereas some other dominant orders of the Church still remain in the more medieval mode of monastic life. This fundamental difference between the Jesuits and the rest of the Church shows a concern in Early Modern Spain for ecclesiastical social action. This is a quality that Cervantes' dog-character admires in them, since he represents here the very bottom of the social scale. Yet he has not received equal treatment from the fathers of the Company; he has only "heard it said." Above all, their main quality is to be the *mirrors* in which the deep and true nature of the human soul reflects itself. This notion of specularity in reference to the practitioners of the spiritual exercises is particularly relevant since it points to the confrontation of the human believer with his true nature.

From the observations of these canines, we can conclude that the young writer Miguel de Cervantes had gone to Rome into his new position as chamberlain of the General's nephew with confidence and interest in the Jesuit order which he admired for the reform of the educative system and their interest in social and individual action. Maybe Andres Trapiello takes this Cervantine 'affection' for Ignatius and his order a little too far when he proposes "que Cervantes pudiese conocer, leer y admirar sus *Ejercicios Espirituales*, como de hecho se trasluce en el comento del *Coloquio*" (28).[15] The passages we have just been commenting on do not suggest in any way that the Spanish author had undergone the four weeks of spiritual withdrawal under the direction of a director. Nonetheless, given the period and his itinerary, it is highly probable that he would have come in close contact with the practice or would have heard accounts from former exercitants. Indeed, Cervantes' second most important encounter with the rising Jesuit order in Rome confirms a certain sympathy for their cause. However, it is a form of sympathy that allows great space for criticism, in the fashion of the Jesuit education itself. The enigmatic nature of Cervantes' existence prior to his retirement and the composition of his masterpieces does not allow us to draw conclusions concerning his appreciation of the *Spiritual Exercises*. One thing is certain, though: Cervantes was familiar with this text and the practice that derived from it and he had witnessed how this method affects the Church of Rome in its re-structuring process after the Reformation. By the end of his life—and when he is most productive as an author—we might observe in his works a questioning of the function of representation. Even though he might admire the Jesuits for their capacity to adjust and adapt mental images to individual circumstances, Cervantes proposes to explore the limits of such visual projections in his most famous masterpiece.

Don Quixote, an Excessive Projection in a Greater Narrative

Cervantes and Loyola have in common the root of Humanism, its impulse for reformation, its rich literary panorama, and the many travels that it requires. *Don Quixote* is in a way Cervantes' response to the Humanist experience,[16] but it also inaugurates a revolution in representational modes: it reverses the artistic perception of the world and modifies the laws of representation, in the same fashion that the exercises bring changes to the setting of sacred interiors. This is how we need to understand Michel Foucault's expression when he states that: "Don Quichotte dessine le *négatif* du monde de la Renaissance; l'écriture a cessé d'être la prose du monde; les ressemblances et les signes ont dénoué leur vieille entente; les similitudes déçoivent, tournent à la vision et au délire" (61). The photographic terminology he chooses—*négatif* means in French 'negative print'—reflects indeed the entire transition toward the Baroque age that we have been discussing so far. It is the art of playing with contrast, as one can observe in the *chiaroscuro* technique in most paintings by Caravaggio. As a matter of fact, Cervantes' masterpieces (both *Don Quixote* and the *Novelas Ejemplares*) emphasize an interest in the depiction of violence in the new representational modes, just as the work of contemporary painters does: they use contrasts and negative prints when possible.

In order to create a negative print of reality, the artist needs to perceive its contrasts and ignore the Renaissance attraction to harmonies in Nature. He needs to stress the mechanisms of human desire and the many triangular configurations that motivate it. He cannot ignore the vicious and the horrific dimensions of the human mind, and ultimately the great absence of sense in the universe. Foucault's 'negative print' functions as a landmark in his epistemological division: it symbolizes a rupture with the stability in Renaissance artistic representation. It also determines Cervantes' most celebrated production, since his earlier works do not belong in this new age of representation. By the turn of the seventeenth century, the Jesuits and Cervantes have more in common: they have stepped into the next generation of Humanists whose main concern is the double perception of the surrounding world, that is, simultaneously through beauty and violence. Does this necessarily mean that Cervantes' hidalgo draws a negative print of the *Spiritual Exercises*?

The correspondence between Ignatius of Loyola and Cervantes' Don Quixote as characters in a fiction has been noted several times since Miguel de Unamuno, and I have already commented on these approaches in the first chapter when discussing the formation of an image reservoir in the *Spiritual Exercises*. Now we are going to try to envision the question from a different angle and not compare Loyola with the hidalgo; instead we will concentrate on some of the visual dynamics found in *Don Quixote* and analyze them in the light of the Ignatian exercises. The influence of these techniques on the evolution of the 'first modern' character in the history of fiction is somehow obvious, but yet a complex matter when it comes to identifying them in the text. Critics in the past have tried various approaches to the problem. For instance, Ernest A. Siciliano comments in *The Jesuits in the Quijote and other Essays* (1974) on the work done by Helmut Hatzfeld in 1962:

> Helmut Hatzfeld has already touched upon our present topic as he demonstrates the influence of *Jesuitismo* upon the society of the Counter Reformation. He points out

that the *Exercitia spiritualia* of Ignatius of Loyola, in regard to the scrupules, is reflected in the *Quijote*; the words *escrúpulo* and *escrupuloso* are counted seventeen times. Merely for the record, we should like to observe that Mr. Hatzfeld seems to have missed the several uses in II, 33 and the one in II, 74 (10)

This example shows that the concerns of many literary critics have revolved around philological considerations; a simple word count works as an element of comparison and conclusion. This method seems very limited, however, to the contemporary reader. The vocabulary used in Cervantes is indeed similar to the one found in the *Spiritual Exercises*, or in Pedro Ribadeneira's *Vida de San Ignacio*, but it is a logical consequence of Cervantes' training in *gramática* with the Jesuit fathers, and does not prove anything else.

More recent studies have envisioned the same question with a more productive eye, but remain in the realm of comparing Don Quixote with Ignatius instead of his exercises. An instance of this approach is E.C. Riley and his *Cervantes's Theory of the Novel* (1992), in which he points to the following factor:

> [Don Quixote's] imitation of the heroes of chivalresque novels aims at such completeness that it becomes an attempt to live literature. He is not inspired to a vague sort of emulation, nor does he merely ape the habits, manners, and dress of knights errant; he does not simply adapt chivalresque ideals to some other causes, like St. Ignatius Loyola; he is not even acting a part, in the usual sense. He is content with nothing less than that the whole of the fabulous world—knights, princesses, magicians, giants and all—should be part of his experience. Once he believes he really is a knight errant, and believes in his world of fiction, he steps off the pinnacle of inspired idealistic emulation into madness. He cannot play his part as he would like except in this fabulous world. In this sense he is trying to live literature (36–7).

Although this perspective opposes Loyola to Cervantes' character, it still underlines a crucial parameter in the question we are analyzing here: Don Quixote is a character that transforms the reality around him in order to comprehend it within the *interpretative codes* of another fiction, that is, the world of Chivalry. In the preceding approach, however, Riley suggests that Ignatius "simply adapts" the motifs of one tradition to a different one, whereas I believe it is a more complex process. In *The Sanctification of Don Quixote* (1991), Eric J. Ziolkowski draws more balanced conclusions and points to the heart of the matter, that is, the anxiety around representation. For Ziolkowski, the equation is simple: "the rivalry between the real world and the representation that we make of it for ourselves" is the essence of the Quixotic principle (17). It is in this tension that we find the technique of the spiritual exercises reproduced and transformed in the journey of the hidalgo.

Ziolkowski offers in this sense the most comprehensive point of view in the debate and expands on the satirical nature of *Don Quixote* in relation to Loyola's *Spiritual Exercises*:

> Even before the Council of Trent instituted its stringent ex cathedra policies, St. Ignatius had expressed his solidarity with the ecclesiastical hierarchy by suggesting, among the other rules in his *Spiritual Exercises* (composed 1521–41), that rather than to search for truth and reality on one's own, the adherent should conform his own perception of appearances with the church's dictates. In order not to err, "we should always be ready to accept this principle: I will believe that the white that I see is black [*que lo blanco que yo veo, creer que es negro*], if the hierarchical Church so defines it" (Loyola 140). This rule demonstrates the bearing of conflict of faith and reason on the appearance-reality dichotomy: Ignatius asserts the primacy of obedience to the human reason, which, were it to operate freely, would hold that white is white, and black, black. The *Quixote* satirize the Ignatian rule by having the knight invoke those same terms to argue that the basin which he has stolen from a barber is really a helmet (. . .) The similarity between the Ignatian principle and the method that Sancho perceives in his master's madness is striking (29).

Maybe this is the strongest point of departure for the analysis developed in this chapter, since it parallels the techniques of unconditional visual belief found in the *Spiritual Exercises* with the transformation of reality operated by the eyes of the hidalgo in the novel. Yet, the similarity goes further if we consider that the Ignatian principle rests on a total creation of sensorial perceptions in which the subject is locked. Don Quixote and Sancho are also going through a period of withdrawal in the enclosed Castile. They walk from episode to episode without a map,[17] following often repetitive patterns and want to accumulate *hazañas* (deeds). The reality they penetrate is in the same fashion a total creation. In other words, Don Quixote takes the novels of Chivalry as his initial narrative and builds on it his own fantasy: it is the basic image reservoir on the basis of which he is going to invent his own "greater narrative" and projects himself into a reality that he entirely designs. The borders between the real world and its representation are going to be blurred in the process. Like an exercitant doing a retreat, he uses reality as a territory for simulation where he can finally envision himself as the continuation of knight-errantry, as the successor of Amadis, as the new dominating figure in the continuity of this narrative tradition. In order to achieve these goals, he will need to envision the surrounding reality in terms of "orders of corruption" in which his identity is transformed and evolves constantly toward a new definition. Interestingly enough, through this process, Don Quixote slowly transforms himself into a corruptible body, and becomes in the second part of the novel a living relic. In order to comprehend this progression of the character, let us look at several passages in which Don Quixote enters in his "greater narrative" and simultaneously in the tension of its orders of corruption.

With *Don Quixote*, the reader gets the opportunity to enter into this universe of contrasts, because s/he is maintained in tension between two "standards," in a constant *dialectical mode* where violence, desire, free will, madness, and reason are all participants. As we have seen previously, this characteristic is typical of the *Spiritual Exercises* and the spirit of Counter-Reformation Catholicism. Ultimately, it becomes one of the principal parameters of definition for the Baroque. Christine Buci-Glucksmann makes in this respect a very general statement supported by Hegel: "Toute étude philosophique dialectique exige donc que l'on tienne compte de ce moment privilégié de la modernité qu'est le baroque. "L'apothéose baroque est dialectique. Elle se réalise dans le renversement des extrêmes."" (41). Reality needs to be perceived by the main character in terms of tensions between opposite poles of attraction. This problematic has been studied in an almost infinite number of possibilities and we could not possibly sum up its history here. However, the notion of *dialectics* is central to the processes of world perception in *Don Quixote* and this narrative would not work as a Modern novel otherwise. Following the lines of reflection opened by Lukács and Bakhtin, Foucault recognizes it where he sees in *Don Quixote* "la première des oeuvres modernes puisqu'on y voit la raison cruelle des identités et des différences se jouer à l'infini des signes et des similitudes" (62). From his point of view, the tension is set up as facing mirrors and therefore creates an infinity of possibilities for the narrative simulation in which the subject engages. This infinite play of signs and similarities emerges, for instance, through the dialogues between Sancho and Don Quixote, and these are ultimately transformed in dialectical response to the world.'[18]

The "Dialectical Other" is essential for the character's *semiophany* and, as a result, the exchanges between the two main characters become the basis for the narrative format. But we find similar dynamics in literary works that precede the *Spiritual Exercises*: How would Christ present his teachings if the disciples were not asking the right and wrong questions? How would Dante the Pilgrim decipher the *interpretative code*[19] of the underworld and Purgatory without the interaction with his guide Virgil? In that sense, the 'play of identities and differences' defined by Foucault was not born with the *Exercises* or *Don Quixote* for it has antecedents in various literary traditions. In this respect, Sancho mirrors the fantasy of his master and multiplies it. In Chapter XXI, for instance, the squire projects his master into a fantasy in which he represents for him the greater triumphs of a knight-errant, including crowns and princesses. However, Don Quixote's reply is very direct:

> - No dices mal, Sancho—respondió Don Quijote–, mas antes que se llegue a ese término es menester andar por el mundo como en aprobación, buscando las aventuras, para que acabando algunas se cobre nombre y fama tal, que cuando se fuere a la corte de algún gran monarca ya sea el caballero conocido por sus obras, y que apenas le hayan visto entrar los muchachos por la puerta de la ciudad, cuando todos le sigan y rodeen dando voces, diciendo: "Éste es el Caballero del Sol" (193).[20]

The squire's purpose in the journey is to enhance the projection into this 'Other' reality. Nonetheless, Don Quixote emphasizes here the importance of the process over that of the goals they are setting. In the first part, Sancho's tendency is to accelerate this process as much as he possibly can in order to reach the goal (the island he will govern). Don Quixote, on the contrary, understands that the goals are set in order to motivate the simulation process in which he wants to engage, but he chooses to keep these goals always at a distance. In this passage, we can see that the *término* (the outcome) is painted in an excessive fashion by the hidalgo as if it alone served a purpose of motivation: Don Quixote pictures himself as a victorious figure entering the city with the warm welcome of the children, and echoes the episode of Jesus' joyful entrance into Jerusalem. This 'fiction within the fiction' serves the purpose of inserting the characters in a narrative greater than the one in which they actually are.[21] It only gives a sense of direction to the character, and that is why Don Quixote insists on perceiving himself as a probationer first. This might be the destiny of the Modern character: knowing that the goals that he has set for himself are not to be reached. This justification of his mission as knight-errant echoes in this passage the entire economy of salvation as it is defined by Counter-Reformation Catholicism, and particularly by the Jesuits and the *Spiritual Exercises*. The fictive entrance into an imaginary city reflects here the salvation obtained for the quantity of works during one's lifetime ("*conocido por sus obras*"). Don Quixote's conception of knight-errantry is therefore, in that sense, a reproduction of the Loyolan definition of salvation and parallels it.

The processes might be very similar in this respect, but the outcomes (the *términos*) diverge. *Don Quixote* is a novel marked by the absence of God and the loss of faith. The goals set by the protagonist are hardly of a Christian nature. As Jesuit philosopher José Eduardo Pérez Valera described it recently, the relation to salvation changes with Don Quixote: "Es cristiano pero no se ha convertido totalmente en un cristiano. Esa convicción pone a la opción vital por la que el hombre decide hacerse a sí mismo en el centro de la reflexión filosófica. Se trata de una nueva etapa en el movimiento de retorno al sujeto" (25).[22] The principle of the *Exercises* is used so that the subject/exercitant can engage in an anagogic communication with his own self. Of course, no one can claim that Don Quixote refuses Christian principles, but he uses his own person as an instrument of inversion of these principles.

Loyola invents a totalitarian system of sensorial perception that requires representations prior to the imaginative act in the exercitant's mind; Cervantes exaggerates this process and presents a character that has already configured the world according to fictive representations. The exercitant of the *Exercises* and Don Quixote have different aims, but attempt to reach them by using similar visual dynamics in their quest. Once again, one could perfectly well see in the hidalgo an act of parody or a encoded message on Cervantes' part, but it would limit the appreciation of *Don Quixote*. It has been observed that the hidalgo was a spiritual director for his squire, and that the two characters progressively reverse roles.[23] In fact, the couple Quixote/Sancho does not reflect literally the dynamics of a director with his exercitant.

The narrative demonstrates that, in the case of the hidalgo and his *escudero*, it becomes difficult to determine which one occupies the position of director and which one receives spiritual guidance as an exercitant. These functions could therefore be interchangeable. This is exactly where the Baroque play of identities and differences takes place. There is no definitive determination of the Dialectical Other. Even the hidalgo points it out to his squire in one of his deepest moments of literary criticism directly applied to his own narrative:

> ¿Que es posible que en cuanto ha que andas conmigo no has echado de ver que todas las cosas de los caballeros andantes parecen quimeras, necedades y desatinos, y que son todas hechas al revés? Y no porque sea ello así, sino porque andan entre nosotros siempre una caterva de encantadores que todas nuestras cosas mudan y truecan, y las vuelven según su gusto y según tienen la gana de favorecernos o destruirnos; y, así, eso que a ti te parece bacía de barbero me parece a mí el yelmo de Mambrino y a otro le parecerá otra cosa (237).[24]

Once again, this is a quite Jesuit perspective coming from the hidalgo. He accuses Sancho of failing to see clearly through the play of representations, illusions, and interpretations in which they have engaged and of not understanding that things around them are voluntarily "metamorphosed into the reverse of what they are," according to Smollett's translation. Don Quixote, in this episode of penitence, reveals the artificiality of his quest. Seeing—and perceiving reality through other senses in general—is all relative and depends on the individual who projects his desires onto reality. This is both a Modern concept and a principle of the *Spiritual Exercises*.

There is no doubt that Cervantes is attentive to the central dynamics of the

Spiritual Exercises and especially to the relationship established by Loyola between a director and his exercitant. This has been demonstrated in relatively recent investigations in which critics conclude that Don Quixote and his Dialectical Other Sancho form together a parody of this fundamental spiritual practice.'[25] On the contrary, I argue that this process is in fact observable within each of the two characters *separately*. In other words, Sancho internalizes the dynamics of the director/exercitant relation when he looks at Don Quixote: he also learns how to become a director for the exercitant in himself. Don Quixote is not a director for Sancho, nor vice versa; Sancho is simply doing a parallel mental pilgrimage and benefits from Don Quixote's greater capacity to establish a structure within his own mind. Adopting the tone of a spiritual director, Don Quixote is no less than an exercitant engaged in a process of *semiophany*, that is, an endless process comparable to the desire that motivates it and, by the same token, a great generator of narrative.

For the hidalgo, the structuring of his *persona* of knight-errant will therefore have to take the form of initiation stages. The act of combining director and exercitant in one individual demands such a pilgrimage in stages, and often appears to be in conflict with spiritual enlightenment, especially if we look at Don Quixote's evolution in the light of his 'madness.'[26] Like the progress of the exercitant, the story of the hidalgo is constructed in *episodes* held together by its own 'greater narrative,' and each single episode gives the reader a different perspective on the whole character. They are independent *views* on the character's search for his missing referents. Cervantes' novel is made of *compartments* that can be isolated from one another and comprehended as distinct narrative entities. In this sense, Cervantes's imaginative strategy is close to the one we encounter in the *Spiritual Exercises*. The narration transports the reader from one episode to the next with very little transition. Again, this is not a purely Cervantine technique and we can observe similar narrative effects in pre-Modern works such as Boccaccio's *Decameron* or Rabelais' *Gargantua*. Nonetheless, it seems that the author emphasizes the ridicule of such *compartmentalizing* and division into episodes. *Don Quixote* is not a novel that seeks to conform to pre-established formats. On several occasions, the narrative structure appears to be sabotaged,[27] as if it wanted to reflect the natural disorder of the human mind when forced into a series of exercises. Ultimately, this is what Don Quixote comes to represent: a negative print of the Renaissance obsession for spatial division.

Don Quixote takes Sancho along so he can teach him the values of imagination and free will. At several stages, he reveals the fundamental truth of the novel: every human perception is different. Of all Catholic orders, the Society of Jesus is the one that places most importance on casuistry and the relativity of perception, always varying from one individual to the next. We have here an example of casuistry's influence on the formation of the Modern subject. José Antonio Maravall confirms this point of view in *Utopia and Counterutopia in the Quixote* (1991):

> Thus Don Quixote affirms the central thesis of the Counter-Reformation, in defense of which Erasmus too had taken the side of the Church by arguing against Luther. There is nothing in the world that "can move and compel the will . . . [for] our will is free" (I:22). Because we are free to do as we wish, merit is possible, for what each individual does may be imputed to him and to him alone. The unavoidable freedom of the human person, that colossal force of the individuality, is consequently the great means by which one can reach, through one's own efforts, the highest level. Freedom, says Don Quixote, "is one of the most precious gifts that the heavens have bestowed on man; with it the treasures locked in the earth or hidden in the depths of the sea are not to be compared" (II:58). (70–1)

Freedom and desire are intertwined and depend on the same factors from the point of view of Jesuit casuistry as well as from Don Quixote's. It is at least one of the fundamental values that he teaches to the squire through their pursuit of adventures. As a consequence, the squire will understand progressively the importance of *hazañas* (simultaneously adventures and good deeds) over that of set goals. It is through the long chain of episodes that the casuistic worldview of the two wanderers becomes defined.

The Loyolan "*code interprétatif*" underlined by Jean Starobinski and discussed earlier is also present in the play of representations underlined here by Don Quixote. After his first sally, the reader is forced to enter into the double perception of reality that is going to follow. This separation of possibilities provokes the freedom of the subject. Ignatius rides his horse on the way to Montserrat and is faced with two diverging paths: he then understands what free will really means. Don Quixote remains constantly in this situation throughout the novel; but he understands that this is the purpose of his journey. The double perception is therefore necessary for the spiritual exercises in which both characters engage. In formalist terms, *signifiers* take double *signifieds*: an inanimate object could be a giant or a windmill; any female could also be at the same time a noble princess and an inn prostitute. For instance, the following passage has become famous for it sums up the essence of *Don Quixote* in this respect:

> Mire vuestra merced—respondió Sancho—que aquellos que allí se parecen no son gigantes, sino molinos de viento, y lo que en ellos parecen brazos son las aspas, que, volteando del viento, hacen andar la piedra del molino.
> -Bien parece—respondió Don Quijote—que no estás cursado en esto de las aventuras: ellos son gigantes; y si tienes miedo quítate de allí, y ponte en oración en el espacio que

yo voy a entrar con ellos en fiera y desigual batalla (75).²⁸

Once again, the hidalgo accuses his squire of not playing the games, or in other words, of refusing the visual exercise. It seems obvious in this passage that Don Quixote is aware of the illusion he has created for himself. Outside of the fact that windmills were a relatively new technology unknown to Don Quixote,²⁹ this most celebrated passage shows that the knight-errant uses reality as a territory for simulation. He voluntarily pairs up two signifiers in order to underline what they might have in common.

These pairings are not innocent because there is an obvious correspondence between their elements, but they emphasize a misinterpretation of reality due to spiritual misguidance. In each case, these opposite images represent two Loyolan 'standards' that maintain our protagonist in tension. The 'author' steps back from the determination of the choices the reader has to make about the main character. This is a very Loyolan component of Cervantes' text: the 'double gaze' in *Don Quixote* allows the narrative voice to be distanced from any decision making.³⁰ It is a process very similar to that of the *Spiritual Exercises* if we follow the argument of Vernon Minor about the 'mind's eye' technique found in the exercises developed in *Death of the Baroque* (2006):

> This kind of visualization, which seems natural enough, something we can all do, is in fact profoundly complicated in terms of the meaning that it creates. First of all, there is a highly problematic relationship between the mind's eye and the external eye. The mind's eye would seem to constitute a synthesizing capacity of the brain (mind) to draw from memory as much data and as many impulses as possible to create an analog to the information originally brought in by the external eye. This over-determinated image called up by the mind then becomes a 'place' where the exercitant can situate himself or herself (22).

Don Quixote, who believes in his mind's eye "so implicitly that in his opinion the Holy Scripture [is] not more true" (Cervantes 46), proves to be an obedient exercitant and takes the visual mechanism described above to its most exaggerated version: he interchanges the role of the mind's eye with that of the external eye. His sense of discipline is based on *synthesizing capacities* he has learned from his director's part, that is, the part of him that sets the scene. As Minor points out, the purpose of this process is to insert oneself into a place. In the case of Don Quixote, this place is the 'greater narrative' of Chivalry.

In order to insert his *hazañas* within this narrative, Don Quixote needs to violate one of the fundamental principles of the exercises: he must combine the capacities of director with those of exercitant and alternate between the two roles.

But this violation reflects that of Cervantes. For reference, the *Spiritual Exercises* begin with this assumption: "the one giving the Exercises ought not to lean or incline in either direction but rather, while standing by like the pointer of a scale in equilibrium, to allow the Creator to deal immediately with the creature and the creature with its Creator and Lord" (125). In the case of the hidalgo, there is not much room for any Creator outside of Cervantes himself. In this sense, the author assumes in the Modern novel the position of the spiritual director. The interpretation derives from the bond formed between the reader (exercitant) and the author (Creator). Otherwise Cervantes would not insist so much on this dimension in both of his prologues and at the very end of the novel. Let us turn to these passages briefly: "aunque parezco padre, soy padrastro de Don Quijote" (7), "esta segunda parte de *Don Quijote* que te ofrezco es cortada del mismo artifice y del mismo paño que la primera, y que en ella te doy a don Quijote dilatado, y finalmente muerto y sepultado, porque ninguno se atreva a levantarle nuevos testimonios" (546), and ultimately "para mí sola nació Don Quijote, y yo para él: el supo obrar y yo escribir" (1105).[31] In other words, the author assumes at several points the position of indirect Creator, a position that is difficult to distinguish from that of director. *Don Quixote* deconstructs at many levels the structure of the *Spiritual Exercises* since it adapts it to various parameters of the text. This is why I believe that considering the hidalgo as a spiritual director limits considerably the appreciation of the text.

Let us now see how these transformations and deconstruction occur. First, we need to understand what the two texts have in common. *Don Quixote* as a novel is indeed a form of art inspired by the Ignatian technique of sign complementation: the central *theophany* of the exercises is transformed into a *semiophany*.[32] One could directly apply Barthes' analysis on Loyola's *Exercises* to *Don Quixote*: "il cherche à dépasser le signifié de l'image (. . .) par les sens imaginaires, il essaye de percevoir tous les attributs circonstanciels" (66). He seeks to perceive *beyond* any signified. Both Ignatius and Don Quixote achieve this kind of world perception through the strict imitation of their models. We have discussed how the saint prescribes a *christomorphic* approach to imitation; in the same fashion, the hidalgo attempts a metamorphosis: "propuso de hacerse armar caballero *del primero que topase*, a imitación de otros muchos que así lo hicieron" (Cervantes 79).[33] He envisions himself as the signifier of a disappeared signified: for Ignatius, Christ has not abandoned the world since his Lord keeps coming back in the practice of the exercises, and for Don Quixote, knight errantry is a practice that he can resuscitate as well. Christopher Braider makes the connection between Cervantes' Quixote and the Christian concept of *imitatio Christi* that we discussed earlier:

> The knight errantry of Don Quijote, *luz y espejo de toda la caballería andante*, light and mirror to all knights errant [...] increasingly assumes the character of an *imitatio Christi*: an attempt to lead, in the baffling realm of fallen corporal appearances, a life fully answering to the pattern laid down in that mirror and example that was the life of Christ (107).

As a matter of fact, the mechanisms are parallel, and Don Quixote is at once a 'self-maintaining machine'[34] and an exercitant whose 'spiritual exercises' have been the novels of Chivalry. Again, the chain of imitations appears to have no limits in the play of representation. In Barthes' terms, one could say that the image reservoir the exercises contain has filled the entirety of Don Quixote's mental territory. His perception of the world also obeys the laws of a totalitarian system, and that is why he modifies the signified to each signifier that he comes across.[35] In this respect, one could argue that there is a reproduction of the mental visualization found in the *Exercises*. But this is precisely where the deconstruction of the Ignatian techniques happens. In less Barthean terms it could be argued that Don Quixote is simultaneously exercitant and spiritual director in his Modern double-dimensioned mind. The definition of roles is voluntarily blurred and they cancel one another out. The hidalgo stays in a world perception process that he understands as a director (reader in his library) before he actually gets to experiment scrupulously with the practice of it as an exercitant (parody of a knight-errant in the outside world). And this is what makes him a Modern hero *par excellence*: he prepares for himself an imaginative methodology and combines the roles of director and exercitant.

Above all, *Don Quixote* is a projection of the *order of corruption* we have been discussing in the previous chapters. We should not see him merely as a parody of Loyola, or as a Modern representation of the human flaws in spiritual guidance. Maybe his progression in episodes also alludes to the fact that he is essentially an *exercitant* with an artificial anagogic correspondent (knight-errantry, the *edad de Oro*, Dulcinea del Toboso, etc.), but that is often the position of Modernity. In other words, his capacity to be director exists only for the purpose of entering the position of the 'guided one,' that is, the only position that guarantees the contact with the order of corruption. During the entire novel, Don Quixote is (in) a territory of great spiritual conflict, with a slight difference between the two parts of the novel: in the first part (1605), he experiences the contradictions between fiction and reality, in the second part (1615), he becomes an element of fiction for his surrounding reality and is expected to conform to this role. Nonetheless, the permanent tension between the two 'standards' is present on two levels: first, at the level of his fictional configuration (God and Satan as narrative elements of the novels of Chivalry) and second at the level of discourse itself (the epistemological 'standards' in Cervantes' Spain). We have already discussed the function of the *order of corruption* in the novels that both Ignatius and Don Quixote read. As a Modern novel, however, *Don Quixote* operates a transfer of these standards (Christ and Satan) to socio-political issues through its *code interprétatif*.

For instance, the 'double gaze' in the case of the 'noble princess' who turns out to be a prostitute, or the 'giant' that turns out to be a windmill, is a narrative instrument that adapts the ancient tension to the new epistemological configuration. Cervantes attributes a correspondence between 1) the standards of Chivalry that maintain the 'noble princess' and the 'giants' in a tension, and 2) the standards that place the windmills and the prostitutes in a comparable tension, that is, new standards yet to be defined. Windmills and prostitutes are indeed representative of an age of technology and social interaction in emergence, yet Don Quixote comprehends them within the 'outdated parameters' of his fictional world. In many ways, the *Spiritual Exercises* seek to implement in the exercitant a similar worldview, an always atemporal perception of reality in terms of opposite standards and *orders of corruption* that s/he has to penetrate in order to decipher its signs. The purpose of such a transfer could be to use Don Quixote as a mirror in which all of Spain's socio-political problems at the turn of the century come to be projected.

It is particularly interesting to see how Sancho Panza begins to reflect on this issue as the two men progress in an exclusively Spanish territory: "¿Está por ventura España abierta, y de modo que es menester cerrarla, o qué ceremonia es está?" (956).[36] This supposedly innocent comment by the *escudero* is extremely relevant since it points to Spain's relative isolation from the rest of Europe—with the exception of Rome—during the era of religious wars. Yet, it is Cervantes' choice to limit the novel to the spatial dimensions of his country, unlike many other contemporary works of fiction in the seventeenth century.[37] Don Quixote and Sancho never truly imitate the great models of knight-errantry since they do not cross the geographical borders that Cervantes has crossed during his own time. Their focus is therefore on Spanish society and their gaze follows the pattern of an *order of corruption*. In other words, they evolve in an enclosed space—mostly Castile—and only go beyond its physical limits with the mind's eye, but certainly not with the external one.

This absolute focus on Spain is part of the novel's rhetorical exercise. After a lifetime of observing the evolution of political trends, military strategies, and literary genres, the author of *Don Quixote* recapitulates the contrasts and contradictions that have configured his own nation during the Renaissance. One could argue that the hidalgo plays a metonymic role in this discourse that goes beyond Foucault's definition of 'negative print.' Don Quixote is a textual figure made of several narrative layers, a condensation of previous literary genres, and this ultimately makes him a 'body in corruption,' because he has been the very instrument of an imaginative transformation (for himself, for Sancho, and ultimately for the reader). This corruption is literal in the evolution of the character: his physical decline is implicitly announced since the very beginning of the novel; the narrator presents him as an old man with his life behind him, and whose brain has been 'dried up' by the activity of reading. As if this were not enough, he denies his character the right to social existence by 'erasing' the name of the hidalgo and the location of his hacienda, when it is traditionally the first piece of information a narrator gives to the reader. Moreover, the age and physical condition of the hero contradicts the definition of heroes and conditions the reader: s/he knows from the very beginning that s/he is a witness to the physical downfall of this pseudo-heroic figure. In this sense, Don Quixote appears as a typically Baroque *memento mori*, and seeks to immerse himself in the greatest orders of corruption a knight can find in the whole of Castile.

The episode that most emphasizes this dimension of the text is the descent of the hero in the Cave of Montesinos, in the second part of the novel. The "descent into Hell" stage of a narrative is quite common, and has been observed in canonical works of literature since Homer's *Odyssey*. As Hutchinson observes, "echoes of every other underworld known in literature up to that time resonate in the cave of Montesinos" (190). However, it was never meant in any preceding work to be such a comprehensive vision of all the elements of Don Quixote's 'greater narrative.' All are present who contribute to the formation of the hidalgo's image reservoir. This incident is special in that Don Quixote narrates it after it has taken place. The narrator does not follow the hidalgo into the cave, but stays outside with Sancho and the men from the village. In this passage, Don Quixote is going to be on his own and will go down into the renowned cave without any eye-witness of his *hazaña*. Yet, it is probably the most significant of all spiritual exercises undertaken by the knight-errant. E.C. Riley underlines the peculiarity and the enigma around this central episode in the second part of *Don Quixote*:

> [The novel] contains plenty of mysteries and odd happenings, but all of them are rationally explained to the reader sooner or later, with the exception of three. These are the question of Benengeli's reality, that of Avellaneda's Quixote and Sancho, and the incident of Montesinos Cave (. . .) The third is left unexplained, a deliberate mystification. Even Benengeli washes his hands of the matter and thrusts responsibility for the story on to Don Quixote who told it. Cervantes strews contradictory clues about, hedges the incident around with talk, and finally leaves the reader to judge for himself (II, 24). It is useless to ask if what Quixote related was a dream, a willful fabrication, or anything else. Cervantes never intended us to know (187).

Nonetheless, we can envision this projection of the reader into the difficulties of free will as a typically Derridean *hors-texte*. It is also interesting to see the episode as a "deliberate mystification," since it implies and simultaneously denies the anagogic nature of Don Quixote's spiritual quest in the cave. Riley is right to underline it as a fundamental and central episode of the second part, since it finalizes the order of corruption that the hidalgo has been constructing for himself. As Avalle-Arce once pointed out, we cannot distinguish this 'incident' from the previous episode in the novel, that is, the penance of Don Quixote in the Sierra Morena. It gives to the episode of the Cave the *verticality* that it requires: "la cueva de Montesinos es donde, efectivamente, don Quijote desciende a la sima del *desengaño*. La correspondencia de los episodios ha alcanzado el punto de simetría" (Avalle-Arce 174). The contemplative mystic act in which the protagonist engages follows the lines of Ignatian contemplation. It forces him to comprehend the surrounding reality-fantasy in terms of *vertical opposites*. In the *Spiritual Exercises*, Loyola often forces the exercitant to enter these plays of drastic contrast, and we have seen earlier how this movement is recycled in church architecture. In the same fashion, Don Quixote prepares his descent into the fabulous cave in a reflexive moment of ascension in the Sierra. Once again, salvation is to be obtained by the constant exposition of natural opposites.

Before his descent, the hidalgo has already programmed how he is going to use this moment of isolation from the rest of the characters (and the reader as well) in order to enter his 'greater narrative' through the dynamics of an order of corruption: "Yo voy a despeñarme, a empozarme y a hundirme en el abismo que aquí se me representa" (721). Half an hour later, when he returns to reality, the hidalgo will claim: "me habéis quitado de la más sabrosa y agradable vida y vista que ningún humano ha visto ni pasado" (722).[38] It is particularly interesting to see how the hidalgo compares his experience to contemplation. The concepts of *vida* and *vista* are intertwined here to underline that the mind's eye is going to be intensively at work: it is going to merge life and sight into one single experience. He expresses very strongly here his desire to be totally submerged in this sensorial activity. The dark abyss turns out to be the *locus* of his long awaited epiphany as a knight-errant since it will enable him to cease all other kinds of sensorial connection to reality. In this respect, the attraction of the cave reflects the desire of an exercitant to enter the retreat in which he will be able to engage in simulative contemplation of reality.

The nature of his 'visions' reflects that of the *Spiritual Exercises* since it transgresses narrative boundaries in the same fashion. For instance, in several meditations of Loyola's text, the director guides his exercitant into mental territories in which s/he can juxtapose the tower of Babel with the Holy Virgin, bringing together two different traditions (the Old and the New Testament). Don Quixote also draws a total perspective on the various traditions that make the genre of Chivalry. Steven Hutchinson points out how the mental line is drawn in the hidalgo's mental territory and why this episode finally makes an expected connection between his desire and his visions:

> In an odd mixture of tradition and experience Don Quixote brings an imaginary past, represented by Montesinos, Durandarte, Belerma, Lancelot, and the rest, into a likewise imaginary present, represented by himself and Dulcinea; he thus assumes a continuum between them and merges them in the same time and place (191).

Montesinos appears to introduce him to characters drawn from different tales: "Éste es mi amigo Durandarte, flor y espejo de los caballeros enamorados de su tiempo. Tiénele aquí encantado, como me tiene a mí y a otros muchos y muchas, Merlín, aquel francés encantador que dicen que fue hijo del diablo" (725).[39] This passage underlines the ongoing quality of the narrative: Don Quixote arrives *in medias res*, and Montesinos obliges him to participate in the action right away. In this simulation process, the hidalgo engages in an active contemplation that rapidly transforms into a narrative in which he is the center:

> Sabed que tenéis aquí en vuestra presencia, y abrid los ojos y vereislo, aquel gran caballero de quien tantas cosas tiene profetizadas el sabio Merlín, aquel Don Quijote de la Mancha, digo, que de nuevo y con mayores ventajas que en los pasados siglos ha resucitado en los presentes la ya olvidada andante caballería, por cuyo medio y favor podría ser que nosotros fuésemos desencantados, que las grandes hazañas para los grandes hombres están guardadas (727).

At this point, not only has he become the center of the contemplative activity, but the course of the history can be modified by his action and presence. It is interesting to see that Cervantes diverges here from Ignatius of Loyola: the Jesuit saint uses the imagery of the novels of Chivalry as a decorum in which he projects the willing exercitant in order to make him perceive the centrality of the divinity (generally speaking, Christ) through the corresponding centrality of the mind's eye. Cervantes, on the contrary, exaggerates the obsolete nature of this setting, and places in it an 'exercitant' who abuses his central position and quickly turns himself into the main object of contemplation.

However, this abuse will not be pass the test of his squire: Sancho's response to the account that we get once the hidalgo is out of the cave is rather severe, since the exaggerated part played by Don Quixote in the deliverance of Montesinos and Durandarte goes beyond the purpose of the exercises in which the two men have engaged. In a way, Don Quixote has gone over the limits of any contemplative act with the episode of the cave, and it already announces his downfall. Nothing after this episode will have a similar effect on the hidalgo, and nothing will reunite him with his squire in collective hallucination. The withdrawal experience in the cave has followed the pattern of the *Spiritual Exercises* since the images projected onto the exercitant during his isolation are still in his mental territory once he is back in the outside world. He carries the visions with him and will pursue his search for signs of his 'greater narrative' in the surrounding reality.

In conclusion, the constant merging of reality and fiction maintains the orders of corruption in their corresponding tension. *Don Quixote* invites its reader to participate in an aesthetic experience whose 'represented object' is reality itself, with death and disillusion as part of it. Its 'standards' parody those of Loyola, but it becomes impossible to identify Hell and Heaven in the perpetual play of representations. The *fantasy* stresses the importance of *reality* and vice versa: Cervantes applies the standards to these two poles of attraction. Unlike the *Spiritual Exercises*, this novel seeks to follow literary realism and makes all of literature progress into it. This is at least what Erich Auerbach proposed in his most celebrated work *Mimesis* (1968). Auerbach argues that reality is what constantly comes back in the face of the hidalgo's fantasies. In many ways, it is the surrounding reality that puts limitations on Don Quixote's existence and defines its 'madness.' Reality becomes the Dialectical Other of his madness. Don Quixote is to the world what Alice is for Wonderland, but in an opposite and reverse way: his incompatibility with the world is precisely what enables him to re-present it. He has the capacity to perceive reality beyond its socio-political limits and he draws this capacity from his own spiritual exercises. It is a result that contradicts the purpose of the *Spiritual Exercises* in many ways since it reverses the work's purposes: Loyola uses the fantastical image in order to bring the exercitant back to reality; Don Quixote exhausts this process so much that he ends up bringing reality into his fantasy. Nonetheless, the goals of the exercises are achieved since he succeeds in transforming this reality and virtually obtain salvation in the process.[48] Auerbach claims that "the theme of the noble and brave fool who sets forth to realize his ideal and improve the world, might be treated in such a way that the problems and conflicts in the world are presented and worked out in the process" (344). He is the only one to possess this capacity in the novel, but progressively, the other characters will seek to imitate him. Was Cervantes trying to propose a model in his Don Quixote? That will remain a debate for criticism; however, one thing is certain: contact with corruption turns out to be productive for the Modern novel since it starts questioning, as a genre, its capacity to perceive and represent the world. Cervantes was not a Jesuit, and probably did not practice Loyola's spiritual exercises, but his late works reflect how this method of conversion transmits its modes of perception and representation to Literature, another territory to be conquered. The lack of direction in Don Quixote's journey reflects Cervantes' own trials and struggles with the processes of novel writing, a process that seems to maintain him in a tension similar to that of the *Exercises*. This is probably why the *Persiles*, his last masterpiece, never obtained the success of *Don Quixote*.

The Last Pilgrimage: Cervantes' Representation of Rome in *Los Trabajos de Persiles y Sigismunda*

It is interesting to contrast our conclusions about *Don Quixote* with the one we can draw from a reading of Cervantes' last text, since the first is recognized as his masterpiece, and the latter has often been considered a failure.[41] As we know, the *Trabajos de Persiles y Sigismunda* was an ongoing project paralleling the writing process of both *Don Quixote* and the *Novelas Ejemplares*. According to David Castillo in his recent *(A)wry views* (2001), "*Persiles* is (. . .) an anamorphic mirror that *inverts* or, at the very least, *distorts* the symbols of Counter-Reformation" (94–5). Although *inverting* and *distorting* are two different matters, I agree that Cervantes' last work definitely also participates in the 'transformation' of the visual culture sprung from the Loyolan conception of spirituality. From the prologue of this novel, we also know that the author was completing it in agony and that he actually died within hours after putting the final period to this account of a pilgrimage. This less studied work of Cervantes has often been considered a conscious backlash against the modernity of *Don Quixote*, when the aging author prefers to return to the writing of *romance*.[42] E.C. Riley sums up the movement in the following fashion: "The *Novelas* were varied enough to have something for all tastes; the *Quixote* was at once a work of art and a best seller; the *Persiles* patently an attempt to give the novel the intellectual prestige of epic and the popular appeal of romance" (113). It is therefore difficult to envision the *Persiles* from the perspective of modernity in that respect. However, this work heavily charged with symbols and responds to Cervantes' experience as a young writer in Rome, as well as his perspective on his career as an old man. It can be seen as a last exercise in the discipline of writing. For this reason, in the prologue, he calls himself "el manco sano" in order to emphasize the quality of his handicap (age combined with a missing arm) and its effect on reason and creativity. Although it is difficult to engender another literary monument after *Don Quixote*, Cervantes presents us in the *Persiles* with a unique perspective on Spain, Catholicism, and their inscription within the greater picture of Western European politics at the beginning of the seventeenth century.

In the *Trabajos de Persiles y Sigismunda*, the two heroes Periandro and Auristela make their progress as pilgrims from the *tierras septentrionales* toward the city of Rome. If *Don Quixote* represented an exploration of Spain from within, the peregrination of these two characters serves the opposite purpose: it presents an image of Spain from without, and emphasizes its strong politico-cultural connection with the city of Rome. For this reason, it recapitulates very well Cervantes' perception of the effects of Counter-Reformation spirituality on his own nation as well as the surrounding Catholic kingdoms. With the *Persiles*, one can observe how the Loyolan concept of immersion in orders of corruption has been integrated as a central part of the redefined spiritual practices. The first half of the novel takes place in a rather unknown and imagined European North, whereas the second part unfolds when the pilgrims arrive by boat in the port of Lisbon, that is, in Cervantes' reality. From this moment on, their progress through Portugal, Spain, France, and finally Italy will turn out to be a long and progressive visual experience in preparation for the revelation and acceptance of the Catholic faith in Rome. Their journey is radically opposed to that of Don Quixote and Sancho, since they are not originally from Spain and only walk through it toward a remote destination. It is therefore important to envision their pilgrimage within different parameters: their perception of Southern European reality is not doubled but rather complemented by the stories they hear during their travels. We should envision the *Persiles*, however, as a complement of *Don Quixote* since their perspectives supplement each other. Hutchinson underlines in *Cervantine Journeys* why this is so: "these novels are episodic, periodically thickening and thinning out and thereby making possible all the diversity that comes their way. How else could practically all of Spain figure into the *Quixote* and the *Coloquio*, or much of Europe in the *Persiles*?" (201). It is true that Cervantes' last work opens up a new dimension of observation on a Southern Europe marked by the spirit of Counter-Reformation that goes beyond the borders of Spain. But there is another major difference between the *Quixote* and the *Persiles*: the latter has a sense of direction that rules the entire narrative. The two pilgrims are making progress toward the city of Rome and will eventually arrive there, unlike Don Quixote who gets to Barcelona instead of Saragossa. In this respect, Hutchinson adds that this "journey narrative already has the road inscribed in its episodic itinerary" (201).

The first half of the *Persiles* is marked by a series of interruption in the narration. Even if the novel starts *in medias res*, the main storyline is given to the reader in small increments. The typically Cervantine *novela intercalada* seems to be given priority over the story of Periandro and Auristela. As I said, the Northern setting in which the characters meet and interact is more legendary and fantastic than the South they discover in the second half. As a matter of fact, this North serves as a margin to define the center of the universe to which they are aiming: Rome (Baena 75–6). Yet it is an order of corruption composed of several islands on which the standards of Good and Evil are maintained in tension. The standards of the *tierras septentrionales* are encoded differently and each of its islands stands in opposition to the civilized world. Castillo declares: "Policarpo's island emerges as an allegorical inversion of spiritual Rome" (100). He is right in affirming that these Northern islands are an imaginary projection that will make the image of Rome stand out in contrast. As an other instance, the story opens on the deliverance of Auristela; she has been kept on another 'allegorical island' in which men's hearts are burned and women are kept locked in a golden prison.

The *Persiles* does not seek to reflect a reality familiar to the Spanish reader. On the contrary, it seeks to develop the *fantasy* that had no space in *Don Quixote*. The Barbaric Islands are remote and distant from Spain, therefore Cervantes enjoys more freedom to make allegorical entities out of them. For instance, a Spanish visitor gives an account of his interaction with the wolves that govern one of the islands, and reports what they have told him: "Español, hazte a lo largo, y busca en otra parte tu ventura, si no quieres en ésta morir hecho pedazos por nuestras uñas y dientes; y no preguntes quién es el que esto te dice, sino da gracias al cielo de que *has hallado piedad entre las mismas fieras*" (77).[43] The *tierras septentrionales* are a virtual world into which Cervantes projects his characters so that they can simulate the reality to come in the fantasy of the foreign land. The wolves are beasts, yet they show pity: it serves as a preparatory 'negative print' of the reality that they observe in the second half in which humans will not show any pity whatsoever in their acts. They underline the piety that can be found amongst the supposedly most ferocious creatures on the planet in order to prepare the pilgrim for the cruelty of the civilized world (Portugal, Spain, France, and Italy). Later on, we will find this chiastic opposition of men and beasts developed to its extreme in Gracián's *Criticón*.

All characters in the novel have been driven by the force of their destiny to hostile lands where their senses have been exposed to these representations of intermingled good and evil. They voluntarily engage in experiences in order to have contact with evil. Antonio, a follower of Auristela and Periandro on their pilgrimage, comes to the general conclusion that: "no hay mejor asilio que el que promete la casa del enemigo" (75).[44] He acknowledges that humans as pilgrims should precisely seek the corruption in the darkest places of this world. This assertion also sums up a great deal of the Counter-Reformation spirit, and particularly the philosophy behind Loyola's *Spiritual Exercises* since this practice encourages the exercitant to be familiar with the enemy at all times:

> When we are in desolation we should think that the Lord has left us in order to test us, by leaving us to our own natural powers so that we may prove ourselves by resisting the various agitations and temptations of the enemy (203). A person who desires to make progress in the spiritual life ought always to proceed in a manner contrary to that of the enemy (Loyola 210).

In this sense, the Northern lands function as a territory for simulation in which the characters voluntarily engage and verify this prescribed interaction with the enemy. In general, Loyola gives to this 'enemy' an importance that is fundamental to God's divine plan for salvation: the temptation that comes out of Him is necessary from the Jesuit's point of view. In the same fashion, Cervantes projects his characters into the midst of this indispensable stage of life experience.

There is an order of preparation in the story of the pilgrims: they need to be acquainted with the works of the enemy, and eventually learn how to recognize them. In the fantastic world of the *tierras septentrionales*, they listen to various accounts in which subjects have experienced the exercise and are offering their testimony to the audience. The supernatural is omnipresent on the many islands that compose the territory in which the characters evolve, but it is treated within an 'understanding of salvation.' For instance, in many stories, one can identify the motif of metamorphosis from men to beasts and vice versa. Amongst the many speakers in these storytelling sessions, an anonymous voice (*"el que me hablaba"*) comes to the conclusion that the supernatural dimensions of their experience are artifacts of God's plan:

> Puedes, buen hombre, dar infinitas gracias al cielo por haberte librado del poder destas maléficas hechiceras, de las cuales hay mucha abundancia en estas septentrionales partes. Cuéntase dellas que se convierten en lobos, así machos como hembras, porque de entrambos géneros hay maléficos y encantadores. Cómo esto pueda ser lo ignoro, y como cristiano que soy católico no lo creo. Pero la esperiencia me muestra lo contrario. Lo que puedo alcanzar es, que todas estas transformaciones son ilusiones del demonio, y permisión de Dios y castigo de los abominables pecados deste maldito género de gente (92).[45]

It is therefore convenient for Cervantes to displace the action in the first half of the *Persiles* to this remote land where people have the reputation of wickedness. In this short speech, we notice the tension between the reasons of the faith and those of experience. The character is therefore placed between the two options and must come to a conclusion by merging these two opposite forms of perception. But above all, this passage shows how the supernatural has been integrated as a virtual artifact in the pilgrim's journey. God allows Satan to use 'illusions' in order to train the pilgrim in his/her spiritual exercises. It is also interesting to notice that the monstrous figures mentioned here no longer follow the limitations imposed by nature upon them: gender and physical parts are intermingled so that the pilgrim concentrates only on centers as a subject in front of the illusion, supposedly engineered for his/her salvation.

The characters seem to give a great deal of importance to the senses and the role they play in their progression through these supernatural orders of corruption. They associate them with all the activities of their journey, such as sleeping, loving others, and eating. For instance, we can find several occasions in the text where the senses are described in terms of a territory to be conquered, such as "tomar posesión de los *sentidos*" (55), or of a territory to be reconfigured, such as "borrándome de los *sentidos* el sentimiento" (76). In both cases, the senses appear central to the activity in which they are involved, and Cervantes underlines here that all depends on the perception through these senses. Unlike the followers of Loyola, however, Cervantes' pilgrims—and all of his characters in general—expose their senses to their desire and their actions are often determined by it. The *Persiles* opens with statements such as "tal vez las leyes del gusto humano tienen más fuerza que las de la religión" (58)[46] in order to emphasize the tension in which the pilgrim has been naturally placed. Their senses are therefore focused on desire (*gusto*) as much as it is on religion and faith. This opposition will maintain Periandro and Auristela in the necessary state of tension prescribed for the Modern pilgrims in the *Spiritual Exercises*. In their progression, they will be constantly exposed to the same choice: *gusto* or *religión*?

Nonetheless, the attraction to the Catholic religion is already part of the initial motivation of these characters. The only way to resolve the tension between *gusto* and *religión* is to make the *religión* an object of the pilgrim's *gusto*. There is no physical presence of the religion in the *tierras septentrionales*, yet very soon after her deliverance from the island Auristela "había prometido de ir a pie hasta Roma" (283). The desires are very present in the characters so that they serve as elements helping to unify the marginal North with the central Rome. And Auristela stands as the female pilgrim whose faith only equals her legendary beauty. She becomes desirable for her capacity to reunite *gusto* and *religión*. Even though she has never had direct contact with the Counter-Reformation, she hears the entire version of the Catholic Credo from Ricla, a barbarian woman, and feels an immediate attraction to the still unknown faith: "Con cuya variable historia, admiraron a los presentes, y despertaron mil alabanzas que les dieron, y mil buenas esperanzas que les anunciaron, especialmente Auristela, que quedó aficionadísima a las dos bárbaras, madre y hija" (83).[47] The reaction to the Credo's enunciation proves that Auristela has been living in a 'faithless world,' but she is now able to understand why her reality is encoded according to God's salvation plan. In a way, her mental progression as a pilgrim is the opposite of that of an exercitant performing the exercises since she receives the interpretation of the Credo after having engaged in the perception of the world. An exercitant, on the contrary, is reeducated in his/her perception through the practice of the spiritual exercises, but is exposed to the codification of reality first. In this sense, Auristela and Periandro are pilgrims who perform their spiritual exercises in reverse gear.

During their journey, the two characters come to an understanding of Christianity and Catholicism in a way radically opposed—but yet complementary—to that of the Jesuits on a mission. Instead of leaving Rome for Barbarian countries, they leave those lands for the city where missions are designed. It is Cervantes' response to Counter-Reformation Catholicism. In *Cervantes' Christian Romance* (1972), Alban Forcione emphasizes this Humanist impulse in the *Persiles*, but this argument has been challenged ever since by critics who have shed a different light on the work. David Castillo, for instance, argues that "in the case of *Persiles*, we can find oblique views of the myths that sustain the ideological field of Counter-Reformation Spain, especially the belief in 'our' spiritual superiority as leaders of the Christian Roman world" (106). This view is extremely valuable if we consider the many episodes in which the characters are confronted by slightly negative aspects of the faith they are about to adopt. We should indeed envision the *Persiles* as the narrative of a highly representational pilgrimage: its goal is to bring the eye back to the epicenter of the Counter-Reformation, Rome. But its representation carries a heavy load of criticism.

Several narrators on their path add elements to the construction of the faith they are seeking. However, they are also exposed to criticism and warnings. For instance, la Cenotia, another Spaniard they meet on their journey, presents them a dark perspective on the Inquisition and its action in Spain. She was forced to leave Spain for unmentioned reasons, and gives an account of her escape from Spain, as well as a recapitulation of her anxiety:

> Dígote en fin, bárbaro discreto, que la persecución de los que llaman inquisidores en España, me arrancó de mi patria; que cuando se sale por fuerza della, antes se puede llamar arrancada que salida. Vine a esta isla por estraños rodeos, por infinitos peligros, casi siempre como si estuvieran cerca, volviendo la cabeza atrás, pensando que me

mordían las faldas los perros, que aun hasta aquí temo (202).[48]

Obviously, the character's anxiety stands in opposition here to the enthusiasm of the two pilgrims to discover a religion of liberating revelation. This female renegade underlines the dominion and the omnipresence of this powerful institution. Yet, in her case, the religion has made sure that she would only survive in the marginal circles of the world. Her refuge logically becomes the *tierras septentrionales* and she crosses the path of the two main characters when she is going in an opposite direction from them.

Beyond this warning against the omnipotence of the Inquisition, another form of criticism that we find in the *Persiles* focuses on the greed associated with the hierarchical Church of Rome. Auristela and Periandro meet in their journey other pilgrims on their way to the Eternal City and soon figure out that there is an entire economy revolving around the religion and the faith they are seeking. They are therefore initiated into this specific parameter of Catholicism prior to their arrival in the city. For instance, the dying count whom the pilgrims help in the Quintanar de la Orden de Santiago tells them how the purpose of his pilgrimage has been undermined by his sickness:

> Yo salí de mi casa con intención de ir a Roma este año, en el cual el Sumo Pontifice ha abierto las arcas del tesoro de la Iglesia y comunicádonos, como el año santo, las infinitas gracias que en él suelen ganarse. Iba a la ligera, más como peregrino pobre que caballero rico; entré en este pueblo (. . .) y por reparar a ajenas vidas, he venido a perder la mía (337–8).[49]

The dying man reveals on his deathbed the true intention behind his journey to Rome: the accumulation of capital. Somehow, this pilgrim who can barely decide whether he is a *peregrino rico* or a *caballero rico* has been punished by the laws of nature. Apparently the line between these two identities is very thin from his point of view. Interestingly enough, this confession comes out of a body in the process of corruption. It proves that even other pilgrims going in the same direction can play with illusions and pretend to be the opposite of what they truly are. In this sense, the pilgrimage acquires the function of a carnival since it allows any member of society who can afford it to look poor in order to obtain more capital. This aristocrat pays the price of his *engaño* and proves to the other pilgrims that even the journey of the faithful to Rome is in itself an "order of corruption" in which pilgrims become illusions.

This episode happens after the arrival of Auristela, Periandro, and Antonio in Southern Europe. It is part of a longer chain of encounters for the Northerners.

As a matter of fact, the second half of the *Persiles* deals only with their progression toward Rome and the many interactions they have on the way with corrupted elements, such as the dying count. In contrast with the corruption, the city of Rome stands as a representation of the standards of Heaven, an image that requires admiration. Once they finally arrive close to the city, they stop to admire it from the top of a hill. An anonymous voice starts to recite verses of admiration:

> ¡Oh grande, oh poderosa, oh sacrosanta,
> Alma ciudad de Roma! A ti me inclino,
> Devoto, humilde y nuevo peregrino,
> A quien admira ver belleza tanta.
> Tu vista, que a tu fama se adelanta,
> Al ingenio suspende, aunque divino,
> De aquel que a verte y adorarte vino
> Con tierno afecto y con desnuda planta.
> La tierra de tu suelo, que contemplo
> Con la sangre de mártires mezclada,
> Es la reliquia universal del suelo.
> No hay parte de ti que no sirva de ejemplo
> De Santidad, así como trazada
> De la ciudad de Dios al gran modelo (426).[58]

The function of this sonnet is to prepare the two pilgrims for the visual contemplation in which they are going to be immerged once they pass through the gates of the city. The urban order is already an object of the spiritual practice: *tu vista ... al ingenio suspende*. This sonnet mentions the martyrs and the relics and the importance of the blood that was shed on the ground: it has transformed Rome into the 'universal relic.' The 'city as relic' is a motif that Cervantes had already adopted in the *Licienciado Vidriera*, as we noted commented earlier. The entire urban fabric is composed of religious components, and the pilgrims should use their visual powers in order to consider them as *examples*. In this sense, the story offers a very Loyolan perception of the urban reality. Just as Ignatius pauses in prayer and visual contemplation at La Storta outside Rome prior to his arrival, so do the pilgrims of the *Persiles*: with the mind's eye. They have to mentally superimpose the image of the historical Rome with the picture of the Modern urban fabric they are contemplating.

David Castillo adds that "the entire narrative of *Persiles* orbits around the symbolic presence of Rome, the erected Guarantee of Meaning" (106) and that ultimately "Rome is presented as another Barbaric Isle" (108). These two perspectives on the city coexist in the perspective that Cervantes offers in the *Persiles*. Rome is simultaneously the 'Guarantee of Meaning' described once by Žižek[51] and the ultimate kingdom of human violence. It is a reality that Ignatius of Loyola had already foreseen: the city was to be a territory in which the two opposite poles could be felt at all times. In this sense, the Rome that Periandro and Auristela penetrate is extremely Loyolan—not to say Jesuit. It is a territory of confusion on all levels since it desperately ties the Catholic faith with its antagonists. Rome as a 'Guarantee of Meaning' needs elements of contrast and contradiction around its most sacred buildings in order to stand as the guardian of the faith. This is why the author adopts the type of urban representation we find in the *Persiles*.

The order of corruption reunites the 'Guarantee of Meaning' with its most threatening adversaries, such as witchcraft and Judaism. It is no coincidence therefore that the first Roman people who come to interact with the Northerners are Jews. It is no coincidence that these Jews will later reappear to save Auristela's life with their 'witchcraft.' They belong to the elements of contrast that make Rome an order of corruption. In Cervantes' perspective, the Jews are part of the total structure designed by God. When it comes to using Jewish witchcraft to save Auristela, this is how Hipólita presents the dilemma:

> Acudió a la judía a pedirle que templase el rigor de los hechizos que consumían a Auristela, o los quitase del todo. (. . .) Hízolo así la judía, como si estuviera en su mano la salud o la enfermedad ajena, o como si no dependieran todos los males que llaman de pena, de la voluntad de Dios, como no dependen los males de culpa (457).[52]

This is quite a problematic statement if we consider the *Persiles* a 'Christian Romance.' The two pilgrims receive their first 'salvation' from the hand of a Jewish woman who 'pretends that God's will does not count.' In this sense, Castillo is right to call Rome in the *Persiles* another "Barbaric Isle" (108). The supernatural remains present in the progression of the two pilgrims, even when they stand next to or within the "Guarantee of Meaning." This episode ties their experience of the faithless North with their immersion in the urban fabric of Rome: the outcome of this juxtaposition produces salvation for both of them.

Of course, Rome is not only a territory for corrupted elements. It is also the palimpsest that we discussed in the third chapter: it invites its *flâneur* to contemplate images constantly. This is part of the construction of meaning that will lead to the adoption of the faith by the two pilgrims. Auristela and Periandro are invited to get involved in the visual exercises of the *Roma Ignaziana*. Following the Licenciado Vidriera's footsteps, they begin with the traditional "andar las siete iglesias" (440). But before this central part of the pilgrimage, they are initiated into the profound meaning of religious images:

> Mostráronle la muerte de Cristo, los trabajos de su vida, desde que se mostró en el pesebre hasta que se puso en la cruz. Exageráronle la fuerza y eficacia de los sacramentos, y señalaron con el dedo la segunda tabla de nuestro naufragio, que es la penitencia, sin la cual no hay abrir la senda del cielo, que suele cerrar el pecado. Mostráronle asimismo a Jesucristo Dios vivo, sentado en la diestra del Padre, estando tan vivo y entero como en el cielo, sacramentado en la tierra, cuya santísima presencia no la puede dividir ni apartar ausencia alguna, porque uno de los mayores atributos de Dios, que todos son iguales, es el estar en todo lugar, por potencia, por esencia, y por presencia. Aseguráronle infaliblemente la venida deste Señor a juzgar el mundo sobre las nubes del cielo, y asimismo la estabilidad y firmeza de su Iglesia, contra quien pueden poco las puertas, o por mejor decir, las fuerzas del infierno. Trataron del poder del sumo pontífice, visorrey de Dios en la tierra y llavero del cielo. Finalmente, no les quedó por decir cosa que vieron que convenía para darse a entender, y para que Auristela y Periandro los entendiesen (436).[53]

This quite systematic presentation of the Catholic faith appears as an adapted message, since Auristela and Periandro learn it in a way they can understand ("*que convenía para darse a entender*"). Following the logic of the *Spiritual Exercises*, the pilgrims have to visualize God's salvation plan according to their intellectual capacities. This passage is also interesting for the tone adopted by Cervantes: the sentences are long and emphasize the mechanical nature of the Counter-Reformation Credo. The verb *mostrar* is linked to *exagerar* in order to stress the scale of the religious image: Rome as a "Guarantee of Meaning" is the *locus* of exaggeration *par excellence*. Also this passage shows the absence of signifiers in the discourse of the faith that Julio Baena has identified in *El Círculo y la Flecha* (1996): "Aquí lo que tenemos *dado* son precisamente esos discursos, es decir, las explicaciones de la existencia humana dadas por la Iglesia Católica. (. . .) Cervantes tiene los significados; le falta el significante, que tiene que construir" (85).[54]

Ultimately, Rome stands as the 'order of corruption' above them all. If we consider that it becomes the Barbaric Island on which the pilgrims discover the mechanisms of the faith, we need to also envision that this faith becomes theirs through an acceptance of the surrounding corrupted elements, and the simultaneous acceptance of their own corrupted nature. Auristela and Periandro will have to invent or seek the missing signifiers of Counter-Reformation faith, but they will not strictly follow the guidelines of the *Spiritual Exercises*. The narrator does not even mention or name the practice during the Roman journey of the pilgrims. Yet it is obvious that Cervantes has a precise narrative design in the *Persiles* and draws the two characters toward a very close contact with corruption in the city of Rome. Auristela experiences unconsciousness and agony at the same time as she accepts to make the Catholic faith her own. Her state is one of physical corruption, yet necessary to obtain salvation. Her withdrawal from reality and her death-simulation experience makes her finally understand a truth beyond the faith, or in other words, she finds the missing 'signified.' When she comes back to life, she talks in private to Periandro to share with him the revelation she has obtained from this experience of corruption:

> Nuestras almas, como tú bien sabes, y como aquí me han enseñado, siempre están en continuo movimiento y no pueden parar sino en Dios, como en su centro. En esta vida los deseos son infinitos, y unos se encadenan de otros, y se eslabonan, y van formando una cadena que tal vez llega al cielo, y tal se sume en el infierno. Si te pareciese, hermano, que este lenguaje no es mío, y que va fuera de la enseñanza que me han podido enseñar mis pocos años y mi remota crianza, advierte que en la tabla rasa de mi alma ha pintado la experiencia y escrito mayores cosas (458–9).[55]

Auristela draws here a conclusion that could possibly sum up Cervantes' last view on Counter-Reformation spirituality: beyond the faith, everything is a matter of *gusto*, that is, the sensuous perception of reality. The religious experience only drives the subject toward a visual contemplation in which a greater truth will be revealed, and for each exercitant, it will be a different and individual truth; in Auristela's case, she comes to the understanding that existence is about being placed within a vertical dimension (*cadena*) in which her desires connect her to the standards of Heaven as much as they connect her to those of Hell. She acknowledges in this moment of confession that humans have to deal with the ongoing back-and-forth movement between the two poles. And none of the Northern Barbaric Islands have been able to teach her this fundamental truth; only the city of Rome, with its omnipresent incitation to contemplation, has been able to truly *convert* Auristela to the conclusions she draws here. Her experience has been one of retreat in which she has been enabled to understand her position within the Counter-Reformation cosmos, and ultimately in the Christian God's salvation plan.

Conclusion

We have seen three different yet complementary steps in Cervantes' reflection on the Jesuits, the Counter-Reformation, and Rome: the *Novelas Ejemplares* present a certain admiration for the Jesuit visual representations derived from the *Spiritual Exercises*; *Don Quixote* exaggerates its use of the mind's eye that projects the subject in 'orders of corruption' and constructs for him a greater narrative in which he becomes the center; and finally the *Persiles* defines the true goals of pilgrimage through critical representations of Southern Europe and ultimately Rome. In his novels, these three parameters are not treated separately as entities, but rather as a whole whose influence is general and epistemological. They follow a progression that remains unfinished unfortunately; we could very well picture how Cervantes could have elaborated on these topics as he died in a time of transition and development for Counter-Reformation spiritual practices. This transformation in Cervantes' works proves that the guidelines of Ignatian spirituality have been diffused and rapidly integrated into Spanish culture.

The novel becomes indeed a profane space where visual techniques can be transformed, parodied, or criticized. Above all, the processes of visual education found in the *Spiritual Exercises* are transferred onto the writing process: no one demonstrates this phenomenon in a more obvious fashion than Cervantes, since his novels are often about the writing process itself (as investigated and proven by E.C. Riley). From Cervantes on, one observes a deviation from the previously religious objects of contemplation toward the Modern human subject. The following decades of Spanish literature will confront the tension between Modernity and the temptation to bring the subject back toward religious conceptions of novel-writing. As we will see, it will often result in more drastic transformation and parody. Nonetheless and simultaneously, authors will still entertain a great deal of fascination with Loyolan techniques, in spite of their desire to adapt them to Modernity and the many questions it raises about the nature and use of senses.

CHAPTER V

Transforming the Orders of Corruption in *El Criticón*

The Case of Baltasar Gracián, a Jesuit Preparing the Way for the Enlightenment

You can find all kinds of Jesuits, including atheists . . .
                                                    Denis Diderot

Pre-Enlightenment Coming Out of the *Exercises*?

After Cervantes, Spain continues to grow in an age of tremendous experimentation with literary genres. The generation of writers entering the realm of literature in the first half of the seventeenth century is aware that the age of Absolutism is no time for conservative attitudes in the arts. Quevedo, Góngora, Calderón, or Gracián are great instances of the many directions that literature takes. These oppositional conceptions of literature lead to a great many debates; for this reason, the Quarrel of the Ancients and the Moderns begins in the peninsula almost a century sooner than in France. Spanish Golden Age literature has a deep influence on the development of French literature at the turn of the eighteenth century because it has already discussed such issues.[1] Moreover, the Jesuits are active participants in the expansion of literature, and therefore in the many debates around it. Their interaction with literature is often perceived as controversial, since they emphasize the role of imagination while condemning the fact that literature can use imagination for vicious purposes. In order to analyze this problematic in the perspective that we have been discussing so far, I would like to demonstrate in the present and following chapters that the Jesuits and their students are paradoxically if only partially at the origins of the Enlightenment since they often produce counter-arguments to the Counter-Reformation they themselves had so crucially helped to shape. The omnipresence of Loyolan visual techniques diffused by the Jesuits throughout Southern Europe soon invites artists to transform and reconceptualize its dynamics. As a result, they demand greater artistic freedom.

In this respect, the Aragonese Jesuit Baltasar Gracián demonstrates the most determination to transform the visual dynamics of the *Spiritual Exercises*. Nonetheless, we need to acknowledge the paradoxes surrounding the phenomenon: the principle of 'constructing visions for contemplation' (what Ignatius called the *composición de lugar*) so central to the *Spiritual Exercises* remains what determines the act of writing for Gracián. His Modern writings often depict a reality that reflects the omnipresence of corruption and the need for the human soul to understand corruption through total immersion in it. But Gracián's text also seeks to follow a clear order in the tradition of Dante's *Divine Comedy* and other classic writers whom he admires, and not necessarily within the 'greater narrative of Christianity.' Gracián represents the world in the form of excessive allegories, and this form of codification allows a greater casuistry for the reader: each of Gracián's allegories stands at a crossroads where the reader has to give up his controlling mind[2] and let free will chose the path of interpretation. The world to which Gracián exposes his reader is one of contemplation: the orders of corruption he presents are usually associated with natural monstrosity, feminine figures, and the urban world of Rome, as we will see in the development of this chapter. We will envision these three dimensions in his most satirical work, *El Criticón*. But simultaneously, we will consider the socio-political circumstances attending the writing process in this work. In many ways, Gracián goes further in Cervantes' direction: he shows how a Jesuit casuistic[3] worldview can easily turn into a pessimistic depiction of the Creation, where the human being has lost touch with his/her origins. We can contemplate in his texts the Modern desire to rise above the human condition and gain access to intellectual power and freedom. His works are widely printed and read in late seventeenth and early eighteenth century France in times of turmoil between two opposing systems of education: the Jesuit *ratio studiorum* and Port Royal Jansenism. For this reason, Gracián is a complex figure, at the crossroads of

Ancients and the Moderns, of the Loyolan imagination and its upcoming philosophical challengers in the Enlightenment, a rebellious Jesuit who takes the very principles of his education system to forbidden spheres.

First, let us analyze what makes Gracián's satirical work so paradoxical in its nature as much as in its criticism of human nature. Should we attribute Gracián's satires and literary activity to his affiliation with the Society of Jesus? Gracián is far from being the only Jesuit who finds the exercise of letters attractive. Pedro Calderón de la Barca is another major figure in Spanish Golden Age Literature coming out of the Jesuit tradition in the generation of writers emerging after Cervantes, but his literary production is essentially dramatic—and we will not be dealing with his works here since we limit this study to the production of prose. Gracián, by contrast, dedicates the end of his life to the writing of modern forms of prose (maxims, satires, novels). Manfred Barthel comments that "the profession of literature, rather than theater, might seem like a more appropriate outlet for the particular talents cultivated by the Jesuits" (130). Even though Barthel does not justify this judgment, one can see how it applies to Gracián. On the one hand, we can effectively consider Gracián's works to be Jesuit since they carry on Loyola's imaginative worldview into the age of Absolutism. On the other hand, Modern prose, partially owing to the distance it takes with respect to the rules of poetry, offers greater flexibility in the representation of the particular case, of individual desire.

Gracián, who was for a time a Jesuit priest, will envision literature as a means of transgressing the boundaries between religion and the world. Indeed, one can see in the works of Gracián a certain detachment from Ignatian devotion and an interest in exploring the origins of humankind, as well as in defining its nature as essentially animal or monstrous. His fellow Jesuits will condemn his writings for the overly scientific and philosophical questions they raised. Nonetheless, the presence of the *Spiritual Exercises* in his works is undeniable; Nicholas Spadaccini, editor of *Rhetoric and Politics: Baltasar Gracián and the New World Order* (1997), envisions this paradox in Gracián's work as a consequence of his affiliation with Loyolan imagination:

> To understand Gracián and the importance placed on rhetoric, we might recall that the Jesuit order, to which he belonged, was rooted on a contradiction that arose from the very personality of Ignatius of Loyola, its founder. A soldier and later on an ascetic, Loyola never separated action from contemplation (xxii).

Indeed the works of Gracián have the following rhetorical characteristic in common with the *Exercises*: they never completely articulate a truth. In the Baroque age, however, such separation between action and contemplation needs to be reconsidered. In the case of the *Oráculo Manual y Arte de Prudencia* (1647), for example, the tone of the maxims reflects the political climate of the Absolutist court where new *interpretative codes* need to be found. A century after the publication of the *Spiritual Exercises*, Spanish society has lost the enthusiasm of the Renaissance; and the works of Gracián reflect the need for encrypting the meanings in the text.

For instance, the text according to Gracián should be wisely encoded and only reveal half of its entire message, in the Classical form of the Oracle that Ancient Greeks went to consult in Delphi. In the *Oráculo Manual*, Gracián mentions that truth should only be 'half-said' (Aphorism 25).[4] The text invites readers to make an effort to participate in the making of the sign produced in the text. In this sense, Gracián minimizes the experience of the *Exercises* in each of his aphorisms: it is an incomplete sign that requires an effort on the part of any meaning seeker, that is, a minimalized *semiophany*. In most cases, even the grammatical structure of the maxims reflects the Baroque inversion that encourages this intellectual/spiritual process. Michel Foucault once commented that "Each reversal seems to be on the road to an epiphany; but in fact each discovery only makes the *enigma* more profound, increases the uncertainty and never reveals an element except to conceal the relationship existing among all the other elements" (Carrette 79).[5] For instance, the following aphorism from the *Oráculo* (#251) illustrates this chiastic Loyolan principle: "Do things in a human way as if there were no godly way; do things in a godly way as though there is no human way" (Barthel 131). In this example it is easy to recognize the Jesuit influence and the encouragement to transgress the boundary between the institution of God and man; but at the same time, this aphorism requires complete observance of the principle that it transgresses.

These maxims are not supposed to work as a general message, but rather should find their completion in the particularity of the situation at which they are aimed; that is, each reading of an aphorism will have a different meaning in the world depending on its reader. The reader's experience comes into contact with the aphorism and they create meaning together, on the mode of Jesuit casuistry and adaptation to particular needs. Malcom K. Read concludes that "Gracián's attitude to language was perfectly consonant with his order's religion of exteriority, not to mention its cultivation of refined casuistry" (Spadaccini 119). In the meantime, Gracián works in enigmas and demands from his reader a higher knowledge of classical literature and mythology. Casuistry and enigmas are therefore parts of the same process of meaning-creation. The world represented in his late literary production is envisioned as an *enigmatic* and *monstrous* immanent system that only the wise will be able to decode: each element follows its *interpretative code*.

Through this, the author assumes the position of a spiritual director, but changes the method by placing it in an enigmatic dimension. In the *Spiritual Exercises*, Loyola proposes an internal representation of Hell and emphasizes that the kingdom of Satan is not a remote reality but can be felt within the soul of the believer. Gracián recycles this process of internalization in his own writings, but modifies its basic parameters, and emphasizes the enigmatic nature of his communications in an almost anagogic mode that requires spiritual detachment from reality. L. Stinglhamber stresses that Gracián follows in the footsteps of Ignatius in this respect since his meanings are only partially communicated:

> Comment cet appel à l'indifférence n'évoquerait-il pas invinciblement le souvenir de la première semaine des *Exercices* de Saint Ignace ? (200) C'était le fort d'Ignace de ne *communiquer que partiellement, progressivement*, en ménageant toujours ses réserves (205).

Nonetheless, this parallelism is only concerned with the rhetorical and semantic analysis of both texts. Some of the Rules found in the *Spiritual Exercises* do compare perfectly with Gracián's aphorisms.[6] But these two texts differ drastically in their focus since the *Exercises* are concerned with meditations outside of the world—as a simulation of experience—whereas the *Oráculo* encourages meditations from within it and provides quicker answers to existential dilemmas in the political, spiritual, and social spheres. This conceptual work also reflects certain anxieties regarding Absolutist Spain and its overly encoded society; therefore it is more concerned with social salvation.[7]

For this reason, we need to consider Gracián's social position in order to understand the paradoxical nature of his texts. Unlike Cervantes, who remains a secular figure, Baltasar Gracián will take orders as a mentor of the Society. He will nevertheless follow in Cervantes' footsteps in his profane use of Jesuit-inspired prose. It is more problematic in his case since, in addition to being a priest, he was the rector of the Jesuit University of Tarragona. A professor of Greek and Latin philosophy, and of Catholic theology, Gracián also served as confessor to the viceroy of Aragon during a time of political turmoil.[8] In other words, he was a professional 'spiritual director,' therefore able to envision the educational system from both ends of its spectrum. He was simultaneously within and outside of the institution, arguing for the supremacy of philosophy and educating generations of young men in the tradition of the *Spiritual Exercises* and, generally speaking, in the politics of Counter-Reformation. His 'paradox' could be summed up in the following manner:

> Ostensibly, the problem was that he was preoccupied with the occult, which immediately seems like a pretext, since the same charges could have been leveled against almost every intellectual in those days. Actually the problem was that Gracián had had extensive firsthand experience of the state of education in the colleges, which he sharply criticizes in his writings (Barthel 130).

Gracián suggested—but never explicitly articulated—in writings such as *El Oráculo* or *El Criticón* that Jesuit education did not offer an adapted response to changes in the relationship of the individual to the universe and to society. His project was different: he hoped to separate very clearly the use of philosophy as a tool for man's consciousness of himself as a social being from the use of religion for spiritual matters. Gracián's satire *El Criticón* offers criticism of the Jesuit relation between action and contemplation by turning the images of his teachers into monstrous allegorical figures. The Jesuit insistence on simulation is present in the text in that he acknowledges the essential role of spiritual directors, but transgresses the boundaries of the system: the salvation he advertises in *El Criticón* is more private, social, and intellectual rather than universal and religious. Moreover, the abundance of deformed Loyolan images in his text surpasses the minimalist aspect of the *Spiritual Exercises* and forces the reader to envision history outside of Christianity. The preeminence of Graeco-Latin mythology in Gracián's works is in this sense a major confrontation with the Jesuit *ratio studiorum*. Also, he breaks with the Catholic linear conception of time and proposes a circular image, as has been suggested by Jorge Checa. As a result, the Jesuit provincial of Tarragona forbids him to publish a text that would contradict the very principles of Jesuit education, and Gracián asked to be released from his vows.

None of his previous writings represented a threat to the Society as did *El Criticón*. What part or element of it can endanger so drastically the Jesuit educative mission in the Spain of the 1650s? Maybe it is its excessive style and its repetitive meditations. After the minimalist style of the *Oráculo Manual*, the Aragonese writer needs a greater project in which he can elaborate on his concerns about post-Counter-Reformation Europe. Gracián's epic satire, the *Criticón*, becomes his pessimistic representation of this world since it deals with the tyranny of desires over the human being in geo-political spheres. In this long pilgrimage, a Spanish Christian named Critilo teaches and shows[9] to the ingenuous 'savage' Andrenio how the world works according to its immanent wickedness and how every vision becomes a text in which this savage/exercitant has to practice his understanding of the struggle between vice and virtue. Their pseudo-epic journey begins when

Critilo wakes up on a virgin island after an allegorical shipwreck. There Critilo meets Andrenio, who is still living in a pre-Adamic state; in opposition to the native man—his Dialectical Other–, Critilo represents the fall of the race as well as the perversion of modern man. In spite of this condition, the Christian assumes the position of 'political director.' After educating and preparing Andrenio for the many *orders of corruption* of the Christian world, the Spaniard will take the innocent islander on a long journey through the many regions and capitals of Europe and will interpret for him the atrocious allegories they find on their way. Andrenio is deprived of sinful thoughts, and therefore deprived of full understanding of sinful mechanism at the beginning of the journey, but will learn how to master this art through an extremely repetitive series of exercises.

One of the first lessons he receives from Critilo is very Ignatian since it is about the tensions between opposite standards that determine human life and the constant struggle that happens between them; the following passage reflects the presence of Loyolan imagination in Gracián's literary production:

> No hay cosa que no tenga su contrario con quien pelee, ya con vitoria, ya con rendimiento; todo es hazer y padecer: si hay acción, hay repasión. Los elementos, que llevan la vanguardia, comiençan a batallar entre sí; siguen los mistos, destruyéndose alternativamente; los males assechan a los bienes, hasta la desdicha a la suerte (91).[10]

Once again, Baltasar Gracián chooses to explore the origins of humankind through the figure of Andrenio, a representation of the purity of human reason that got lost through the centuries of history. However, the savage loses his innocence as soon as he becomes aware that existence follows the patterns of *orders of corruption*. After this moment of realization, there is no hope for a recuperation of his lost condition in the development of the satire; there only remains a certain desire in the character to apply the morals developed earlier in the *Oráculo* to an allegorical work of fiction.

According to this principle, there is absolutely no reason to practice the *Spiritual Exercises* or to pursue salvation through withdrawal from the world. On the contrary, the 'savage' needs constant confrontation with the corrupted spaces of Christian societies. Andrenio's only salvation lies in a philosophical awareness of his social condition. In this respect, the introduction of the innocent savage in a philosophical work of fiction announces a recurrent motif that will develop in eighteenth-century Western literature.[11] Even though Gracián's texts are highly encrypted, they announce the project of the Enlightenment to surpass the limitations of a scholastic worldview based on outdated dichotomies and to understand the world in terms of Nature instead of God.

As Alban Forcione puts it, the world as it is for the two pilgrims "is an 'agregado de monstruosidades'" (Spadaccini 45). Yet it is a surprise—if we consider the Jesuit faith in conquering the world in all of its opposing parameters—to have such a pessimistic view of Nature exposed in the *Criticón*. But a casuistic perspective on the world and its elements brings out the vice and the perversity of human desires. Forcione pursues his analysis:

> [Gracián's response to the] decisive changes in the relationship of the individual to the cosmos was not in aesthetics, in epistemology or in literary innovations of the type we associate with Cervantes and Góngora, two great visionaries of man in a world of his own making. It was rather in his wordly philosophy, in his understanding of a major alteration in this period in man's consciousness of himself as a social being (Spadaccini 43).

This critic considers Gracián to be the last and most complex of Christian Humanist writers, but in the same fashion we can envision him as a writer fundamentally dissociated from both the world of the Renaissance and the *Spiritual Exercises*. His works reflect the anxiety that we typically associate with the Baroque age. He questions the entire cosmological order during his existence as a writer in a more explicit way than Cervantes' Don Quixote. For the hidalgo de la Mancha, the world still makes sense, but this 'sense' was different from the commonly accepted one. For Gracián and his characters, however, the representation reflects a constant anxiety arising from a lack of meaning in the cosmological order. According to David Castillo, *El Criticón* is "an allegory of man's peregrination from animality to humanity" (Spadaccini 203). It is certain that there are numerous attempts in this work to discover a sense of order in Creation and humankind. Nonetheless, one could argue that the pilgrims confront an 'animality' heavily intermingled with humanity and vice versa.

There are divergent conceptions of Nature as an immanently perverted system that challenges Catholic perspectives on the place of man in the universe beyond the modernity of Cervantes' works. Gracián's worldview is one of them and that is why the peregrination in the *Criticón* is a rather pessimistic one; it introduces the uniquely Spanish notion of disappointment intermingled with disillusion, the *desengaño*.[12] This often internal and individual outlook on one's condition leads artists and writers to depict the monstrous nature of the human. This is what clearly separates the Renaissance from the Baroque. In Spain, this phenomenon has a name: '*caer en la cuenta.*' This expression perfectly translates the Baroque relationship between the subject and representation: it is vertical and implies a fall (associated to the original sin). In the *Criticón*, El Sabio gives the two pilgrims the secret to avoid this infernal sensation: "Todos entran como visteis, cantando, y después salen solloçando, sino son los envidiosos, que proceden al revés. El remedio para no despeñarse al fin es *caer en la cuenta* al principio" (227).[13] In other words, the recommendation is simple: the subject needs to *practice simulation* and must begin his/her journey with a simulation of the fall, as exercise, and get used to the feeling so it is never repeated in the future.

This is altogether a very Ignatian technique: the exercitant needs to get used to the horror of reality through simulation in order to recognize it and become 'immune' to it. We can see how the *desengaño* is derived from the *Spiritual Exercises* in this sense when the pilgrims receive the following advice:

> Razón tenéis de quexaros del desconcierto del mundo, mas no habéis de preguntar quién assí ordenó; no quién lo ha dispuesto, sino quién lo ha descompuesto. Porque habéis de saber que el *artífice supremo* muy al contrario lo traçó de cómo hoy está, pues colocó el Desengaño en el mismo umbral del mundo y echó el Engaño acullá lexos donde nunca fuera visto ni oído, donde jamás los hombres lo encontraron (635).[14]

The world for Gracián is also a structure in which orders have been purposefully corrupted and rearranged in order to invite the human being to a constant *exercise* of recognition and decoding. The *Desengaño* is an artifice, an illusion, a façade that stands where absolute truth should be found.[15] Nonetheless, the *repetitive practice* offers itself as a solution that turns the illusion into fundamental truth.

This factor was, of course, already present in Cervantes' *Don Quixote*, since he had the capacity to see fantasy through reality (or vice versa?) and to also turn the *desengaño* into its opposite. *Don Quixote* is a constant source of inspiration for Baltasar Gracián. García Gilbert mentions a "secreta y conmovedora influencia del *Quijote* en Gracián" (107) and has researched extensively the many parallels between this novel and the *Criticón*. Both texts share—along with the *Spiritual Exercises*—the same purposefully arranged architectonic perplexities. A great deal of Baroque art reflects the negativity of an image—that is, its 'corrupted' version—in order to provoke the perplexity of the observer. The hidalgo was only standing at the gate of a new age in which the subject was going to fall (*caer*) constantly in the anxiety of representation. The subject in Gracián, however, can no longer claim to see fantasy through reality.

We have mentioned the 'double gaze' common to the *Spiritual Exercises* and to *Don Quixote*. In *El Criticón*, however, the many directors (such as Chiron, El Sabio, the old blind man, Critilo, Gracián himself as the autor, and eventually Andrenio at the end of the journey) emphasize the importance of a double gaze combined with a multiple use of the associated senses, therefore superseding an already outdated two-dimensional perception: "¿Qué arte puede ser essa tuya, qué habilidad, que sobrepuje al ver con *cien ojos*, al oír con *cien orejas*, al obrar con *cien manos, proceder con dos rostros*, doblando la atención al adivinar cuanto ha de ser y al descifrar un mundo entero?" (639).[16] Gracián therefore invites his reader to combine capacities in the exercise of decrypting reality. It is only through this 'aesthetical' experience *avant la lettre* that the subject is going to be able to move forward in the world. This explains why Gracián is widely read in France by thinkers such La Rochefoucauld and Voltaire, and plays its part in the emergence of modern Aesthetics.

His two pilgrims walk through the world in order to perceive the cosmological tension and to eventually achieve immortality. They combine, in this sense, the goals of Dante and Virgil with those of Voltaire's Candide and Pangloss. Critilo warns Andrenio once they have entered the corruptible reality "Comiença a medio vivir quien poco o nada *percibe*" (287) and declares therefore that existence is about perception. In the same fashion, Gracián admires Cervantes' hero since he has the capacity to perceive and then depict the flaws of the system. Again, both authors are aware that Spain stands as an isolated political power whose ally is the Counter-Reformed Roman Church and whose only economic power depends on the conquest of the New World.[17] It is therefore no wonder if they share some fascination with the many possibilities of perception.

We would need to go back to sources older than *Don Quixote* to fully understand the historical depths of the *orders of corruption* depicted in *El Criticón*. Because of its political motivations and its fascination with exploring underworld, *El Criticón* follows the tradition of *The Odyssey*, Virgil's *Aeneid*, and Dante's *Divine Comedy* as well as Cervantes' *Don Quixote*,[18] but this literary work is much more attached to wordly circumstances than its predecessors.[19] As I said before about the *Oráculo*, it requires from its reader a great knowledge of classical literature. Moreover, it is addressed to a specific public: the educated elite of Spain, preferably with a connection to the court or with any other source of political power. A reader who has little or no previous background information about the early days of absolutist Spain will have a rather difficult time following the adventures of Critilo and Andrenio. One could argue that this regime has taken the Roman baroque to its extreme, and Gracián is educated in a very hybrid tradition that conjoins the respect for the religious institution with a scientific interest in new discoveries. Artists revive the classical models in order to give them a Christian meaning, but do not always sound very convincing in the process.[20] Consequently, the amount of play in their representation becomes more complex.

Gracián writes his *Criticón* in an age of intellectual confusion where simple formulas are no longer an option. In this sense, this excessive text stands in complete opposition to the *Spiritual Exercises* and Loyola's intention to make it a simple, accessible, and universal text. Also, Gracián's long exposure to the Jesuit *ratio studiorum* makes him a more educated figure than Loyola and Cervantes and therefore a much more complex writer. Very early in his life, Gracián decides to blend this acquired knowledge with experiences in the political sphere,[21] in Aragon as well as in the Madrid of Philip IV. But in many ways, his observer's gaze has already been configured by the visual dynamics of the spiritual exercises and he admits voluntarily his attachment to them: "las cosas espirituales se pintan en figuras de cosas materiales y visibles", or again "lo que no se ve es como si no fuese" (García Gilbert 113).[22] In the *Criticón*, he brings the skills acquired by the practice of the exercises to his political criticism and depicts an infernal reality. This satire is extremely repetitive and yet prepares the way for some of the most central debates of the Enlightenment, such as the role of aesthetics, the arguments of the Moderns around the role of literature, or the absence of religious purpose in the exercise of writing. As Voltaire, Diderot, and Sade will also do in the next century, Gracián seeks to exaggerate his literary figures in order to emphasize the true nature of things and approach the real issue closely.

The Exercise of Decoding Monstrosity

Let us now analyze how the exercise of decoding operates in *El Criticón*. The extremely repetitive apparition of monstrous figures in the journey of the two pilgrims underlines the invitation to an aesthetical experience. He is not a writer concerned with marginal figures of Spanish society such as we could find them in Cervantes' *Novelas Ejemplares*, but on the contrary, his focus is on the very center of this society: the court of the absolute king who proclaims all the victories of the Counter-Reformation as well as the dominion of his country over the New World.[23] As far as Gracián is concerned, demons and monsters are to be found everywhere in the halls and corners of the Escorial, where the court evolves as the greatest example of animality intermingled with humanity. It is no wonder that he chooses a 'virgin land' as the setting for the beginning of the book: it is a necessary *genesis* to his work where he underlines the fundamental difference between the innocent perceptions of the yet-to-be-evangelized native and the visible corruption of the Christian world. Alban Forcione identifies here a direct relationship between Gracián's writings and these political circumstances:

> Gracián would later provide a glimpse of the demonic realities of seventeenth-century politics that he was to imaginatively develop in the spectacle of enslaving representa-

tion that Andrenio and Critilo witness in their subsequent encounter with the *monstrous*, 'invisible' politician in Spain (Spadaccini xxiv).

Gracián perceives a 'labyrinth of interpretations' when he observes the many illusions of Spanish politics and wants to propose a remedy for it. The *Oráculo* was a encoded message, a warning in 'half-words' against the illusion makers, but the *Criticón* is a much bolder statement about it. It is so impregnated with political satire that we cannot possibly classify it as a 'novel' or even a work of fiction. Rather it is what Northorp Frye and Mikhail Bakthin would have called a "menippean satire."[24] In other words, it is a fictional mode where voices co-exist and answer each other; it combines fantasy and morals often with the tone of allegory and in a quite *encyclopedic* fashion at times. In fact, a totalitarian intention is more obvious in Gracián than in Loyola. The menippean satire is in itself a monstrous form of narrative since it combines a variety of elements from different traditions in the mode of *palimpsest* discussed in preceding chapters. Yet, it seems to be the only one that can contain the kind of criticism that the author makes about the political system in which he lives. This confrontation of genres and the chaotic textual space that we have in our hands when we read the *Criticón* are two parameters that would not scare a Jesuit like Gracián since it reflects contact with corruption, the only contact from which salvation and immortality can be obtained.

In the Baroque age, monsters are often a place of artistic independence and freedom, a place where painters and writers do not have to limit their fantasy as much. Since the Council of Trent in 1562, the Church has proclaimed some stricter rules in relation to the representation of Heaven, the afterlife, angels, demons, and anything relating to Satan and Hell. The debate around salvation makes Heaven much more difficult to depict than Hell. In 1649, for instance, the Spanish Inquisitor Francisco Pacheco publishes his *Arte de la Pintura* in order to limit and restrict these infernal spaces of fantastical representation that he often judges to be deviant. After all, all seem to agree on the horrible nature of the underworld. As a consequence, artists associate these *orders of corruption* to spaces of artistic innovation. Hilaire Kallendorf defines it as "a *liminal space of artistic freedom* in which the artist could paint whatever he pleased" (5). In the time of Gracián, this kind of representation becomes even more regulated. But the increased regulation does not seem to limit innovation; on the contrary, it encourages it. The incidence of monstrous figures in this satire is indeed enormous and also needs to be connected to the visual dynamics of the *Spiritual Exercises*. Andrenio and Critilo progress on a path in which they encounter these corrupted elements one after the other, in an extremely orderly fashion. Nonetheless, these are allegorical figures only and do not compare to the *monsters* that we find in Renaissance literature.[25] Yet, the monsters share the same kind of fascination with them.

This is quite an evolution from the *Spiritual Exercises*, and it is no wonder that the Society of Jesus is not satisfied with the works of this Aragonese member, who is also rector of one of their main novitiates in Tarragona. Gracián writes the *Criticón* toward the end of his life with a detachment similar to that of Cervantes in his *Quixote* and *Novelas Ejemplares*. He does not seem to fear expulsion from the order. Nonetheless, *El Criticón* is not such a 'deviation' from the *Spiritual Exercises* and reveals much about the relationship between director and exercitant that partially defines the Baroque orders of corruption. Let us remember that visualization of infernal scenes is essential in the practice of the exercises in order to simulate the 'horror of sins' in one's lifetime. Gracián understands that it is important to cultivate this 'neurosis' (one of Barthes' terms for Loyola's project) in the citizen's mind, but he seems on the surface to be more concerned about political survival than spiritual salvation. In this sense, he remains faithful to some of the fundamental principles of his order: the great majority of 'monsters' that Critilo and Andrenio encounter are allegorical figures that symbolize perdition, and Critilo is familiar with them. These allegories, as we have just seen, are extremely visual and remind us of some of the late representations of Hell by Hieronymus Bosch, another figure that Gracián deeply admires. Chiron the Centaur,[26] who guides the two pilgrims part of the way on their journey, confirms this artistic affiliation: "- Haced cuenta, dijo Quirón, que soñáis despiertos, ¡oh, qué bien pintaba el Bosco, ahora entiendo su capricho!; cosas veréis increíbles (. . .) No hallaréis cosa en cosa y a un mundo que no tiene ni pies ni cabeza, de merced se le da el descabezado" (Gracián 133).[27] This reference to another great actor of visual culture in Renaissance is essential: Gracián valued anyone who had contributed to the depiction of corruption and its development.

Monstrosity becomes somewhat of a repetitive territory for allegories and chaotic fantasies. At least it reflects the unbalanced nature of the world and the 'horrendous nature' of human desires. But Gracián's project goes further than this; his monster is multiform and omnipresent and certainly difficult to define: "Y no son todos hombres los que vemos, que hay horribles monstruos y aun acroceraunios en los golfos de las grandes poblaciones" (225).[28] Somehow, Gracián transfers the Loyolan dynamics to political reality and recommends to use the world has a simulation territory for the visualization of the standards of Hell: not all are men; the agents of the Devil are amongst them, and the wise need to learn how to recognize them! That is the very ambition of the *Criticón*: it should educate its reader and train him/her to develop this capacity to see through things.

Once again, in the Renaissance, the monster represented the limits of human knowledge, the unknown phenomena of nature. Loyola himself makes a clear distinction between the natural orders at the very beginning of the *Spiritual Exercises* to avoid any confusion in the exercitant's mind: "Human beings are created to praise, reverence and serve God (. . .) The other things on the face of the Earth are created for the human beings" (130). In the Spanish Baroque that Gracián represents, however, humans are not separated from their animal condition in the same manner; the monster reflects the very essence of the human, including his wisdom, his philosophy and his historical circumstances: it becomes an allegorical manifestation of the Spanish courtier. At the beginning of the chapter titled "Moral Anatomía del Hombre," we can see how this inversion functions in the satire; the narrator (director) reminds his reader of some essential rules, in a very Ignatian way, including this quite bold statement:

> [los hombres] tienen unas entrañas más dañadas que las víboras, un aliento más venenoso que el de los dragones, unos ojos envidiosos y malévolos más que los del basilisco; unos dientes de un perro, unas narices fisgonas, encubridoras de su irrisión, que exceden a las trompas de los elefantes; de modo que solo el hombre tiene juntas todas las armas ofensivas que se hallaban repartidas entre las fieras, y así el ofende más que todas (102). No hay salteadora esfinge que así oprima al viandante (digo viviente) como la ignorancia de sí (214).[29]

He compares here ignorance to a 'jumping sphinx' and combines therefore the enigmatic nature of the human quest with its constant mobility and its hybrid powers. But above all, he stresses in one of his typical puns that men are just made of flesh and that is all there is to it if ignorance is not superseded. According to the Jesuit in him, if humans do not encounter the missing part of the signs they come across on their path, they are just monstrous packs of flesh. Existence is horrendous since it is incomplete and in need of constant interpretation, just like the mythological sphinx that he mentions here. In consequence, each form of monstrosity needs to be envisioned as an element in an endless chain of symbols that never provides any answer to the existential questions. The monster in Gracián is a literary image above all, but should be considered as sharing the nature of the aphorism: it is an *oracle* because it also deliberately proposes an incomplete sign open for interpretation and representation.[30]

In this exercise, the designated exercitant is Andrenio. His indigenous condition guarantees the virginity of his perception—and we know how much the Jesuit cherished this quality in the natives of Amazonia when they established their mission there. As an exercitant, Andrenio reacts *totally* and not *partially* as any 'sinner' would do. Similarly, his perception of the *order of corruption* is total and greater than Critilo's. His virgin eyes have more difficulty facing horror in his entirety, yet this unaltered vision benefits Critilo and an old blind guide who accompanies them for part of their journey:

> ¿Qué tienes? ¿Qué ves?, le preguntó el anciano.—¡Qué he de ver! Lo que no quisiera ni creyera: veo un monstruo, el más horrible que vi en mi vida, porque no tiene pies ni cabeza, ¡qué cosa tan desproporcionada! No corresponde parte a parte, ni dice uno con otro en todo él; ¡qué fieras manos tiene! Y cada una de su fiera, ni bien carne, ni pescado, y todo lo parece, ¡qué boca tan de lobo, donde jamás se vio verdad! (182).[31]

Imitating Dante, who is almost forced to close his eyes at times during his descent into Hell,[32] Andrenio learns how to familiarize his vision with the nature of things. In the *Criticón*, the reader perceives the presence of monster through his eyes-in-training. The relationship between the old blind man and the young man mirrors the model of spiritual guidance advertised in the *Spiritual Exercises* since his vision is personal and individual-oriented; moreover his 'director' must not have access to it. In this case, he is literally blinded.

All in all, Gracián emphasizes in a succession of episodes that spiritual guidance is a very male-oriented exercise, leaving no alternative for women. It is an aspect of Loyola's text that we have not treated so far in our analysis, but the *Criticón*, as an exaggeration of many principles of the *Spiritual Exercises*, enables us to see the fundamental division that the first generation of Jesuit thinkers make between men and women. The monstrosity that they both emphasize is often of a feminine nature. Luis Avilés has studied this phenomenon from a Lacanian angle and acknowledges this tension in the *Criticón*: "la mujer, en la etapa histórica de Gracián, se ha convertido en un monstruo que ha logrado socavar los valores masculinos de la virtud y el valor," and he adds later on that the word *monstruo* should be understood as *prodigio*, that is, "toda entidad que adquiere características que no le corresponden, diferentes a su supuesta naturaleza" (84).[33] There are places in Loyola's text where this connection is already announced. Women, by the way, are not immediately welcome to the practice of the exercises and will barely have access to it until the twentieth century. Let us remember what Ignatius of Loyola had written in the *Exercises*:

> The enemy conducts himself as a woman. He is a weakling before a show of strength, and a tyrant if he has his will. It is characteristic of a woman in a quarrel with a man to lose courage and take to flight if the man shows that he is determined and fearless. However, if the man loses courage and begins to flee, the anger, vindictiveness, and rage of the woman surge up and know no bounds (145).

Because of their transformational powers, women are therefore included as active participants in the order of corruption that men have to face during their lifetime. Nevertheless, Loyola limits his comparison between Satan and woman to this assertion. For Gracián, however, this relationship deserves more research and reflection. The Aragonese Jesuit makes monstrous feminine figures omnipresent in the *Criticón*, and that is why they deserve to be explored thoroughly. From the very beginning of the story female figures are absent from the main action. For instance, no mention of female characters is made while the two men are on the island at the beginning of the book, since they are *isolated* from the corruption that they represent. Later on, when they find female figures on their path, they are usually monsters in the mode of Classical figures.

They represent chaos and reflect the cosmological confusion of the period. Gracián recycles the myth of Eve, the first human tempted by the enemy and mother of all corruption, and makes a non-Biblical version of it: he includes the story of the first woman in the *Criticón* and blames her for opening the cave where God had locked up all the vices and corruption. She becomes a sort of Eve-Pandora hybrid. In other words, he synthesizes Judeo-Christian narratives with Ancient Greek and philosophical ones. In the satire, myths and legends are often intermingled: the Fall of Man, the tower of Babel, Plato's Allegory of the Cave are all rhetorical instruments that he uses to rewrite the story of corruption through an historical line of female figures that have led men to perdition. Cosmological confusion is definitely of a female nature in Gracián's worldview.

Francesca Perugini has analyzed this dimension of *El Criticón* and has come to the following conclusion:

> Du fait que la femme concentre en elle les trois pires *ennemis* de l'homme, la chair, le monde et le diable, "procedió", écrit Gracián en suivant une longue tradition, "el apellidarse todos los males hembras, las furias, las parcas, las sirenas y las arpías, que todo lo es una mujer mala" (193).

This analysis sums up the anxiety we encounter in the text. Flesh, World, and Devil—the three elements of Nature that define corruption in all of its senses: carnal, natural, and spiritual—are *concentrated* in one creature. It is no wonder therefore that the exercitant Andrenio is trained very early in the peregrination to contemplate the monstrous result and learn through the horrific visions how to recognize the female dangers and avoid them. One of these first encounters happens right when the young native enters the Christian world and is confronted with a female version of the Greek god Saturn.[34] Interestingly enough, his reaction is extremely strong for a male character who has never had a direct encounter with the female object; he immediately defines her as "aquella *engañosa* hembra" and he screams at her: "¡Oh traídora! ¡oh, bárbara!, ¡oh, sacrílega mujer! Más fiera que las mismas fieras; ¿es posible que en esto han parado tus caricias, para esto era tanto cuidado y asistencia?" (117).[35] Although this discourse sounds inadequate and does not reflect the character's supposed innocence in any way, it surely echoes the message of the old Jesuit author. He associates female creatures with the *desengaño*, this hybrid notion of mingled disappointment and corruption, as well as with the animal order (*fieras*).

Nonetheless, the female orders of corruption are not systematically attached to female creatures in the *Criticón*. As the monster and the human are two elements that oscillate between the standards of Heaven and those of Hell, so do the masculine and the feminine. Since most of the universe is in a state of confusion and constant degradation (corruption), it is impossible to match perfectly a signifier to a signified: therefore everything is an *engaño*, and the female vice can be found at the heart of male virtue. In the Baroque worldview of Gracián, the dichotomies determined by the thinkers of the Renaissance are often cancelled: masculine and feminine no longer exist as such, since reality is fundamentally hybrid. Luis Avilés explains this *crisis* in the following terms:

> [For Gracián] conceptions of crisis in seventeenth-century Spain eroded parameters that define masculinity and feminity as categories of distinction and separation. The boundaries between these concepts became blurred, often resulting in the contamination of each other. As a consequence, men were seen as insufficient, lacking in those characteristics that once defined the male paradigm. Men suddenly became more feminine, and at the same time women were seen as more powerful (Spadaccini 127).

We are truly in the realm of *erosion*, *separation*, and *contamination*, all words that relate to the disintegration of a previously philosophical approach to the body. Even if the purpose of contemplation remains the same from the *Spiritual Exercises* to the *Criticón*, the parameters drastically change from the Renaissance to the Baroque age. Gracián illustrates it, for instance, through the binary opposition Felisinda–Falsirena that keeps the two main characters in a state of tension in the first part of the book. These two female figures point to the extremes of femininity: blissful salvation and lustful perdition are of the same nature. Felisinda represents the feminine ideal for Critilo (*mi dama*), in the fashion of Don Quixote's Dulcinea. Falsirena is her evil counterpart, sharing the same physical appearance and the most dreadful danger to the virtue of Critilo. In other words, he transposes the standards of Heaven and Hell to those of femininity and maintains a balance between the two.

In summary, female monstrous creatures participate in creating a necessary state of tension for a productive peregrination, that is, a spiritual evolution progressing between two extreme and opposing points of attraction. Andrenio is advised to keep his perceptions in balance and does this in a mimetic fashion, always looking up at his spiritual father Critilo. Before leaving the island, Critilo tells the story of his love for Felisinda to Andrenio, and she becomes their common quest and purpose to enter the world. They will need to wander through corruption in order to find her: like salvation in the case of the *Spiritual Exercises*, Felisinda is the reward of the pilgrim for undergoing his immersion in corruption. In the chapter titled "Entrada en el Mundo," the two pilgrims leave the purity of the virgin island to enter the order of corruption, the World. Critilo's last advice to the innocent Andrenio before 'penetrating' this other reality is a quote from Latin thinker Horace: "Medio hay en las cosas; tú no vayas por los estremos. Vé por el medio, y correrás seguro. ¡Vuela por el medio!" (121).[36] With this assertion, Critilo assumes totally his position of spiritual director whose function is to indicate to his exercitant the 'extremes,' or in other words, the distinction of Standards announced by Loyola in the *Spiritual Exercises*: "The director should encourage and strengthen the exercitant for the future, *unmask the deceptive tactics of the Enemy* of our human nature. The rules on different kinds of spirit are too subtle and advanced for such a one to understand" (123).

At the same time, this director recommends that we learn how to maintain the balance between the two standards while in a state of peregrination. This is, of course, a very Ignatian approach to the journey they are about to begin. Also, this peregrination is composed of 'compartments,' just as we have been observing in the *Spiritual Exercises*, in the Roman churches that reproduce their dynamics, and in the division of episodes in *Don Quixote*. In the same fashion, Critilo will *isolate* Andrenio in separated perspectives of contemplation in which his discourse can be oriented toward a specific target (monstrous nature of men, warning against female evils, political corruption, etc.). With this format, the author can deal with each dimension separately, always showing the two extremes that maintain his characters in a state of tension.

The pilgrims will move from a stage of simulation to a stage of confirmation in which Andrenio will apply his training to urban reality. In this sense, their journey follows the pattern of the *Spiritual Exercises*: "For ordinarily the Enemy of human nature tempts under the appearance of good more often when a person is performing the Exercises in the *illuminative life* (First Week) than in *purgative life* (Second Week)" (Loyola 123). This division is translated in the *Criticón* with a contrast between the rural world and the city. Unlike in Dante's and Virgil's poems, the pilgrimage of *El Criticón* is essentially urban: it presents the modernity of Western European cities as the most efficient orders of corruption, that is, the Great Harlots with whom the two pilgrims will learn how to differentiate the temporal from the eternal, the virtuous from the vicious, and where they will eventually obtain their philosophical salvation. In this sense, the purgative life can only happens in simulated visual projections of the urban world.

Contemplating Eternal Arts beyond the *Roma Ignaziana*

Gracián is a well-traveled professor and has seen Madrid, Rome and Paris. German critic Krauss once wrote: "Gracián is the first Spanish intellectual (*Geist*) of truly conscious European orientation" (Spadaccini 312). Even though Spain is in a state of isolation from the rest of endangered Europe and protects its faith in Catholicism from the Lutheran/Calvinist wave, the Jesuits do not feel constrained and continue to travel to the main urban poles of Western Europe. Gracián could not allow his writings to be too critical of femininity, since he was still, in theory, a Jesuit priest. The extreme poles of attraction found in *El Criticón* are not only those set by monstrous female creatures, however. This is why this discourse is transferred and applied to his criticism of early-Modern urban reality and, in this sense, cities also reflect female qualities in the fashion of the Babylon of the *Spiritual Exercises*. The peregrination is composed of a balanced alternation of 'natural' and 'urban' settings. This dichotomy reveals another anxiety in Spanish high-Baroque society: the cities are growing and often project an image of corruption.[37] The Jesuits, as we have seen in the third chapter, have a natural inclination for the urban *decorum*, since they find there the tensions between heavenly and infernal Standards at their highest potential. Salvation is therefore to be found in contact with the feminine/monstrous city and its many orders of corruption. Critilo and Andrenio follow in the footsteps of these spiritual travelers and also contemplate the new urban configuration of these traditionally Catholic cities and progressively get their eyes used to their horrific nature.

The second part of *El Criticón* begins with a warning that the pilgrims are entering the age of Virility, and their first 'vision' of the cities happens from the top of the Pyrenees, in a liminal space between France and Spain. The author places them in this very spot supposedly because it symbolizes the *natural* tension between the elements that Nature arranges constantly. The two countries stand in opposition like God and Satan, according to Gracián's belief exposed in the first part: "todo este universo se compone de contrarios y se concierta de desconciertos (. . .) No hay cosa que no tenga su contrario con quien pelee (...) [como] los españoles a los franceses" (91).³⁸ In the space between, the pilgrims have a perspective on Madrid, Rome, and Paris all at once and practically stand in the middle of this triangle. Their conversation from this particularly exceptional point of view forms most of the second *crisis* of the second part, since Critilo deciphers the urban codes for Andrenio. With one foot in Spain (secured Catholicism) and one in France (unsecured territory half-conquered by the Huguenots), they contemplate the feminine *urba caput mundi* and 'mother of all civilization,' the city of Rome:

> Éssa que te parece a ti andar entre pies de la tierra, es el cielo, la coronada cabeça del mundo y muy señora de todo él, la sacra y triunfante Roma, por su valor, saber, grandeza, mando y religión; corte de personas, oficina de hombres, pues restituyéndolos a todo el mundo, todas las demás ciudades la son colonias de policía (314).³⁹

This heavenly vision confirms the Jesuit belief that Rome has regained its status of New Jerusalem since it has been conquered by Ignatius and his followers. Then they enjoy a view that enables them to contrast the triumphant Rome with Paris and the Louvre at its very center: "Se llama el Lobero (y no voy con vuestra malicia) porque ahí se les ha armado siempre la trampa a los rebeldes lobos con piel de ovejas; digo, aquellas horribles fieras hugonotas" (316).⁴⁰ In summary, the two pilgrims are exposed to three kinds of cities (Rome, Paris, and Madrid) and, by the same token, contemplate the tension between Rome and Paris, a tension with which the court of Madrid is familiar. The new Spanish capital does not seem to match the description of any of its two counterparts. It does reflect, however, the monstrous nature of the early-Modern Spanish man according to Gracián. Nevertheless, when the two pilgrims had previously observed Madrid before leaving Spain, their visions of the city were very different and underlined the fundamentally illusionistic nature of the urban façade. For Andrenio, Madrid reflected the quality of a new Rome that was head of the New World, but for Critilo, this city chosen by the court of Phillip II had nothing to offer but corruption:

> ¿Qué ves cuando miras?—Veo, dijo [Andrenio], una real madre de tantas naciones, una corona de dos mundos, un centro de tantos reinos, un joyel de entrambas Indias, un nido del mismo Fénix y una esfera del Sol católico coronado de prendas en rayos y de blasones en luces.—Pues yo veo, dijo Critilo, una Babilonia de confusiones, una Lutecia de inmundicias, una Roma de mutaciones, un Palermo de volcanes, una Constantinopla de nieblas, un Londres de pestilencia, un Argel de cautiverios (235).⁴¹

This double perspective reminds the reader of the dynamics encountered in *Don Quixote de la Mancha*, before the hidalgo and his squire merge their perceptions.

Every city in this passage is associated with cosmological confusion and disintegration. According to Theodore Kassier, author of *The Truth Disguised*, "the insistent reminders of the pilgrimage's location in Europe's familiar nations and cities serve as an implicit authentication of the startling monstrosities and prodigies represented by the courts, palaces and creatures among which the protagonists move" (28). The new urban reality offers all the characteristics and symbols of the ancient orders of corruption. That is why, for instance, Gracián chooses to rename Paris with its original name 'Lutecia,' in order to insist on the corrupted past in which all of these cities were born. We could compare this perception of Madrid with a similar one found in María de Zayas' *Desengaños Amorosos* (1647) where the city is described in the following terms: "En la Babilonia de España, en la nueva maravilla de Europa, en la madre de la nobleza, en el jardín de los divinos entendimientos (. . .) Madrid, Babilonia, madre, maravilla, jardín, archiva, escuela, progenitora, retrato y cielo" (295).[42] Both authors use the Loyolan image of Babylon to describe the new reality and urban model that Madrid has become. It is a modern Babylon that also lives in a state of tension between its two European counterparts, Paris and Rome. Nonetheless, it is comprehensible that Madrid awakens so much interest and anxiety in the first half of the seventeenth century since it has developed at an incredibly rapid pace and has benefited economically from the conquest of South America. This growth has often thrown the urban reality into a state of excess and lack of control. This intense urbanization in Spain comes after it happens in most major European cities, and Madrid will try to follow the lines of the Roman architectural reformation.[43] As a result, there is a certain anxiety about attaining a similar progress. Critical eyes like those of Gracián or Zayas often perceive this rapid evolution as another sign of the corruption of the times.

After understanding that urban realities are all situated on this scale, the two pilgrims are ready to come down from the mountains and to wander through the cities. Soon they realize that the dynamics of all urban spaces are naturally formed by human violence and corruption. According to Forcione, the cities of *El Criticón* are in this sense the *locus* in which the fusion of all binary oppositions takes place; the animal is merged with the human, the masculine with the feminine, etc: "It is a mass of coiling lines and twisted forms, which grotesquely intermingles the animal and the human orders of being and continually eludes the observer's fixing glance in its restless movements and metamorphoses" (Spadaccini 45). It becomes impossible to recognize the nature of things or to put them in an *order* other than that of corruption. Even if the *Criticón* is an evolution that begins on a virgin island and ends in the utopia of an eternal natural space completely deprived of corruption, the true center of its peregrination is the modern city in its most allegorical forms. This is where the two pilgrims come to understand the path they need to follow to reach immortality. García Gilbert offers in this respect an interesting comparison with the rather rural nature of Don Quixote's and Sancho's itinerary through Spain, and attributes it to the 'Jesuit nature' of *El Criticón*:

> Es sabido que los jesuitas son los primeros que asimilaron la conciencia moderna del hombre urbano, del ser humano como habitante de la gran ciudad. *El Criticón*, en fuerte contraste con el *Quijote*, participa de esa sensibilidad y sus espacios, aunque alegóricos, son esencialmente urbanos (107).⁴⁴

Even though everything in *El Criticón* seems to follow in this sense the guidelines of the Society of Jesus in relation to urban development and landmarking, Gracián's supervisors were actually very unpleased with such controversial piece of literature. But the fascination with the urban order of corruption—which is often described as a 'she' or with feminine attributes—is definitely a common determinant in the spiritual quest of the followers of Ignatius as well as Gracián's two pilgrims.

Andrenio slowly progresses and finally understands the encrypted nature of the urban space through the omnipresence of allegorical monsters. The confusion of signs they represent—what Gracián often defines as 'Babylon'—keeps him from an immediate comprehension of what this space has come to represent in the world, and why cities have become the centers of attraction for the human being. However, he will make progress in this space by cultivating his visual powers in the Loyolan definition of exercitant. He learns the distinction between *ver* (to see) and *mirar* (to look at) through the exploration of allegorical urban spaces (Gracián 290). He is carefully warned before penetrating these realms at the beginning of the second part—the most representative of the 'urban stage' in human life:

> Prométoos que para poder vivir es menester armarse un hombre de pies a cabeça, no de ojetes, sino de ojazos muy despiertos: ojos en las orejas, para descubrir tanta falsedad y mentira; ojos en las manos, para ver lo que da y mucho más lo que toma; ojos en los braços, para no abarcar mucho y apretar poco; ojos en la misma lengua, para mirar muchas vezes lo que ha de decir una; ojos en el pecho, para ver en qué lo ha de tener; ojos en el corazón, atendiendo a quien le tira o le haze tiro; ojos en los mismos ojos, para mirar cómo miran; ojos y más ojos y reojos, procurando ser elmirante en un siglo tan adelantado (294).⁴⁵

This totalitarian dominion of the eye as superior organ is directly linked here to the anxiety around urban development (*siglo tan adelantado*). Because of the excessive nature of the Modern city, all other senses need to be replaced by the only one that can prevent its dweller from perdition and lead him to salvation. The long initiation of the innocent exercitant follows therefore the chain of interpretations identified in the *Spiritual Exercises* through the visual imperialism imposed by the spiritual director. The eye needs to be overly developed in times of urbanization because cities require a greater capacity for perception. Christine Buci-Glucksmann perceives this phenomenon as a consequence of the "apologie post-tridentine des images et de l'impérialisme visuel" (97) that she attributes to Ignatius of Loyola.[46] Eventually, Andrenio enters this extremely visual 'symbolic order of corruption' when Critilo suddenly recognizes him as his son, in the second part of the satire. This dramatic twist in the course of *El Criticón* confirms Andrenio's total acceptance of Critilo's guidance through the world, and it happens right at the moment when their visual powers are finally calibrated for each other. Critilo turns out to be Andrenio's father not only because he has given life to him, but also because he has restored him to sight and has taught him how to use the visual capacity in a beneficial way. As a matter of fact, the second half of the satire will no longer be about initiation and training in visual encryption, but rather about a common quest toward enlightenment. All in all, after going through these modern allegorical cities, the director has succeeded in the visual education of his exercitant.

In summary, whether we are dealing with monstrous figures, with female creatures, or with modern urban spaces, Gracián places the emphasis of perception on the eye and the gaze. It is the very organ of this entire peregrination. But as we can see in the previous quote, the eye has come to cover the entire body and Modern man is slowly transforming into a gazing creature. The perception of orders of corruption (monstrous, political, feminine, urban) through the eye—what Loyola recommended when he wrote "to see with the eyes of imagination"—is therefore the most repeated exercise of *El Criticón*. In spite of the tension that it produces between the Society of Jesus and Baltasar Gracián, this satire takes the Loyolan '*composición de lugar*' to greater lengths: it develops the initial images and uses the *Exercises* only as a base and implements these mental pictures with elements of corruption derived from contemporary geo-political circumstances. Also, the director and the exercitant somehow 'merge' in their mission and become one symbolic figure: the father reunited with his son. The casuistic worldview presented here turns out to go beyond the limits of fantasy allowed by the Jesuits in the practice of the exercises. For instance, the mythological dimension takes over the theological one, and the pilgrims show very little concern for the Scriptures or the divine figures of Christianity throughout their travels. Nonetheless, there are some fundamentally Loyolan factors in the evolution of the two characters, like those we have already witnessed in *Don Quixote*: *El Criticón* is a concentrate of the visual dynamics prescribed by Ignatius and could indicate the agenda of its author.

In the tradition of Ignatius' life journey from Loyola to Rome, and that of the two pilgrims of Cervantes' *Persiles*, Critilo and Andrenio will follow an allegorical path that will eventually lead them to the capital of the Counter-Reformation, what we have previously identified as the 'Roma Ignaziana.' It is interesting to see that Rome stands at the very end of the journey and gives, again, a sense of perspective to the entire journey of the two wanderers. Rome's presence, as we have seen, has been previously underlined in the narrative, but the two heroes have only seen it from a distance. When they eventually reach the third and final stage of their human progress, they are finally ready and prepared to enter the urban reality of the sacred city and to fully perceive it as another allegorical and monstrous order of corruption. Their first perception, however, is based on Gracián's insistence on the most sacred nature of the city, above them all:

> Trataron, ya vitoriosos, de encaminarse a triunfar a la siempre augusta Roma, teatro heroico de inmortales hazañas, corona del mundo, reina de las ciudades, esfera de los grandes ingenios, que en todos siglos, aun los mayores, las águilas caudales tuvieron necesidad de volar a ella y darse unos filos de Roma hasta los mismos españoles (. . .) Trono de lucimiento, que lo que en ella luce por todo el mundo campea, fénix de las edades, que cuando otras ciudades perecen ella renace y se eterniça, emporio de todo lo bueno, corte de todo el mundo, que todo él cabe en ella; pues el que a Madrid ve a sólo Madrid, el que a París no ve sino a París y el que ve a Lisboa ve a Lisboa, pero el que ve Roma las ve todas juntas y goza de todo el mundo de una vez, término de la tierra y entrada cátolica del cielo (727–8).[47]

The author has no other option but to exaggerate the 'eternal' nature of Rome, and this seems to be one of the most religious passages found in *El Criticón* in terms of the reaffirmation of the Catholic faith. Nonetheless, we could also consider that it refers to the ancient roots of the city and its role as the capital and founding city of Europe. It is also obvious that Gracián underlines the Spanish presence in/dominion of the city; Critilo had previously suggested that "con el humo de España se luce Roma" (684). According to the outline of the epic journey, Rome is truly the *axis mundi* of the world that the two pilgrims have been exploring. As Dandelet points out:

> By the first decade of the seventeenth century, with the Spanish monarchy enjoying unprecedented influence in Rome and the Spanish community in the city at its peak, a final theme emerged in the Spanish myth of Rome to match the moment: the rhetoric of praise. Gone were the days of criticism. As the preeminent foreign power in the city, Spaniards felt increasingly positive about Rome, a fact reflected in Spanish writing celebrating the *spiritual city*, the mother of the church, the most holy center of Christendom (98).

One of the first figures to favor this movement in literature was Jerónimo Gracián, a Carmelite from Granada, who had no relation to the author of *El Criticón* (Dandelet 99). Since the triumph of Ignatius of Loyola and his *Spiritual Exercises* in the reconstruction of the Catholic faith, Rome is deeply under Spanish cultural influence, and Spanish pride is reflected in Gracián's works as well, since we can perfectly observe the "rhetoric of praise" in the preceding passage.

The contemplation of Rome from the exterior—what Barthes once called a 'vue ignacienne' (*Sade*, 58)—always seems to carry a great deal of spiritual reverence; it is a necessary stage for anyone coming to Rome from the outside. The superlative nature of the designated urban space is due to its unbeaten collection of historical events: it has collected the essence of human nature more than any other city. Gracián seeks to emphasize this unsurpassed dimension of Rome. In this sense, the exterior perception of Rome echoes the Loyolan imaginative depiction associated with the eternal city. Rome is not only a vision in the distance. It is a space that the two pilgrims are going to explore from its interior, where they are going to exercise the skills acquired on their journey. This is why the moment of external contemplation plays a fundamental part: its discrepancy with the interior reminds us of the Deleuzian notion of 'baroqueness' as an invitation by the exterior to enter a saturated interior, as we have noted in the third chapter.

The admiration for the interior urban space is based on different criteria, however. The city functions like any other sacred interior: the pilgrims are guided by the images projected onto them. They quickly come to the conclusion that it is the constant contrasting of orders, i.e., its chaotic nature, that makes Rome the unique spiritual city that it is:

> Fuelos introduciendo en una tan espaciosa cuan especiosa plaça coronada de alternados edificios, unos muy magestuosos, que parecían alcaçares, otros muy pobres, como casas de filósofos; hasta pabellones militares, entre patios de escuelas. Quedaron admirados nuestros peregrinos de ver tal variedad de edificios (667).[48]

This could be the definition of a perfect urban 'order of corruption' since it is through the contrasts of architectural forms and political/social classes that the true beauty of the city appears. This variety so typical of the *axis mundi* of Christendom is what makes Rome a recapitulation of all urban history. Obviously, Rome had already kept a quality that other urban centers in seventeenth-century Western Europe were slowly eliminating: the cohabitation and compilation of its various architectural styles, and generally speaking, its taste for eclecticism. On the other hand, Paris and Madrid were under the dominion of still recent artistic concepts serving the needs of Absolutism.[49] They were eliminating their atemporality and their contrasts in the process. Rome, on the other hand, was the only site where one could contemplate the 'greater narrative of Christianity' as well as the oddest juxtapositions.

The pilgrims have gone from the virgin island to the eternal city with a clear purpose in mind: they are going after Felisinda, the one figure who will be a mother for Andrenio and a wife for Critilo. Their quest ends naturally in Rome where the third member of their trinity—what they need to form a reunited holy family—is supposed to be found. But the pilgrims still have to demonstrate their capacity to decipher the urban space in which they are immersed in order to gain access to this complementary figure. Through the illusion of the city's façades, they will learn the capacity to see the 'true nature of things.' Critilo and Andrenio rapidly notice the new tendencies in Roman architecture that invite the observer's gaze: "inculcan estatuas mudas entre colunas pesadas para adorno de las vistosas fachadas" (667).[50] This reference is clearly directed to the brand-new church of Il Gesú, whose façade has turned into a paradigm for many other churches throughout Rome—and soon after, throughout the rest of the world—and also features two 'mute statues between columns:' one of Ignatius of Loyola and another of his beloved Francisco Javier. These statues might be 'mute' in their principle, but, after detailed contemplation, the pilgrims come to the conclusion that these are actually "animadas piedras hablando con lenguas de inscripciones" (668).[51] The pilgrims follow here in the footsteps of Virgil and Dante in Purgatory, when in the spiritual director shows his exercitant the statues on the walls. In Canto X, Dante observes the frescoes and comes to the conclusion that:

> In front of us appeared so truthfully there sculptured in a gracious attitude, *He did not seem an image that is silent*. One would have sworn that he was saying *Ave* (. . .) Around about him seemed it thronged and full of cavaliers, and the eagles in the gold above them visibly in the wind were moving. The wretched woman in the midst of these seemed to be saying: "Give me vengeance Lord, for my dead son, for whom my heart is breaking." (. . .) He who on no new thing has ever looked was the creator of *this visible language*, novel to us, for here it is not found. I delighted me in *contemplating the images* of such humility (56–7).

Dante the pilgrim is intensively trained throughout the Divine Comedy in the art of contemplation, and only his constant visual exercising enables him to hear the sounds coming out of the statues and to see them moving.[52] Gracián's pilgrims are experiencing with very similar contacts with the contrasting works of art. In his highly acclaimed *Graciáns Lebenslehre*, Werner Krauss underlines that "no one [outside of Gracián] had dared to attempt a collective display of the intellectual and moral world through the developmental tendencies of the novel with such scope since Dante" (Spadaccini 24). Rome naturally displays her own collection in this sense and participates in the general intention of *El Criticón* as menippean satire.

This exceptional quality in the act of representing is peculiar to Rome since the city derives it from its 'eternal' nature. The statues are not the only representations that have the capacity to talk to the pilgrims and make their aesthetical experience complete. Gracián does not attribute this capacity of the urban space to the Christian nature of Rome, but on the contrary, acknowledges the success of Catholicism through its association with a city that was already configured for the development of artists of exception, prior to the avent of Christianity.[53] This is precisely where Gracián's text diverges slightly from the Jesuit conception of a guided pilgrimage to Rome: the importance placed on pre-Christian art is too great. Instead of considering Rome as part of the linear Catholic 'greater narrative' of Christianity, Gracián envisions on the contrary Catholicism as part of the circular Roman 'great narrative' and will be followed by Sade in the next century. Moreover, his belief in literature as the highest form of visual art contradicts the supremacy placed by the Jesuits on painted, enacted, or sculpted images.

Beyond its architecture, the rest of Roman arts follow the same rule of exceptional significance. Rome not only reveals to the pilgrims some fundamental truths about their spirituality and how it is exhalted in the arts. It also teaches them to recognize some extremely secular phenomena associated with the production of art in the eternal city. Rome has not only been a home for the Catholic Church, but it has also sheltered some of the most significant non-Christian authors (Virgile, Horace, Marcial, and Pliny). Gracián acknowledges their influence as fundamental in the election of Rome as center for the development of a renewed religious tradition. The divergence of architectural styles and the erosion process of the buildings underline the temporality of most forms of arts. Therefore, the pilgrims come to identify literature as the supreme form of art since it is the only one that transcends both time and space:

> Mayor reparo es el mío—dixo Andrenio—y es cuál sea la causa que los príncipes se pagan más y les pagan también a un excelente pintor, a un escultor insigne, y los honran y premian mucho más que a un historiador eminente, que al más divino poeta, que al más excelente escritor. Pues vemos que los pinceles sólo retratan el exterior, pero las plumas el interior, y va la ventaja de uno a otro que del cuerpo al alma. Exprimen aquéllos cuando mucho el talle, el garbo, la gentileza y tal vez la fiereza; pero éstas el entendimiento, el valor, la virtud, la capacidad y las inmortales hazañas. Aquéllos les pueden dar vida por algún tiempo, mientras duraren las tablas o los lienços, ya sean

bronces; mas estas otras por todos los venideros siglos, que es inmortalizarlos. Aquéllos los dan a conocer, digo a ver, a los pocos que llegan a mirar sus retratos; mas éstas a los muchos que leen sus escritos, yendo de provincia en provincia, de lengua en lengua, y aun de siglo en siglo (670).[54]

This 'fundamental truth' comes to Andrenio at the climax of his pilgrimage, but also contradicts the spirit of Counter-Reformation Rome altogether. The *Roma Ignaziana* is an architectural construction that favors the 'temporal arts' and Gracián emphasizes here the supremacy of the 'eternal arts.' The Loyolan principles of excessive training in visual decipherment are therefore to be applied to the sphere of literature, according to the author of *El Criticón*. In other words, the purpose of the *Spiritual Exercises*—that is, a conversion method that requires the exercitant to envision his own existence within the greater narrative of Christianity—is radically modified through the supremacy of the eternal arts since they force their exercitant—the reader—to envision Christianity as a mere component of the philosophical evolution of humankind. Christianity becomes an episode in a narrative greater than its own in Gracián's *Criticón*.

Eventually, the greater moment of contemplation in the satire happens on one of Rome's seven hills when the two pilgrims, in the company of the Courtier, are faced with the Wheel of Time: "os convido a ver, no sola Roma, sino todo el mundo de una vez, desde cierto puesto de donde se señorea. Veréis, no solo este siglo, esta nuestra era, sino las venideras" (741).[55] In their experience of Rome, the pilgrims are therefore going to experience a third and last moment of contemplation; after seeing Rome from the exterior, and then from its interior, they will be invited to contemplate the city outside of this interior/exterior dichotomy. This third and deconstructive stage is antithetic to the process of the *Spiritual Exercises*. As I pointed out earlier, Jorge Checa sees in the Wheel of Time a major confrontation with and contradiction of the Catholic notion of linear time: "Past, present and future are displayed in the Wheel of Time synthetically and almost simultaneously, and the Wheel proclaims the circularity of history along with the 'easy and secure' nature of the predictions derived from it" (Spadaccini 170). Again, with the Wheel of Time as supreme object of the pilgrims' contemplation, Gracián emphasizes the eternal and repetitive over the temporal. Circular time confirms the value of envisioning art within an eternal perspective, and therefore confirms the role of literature. The act of contemplating the Wheel confirms the nature of Rome as the most intact urban space after the passing of time. It makes perfect sense that the pilgrims finish their journey with this awesome vision of the Wheel over the eternal city since nowhere else can the pilgrim realize how repetitive time is; Rome has collected the marks of historical events and the observer can juxtapose these different marks and come to the same conclusion: "Lo que sucedió dozientos ha, esso mismo estamos viendo agora" (745).[56]

In summary, *El Criticón* ends with the affirmation that History is just a repetition of itself, but Gracián does not dare to imply that Christianity is therefore another repetition of previous spiritual traditions already existing in Rome. It is strongly suggested in this final part, however, even though never actually articulated. It is no wonder that the Jesuit provincial would demand the total prohibition of Gracián's satire: this work recycles the contemplative act in its most Loyolan dynamics, but literally transforms its core objectives by making the exercitant envision a temporal reality in which he can integrate the 'greater narrative of Christianity.' The conclusion of *El Criticón*, on the contrary, already announces one of the Enlightenment's central debates: History is made of repetitive acts. Rome stands at the center of the world, but no longer in a Loyolan sense, and no longer in order to proclaim the victory of Counter-Reformation Catholicism. Gracián envisions Rome in its atemporal value as an urban space primarily, but through a typically Jesuit act of contemplation. *El Criticón* stands at the crossroads of Loyolan imagination—for the dimensions of its visions and contemplations—and the Sadean Enlightenment that we will analyze in the following chapter—for its extremely repetitive nature and the constant questioning of linear conceptions of time.

The Enigmatic Parallel Writing of *El Comulgatorio*

Interestingly enough, *El Criticón* is not the only manuscript on Gracián's desk in this final stage of his life. It is the only one he publishes under a false name, however, since he does not want to be too closely associated with the idea the satire contained. He decides to divide the story of the two pilgrims into three parts according to the three stages of a man's life, and the third part corresponds to 'old age.' But in the meantime, he works on a quadripartite project for which he wants to be recognized, published under his real name; it is a book of meditations and spiritual exercises for novices and educated parishioners that are about to receive communion. This work, entitled *El Comulgatorio*, is published in 1655, right between the publication of the second and the third parts of *El Criticón*. As mentioned previously, there are great tensions between the author and the Society, and one could think that Gracián needs to reassure his superiors by demonstrating a dedication to the development of Jesuit spirituality. It is true that *El Comulgatorio* corresponds more to his vocation in this sense, but on the other hand, it seems difficult to conceive that the Aragonese would work on a project that would radically contradict the literary orientation of *El Criticón*. As Aurora Egido writes:

> Lo chocante no es que el jesuita escribiera un libro sobre la comunión, sino que lo hiciera al final de toda una vida dedicada a la elaboración de un corpus eminentemente profano y distanciado de las ocupaciones y preocupaciones de la Compañía (xvi). Lejos de esta obra quedaba la corriente escéptica de Gracián hasta *El Criticón*. En *El Comulgatorio*, por contra, no cabe la duda sino la fe ciega. La Eucaristía no implica *crisis* ninguna, sino verdad aceptada (xxxv).[57]

The extremely religious nature of this book of meditations might explain why *El Criticón* is so deprived of Catholic images: Gracián concentrates all of them in this spiritual writing. Furthermore, most of Gracián's literary production goes against the prescription of the Society,[58] and it seems that *El Comulgatorio* is Gracián's last attempt to be an obedient Jesuit. Egido acknowledges in her analysis that these works stand at the two extremes of Gracián's output: literary criticism has obviously devoted its attention to the one work that featured most doubt, crisis, anxiety, and skepticism. How can we reconcile such opposed masterpieces when they truly contradict each other in every possible way?

Indeed, *El Comulgatorio*, this 'Dialectical Other' of *El Criticón*, has a lot to tell us about its counterpart, since it represents the opposite pole of attraction of the menippean satire for the Jesuit writer. It is in fact a very traditional book of mental exercises that involves the extensive use and development of the visual powers through mnemonic practices. It confirms Gracián's controversial relation with the Society of Jesus. The exercitant of the meditations contained in *El Comulgatorio* is not guided by any director since it is a book of meditation originally written for those 'giving the exercises,' that is, potential directors already at a higher level on the road to spiritual enlightenment. The text is divided into four categories of meditations and follows a progression accordingly, reminding any Jesuit reader of the similar repartition in the *Spiritual Exercises*, and their division into four weeks. Some of these 'meditations' are entire exercises based on a complex '*composición de lugar*'. If we take for instance Meditation XLI, called 'Los Pasos de la Pasión' (the Stages/Steps of the Passion), we find a series of extremely graphic 'Loyolan images':

> Imagina cuando comulgas que llegas al huerto y que le enjugas el copioso sudor sangriento con las telas de tu corazón, que te acercas a la columna y le desatas para enlazarle en tus brazos y curarle las heridas, poniendo en cada una un pedazo de tu corazón; haz cuenta que le aprietas en tu seno coronado, aunque te espines, y que le sientas en el trono de tu pecho; que le trasladas de los brazos de la cruz, donde con tanto afán pende, a tus entrañas, donde descanse (174).[59]

A century after the triumph of Loyola, *El Comulgatorio* recycles the images of the *Spiritual Exercises* and increases tremendously their effect on all the senses. The style is more sophisticated than Loyola's and definitely typical of Gracián's works, but the mental inspiration and composition is without a doubt Ignatian.[60] Obviously here, the emphasis is placed on the visualization of a body in corruptible contact with the body of the exercitant. Christ is no longer an object of distant contemplation but a model for virtual sufferings based on an internalization of his dying body in the mind of the believer. Egido stresses that the bloody image we find in such passages is "vinculada además a los *Ejercicios Espirituales* de san Ignacio, que tanto peso tienen en esta y otras obras gracianas, ya que ubican las imágenes recreándolas en el lugar, punto por punto, con todas las potencias y sentidos en el juego" (xxxii).[61] No wonder that this highly metaphorical text co-exists with the story of the two pilgrims: the dynamics of the *Exercises* can be incorporated in this larger fiction, but fiction has very limited power in the genre of meditation books. This is why *El Comulgatorio* stands as a negative print of *El Criticón*: Gracián makes the experiment of contemplation in its two extremes and presents two texts that complement each other in this sense.

With *El Comulgatorio*, however, the 'spiritual exercises' as a literary genre[62] are starting to face a very serious problem: they are popular but are also coming to a point of exhaustion in the extremely graphic quality of their images, as we can see in the previous passage. In this book of meditations, for instance, the incorporation of the "greater narrative of Christianity" is increased: a Protestant point of view could highly criticize Loyola's *Exercises* for the freedom they take in 'directing' the evangelical scenes with images that are not drawn from Scripture but from imagination. Gracián's *Comulgatorio* takes imagination to a new frontier in this sense, since it exaggerates the details in the imaginary construction. The following comparison of passages illustrates this major difference between Loyola's exercises and Gracián's. The structure of the meditation appears as such in the *Exercises*:

> Christ our Lord remained in Jerusalem, and his parents did not know it. After three days, they found him seated among the doctors and conversing with them. When his parents asked him where he had been, he replied: "Did you not know that I must be about my Father's business?" (186)

In Gracián's *Comulgatorio*, the same meditation leaves much less space for imagination:

> Sale la Virgen Madre en busca de su Dios Hijo, tan deseado cuan amado; no le busca como la esposa en el lecho de su descanso (. . .) Entra la Virgen en el templo y descubre en medio de los dotores la sabiduría del Padre; fue su contento desquite de su

> dolor (…) Fue siempre la Virgen Madre tan agradecida cuan graciosa; volvería a entonar a Dios otro cántico nuevo, por haberla vuelto de nuevo su amado Jesús (…) ¡Cómo guardaría su Niño Dios en adelante, nunca perdiéndole de vista, previniendo con agradecimientos los riesgos de volverle a perder! (158–60).[63]

Gracián's female protagonist in *El Comulgatorio* resemble the Greek figures of tragedy, such as Antigone or Phaedra, and they are almost too tragic to be considered worthy of the Jesuit tradition. The Virgin Mary of Gracián's book of meditations seems desperate, barely bearing the anxiety of being physically separated from her son, and the meditation entirely focuses on her. Loyola's Mary, on the other hand, does not show any of her feelings and the focus of the action is on Jesus' strong determination. We know for a fact that *El Comulgatorio* did not turn out to be Gracián's masterpiece. But maybe this is due to the overly tragic nature of his images and the excess of his descriptions. This text is another form of transgression in Gracián's literary production since it does not respect the Loyolan principle of distancing oneself from the exercitant's imagination: "The one giving the Exercises *ought not to lean or incline in either direction* but rather, while standing by like *the pointer of a scale in equilibrium*, to allow the Creator to deal immediately with the creature and the creature with its Creator and Lord" (Loyola 125). In order words, Gracián does not respect the distance and imposes a direction to the imagination of his reader/exercitant.

The 'contradiction' in the simultaneous writing of *El Criticón* and *El Comulgatorio* disappears with the common parameter of excess: whether he writes a satire or tries to provide the Jesuit with a highly ornamented version of the *Spiritual Exercises*, Gracián does not simplify any of his literary constructions. Both works have in common that they project the pilgrim/exercitant in the same object, that is, in *orders of corruption*. Moreover, they complement each other in an interesting way, since *El Criticón* is radically deprived of religious images and yet reproduces the spiritual progression of an exercitant's visual training, and the other takes the religious image to its extreme in order to satisfy the exercitants who would not have exhausted the practice of Loyola's *Spiritual Exercises*. *El Comulgatorio* proves that Gracián makes a clear division in his writing between exercises for the intellect and the act of politics, and exercises for the spirit in search of its divinity. He clearly seeks to separate religion from philosophy, like two opposite standards between which the human pilgrim navigates.

Conclusion

Given the omnipresence of corrupted elements in *El Criticón*, we might find it puzzling that the satire follows a structure in radical opposition to that of the *Spiritual Exercises*, their tradition, and above all, to the rest of Gracián's production, such as *El Comulgatorio*. Krauss, in his analysis, answers this question: "The extremes [in Gracián's texts] are juxtaposed in their breadth: vice and virtue, truth and deception. The hero, who must reach perfection, is not spared the stages of madness and foolishness as touchstones of their work" (Spadaccini 313). This principle applies to *El Criticón* as much as to *El Comulgatorio*, even though the rest of the author's works are maxims, aphorisms, theoretical writings, etc. *El Criticón* stands as an entirely *practical* piece of writing, in which the principle of contact with the orders of corruption (the 'juxtaposed extremes' for Krauss) is applied, and not theorized. Gracián compares the very act of writing it to a practice of the exercises threatened at all time by corruption itself, and therefore recommends to add salt to the text: "Salan mucho los cuerpos de sus obras porque nunca se corrompan" (306).[64] It is a text full of deliberately placed corrupted elements and somehow, according to its author, this corruption comes to threaten the very existence of the text. In *El Comulgatorio*, the meditations are arranged in a specific order so that the exercitant is also forced to follow a planned progression toward the corrupted elements in an excessively tragic re-writing of the Gospels. As a follower of Ignatius and the Jesuits, Gracián has gone beyond the limits of Loyolan imagination. As a follower of Cervantes, Gracián envisions the exercise of writing as an experiment. Both of the works we have been comparing here are recipes-in-progress that Gracián proposes in the contrasted forms of satire and a book of meditations, but neither one stands as a definite report of his most precious spiritual recommendations. This is why these texts turn out to be experimental pieces of literature and have not quite made their way into the literary canon of the Spanish Golden Age. They are usually considered too esoteric, too obscure and too descriptive.

These patterns in Gracián's works reflect Georg Lukacs's line of thought regarding *Don Quixote* in that sense, since their excessive presence also has the potential to suggest that God has abandoned the world. Egido comes to the conclusion that

> Gracián lleva hasta los últimos extremos la unión de Eucaristía y sacrificio, consubstancial al sacramento, convirtiendo la tragedia de la muerte en salvación. *El Criticón* hablará de un tránsito muy distinto, en el que el hombre, *sin más auxilios* que los de la virtud y sus obras, deberá encontrar, *en soledad* y *sin otra ayuda* que la de sus propias fuerzas, el lugar incógnito de las "inmortales puertas" (LXXVI).[65]

As she emphasizes here, the human hero of *El Criticón* is an exercitant on his own whose search is no longer about the divinity, but about his own humanity. In a way, these two works of literature feature exercitants who apply the anagogic communicative level of the *Spiritual Exercises* to their own selves. Don Quixote is always after images of himself and in search of his humanity, and never reaches the goal at which he initially aimed: the director and the exercitant merge in him in order to emphasize his human dimensions and exaggerate them to the point of madness. Andrenio and Critilo symbolically merge into one *persona* that is self-sufficient and no longer needs the complement of the divinity to enter the realm of immortality. *El Criticón* exaggerates the corrupted nature of both reality and humanity, saturates the literary space with *memento mori* images, entertains a certain paranoia about the dynamics of Spanish politics, but ultimately does so in order to educate the eye. This education of the eye turns out to be the human's first weapon in a world abandoned by its God—although it is never verbalized as such in the text–, and this methodology derives precisely from the most Jesuit of all techniques: the spiritual exercise, that is, the exercise that trains the human eye to be divine. Ultimately, as in the *Spiritual Exercises*, the eye will stand in the position of the divinity and occupy the highest point in the order's vertical scale. Let us remember than Loyola expected his exercitant to arrive at this moment of contemplation during the second week and to occupy the divine throne. Observe, for instance, this mechanism of progressive substitution at work in the following passage:

> I will see and consider the Three Divine Persons, seated, so to speak, on the royal throne of their Divine Majesty. They are gazing on the whole face and circuit of the earth; and they see all the peoples in such great blindness, and how they are dying and going down to hell. There I will reflect on this to draw some profit from what I see. I will see what the persons on the face of the earth are saying (...) I will consider what the people on the face of the earth are doing (149).

Cervantes and Gracián pursue this effort and transform the original purpose of the spiritual exercise: its object in the rising novel is therefore no longer the divinity but humanity, in order to transform the exercitant (the reader) into a "prophet of his own existence," according to Ricoeur's expression. The human being occupies the position of the divinity and arrives at it *without any help*. This is why the transformation of visual dynamics operated in their texts is partially responsible for the Enlightenment. The purpose of the successful spiritual exercise is transformed in their works of literature to bring about the Modern subject with its no-less modern gaze.

Vernon Minor writes about contemporaries of Cervantes and Gracián that "whether consciously or not, many baroque painters created rhetorical structures that represent Ignatian mental images" (*Baroque*, 47). The same conclusion could be drawn about the two Spanish writers of prose we have been analyzing at the rise of Modern fiction. It would be hard to determine whether we are dealing with an absolutely conscious move, but it remains a transformation in which the subject evolves toward an anagogic communication with his/her own self through the projection of the same kind of images. After Gracián, the literary production of Spain enters a crisis of creativity that it will not overcome very easily. For two centuries after Gracián, literature is still very limited and controlled by the Inquisition. Nonetheless, the transformations I have analyzed in this chapter have a direct influence on other Western European literatures. The works of Gracián are translated into French very rapidly and widely read in the second half of the seventeenth century, when France enters the age of Absolutism and seeks some wisdom in the works of the Spanish Jesuit. Both Cervantes and Gracián become extremely well-known figures in literary circles and models to imitate for mid-seventeenth-century French writers. Alexandre Cioranescu, who has left us the greatest research on this transition from the Spanish Baroque to French Classicism, sees in these two authors—along with others not discussed here—the precursors of the Enlightenment that will take place in France during the following century. Cioranescu comes to the following conclusions:

> Presque toute la production littéraire qui dépend d'une façon ou d'une autre des modes espagnoles, se caractérise par une préoccupation fondamentale, plus ou moins transparente, plus ou moins expliquée: la conscience d'un monde trompeur, des fausses apparences dont nous sommes les victimes, de l'*engaño*, ou faculté de tromper, du monde réel et de notre imagination, avec, comme contre-partie, la conscience du *desengaño*, fruit de l'expérience qui représente la vie (235). Sur ce point tout le monde est d'accord, le roman est un produit espagnol (391).

Consciously or not, the vertical orders of corruption are a part of the literary dynamics that we find in the rise of the new genre. Spanish or not, the seventeenth-century novel will keep on transforming the search for the missing sign initiated in the *Spiritual Exercises*.

CHAPTER VI

From Loyolan Imagination to Sadean Enlightenment

Parodistic Inversions of the *Spiritual Exercises* in the Novels of the Marquis de Sade

> *O! Dieux, faut-il qu'un chétif hypocondre comme vous soit la condamnation de toute la Société, et que vous fassiez éclipser mille Soleils en votre Compagnie par la seule interposition de votre épaisse révérence, et que saint Ignace, depuis un siècle qu'il est au Ciel, boite encore en vous tous les jours . . .*
>
> Cyrano de Bergerac, « Lettre à un jés . . . » (1651)

Philosophical Criticism of the Loyolan System in Early Enlightenment France, from Descartes to Voltaire

In the preceding chapter, we established that Baltasar Gracián was a pre-Enlightenment figure, and that the transformative nature of his works in terms of the visual dynamics of the *Spiritual Exercises* contributed to the rise of the Modern conception of literature. With the rise of philosophy, this transformation will lead literary figures educated in this tradition to negate their principles. In the same century and the following, this operation will continue in France, where the Jesuits have the monopoly of the most renowned schools. These Jesuit institutions are going to be initiation points for many significant Enlightenment philosophers who will rebel against the Society of Jesus, following in Gracián's footsteps. Their exposure to and understanding of the Loyolan *orders of corruption* will lead them to criticize them in many ways, including parody them. This critical reproduction of the *Spiritual Exercises* will develop in the works of Descartes, Voltaire, and Diderot—all educated by the Jesuits—but will culminate in the works of the marquis de Sade during the French Revolution. This is the tension I propose to analyze in this final chapter. But in order to comprehend the parody and the negation of Loyola's text in the novels of Sade, it is necessary to envision and replace these novels in a clear perspective. They can be seen as the confluence of various influences. Many of Sade's sources of inspiration have a strong connection to the Jesuit educational system, just as he did as an ex-student of the famous Jesuit lycée Louis-le-Grand.

Most educational systems have their rebellious students. Moreover, such students often reveal the limitations of the systems involved. Education comes with a philosophy and the fixed set of principles on which that philosophy is based, and as a result, can never please everyone. Sometimes its orientation will lead students in a direction that will eventually contradict the original intentions behind the system. In the seventeenth and eighteenth centuries, the schools of the Society of Jesus flourish all over France, Italy, and Spain and benefit from great political support from absolutist monarchs and the Holy See. They become the most renowned centers of intellectual activity, always located at the heart of the urban fabric. In Paris, for example, the Jesuits take over the control of the Sorbonne and found the Lycée Louis-le-Grand right across the street, in order to prepare the most distinguished students. Nevertheless, in the case of these Jesuit schools, we can count an admirable generation of rebels against their teachers.

From its beginnings, the Society of Jesus, founded by Loyola in the tradition of his *Spiritual Exercises*, based its educational principles on the *ratio studiorum*, an academic design that combines visual and interdisciplinary approaches to the study of the arts and sciences. In the early modern period, this system will train an impressive range of intellectual figures, all significant in the parallel rises of modernity, aesthetics and the novel: among them, Miguel de Cervantes, Baltasar Gracián, René Descartes, the Abbé Prévost, Crébillon fils, Diderot, Voltaire, and the marquis de Sade. In this list, we can already identify a pattern of increasing criticism of the system, often based in claims of intellectual freedom. These writers all distance themselves from the principles they receive in their education, and generally do so by transforming, parodying or competing with it. In this sense, the Society produces the intellectual figures who will work for its destruction in the Enlightenment. But interestingly enough, the Jesuits acknowledge a certain continuity between their system of education and the project of the philosophers who condemn them. The Abbé de Caveirac, one of the last Jesuit professors at Louis-le-Grand prior to the Society's expulsion from France in 1762, writes in his *Appel à la Raison* that, despite their hostility to Jesuit teachings, the *Lumières* are a product of the Jesuit system:

> Si ce siècle irréligieux et corrompu pouvait être sensible aux biens spirituels, nous ajouterions que les jésuites, obligés par leur état de vivre au milieu du monde, n'en font pas le scandale, que ceux même qui sortent de la Société par dégoût, ou qu'elle rejette par sagesse, font encore plus d'honneur à l'humanité qu'une infinité d'autres citoyens qui n'ont pas reçu cette éducation. Nous n'appellerons pas ici en témoins ces hommes illustres par leurs emplois et par leurs talents, on les regardera avec raison comme des phénomènes ; nous nous bornerons donc à demander que l'on jette les yeux sur cette multitude d'ex-Jésuites répandus dans le Royaume (14).

Caveirac takes pride in pointing to the figures of the Enlightenment who have become the worst enemies of their old masters, those who have left the Society to carry on a different project. There is irony in his tone, of course, and a suggestion that no one ever completely separates from the system, that Jesuit education is implanted in one's soul for all eternity. Nor did these arguments save the Company. But was Caveirac right to claim that Jesuitism could survive its own destruction, and if so, in what capacity?

Thirty years later, the marquis de Sade continues to entertain a certain fascination with the vanished Society in his novels. I propose to analyze here this dimension of Sade's work. The 'teachers' in his novels (such as Dolmancé in *La Philosophie*, Juliette or the four masters of Schilling in the *Cent Vingt Journées*) perpetuate the practices of Jesuit education through a systematic inversion of its principles. Loyola's *Spiritual Exercises* are transformed in such a way to emphasize that the mechanisms remain the same. But, of course, the theological content is replaced by a rather radical late Enlightenment philosophy. In order to elucidate this dimension of Sade's works, I would like to devote the first part of this analysis to a brief history of the 'ex-Jesuits' who prepare the way for Sade, and particularly concentrate on the apparently paradoxical connections made in French literature between the Jesuits and the Libertines. Then, in a second part, I would like to focus more in detail on the role of systematic parody in Sade's novels

As we have seen, Ignatius of Loyola formulates in the middle of the sixteenth century a method for recuperating the Roman essence of Christianity through the diffusion of the *Spiritual Exercises*. This text will become the founding doctrine of the Jesuits, and will serve as a pillar for Counter-Reformation thought in a time of epistemological crisis. In sixteenth-century France, precisely where the Spaniard Loyola founded the Society of Jesus, the experience of religious wars seems to have generated a certain questioning of religion as a whole. After all, it is the country where the satirical writer Rabelais formulated the notion of 'atheism' for the first time in the history of language.[1] In the late sixteenth century and early seventeenth century, unbelief appears to be an alternative to Christianity and other forms of religion. The enthusiasm for scientific discoveries also contributes in creating a climate for spiritual renewal. At the end of the Renaissance, the epistemological configuration in Europe has progressively turned into the chaotic amalgam of cosmological confusions identified by Michel Foucault:

> Il nous semble que les connaissances du XVIè siècle étaient constituées d'un *mélange instable de savoir rationnel*, de notions dérivées des pratiques de la magie, et de tout un héritage culturel dont la redécouverte des textes anciens avait multiplié les pouvoirs d'autorité. Ainsi conçue, la science de cette époque apparaît dotée d'une structure faible ; elle ne serait que *le lieu libéral d'un affrontement* entre la fidélité des Anciens, le goût pour le merveilleux, et une attention déjà éveillée sur cette souveraine rationalité en laquelle nous nous reconnaissons (. . .) Le monde est couvert de signes qu'il faut déchiffrer, et ces signes, qui révèlent des ressemblances et des affinités, ne sont eux-mêmes que des formes de la similitude (47).

As a matter of fact, religious factions, independent philosophers, and even novelists, such as Cervantes and Gracián in Spain, all coming out of the humanist experience, propose their own projects to remedy this epistemological instability. Two particular and apparently 'opposite positions' are going to rise from the 'liberal space of confrontation' cited by Foucault, and are going to be the subjects of our analysis here: the Jesuits and the libertines.

On the one hand, in the seventeenth century, the Society of Jesus becomes a powerful branch of the counter-reformed Catholic Church and an influential source of counsel for the political powers of southwestern Europe. On the other hand, the desire for freedom from religion and the demand for unconditional spiritual liberty in thought give birth to *libertinage* among French intellectuals in the first half of this same century. What seems to be at first a simple rejection of the notion of God, or a simple recognition that what religion has named God is no longer present in the world, develops into a philosophy, a lifestyle, a project for humanity that is going to influence the arts and society until the French Revolution. The period of Jesuit influence in Southwestern Europe parallels that of the libertines. Both spiritual movements originate in the same epistemological crisis and come to an end at the turn of the nineteenth century, when the *episteme* once again undergoes a complete restructuring.

Jesuits and libertines have in common an interest in the origins of humanity, in the human potential in imagination, in the corrupted nature of creation, and in the desires of the individual. Nonetheless this interest is more problematic for the Jesuits since it forces them to step outside of the boundaries of religion. Therefore, the Jesuit transgression will progressively become a figure in libertine fiction since it serves as an example of the contradictions with Christianity as a belief system. In France, however, though supposedly radically opposed to the Jesuit project of reconstructing the Catholic Church, the rise of *libertinage* shares the Jesuit effort to provide a sensualist answer to post-humanist cosmological confusion and the need to reform the belief systems of Western European societies. It offers an alternative to the spiritual crisis that France enters at the end of the Renaissance. As Raymond Trousson explains "utilisé d'abord par les protestants, le mot [*libertinage*] figure ensuite, dans la seconde moitié du siècle, chez les catholiques, qui dénoncent eux aussi l'interdépendance entre libération de l'esprit et dépravation des moeurs" (III). But *libertinage* is a complex philosophical set of beliefs that manifests itself in various generations and streams that should not be conflated or confused; the first generation of libertines, usually aristocrats and intellectuals, arrives under the reign of Louis XIII, during the first half of his reign, and is then reduced to silence by the *retour à l'ordre moral* of Cardinal Mazarin. The first half of the reign of Louis XIV also celebrates the senses and pleasure, but as the king gets older, his aristocratic entourage seems to go in the direction of devotion and to abandon its libertine ideals (Mittérand 123). The third generation is the one that adopts a libertine lifestyle, philosophy, and artistic values by the middle of the eighteenth-century during the Enlightenment. This generation has a much more mature philosophical tradition divided into *libertins de moeurs* and *libertins d'érudition*, two groups that we need to define and separate when the movement first begins.

Libertinage in the seventeenth century finds its origin in a lack of faith as much as in the need for new faith. It tends to define all kinds of deviations from Catholicism; it progressively becomes the French equivalent of philosophical heresy. Henri Mittérand sums up this phenomenon in the following manner: "A cela plusieurs raisons: les croyances religieuses sont sorties amoindries des conflits du siècle précédent; le dégoût a parfois engendré l'indifférence; les philosophies païennes, remises à l'honneur par les humanistes, ont concurrencé la vision chrétienne du monde" (123). Libertinage is a reaction against the inflexibility of Church dogma in an age of modernization. It is obvious by 1620 that the hope of reform for the whole of Christianity formulated by the humanists no longer makes sense in a world in which this traditional belief system has divided into different branches in opposition to each other. The aftermath of the Counter-Reformation is clear:

more political power has been given to the Roman institution in France, in Spain, and in Italy, whereas intellectuals hoped for its reduction. The Church of Rome has not reformed its hierarchy or reduced influence on politics, but has reinforced it, partially with the help of the Society of Jesus. As Barthes would put it, the Counter-Reformation has turned into a conquest of the believer's mental territory, but intellectuals demand more freedom and less censorship.

Reviving and promoting pagan philosophies derived from the Greek and Roman mythological traditions, some libertines inspire aristocrats, intellectuals and artists they associate with to look at Christianity as an essentially constrictive form of spirituality. They see in ancient philosophies a greater liberty of action, enhanced sensual experience, and a new orientation toward pleasure in literature and the arts. For them, the Greek and Roman societies of antiquity are a model of both spirituality and sexuality. Libertines of this sort are often called the *libertins de moeurs*, for they are concerned with the limitations that society and religion have imposed on their actions. Libertinage, however, has a second dimension in this first generation, distinguished as that of the *libertins érudits*. It is more difficult to identify in this group any credo or dogma corresponding to a specific belief system, since this is precisely what they are trying to avoid. Most of them, however, are Christians, and some are current or former member of the clergy.[2] This rather philosophical movement encourages the free circulation of thought and a taste for independent reflection. This second variety of libertinage evolves in the space between—and formed by—several parameters such as the critical rationalism of Descartes, the both moral and scientific epicurism of Gassendi, and other streams of 'Rationalist Catholicism' and materialist atheism (Mittérand 123).

Although Descartes was never considered a libertine, we cannot ignore the fact that his *Discourse on the Method* is central to the epistemological debates from which libertinage arises, and greatly influences a whole generation of libertine thinkers at the turn of the eighteenth century. Descartes warns his readers that the single design to strip one's self of all past beliefs is one that ought not to be taken by everyone. In that sense, Descartes stands in the middle of the contest between Jesuits and libertines: there may be a need for spiritual reformation but its methods have to be carefully applied. All the streams of 'libertine' philosophy have on their common agenda a severe critique of Christianity as a belief system. Their arguments will be followed up later on by British thinkers such as Hobbes in his *Leviathan* (1660), and the sensualist John Locke, both of whom urge a revision of Christian historical proofs.

This post-humanist approach to reforming religion through philosophy requires all of them to turn to the very origins of Christianity, and at the same time to the roots of the Western tradition and those of humanity. In France, Gassendi is one of the dominant figures of this vague group, since he comes up with an 'unbelief system' based on Epicurus, at the same time attacking the Cartesian method and the metaphysical meditations derived from them. According to Gassendi, his contemporaries should change their perspectives on the origins of belief systems. Gassendi addresses and attacks Descartes directly regarding the concept of God as an immanent feeling of humankind since the beginning of time in his *Recherche Métaphysiques ou doutes et instances contre la métaphysique de René Descartes et ses réponses* (1642):

> Il suffit d'avoir effleuré ce sujet, qui d'ailleurs est bien connu, pour que vous puissiez voir comment les premiers hommes ont pu se faire quelque idée de Dieu, même s'ils en avaient pas, comme vous prétendez, une idée innée. Ce qui fait que qu'il est inutile de vous demander *pourquoi, s'ils ont pu avoir cette idée d'eux-mêmes, nous ne pourrions pas l'avoir, nous aussi, de nous-mêmes*, puisque vous voyez bien que l'on peut vous répondre que ni ils ne l'ont eue d'eux-mêmes, ni nous ne l'avons non plus de nous-mêmes (Mittérand 125).

Indeed the 'first men' are at the heart of a debate engaged by the libertines that will be continued in the next century. In the discussion that takes place between Descartes and Gassendi, one can observe that proving the existence of God follows the same principles as proving the contrary: Gassendi systematically returns the argument against his opponent.[3] However, this discussion serves as a great example of how the *libertinage d'érudition* in seventeenth-century France constantly generates debates and conversations, but does not find much common ground for the establishment of a single system of un-belief. Within libertinage and its associated streams of thought, including Descartes' rationalism, everything is a matter for contradiction. Even the *Méditations Métaphysiques* (1641), the text at the origin of Gassendi's attacks, opens up with the following statement: "je m'appliquerai sérieusement et *avec liberté* à détruire généralement toutes mes anciennes opinions" (Descartes 27). It is a complex project, however, to envision what these 'old opinions' could represent for this author, since Descartes has been educated in the Ignatian pedagogic system.

It is at the competitive Jesuit college of La Flèche that René Descartes starts studying philosophy and mathematics.[4] Like Gracián, Descartes seeks to reconcile the various disciplines to which he had been exposed by his teachers in order to rise above the dominion of theology and to present a method in which mathematical thought gives structure to the existence of God and man. The Jesuit fathers recognize his genius very early and encourage him to continue his investigations.

He will inherit from them a mathematical dedication to the exploration of reality. We find in the *Méditations*, indeed, a method apparently based on the tradition of devotional meditations that requires solitude and isolation. This is Descartes' own reply to those who accused him of atheism after the publication of his *Discours de la Méthode* in 1637. Nonetheless, Descartes makes a clear distinction between imagination and thought in order to reach the pure nature of thought:

> Je feindrais en effet si je m'imaginais être quelque chose, puisque imaginer n'est rien autre chose que contempler la figure ou l'image d'une chose corporelle; or je sais déjà que je suis, et que tout ensemble il se peut faire que toutes ces images, et généralement toutes les choses se rapportant à la nature du corps, ne soient que des songes ou des chimères (37).

Descartes warns his reader against this negative capacity of imagination because it is often an obstacle in the process he describes. His perspective on imagination is therefore conceptually opposed to that underlying the Ignatian exercises; it needs to be controlled and mastered, not used in order to guide sensual experience. In other words, the Cartesian method would consist in reuniting in one person the roles of the spiritual director and those of the exercitant. Also, Descartes applies the concept of 'spiritual exercise' to geometry more than any other discipline.[5] However, the method, the form that this orientation of thought takes in Descartes's writings, has a lot in common with the Jesuit tactical approach to the conversion experience. Arthur Thomson writes that:

> La dette de Descartes à la tradition des Jésuites est plus manifeste dans le domaine de la méthode et de la psychologie que dans celui de la morale et de la religion ... [I]l a appris de ses maîtres jésuites non seulement certains principes de discipline mentale, mais aussi une psychologie de la pensée et de la volonté en accord avec ces principes (80–81).

Bradley Rubidge, in his commentary on Thomson, adds: "Descartes and Loyola both mention the value of personal experience, the need for application, the usefulness of retirement, the importance of following a clear order, and the advantage of adapting a method to the individual using it" (36). Even though it would be a bit speculative to see in the *Meditations* an adaptation of the *Exercises* to the Age of Reason, we should acknowledge the fact that Descartes is the first thinker at the beginning of the seventeenth century to offer a comprehensive approach to human existence that encompasses, on the one hand, the Jesuit recognition of imagination as a spiritual force and, on the other hand, the libertine intention to reformulate the idea of God outside the boundaries of Christian theology.[6]

At this point, we could consider Libertinage, rationalism, and Jesuit devotion to be part of the same ontological crisis. They are, in a sense, three branches of the same tree whose roots are humanist ideals. In France these three systems communicate through their oppositions. The emphasis they place on sensual experience already creates a dialogue that will become one of the central debates of the Enlightenment. They are all at the origins of what Foucault has identified as the 'episteme of Classicism' in *Les mots et les choses*. Following this theoretical division, Richard Mazzara indicates that "the direction of Descartes' rationalism and psychology was in complete harmony with the Christian Stoicism then advocated by the Jesuits" (619). They often share common concerns in spite of their philosophical differences. If the Jesuit response to the post-Humanist crisis offers this peculiarity in comparison with other Catholic orders, it is because their activity is based on direct immersion in the various *orders of corruption* of the world and on their greater interest in the origins of men.

But Descartes' *Discourse* and his *Principes* (1647) present very contradictory arguments. First of all, the Cartesian method would consist in reuniting in one person the roles of spiritual director and student in order to protect humanity from the abuses of a system such as the *Exercises*. If he had had absolute faith in the Jesuit system, he would not have tried to invent a new method. When he composes his method, he still hopes that the educational system will open up a greater space for philosophy in its curriculum. But he under-estimated the force of tradition. We find in his later work, the *Principes*, a bitter and disappointed philosopher who underlines the obstacles presented by traditional educational systems based on scholastic philosophy. His superior weapon is, like Gracián, his own philosophy. He looks at his old teachers with new eyes and writes. But we can already see in the *Discours* the premises of this criticism:

> Ils me semblent pareils à un aveugle, qui, pour se battre sans désavantage contre un qui voit, l'aurait fait venir dans le fond de quelque cave fort obscure; et je puis dire que ceux-ci ont intérêt que je m'abstienne de publier les principes de la philosophie dont je me sers : car étant très simples et très évidents, comme ils sont, je ferais quasi de même, en les publiant que si j'ouvrais quelques fenêtres, et faisais entrer du jour dans cette cave, où ils sont descendus pour se battre (14).

Even though this attack appears in a text that draws on Plato, the tone and the present tense underline that Descartes is pointing to his religious men. He targets religious orders in charge of philosophical education such as the Dominicans and the Jesuits ("ceux-ci ont intérêt" would not apply to philosophers who passed away millennia before). Only someone who is extremely familiar with a contemporary enemy can speak in such a manner. He uses here the image of the cave to describe a philosophical experience he knows very well. But this experience could be applied to the education he received in the same fashion. He suggests that he has the tool to deconstruct the principles on which this system is based. The practice of the *Exercises* sometimes involved the retreat into dark caves, where students were blinded and, as a result, were not able to see or understand the limits of the space in which they were placed. It also involved a control of the exercitant's mind that does not please philosophers like Descartes; for instance, Loyola writes that "it is very advantageous for the director to be faithfully informed about the various agitations and thoughts which the different spirits stir up in the retreatant" (126). Here Descartes clearly attacks this form of obscurantism used for the noble cause of meditation and its abuses. He seeks to prove that he has transformed the method in order to enlighten the subject, instead of cultivating false visions on mental territories, without the constant control of a spiritual director. As an excellent student of the Jesuits, he has mastered his enemy.[7]

Nevertheless, Descartes' threatening arguments are glancing and indirect in comparison with Blaise Pascal's overt critiques. With the rise of Jansenism, a reformed branch of French Catholicism founded on the principles of Cornelius Jansenius (1585–1638) and based at the Abbaye de Port-Royal to the south of Paris, the Jesuits begin to have more aggressive enemies than the Libertines. According to Blaise Pascal, a follower of Jansenius, Jesuits have crossed too many boundaries: "Pascal associates libertines and Jesuits in the *Pensées* and the *Provinciales*. For him, they have a similar project: the corruption of morals through texts, language generally, and flawed reasoning" (Houle 43). In the *Lettres Provinciales* (1656), he challenges the Jesuit notions of *pouvoir prochain*,[8] divine grace, and casuistry. The conception of grace is central to the violent debate that will take place between Jesuits and Jansenists in the Classical era. Port-Royal believes in the *grâce efficace*, whereas their opponents defend the concept of *grâce suffisante*. The difference between these two conceptions is tremendous, since the Jesuits envision a divine grace granted to everyone that is then submitted to the free will of the individual. The Jansenists, on the contrary, envision a divine grace restricted to a few chosen believers; they are theologically closer to the Calvinist economy of faith. Pascal's letters set out to deconstruct the already traditional opposition between Jesuits and libertines and have these two belief systems stand as a common enemy in opposition to his own. The question of grace becomes so crucial for the making of belief systems in the Classical era that Jansenists like Pascal often consider sufficient grace and casuistry as philosophically closer to the libertine *dérèglement*. In the seventh letter of this collection, Pascal reports the words of a Jesuit father who justifies his belief in the adaptation of ministry to the particular cases:

> Et il me parla des maximes de ses casuistes touchant les gentilshommes, à peu près en ces termes: « Vous savez, me dit-il, que la passion dominante des personnes de cette condition est ce point d'honneur qui les engage à toute heure à des violences qui paraissent bien contraire à la piété chrétienne ; de sorte qu'il faudrait les exclure presque tous de nos confessionnaux, si nos Pères n'eussent un peu relâché de la sévérité de la religion pour s'accommoder à la faiblesse des hommes. Mais comme ils voulaient demeurer attachés à l'Evangile par leur devoir envers Dieu, et aux gens du monde par leur charité pour le prochain, ils ont eu besoin de toute leur lumière pour trouver des expédients qui tempérassent les choses avec tant de justesse, qu'on pût maintenir et réparer son honneur par les moyens dont on se sert ordinairement dans le monde, sans blesser néanmoins sa conscience » (Mittérand 142).

Again, Pascal paraphrases the Jesuit father in order to criticize the Jesuit pretension to fight a religious battle in the world, and their flexibility in response to corruption. We can see clearly in this passage how Pascal insinuates that this pretension is contrary to the very essence of Christianity, for it makes its challenges easier and more accessible to the multitude. Conscience is not pushed beyond its limits in this case, and casuistry becomes "une de leurs plus pernicieuses maximes, et des plus propres à entretenir les vicieux dans leurs mauvaises habitudes" according to Pascal (144–145).

The *Lettres Provinciales* are also a direct attack against the theological treatises of Spanish Jesuits Molina, Escobar, Granados, and Hurtado de Mendoza, who have all formulated a justification for their practices and diffused Loyolan imagination in France. It is rather the abuses of this generation of the Society, and not so much the original features of the Ignatian devotional system, that Pascal seeks to denounce. In this respect, Pascal makes a clear distinction between Ignatian devotion and Loyolan imagination, that is, the system that derived from the *Spiritual Exercises*, enhanced by the politics of Counter-Reformation Rome. The idea that their belief system entertains and maintains vices in the human being is central to the argument of the largest letters of the collection. It will certainly not benefit the credibility of the Jesuits in France. As a Jansenist, Pascal does not have the divided loyalties of a former student of the Jesuits, and illustrates the point of view of Jansenist thought in regard to Loyolan imagination and Jesuit education. For Pascal, the Jesuits and the Libertines have in common a certain inclination for transgressing the limits of their role in the world. On the one hand, from a Jansenist point of view, Pascal understands that each human being is restricted to a limited role. On the other hand, the Jesuit doctrine teaches that, according to the Loyolan system, the 'soldier of Christ' should mediate between 1) formal and theological dicta and 2) the more chaotic data and necessities of everyday life: the nature of the *orders of corruption* invites him to transgress his social boundaries. As we will see later on in this chapter, this peculiar feature of the Company often appears to non-Jesuit Christianity as a transgression of the institutional boundaries.

Also, the Jesuit system encourages the adaptation of a Christian economy of salvation to the particular case of the sinner: this doctrine, called casuistry, is what distinguishes Jesuits from other branches of the Catholic Church. For Pascal, this tailored application of Christian principles is a form of libertinage. Martha Houle points out that: "Both casuistry and libertinage represent a tactical approach to life events and situations by no means random or unreasoned" (43). According to this doctrine, the belief system should offer more flexibility and freedom to deal with the particular sins of an individual. Libertinage in the seventeenth century is also interested in exploring the singularities of the various forms of desire immanent to the human being. We have already established how the Jesuits are an exceptional Catholic order, since they have created their own belief system.

Blaise Pascal is also aware that this system is based on a misleading use of imagination; according to Pascal, "imagination is the power that defines humanity collectively as well as individually; imagination takes its significance not only from individual uses or misuses of imagination but from the imaginative foundations of political and social institutions" (Lyons 99). Pascal understands the Jesuit system within this parameter: they require all of their members, through the *Spiritual Exercises*, to use their imagination in order to simulate sensual experiences, and by the same token, configure them to become the very foundations of such a system. In the meantime, they also require a greater knowledge of the world, including a participation in scientific investigation and debates. Consequently, the Jesuit intellect is pushed to explore new territories. Jesuits do not limit themselves to contemplation and ministry, but to evangelization in remote places, integration of foreign traditions (including religious ones), and building an educational system based on a constant questioning of individual actions. Their project often appears to be a bit too ambitious for a religious order, and certainly more political than religious. Their enthusiasm for reform within the Church has often separated them from the rest of its members, and has even created tensions with other religious orders.

For their Jansenist and Libertine opponents, there seems to be no boundary to the intellect of the followers of Ignatius. In the case of the Jesuits, one also has to consider another parameter of their action, that is, their perspective on literary texts. They seek contact with the *order of corruption in-the-making* that literature represents. As a potential territory for discursive tension, they envision literature as another order of corruption; literature, like the rest of the arts, is another space of confrontation in which the Jesuits need to intervene.⁹ This is due to the generally narrative conception they have of human existence and salvation:

> The Jesuit crosses the boundary between priesthood and laity, between religion and the world. By learning men's corruption the Jesuit has himself become corrupt ("il faut bien que nous allions à eux"). And most crucially, by textually representing the world in the vernacular, the Jesuit has brought the world into existence—that is, into narrative and public space—and, with it, himself as a recognizable character type (Houle 48).

The *Lettres Provinciales* denounce this transgressiveness on the part of the Jesuit system, and only inaugurate a wave of similar criticism. Pascal's followers in this respect will be Molière, Racine, Voltaire, Diderot, and Sade. They will all criticize—with contrasting arguments—the figure of the Jesuit in their fiction.

Accordingly, the figure of the Spanish Jesuit quickly becomes a symbol of sexual indulgence in literature and the arts. Such an ambiguous figure becomes very intriguing in a Classical era in which *faux-dévots* turn out to be *faux-libertins*, as in Molière's *Tartuffe*. Alexandre Cioranescu explains this downfall of an originally respected social character:

> L'idée de morale relâchée et d'indulgence coupable resta accolée insidieusement à l'image du jésuite espagnol. Le Père Escobar, ecclésiastique modeste et pratiquement inconnu dans son propre pays, atteignit en France une popularité dont il se serait certainement dispensé. On connaît la ballade de La Fontaine dont le refrain affirme que pour tous les désirs inopportuns et pour toutes les envies illégitimes « Escobar fait un chemin de velours » (210).

Pascal's *Lettres Provinciales* are largely responsible for this reversal in public opinion. Ironically, Spaniards in general—and not only Jesuits—become suspect of loose morals in the French arts of the Classical era, and have a reputation for flexible morality and irresistible seduction.¹⁰ There is a thin line between moral condemnation and subjective eroticization, since fiction often features the type of character that society would condemn in a given situation. In the *roman galant*, for example, the Spanish male character is always emotionally stronger than the French women he tries to conquer, and is consequently physically stronger than his French male rivals, given the power of his exoticism (Cioranescu 468). 'Spanish' becomes a synonym for 'transgression' and 'passion' in French fiction around the turn of the eighteenth century.¹¹ Jesuit casuistry and the related defense of flexibility regarding morality and the sinful nature of human beings are involved in this process.

This would partially explain why the Jesuit system based on Loyolan imagination contributed to the education of the most radical writers of eighteenth-century libertine novels. After Descartes, the philosophers of the Enlightenment will add to Cartesian method a great many satirical representations of the Jesuit system in their fiction. At the turn of the eighteenth century, many students of Louis-le-Grand seem to join quite rapidly the side of the Enemy. Within a few weeks after his graduation, Voltaire, for instance, joins Parisian libertine circles. Two other figures will make the exact same and rapid transfer: the Abbé Prévost and Crébillon fils. At the time, David Hume's sensualist theories were just arriving from England and Voltaire considered the great potential of British philosophy for promoting social change; the importance placed on the senses in the Jesuit tradition paradoxically echoed the sensualist doctrine that moral and metaphysical ideas derive from the senses. Voltaire was familiar with Jesuit theology but perceived it as a façade of hypocrisy. Unlike Gracián and Descartes, he did not have the intention of justifying the precepts of his education within the project of the Enlightenment. On the contrary, the system was to be attacked and destroyed completely. Interestingly enough, his library contained a notable amount of Gracián and Voltaire mentions the seventeenth-century author with evident admiration.[12] As a reader of Gracián, he seeks to offer a criticism that the Spanish author was never able to articulate a century earlier.

Candide perfectly assumes the position of Gracián's Andrenio, since he leaves his earthly Paradise of Westphalia to explore the world but this time in the company of a pathetic mentor and spiritual director, Dr. Pangloss. Through the story of Candide, Voltaire emphasizes the contradictions in his educators and attacks them in every possible way. In this philosophical tale published in 1759, we return to a much more sarcastic representation of the 'Libertine Spanish Jesuit' (three transgressions in one), since, this time, the philosophical tale takes us to the Jesuit missions of South America. By the middle of the eighteenth century, the Jesuit educational system has spread tremendously; Voltaire himself is an alumnus of the Lycée Louis-le-Grand, Paris's most prestigious Jesuit institution in the eighteenth century. He is familiar with Jesuit theology and has read most of its criticism. Candide will be an innocent voice through which Voltaire can attack his old masters. Before embarking for the New World, Candide meets his master Pangloss by coincidence in Portugal where he has recently arrived, as he is continuously escaping from one country to the next, in search of the ideal system. Candide can barely recognize his old master since his face has been deformed by syphilis. The master then starts telling the innocent Candide how he contracted the disease:

O mon cher Candide! Vous avez connu Paquette, cette jolie suivante de notre auguste baronne; j'ai goûté dans ses bras les délices du Paradis, qui ont produit ses tourments d'enfer dont vous me voyez dévoré ; elle en était infectée, elle en est peut-être morte. Paquette tenait ce présent d'un cordelier très savant qui avait remonté à la source, car il l'avait eur d'une vieille comtesse, qui l'avait reçu d'un capitaine de chevalerie, qui le devait à une marquise, qui le tenait d'un page, qui l'avait reçu d'un jésuite qui, étant novice, l'avait eu en droite ligne d'un des compagnons de Christophe Colomb (16).

Pangloss has been since the beginning of the tale a parody of the mentor, and emphasizes here the ridicule of nobility through this genealogy of the disease. He takes pride in this extreme contact with physical corruption, and his privileged position between Heaven and Hell. Sexual transgression is indeed present in each of these relations of contagion, in spite of the ironically sacred genealogy underlined here by Pangloss. Nonetheless, the Jesuit's contribution to this transmission is distinct from the other modes since it is through two homosexual relations that he passes it on. Moreover, for this Jesuit to have received it from a companion of Colombus' would have meant that he had to be a contemporary of Loyola, one of the very first Jesuits who founded the Society, probably a Spaniard. Voltaire implies here that these religious men have been masked libertines since the very foundation of the order in the sixteenth century. The philosopher makes in *Candide* several connections of this kind between the Jesuit lifestyle and sexual pleasure. He bases his argument on rumors that Loyola himself had contracted syphilis before his conversion and that the anxiety of the disease had motivated him to write the *Spiritual Exercises*, and even that the text had been written under the influence of syphilitic madness.[13]

Candide finally arrives to the Paraguay *reducción*, the Jesuit version of Paradise on Earth in the eighteenth century. At this point, Voltaire denounces the artificiality of their system and their abuse of the indigenous people, an image that obviously contradicts the one presented in Jesuit travel accounts. Even Cacambo, Candide's servant, is able to realize the contradictory nature of the faith system that rules the territory of Paraguay: "Pour moi je ne vois rien de si divin que Los Padres, qui font ici la guerre au roi d'Espagne et au roi du Portugal, et qui en Europe confessent ces rois ; qui tuent ici des Espagnols, et qui à Madrid les envoient au ciel" (38). As Candide and Cacambo enter their 'kingdom,' they come across the Baron, Cunégonde's brother who lived with Candide in Westphalia. This German aristocrat became a Jesuit and was sent to Paraguay for the reasons he reveals to Candide:

Vous savez, mon cher Candide, que j'étais fort joli ; je le devins encore davantage ; aussi le révérend père Croust, supérieur de la maison, prit pour moi la plus tendre amitié : il me donna l'habit de novice ; quelques temps après je fus envoyé à Rome. Le père général avait besoin d'une recrue de jeunes jésuites allemands. Les souverains du Paraguai reçoivent le moins qu'ils peuvent de jésuites espagnols ; ils aiment mieux les étrangers, dont ils se croient plus maîtres. Je fus jugé par le révérend père général pour aller travailler dans cette vigne (41).

Obviously, the relation between homosexual desire and the Jesuits' interest in the Baron is made clear in this passage. Not only is the Society of Jesus an all-male religious order, but it is also based on a close physical contact between directors and exercitants during the practice of the *Spiritual Exercises* and the necessary journey to Rome. This practice naturally leads its opponents to the kind of assertions made by Voltaire in *Candide*. Voltaire compares it to the abuses of Spanish Jesuits on foreigners in general (sexual and political), implying that they cannot fool those of their own kind, so they need to import disciplined Germans.

Also, in this account the Baron skips a very important step: why he went from Rome to Paraguay. It turns out that the Jesuit paradise that Candide discovers in Paraguay is a place of total luxury and lust, where the Jesuits can truly be their real selves: "Un excellent déjeuner était préparé dans des vases d'or; et tandis que les Paraguains mangèrent du maïs dans des écuelles de bois, en plein champ, à l'ardeur du soleil, le révérend père commandant entra dans la feuillée" (63). This image seems very distant from the originally evangelical mission of the Jesuits in South America. Voltaire pictures them as masters of a remote kingdom where they have built their wealth on slavery. The Jesuit utopian society resembles in *Candide* the libertine socio-economic structure encountered in the novels of Sade, where the natural order always justifies that the pleasure of the minority should derive from the pain of the majority. Or is it rather that this libertine world has imitated the Jesuit model?

The satirical philosophical tale of Voltaire prepares the way for later libertine depictions of clerical sexuality in the novel genre. The fictional worlds of libertine writers such as Duclos or Boyer d'Argens include a great many ecclesiastical characters; the priests they feature in their novels are usually experts of libertinage. In Žižek's words, they are the "ultimate bearer[s] of sexual wisdom" and the "agent[s] of fidelity to one's desire" (48). As Jesuits and Jansenists in the eighteenth century are both going to react against that conception and fight the rise of a literary genre that uses their image to depict vice. The novel becomes the most dreaded instrument of unmaking belief after the Enlightenment.[14] Jesuit Father Porée demands of the authorities in 1737 : "Que les lois transpercent (. . .), que les flammes détruisent, et fassent disparaître si faire se peut de tout le territoire toutes les oeuvres empoisonnées des auteurs de romans. Et qu'ainsi on prenne enfin soin un jour de la littérature et de l'État" (Trousson, *Romans*, xxiii). This assertion obviously shows that he was familiar with the object of his attacks. The libertines, however, know exactly how to undo the belief system on which their opponents have built their political power: by placing libertine words in the mouth of fictional characters who physically represent Christianity.[15]

Voltaire and Sade have in common one thing in addition to their fascination with repressed desires: they have both received their formal education at a Jesuit institution and they both chose to represent members of the clergy engaged in sexual acts in their novels. To them, the condemnation of the Jesuits paralleled the decline of the absolutist system, since the Jesuits had been expelled from France in August 1762. According to the trial report, the Order was prescribed as "endangering the Christian faith, disturbing the peace of the Church, and in general building up far less than it destroyed. Moreover it was outraging the laws of nature and as an enemy of the laws of France should be irrevocably expelled" (Barthel 220). Catholicism and libertinage survive thereafter without the Society of Jesus.

Sadean Inversions of the *Spiritual Exercises*

The Jesuits are expelled from France in 1762, and throughout the rest of Europe they also lose most of their power. Along with the order, it is the entire politics of the Counter-Reformation that seems to be questioned. In order to undermine the argumentation of Christianity after the Enlightenment, libertine writers are going to pursue the representation of members of the clergy as engaging in a practice of excessive libertinage. Even Voltaire's hatred of the Jesuit's position against the development of the Lumières does not surpass the violent and graphic philosophical demonstrations that we find in the novels of the marquis de Sade. We have just presented a short history of philosophical opposition to the Jesuit principles in order to understand Sade's attitude toward the disappeared Society of Jesus. Of course, his anxiety develops around the entire Roman Church and all forms of organized religion in general. So he is not only targeting Jesuitism; however the recently disappeared order has made the aesthetics of Counter-Reformation triumph in most urban centers of Western Europe—and the rest of the World— with a success that no other part of the Roman institution had ever reached. The followers of Loyola might have been forced out of France, but their action still remains effective in Sade's present. Consequently, he will pursue the representation of his old teachers as engaged in excessive libertinage as a reflection of the true essence of their system of education. He seeks to reveal the hidden face of the Jesuits in his fiction through an imitation of its principles, as if the practice of the exercises were only one side of the coin, and excessively structured sexual activity its complement.

At the same time, he is very skeptical and does not believe that the Revolution has succeeded in its project of eradicating Catholicism. In the midst of the struggles between republican priests and *réfractaires*,[16] Sade underlines in the essay "Français encore un effort si vous voulez être républicains" (inserted in *La Philosophie dans le Boudoir*) that no revolution has the potential to erase centuries of religious history:

> Il est des vices d'état dont on ne se corrige jamais, avant dix ans, au moyen de la religion chrétienne, de sa superstition, de ses préjugés, vos prêtres, malgré leur serment, malgré leur pauvreté, ils reprendraient sur les âmes l'empire qu'ils avaient envahi, ils vous renchaîneraient à des rois, parce que la puissance de ceux-ci étaya toujours celle de l'autre, et votre édifice républicain s'écroulerait faute de bases. Ô, vous qui avez la faux à la main, portez le dernier coup à l'arbre de la superstition, ne vous contentez pas d'élaguer les branches, déracinez tout à fait une plante dont les effets sont si contagieux ; soyez parfaitement convaincus que votre système de liberté et d'égalité contrarie trop ouvertement les ministres des autels du Christ (...). Hâtez-vous, ne laissez pas à *Rome la sainte*, s'agitant en tout son sens pour réprimer votre énergie, le temps de se conserver peut-être encore quelques prosélites (111–2).

In this essay Sade adopts the tone of a remote philosopher who can contemplate the needs and desires of the two parties in a battle but, as an enemy of Catholicism, he has chosen the side of the Revolution, even though he is not entirely convinced. He compares the Roman institution to a parasite weed whose roots have not disappeared. This image is recurrent in his writings and also compares to some post-modern readings of organized religions. For instance, this argument finds its echo in Lacan's post-modern point of view presented in *Le triomphe de la religion* (1974),[17] two hundred years later:

> La vraie religion, c'est la romaine. Essayer de mettre toutes les religions dans le même sac et faire ce qu'on appelle de l'histoire des religions, c'est vraiment horrible. Il y a *une* vraie religion, c'est la religion chrétienne. Il s'agit simplement de savoir si cette vérité tiendra le coup, à savoir si elle sera capable de sécréter du sens de façon à ce que l'on en soit vraiment bien noyé. Elle y arrivera, c'est certain, parce qu'elle a des ressources. Il y a déjà des tas de trucs qui sont préparés pour ça. Elle interprétera l'Apocalypse de Saint Jean. Il y a déjà pas mal de gens qui s'y sont essayés. Elle trouvera une correspondance de tout avec tout. C'est sa même fonction (82–3).

In this quote, the psychologist points to the Catholic capacity of including the believer within a greater narrative. Lacan's capitulation in the face of the atemporal powers of Roman spirituality contains various Sadean arguments in this sense: they both point to the fact that Rome has found a way to become a religion outside of time, through which all things have already been attributed a signifier for each signified (the Lacanian *correspondence*). Even though we cannot identify such a psychological point of view in Sade, the premises of this post-modern realization are already present in his texts. This is the reason why the novels of Sade are filled with ecclesiastical figures and why he repetitively places them in deconstructive positions.[18] They disintegrate the dichotomies on which the entire system of belief is based by acting completely against their putative social identity. In order to undermine the totalitarian powers of Roman Catholicism that have been tremendously enhanced by the *Spiritual Exercises* in the spirit of the Counter-Reformation, Sade needs to establish a strategy in which the very *correspondences* are kept intact, but parodied in very extreme ways.

The first step is to emphasize the illusory nature of his Roman institutional enemy and, consequently, Sade underlines the double-sided nature of the institutionalized human being. In his novels, we find characters who co-exist with Catholic principles and only 'pretend' to live by them. In this sense, Sade reproduces a model found earlier in French literature: for instance, the vicomte de Valmont in response to the Presidente de Tourvel in Laclos' *Liaisons Dangereuses* represents the archetype of the Libertine wearing the mask of virtue. He studies and reproduces religious behaviors in order to build his own illusion around his pious victim. This representation of double-faced characters—who have the capacity to appear as examples according to the standards of the Roman faith, and can be involved in the worst kind of orgies and crimes at the same time—underlines what he perceives as hypocrisy from the part of the Jesuit system, in the line drawn by his predecessors.[19] Sade's characters are not only simple libertine aristocrats: they are the rulers of this world. The orgy is a projection of Sade's perception of institutions: they organize power exchange. Systematically, when the action progresses from one place to another, we find a structure similar to the one we have just left: those in charge of institutions are always the most perverse beings.

In 1775, Sade is prosecuted by the French justice for sexual molestation on minors and chooses to flee to another country. All of places, he decides to seek refuge in Rome, the capital of Counter-Reformation. Following the advice of Cervantes who claims that there is no better refuge than the house of one's Enemy, he will spend his days of exile exploring the various architectural layers of Rome and become one of its most admirative critics. In order to undermine the argumentation of a Roman Counter-Reformation transforming in Counter-Enlightenment, Sade is going to focus on Jesuit art in Rome and analyze the arguments on which the reformulated faith is based.[20] In his travel accounts (*Voyage d'Italie*, 1772) he rapidly comes to the rather pessimistic conclusion that the Rome of the Jesuits is an attempt to incrust the city within the "greater narrative" of Christianity. But he despises this artistical trend, such as Baciccio's ceiling in Il Gesù : "Il y règne une telle confusion qu'il est absolument impossible de démêler les sujets" (303).

Above all, the marquis de Sade seeks to reveal in his fiction the *illusion* on which Roman Christianity is based through an imitation of its principles, as if the practice of Catholicism were only one side of the coin, and libertinage, the other. This is possible because the association between Jesuits and Libertines has previously been made, as we have seen in the first part of this chapter. Moreover, the Sadean spaces have a lot in common with Roman architecture in terms of the *illusory* effects they produce. As a confirmed structuralist, Barthes has pointed out this dimension at the very beginning of his essay on Sade: "Ici comme ailleurs, c'est la clôture qui permet le système, c'est-à-dire l'imagination" (21). But we know that, in the light of more recent research and through a reading of Sade's travel notes, enclosed spaces are not the only common determinators between Sade and Loyola: the author was largely inspired by Loyolan visual dynamics in architecture, which he recognizes as the very essence of the entire Roman Catholic illusion. They both recognize that the illusion has to be created in order to motivate the movement "as if there were no anticipation of finding anything good" (Loyola 125) beyond the created illusion. One can particularly see how much of an ex-Jesuit Sade is in this sense in his *Voyage d'Italie*, when the young marquis follows the footsteps of Ignatius. Eric Boutoute has analyzed this lesser known text in *Sade et les figures du Baroque* (1999):

> A Saint-Ignace, Rome, Sade "reconnaît le luxe jésuitique," et remarque la "coupole en perspective qu'on y voit et qui fait véritablement *illusion*." L'illusion domine. Le "luxe jésuitique" que Sade y découvre doit ranimer en lui le souvenir de la "splendeur des décors au milieu desquels les Jésuites s'emploient à modeler les jeunes sensibilités dont ils ont la charge," Le Brun rappelant "qu'on perdrait beaucoup à ignorer qu'entre 10 et 14 ans, Sade a constamment sous les yeux cette scène où la magnificence de l'illusion rivalise avec l'illusion de la magnificence" (66).

As another former student of Louis-le-Grand, Sade has had the opportunity to discover early in life the purposes of creating illusions, and has been able to conjugate this experience with a journey to Rome. We will pay particular attention to this factor in our upcoming close-reading of passages from his novels. The illusion is admirable but must remain within certain limits in order to work as illusion: Sade will transgress these limits in order to undermine the power of the illusions associated with spiritual beliefs.

Accordingly, it is no surprise if the novels of Sade construct a world of their own where illusions are conceptualized and even prevail over the most sacred principles of the Enlightenment, such as transparency. The omnipresence of illusions whose principles are revealed by Sade's libertine masters is a major deconstructive tool for him. But the parody of religious illusions is only works in an extremely repetitive mode that parodies in turn the rituals of Roman Catholicism. The libertine characters alternate liturgically their philosophical discourse and their sexual orgies, whether it be in a static mode (*La Philosophie dans le boudoir* and *Les Cent Vingt Journées de Sodome*) or in a nomadic-picaresque mode (essentially in *Justine ou les infortunes de la vertu* and *Histoire de Juliette ou la prospérité du vice*). Sade's novels are based on similar narrative patterns in the tradition of Catholicism, Jesuit education, and the *Spiritual Exercises*, such as retreats in enclosed spaces and repetitive acts.

Repetition is essential to the progress of the characters since it is a continuous confirmation of the philosophical demonstration: as in mathematics, one demonstration is never enough to prove a result, and the operating principle needs to be applied several times to become a recognized method, not only according to Jesuit principles, but also to Descartes. Gilles Deleuze points to this common feature of contemplation in the *Spiritual Exercises* and in the novels of Sade in *Différence et Répétition* (1968): "Le paradoxe de la répétition n'est-il pas dans le fait même que l'on ne peut parler de répétition seulement que par vertu du changement ou de la différence qu'elle présente à l'esprit qui la contemple" (70). In the same fashion, Sade presents us with an extremely structured and repetitive initiation to libertinage. The enclosed spaces and the endless journeys are the only two working formats for the repetition operated in these Sadean novels. Repetition is essential to the progress of the characters since it is a continuous confirmation of the libertine demonstration. Repetition is also the essence of Christianity since its practice is a repetition of the evangelical message and the rituals that derive from it.

We will now turn to four of these novels, all written in the years following Sade's exile to Rome: the *Cent Vingt Journées*, *La Philosophie dans le boudoir*, *Justine* and the *Histoire de Juliette*. In each of these novels, we will identify how the libertines reproduce the Christian/Jesuit practices in order to deconstruct it. Sade's project to offer a fully articulated critique of the Catholic faith in which he has been educated will evolve in these successive writings. The libertine author begins with a presentation of his visual collection of *tableaux*—"la plus inconvenante scène mentale qu'on ait jamais conçue" according to Annie Lebrun (21)—and will end with a picaresque revisitation of Rome in which his main character will conquer Rome and its Church. Through this progression, we will see that a part of Sade's project is to reformulate the Ignatian perception of the world as a structure designed so that vice is in constant struggle with virtue.

Collecting the *Tableaux* in the *Cent Vingt Journées*

At the beginning of the *Cent Vingt Journées*, Sade assumes the position of director for his reader: "Tels sont en un mot, cher lecteur, les quatre scélérats avec lesquels je vais te faire passer quelques mois" (34). It is a clear invitation on his part to withdrawal for contemplation. Of all of Sade's writings, the *Cent Vingt Journées de Sodome* (1785) is structurally the closest to a manual of retreat for libertine exercitants. Barthes has pointed out the peculiarities of the space in which this novel evolves: "au sein des retraites les mieux éprouvées, il existe toujours, dans l'espace sadien, un secret où le libertin emmène certaines de ses victimes, loin de tout regard, même complice, où il est irréversiblement seul avec son objet" (20). Structurally speaking, the similarities between this novel and Loyola's *Exercises* are striking, and it is even more striking that Barthes does not explicitly point to the parallels in the detailed outline of the two texts in *Sade, Fourier, Loyola*. First of all, the dynamics of the space strikingly parody those of the *Spiritual Exercises*. Loyola had underlined the importance of creating a space in which the exercitant would not have any other human contact but that of his director:

> Ordinarily, in making [the Exercises] an exercitant will achieve more progress the more he or she *withdraws* from all friends and acquaintances and from all earthly concerns (...) by taking a different space (127). By being secluded (...) we enjoy a freer use of our natural faculties for seeking diligently *what we so ardently desire* (128).

In *Les Cent Vingt Journées*, the dimension of seclusion as a sine qua non in the quest for *jouissance* is made extremely obvious by the long description of the author in which he emphasizes the many obstacles between the world and the castle of Silling, in which all of the action is to take place: "Dans le fait, la description suivante va faire voir combien, cette porte bien close, il devenait difficile de pouvoir parvenir à Silling, nom du château" (58). Barthes underlines the similarity between this *decorum* and medieval literature: "Ce château est hermétiquement isolé du monde par une suite d'obstacles qui rappellent assez ceux que l'on trouve dans certains contes de fées" (19). More than fairy-tales, the *Cent Vingt Journées* reflects certain features of the world of Chivalry, such as Loyola and Don Quixote read it. Therefore—and in accord with the visual tactics of Loyolan imagination—it is the kind of setting most favorable to the practice of exercises. In this sense, it is compatible with Catholic narrative traditions in which the believer/exercitant is transformed into a soldier/knight of Christ. Yet, as we have seen in the case of Roman baroque churches, the illusion of this *exterior* will drive the reader into a radically different *interior* in which the narrative rules of all previous traditions are inversed and parodies are enacted in an extremely organized and *ordered* way.

Order and rules are everywhere to be found in this text. It is the order that allows the parody, but the parody must remain within the parameters of an ordered *cérémonie religieuse*. For instance, each ceremony performed inside systematically interchanges the functions of its elements. Mariage—the very goal of fairy-tales and novels of chivalry—is parodied in the following fashion:

> Tous deux étaient extraordinairement parés en habit de ville, mais en *sens contraire*, c'est-à-dire que le petit garçon était en fille et la fille en garçon. Nous sommes malheureusement obligés, *par l'ordre que nous nous sommes prescrit* pour les matières, de retarder encore quelque temps le plaisir qu'aurait sans doute le lecteur à apprendre les détails de cette cérémonie religieuse (162–3).

The parody is only possible because the *Cent Vingt Journées* recycles various parameters of the most ordered 'practiced text' in the Roman tradition: the *Spiritual Exercises*. As in the previous example, the reader is not granted visual access to the practices of the libertines before undergoing a long series of Rules, just like in the *Exercises*. These *Règlements* are exposed in the same minimalist fashion, using the same future tense used by Loyola in his Rules. The rules are concerned with the division of the day for the teachers and their students: "On se lèvera tous les jours à dix heures du matin: à ce moment les quatre fouteurs passeront d'une chambre à l'autre ..." (63). The libertines start their day with an immediate morning exercise. This mechanical order imposed on the days is the fundament of the practice in which the libertines engage immediately upon wakening. It is at the root of the Ignatian contemplation, which imposes a set of contemplations as soon as the exercitant opens his/her eyes: "When I awaken I should immediately call to mind the contemplation I am about to make in my desire" (152).

On top of this obsessive ordering of their practices, there is in this text an obsession for the number four. Barthes comments about Loyola (and not about Sade!) that the number four is *par excellence* a number of oppositions: "le nombre 4 (puisqu'il y a quatre Semaines de retraite) renvoie, sans transaction possible, à une figure binaire; c'est le contact abrupt d'une liberté et d'une volonté" (50). The whole structure of Sade's novel is based on this same number four. In the *Cent Vingt Journées*, the motif of 'les quatre fouteurs' encountered later on in *Justine* appears for the first time; the four weeks of the *Exercises* suddenly become four months, one hundred and twenty days. The Loyolan logic of systematic division into four can be applied to the retreat of the libertines in the castle of Silling and the totalitarian division of time. Sade builds the world of his fiction on this logic of opposition that Ignatius of Loyola had elaborated as the basis of his exercises.

In Silling, the teachers and their students spend their days in the practice of inverted Christian rituals, such as wedding ceremonies or scatological imitations of the Communion. But these rituals only punctuate the days and work as frames for the main activity of the days, that is, the act of story-telling. Following up on the parody of fairy-tales and novels of chivalry, the stories (referred to as *passions* or *exemples*) are not only told for entertainment: they are *tableaux*, i.e. visual scenes in which the libertines can see their desire and the nature of their senses reflected. The stories are short and go straight to the point; they have no literary quality. They share the quality of "accurate narration" and "going over the points with only a brief or summary explanation" with the examples of the *Spiritual Exercises*; they take the "story as the authentic foundation" in order to "discover something that will bring a more *personalized* concept of the story" (Loyola 121).[21] In summary, they work as an incomplete structure for the libertine exercitants who use them in order to 'fill the blanks' with *jouissance*. This mechanism is clear in the following passage:

> O terrible effet de l'exemple! Qui l'eût dit? Au même instant, et comme s'ils se fussent donnés le mot, nos quatre libertins appellent à eux les duègnes de leurs quadrilles. Ils s'emparent de leurs vieux et vilains culs, sollicitent des pets, en obtiennent, et sont au moment d'être aussi heureux que le maître des requêtes, si le *souvenir des plaisirs qui les attendent* aux orgies ne les contient pas. Mais ils se rappellent, s'en tiennent là, congédient leur Vénus, et Duclos continue ... (164).

The libertine retreatants experience with mental reenactment prior to a physical application, which explains the paradoxical expression used here: the *memory of pleasures to come* (le "*souvenir des plaisirs qui les attendant*"). In this process of collection, memory is lost and the notion of past, present, and future is also disintegrated. The oral descriptions of *tableaux* by one of the storytellers need direct application on the senses in order to become *personalized*. The function of the *tableaux* is therefore to offer a structure in which the exercitant can 'fill blanks' in order to lose the notion of linear time associated with the 'greater narrative' of the Roman faith. The function of the repetitive storytelling not only gives a sense of doctrine to the unbelief on which their ceremonies are based, but it also replaces the eliminated gospel; the stories of the libertine *passions*—told by a sacred trinity of old libertine women—become a visual representation of their philosophy through a common orientation of their imagination:

> Les trois historiennes magnifiquement vêtues à la manière des filles du bon ton de Paris, s'assirent au bas du trône, sur un canapé place là à dessein, et Mme Duclos, narratrice du mois, en déshabillé très léger et très élégant, beaucoup de rouge et de diamants, s'étant placée sur son estrade, commença ainsi l'histoire des événements de sa vie, dans laquelle elle devait faire entrer dans le détail des cent cinquante premières passions, désignées sous le nom de *passions simples* (88).

The word *passion* underlines here the ambiguity of the libertine mission since it combines its meaning of 'sensual/sexual pleasure' with its Christian meaning of 'suffering for the multitude.' Even the division of space in the castle reflects the sacred interior of a Catholic church, according to Barthes' own drawing of it in *Sade, Fourier, Loyola* (151). In the enclosed space of the castle of Silling, the libertines practice the destruction of Christianity through their extremely transgressive acts, not so much through their verbal argumentation against the religious principles as we will have it later in *Juliette*, but rather through their collection of repetitive acts organized in a logothetic fashion.[22] The entire novel is based on the static mode and the repetition of acts of perversion, but with a clearly defined progression in the educative mode. For this reason, this 'novel' can be seen as a logothetic collection of figures and tableaux, an encyclopedia of libertine acts and a "dictionary of perversions" (Hénaff 57). It also pretends to parody the *Encyclopédie* in a desacralized world with a baroque attitude of totality and excess. Like the action of *Juliette*, the action of this novel repeats itself to a point of exhaustion of all kinds of memory, when episodes cannot possibly be remembered, and they all become a repetition of previous ones. Characters engage in total exercises of submission and follow to its extreme the Loyolan principle of obedience in the *Exercises*; the only difference is the absence of the Divinity:

> The persons who receive the Exercises will benefit greatly (. . .) by offering all their desires and freedom to [the director] so that his Divine Majesty can make use of their persons and of all they possess *in whatsoever way is according to his most holy will* (122).

Loyola invites the exercitant to submit his/her will entirely to the director, and ultimately to the Divine. Sade uses the same vector to orient the desire of the sexual slaves of Silling toward the will of the four masters, who represent simultaneously spiritual direction and the most divine incarnation of Nature. This complete submission, combined with self-destruction and voluntary amnesia, is necessary to the process of deconstruction of the traditional belief system since religion is based on memory, and the act of remembering voluntarily the text on which it is founded. The characters of his novels extensively repeat the same arguments against Christianity because Sade is convinced that a Revolution is not enough to erase the memory of a religious belief system. This is why, at the end of the four-month period, the 'quatre fouteurs' have even destroyed the society they had created, since these acts are a mimetic inversion of the Catholic principles they have condemned. Their own destruction is therefore part of the destruction of the enemy. When Sade completes the first version of the *Cent Vingt Journées*—four years before the beginning of the Revolution—France is entering a state of reformulation of its spiritual beliefs. Sade's contemporaries live under the impression that Christianity as a belief system is going to disappear. In this most difficult text of the marquis, it is not the downfall of this religion that we witness, but rather the self-destruction of libertinage, which corresponds to Sade's strong doubts about undoing an eighteen-century-old belief system with a simple Revolution. The libertine philosophy and lifestyle do not survive the Revolution in France either. After the Revolution, Catholicism is temporarily replaced by the cult of the Supreme Being (*Etre Suprême*), which is, for libertines like the marquis de Sade, a pathetic substitute and marks the failure of the Revolution. According to the characters of his novels, a libertine system of un-belief requires the total inversion of this system and a constant justification of libertinage as an immanent conduct of the human nature. Therefore totality and excess is the only libertine remedy to the new epistemological crisis that France enters after the Revolution, in a world where they have no counterparts, a world temporarily oblivious to Christianity. Yet it seems that Sade comes to a moment of realization in the evolution of his literary production: the collection of *tableaux* is a working motif for an author who seeks systematic parodies of existing rituals, but can certainly be improved by a change from the static mode to the nomadic mode. *La Philosophie dans le Boudoir*—his first major work after the fall of the Ancien Régime—will be his last attempt with the static mode, but he will soon envision similar collections of *tableaux* within the nomadic modes of *Justine* and *Juliette*.

Melting Down the Concept of Spiritual Direction

La Philosophie dans le Boudoir ou les instituteurs immoraux (1795) echoes the fundamental Ignatian relationship between director and disciple. But the novel seeks to reformulate the concept of "mentors" in its entirety. The entire novel is based on a re-conceptualization of education: Dolmancé, the most experienced character in terms of libertinage, teaches the young and innocent Eugénie how to master her senses and imagination through a precise alternation of orgies and philosophical discourses in which strong images are created. The director has been chosen according to the following criteria: "Il est grand, d'une fort belle figure, des yeux très vifs et très *spirituels*. C'est bien la *corruption* la plus complète et la plus entière, l'individu le plus méchant et le plus scélérat qui puisse exister au monde." For his exercitant, these qualities make him immediately attractive: "Je veux être la victime de ses erreurs" (6). Dolmancé is therefore an *instituteur* who reunites spirituality and corruption in a perspective of purposefully arranged mistakes. This most renowned director claims that "l'éducation, il faut qu'elle ait été bien mauvaise, car nous sommes obligés de refondre ici tous les principes inculqués" (167). Eugénie, as a good learner, tells her 'philosophical' director: "ces leçons seront retenues et mises en action" (61). Sade's project is to 'melt down again' (*refondre*) the principles of the 'bad Jesuit' education, but this notion implies that he is working with the same material, only inverting its traditional orientation.

In *La Philosophie dans le Boudoir*, the inversion happens on the most basic level of education: the *instituteurs* do not pretend to envision education as a benefit for their exercitant, but on the contrary intend to draw more jouissance from it, recognizing that "l'acte de jouissance est une passion qui, j'en conviens, surbordonne à elle toutes les autres, mais qui les réunit en même temps" (158). In this sense, the only purpose of *educating* is to obtain *jouissance* from it. The director will receive full benefit of the experiments performed on his exercitant. Eugénie has no other choice if she wants to 'graduate' from the libertine school: she will have to become a teacher at the end of the novel, and use her own mother as her first exercitant. The Libertine *instituteurs* reproduce the Jesuit chain of education that turns exercitants into potential directors.

This strategy is announced from the very beginning of the text, in the "Premier Dialogue," when Madame de Saint-Ange discusses the arrangements with her brother the Chevalier:

> Nous passerons deux jours ensemble ... deux jours délicieux, la meilleure partie de ce temps, je l'emploie à éduquer cette jeune personne. Nous placerons dans cette jolie petite tête, tous les principes du libertinage effréné, nous l'embraserons de nos feux, nous l'alimenterons de notre philosophie, nous lui inspirerons nos désirs (9).

There is a lot of pleasure in the education process on the part of the directors. It generates an even greater pleasure in the exercitant Eugénie by the end of the seventh dialogue. In this respect, this novel recapitulates the parody of the director/exercitant relation in all of Sade's work. It is where it is most apparent in a rather simplified form. The novel in itself has the pretension to 'educate the young ladies' and to be passed along from mothers to daughters. We can see in the *Philosophie* an abbreviation of the principles exposed in Sade's much bigger project: the opposite and complementary stories of the two sisters, *Justine* and *Juliette*. Even though these two novels were written prior to the *Philosophie*, their content reflects similar preoccupations in relation to the reformulation (*refondement*) of education in the post-revolutionary Sadean reality.

Forcing the Exercitant to Desire the Opposite

In the story of *Justine* (1791), the female protagonist is the opposite of Eugénie: she wants to remain virtuous in spite of her many encounters with libertine figures and their repetitive deconstruction of Christian principles. Justine mentally resists the many external attempts to convert her to Libertine ways. Even though she has received the same education as her perverted sister Juliette, she refuses to follow the same path. Her repetitive refusal of its principles and her mental reiteration of Catholic dogma will lead her to experience symbolic crucifixion of/for her beliefs, as well as literal physical tortures. Yet, Justine's perspective on the Roman faith appears to be as firm as Sade's faith in libertine principles. In the following passage, for instance, it is interesting to see how the author applies the rhetoric of libertinage to Justine's inflexible beliefs:

> Dans aucune circonstance de ma vie, les sentiments de religion ne m'avaient abandonnée. Méprisant les vains sophismes des esprits forts, les croyant tous émanés du libertinage bien plus que d'une ferme persuasion, je leur opposais ma conscience et mon cœur et trouvais au moyen de l'un et de l'autre tout ce qu'il fallait pour y répondre (153).

In the form of a picaresque story[23] told in retrospect, Justine exposes such perspectives on her own misfortune. She opposes to the libertine belief an unconditional faith in the Roman credos and denounces the lack of 'ultimate concern'[24] on the part her libertine persecutors (*ferme persuasion*). Altogether, the story of Justine is crafted with greater complexity than the *Histoire de Juliette*, since the author gives a voice to the antagonistic virtue to which he attributes all kinds of misfortunes.

In the middle of her journey, Justine leaves Paris and flees to the south of France. On her way, she feels a sudden need to adore an image of the Virgin Mary for spiritual consolation: "me prosterner aux pieds de la sainte image" (159). She seeks refuge in the monastery of an isolated part of Burgundy. The unwelcoming and suspicious establishment is directed by Father Severino, a close friend of the Pope. Instead of safety in a spiritual haven, she finds depravity and inverted forms of worshiping the holy image. The four teachers who rule the place turn her into an object of sexual satisfaction and have her practice the inverted exercises. They use the space of the monastery for this temporary retreat. The name of the religious order in this monastery is not mentioned directly; we just know that they are involved in educational systems and they have a close connection with Rome. We would not have any proof that these were Jesuits were it not for a footnote left by the author in this episode, making direct reference to a vanished short story he uses here as an inter-text: "Voyez un petit ouvrage intitulé: *Les Jésuites de bonne humeur*" (148). This marginal note points to Sade's intention to have the reader some space for imagination.[25] Another indication in the text that Justine is the captive of Jesuit teachers is the implicit inversion of the spiritual exercises that these orgies represent for them.

The demonstrations she receives from these Jesuit/libertine teachers often take the form of organized and mathematically prepared orgies, the Sadean *tableaux*. In the novels of Sade, these scenes often take place in monasteries, churches, convents, and chapels, "noting that the orgies themselves are most often held in places where large numbers of people are already gathered" (Hénaff 29), and where Justine witnesses how the clergy uses a traditional belief system and its enclosed space to fuel an underground unbelief and practice unrestricted sexual pleasure. Justine realizes that the four masters are in charge of coordinating this retreat from the world, but also of applying the fundamental principle of Loyola's *Spiritual Exercises*:

> If by chance the exercitant feels an *affection or inclination* to something in a disordered way, it is profitable for that person to strive with all possible effort to come over to the opposite of that to which he or *she is wrongly attached* (. . .) One should try to bring oneself to *desire the opposite* (125).

Loyola points to sexual desire as the 'wrong-affection' obstacle for the believer, whereas Sade envisions the Roman faith as the major obstacle *within the very same principle*. Justine will be forced by her directors to desire the opposite. Political and religious orders are duplicated and inverted in the practice of the libertine masters. The process remains geometrical and aesthetic, the libertine only achieves pleasure through a mastered discipline, not through disordering his senses. One of these 'sexual directors' tells her: "Tu n'es entrée dans cette maison que pour en sortir, quand nous serons convenus tous les quatre de t'accorder ta retraite. Tu l'auras très certainement" (229). Justine therefore undergoes nothing other than an educative process in which she will be able to superimpose her familiarity with Catholic rituals on the cruelty of her persecutors.

The parody of the Christian ritual is far from being purely comic, however. The philosophical justification of the libertine act is often in accordance with the purpose of the religious ritual. For this reason, it would be unfair to call it a parody of the Loyolan system, were it not for the logothetic importance placed on 'occupying the mental territory' of the orgy participants through a total sensual experience: "Il était de règle que quand un novice jouissait de telle façon que ce pût être, toutes les filles l'entourassent alors, afin *d'embrasser ses sens de toutes parts*, et que la volupté pût, s'il est permis de s'exprimer ainsi, pénétrer plus sûrement en lui par chacun de ses pores" (203–204). We can see in this example that the totality of the novice's senses are being connected to the sexual/mystical experience he is having, in imitation of the *Spiritual Exercises*. In *Justine*, the sensual experience is generally associated with Catholicism; but in this particular episode, it is clearly related to the Jesuit inclination for sensual experiences of the divine. Sade translates it into experience of Nature. But at the same time, he underlines the similarity between sensuality and religiosity, since they both originate in imagination and require the total use of senses: "une sorte de jouissance dont la cruauté exaltant leur perfide imagination, pût plonger leur sens dans une ivresse plus vive" (198). The gaze of the virtuous Justine helps envisioning this common parameter between mystical experience and libertine sexuality.

Moreover, the Libertine fathers have arranged the space of the convent in the logic of progression. Under the church, there is an entire underground network of rooms and tunnels leading to one another, following the format of the Jesuit novitiates of Rome. Severino, the director of the convent, has conceived this establishment after years of practice in Rome, and has designed a great façade to protect the convent from any suspicion: a miraculous image of the Virgin. This is why the priests admit with pride that: "il n'y a pas maison en France où l'on forme mieux les filles que celle-ci" (202). The female exercitants, who are always in the number of eight, enter through the main church and will exit the progression from the 'other side.' They follow a progression in the underground 'bowel of the earth.' They are eventually rejected in Nature as if they had undergone the many steps of a digestive system. But contrary to the process of digestion, they have been 'purified' of their religious configuration through the series of exercises. Soon it will be Justine's turn to be exposed to the total sensual experience inspired by Loyolan imagination and applied to Libertine philosophy and practices. She undergoes the entire process and discovers the many hidden rooms of this mechanical building. When she approaches the end of this long withdrawal from external reality, one of her directors reveals the philosophical content of the experience and the nature of the illusions on which it is based:

> L'imagination de l'homme est une faculté de son esprit où vont, par l'organe des sens, se peindre, se modifier les objets. Mais cette imagination résultative elle-même de l'espèce d'organisation dont est doué l'homme, n'adopte les objets reçus que de telle

ou telle manière, et ne crée ensuite les pensées que d'après les *effets produits par le choc des objets aperçus* : qu'une comparaison facilite à tes yeux ce que j'expose. N'as-tu pas vu, Thérèse, des miroirs de formes différentes, quelques-uns qui diminuent les objets, d'autres qui les grossissent ; ceux-ci qui les rendent affreux ; ceux-là qui leur prêtent des charmes (. . .) Telle est l'imagination de l'homme, Thérèse ; le même objet s'y représente sous autant de formes qu'elle a de différents modes (214–5).

At this point it almost seems that the four priests have been using excessive sexuality just to demonstrate this theory of imagination to their exercitant. Their awareness of imaginative mechanisms through Jesuit education has forced them to re-apply the special effects of the *Spiritual Exercises* ('*effets produits par le choc*') to Libertine education. Therefore, the fact that Justine is religious makes the educative experience more interesting since they can already use the base of her imagination, already configured by the Roman faith. According to this principle, the Libertine conception of imagination and the visual constructions of Counter-Reformation Rome are not in contradiction: they follow the same mechanisms, but are aiming at opposite goals.[26]

In spite of the extremely complex educative initiation she receives under the direction of Father Severino and his companions, Justine will remain inflexible in her belief, but as Barthes reminds us, it is not Justine who is being educated through this persecution, but the reader: "l'éducation n'est pas celle de tel ou tel personnage, c'est celle du lecteur. De toute manière, l'éducation ne permet jamais de passer d'une classe à l'autre: Justine que l'on chapitre combien de fois, ne sort jamais de son état victimal" (28). The truth is that Justine will never arrive at an actual 'existential destination' such as we find in *Bildungsroman*. Her story ends when she is burned by a bolt of lightning, but her faith remains intact. But her function in Sade's own 'greater narrative' of the two parallel stories of opposite sisters is undeniable: Justine represents the standards of Virtue, the opposite element that comes to corrupt the fundamental beliefs that are being exposed and defended in the philosophical demonstrations of the novel. Justine is a part of Juliette and vice versa; and Justine's discourse maintains a necessary tension in the education of the reader. By presenting the argument of her enemies with so much talent, Justine exists in two dimensions: she speaks from the space of Virtue but she is constantly exposed to the spaces of her enemies, which are in turn her own *orders of corruption*. Sade purposefully presents in *Justine* the realms of libertinage as imaginative constructions in order to guide his exercitant through the corrupted aspects of religious virtue, one by one. In the *Histoire de Juliette*, the principle of confronting the opposite elements (virtue and vice) remains the same, but the perspective changes.

Revisiting the *Roma Ignaziana* in *Juliette*

For the Michel Foucault of *Les mots et les choses*, the complementary stories of the two sisters Justine and Juliette embodies a second moment of realization in the rise of modernity (the first was, of course, the Counter-Reformation): "Peut-être Justine et Juliette, à la naissance de la culture moderne, sont-elles dans la même position que Don Quichotte entre la Renaissance et le Classicisme" (222). Whether we accept these epistemological divisions or not, we have to recognize that there is an inevitable correspondence between Cervantes and Sade through their position relative to the illusory nature of Counter-Reformation aesthetics.[27] In the *Histoire de Juliette* (published in several parts between 1797 and 1801), the reader pursues the education begun in *Justine*, but this time mostly outside of France. Juliette, because of her attachment to vice and prosperity, gets to travel a lot more and farther than her innocent sister.

In the fourth and fifth parts of the novel, Juliette remains exclusively in Counter-Reformed Italy and particularly in the city of Rome. For the purpose of our analysis, we will concentrate on these two parts only. There is in the story of Juliette a certain exploration and criticism of baroque motifs. Several critics have agreed to call the *Histoire de Juliette* a 'baroque narrative' on the strength of its deconstructive capacity for inversions. Michel Delon stresses that "Sade connaît les auteurs d'histoires tragiques du XVIè et du XVIIè siècles, aussi bien que les peintres et les architectes de la Contre-réforme (...) le souvenir baroque traverse son œuvre" (77). Lucienne Frappier-Mazur sees in the *Histoire de Juliette* an "undeniable affinity with baroque conceptions of the sublime" (194). Finally, Eric Boutoute adds that "Le baroque est comme catégorie esthétique le lieu privilégié pour l'imaginaire de Sade" (15). One of the first lessons Juliette receives from her *instituteurs* is an invitation to be more chiastically baroque than the Baroque itself: "C'est à l'homme passionné que l'on doit le *renversement total* de toutes les imbécillités religieuses" (258). This invitation to constant and repetitive *total inversions* will structure Juliette's entire journey. In a very Loyolan spirit, Juliette is going to force herself 'to desire the opposite' but with the Sadean intention of obtaining *jouissance* from it.

If we were to read *Juliette* in parallel with Sade's travel notes taken while in Rome, we would realize that a great deal of the action is based on Sade's own memories of his visit to the capital of the Counter-Reformation and his fascination with Baroque architecture inspired by his Jesuit education at Louis-le-Grand. Both Sade and Juliette underline the challenge to notions of scientific progress posed by the coexistence of post-revolutionary France and a Southern Europe that still lives in the Baroque age. Rome offers itself to Juliette's eyes as the surviving pocket of seventeenth-century epistemology:

> Ce qu'il y a de bien plaisant, c'est que tes arts tiennent du caractère vain et glorieux de ton people. Aucune ville sur terre ne surpasse la tienne en décorations d'opéra, tout est clinquant chez toi, comme ce peuple. La médecine, la chirurgie, la poésie, l'astronomie y sont encore dans les ténèbres (1024).

The protagonist stresses that the *décors* that French society associates with opera—a form of entertainment in which a certain nostalgia for the past is cultivated—are the reality of the urban fabric she is visiting.[28] She emphasizes by the same token that the Roman people live in the illusion produced by purposefully constructed images that shine in their faces (*clinquant*) in order to prevent them from seeing any further. Nonetheless, the *Roma Ignaziana* to which she points is the theater she chooses in order to stage-manage the most imaginative orgies of her entire journey. Adorno and Horkheimer see in Juliette's mission a direct connection between the orgies she conceptualizes and Baroque Rome as their theater. The following quote is a collage of several points they raise in regard to this question in *Dialectic of Enlightenment* (1947):

> These arrangements [the orgies] amount not so much to pleasure as to its regimented pursuit—organization—just as in other demythologized epochs (Imperial Rome and the Renaissance, as well as the Baroque) the schema of an activity was more important than its content (88). The particular mythology which the Western Enlightenment, even in the form of Calvinism, had to get rid of was the Catholic doctrine of the *ordo* and the popular pagan religion which still flourished under it (90). [Juliette] demonizes Catholicism as the most up-to-date mythology, and with civilization as a whole (. . .) Juliette embodies *amor intellectualis diaboli* the pleasure of attacking civilization with its own weapons (94). Her libertinage is as marked by Catholicism as the nun's ecstasy is by paganism (106).

As I have pointed out in previous chapters, Rome reunites all the necessary qualities to be the theater of an *ordo* in the Church's meaning of the word. However, in *Juliette*, we are not dealing with the Catholic doctrine of *ordo salutatis* (order of salvation),[29] but with a parallel imaginative construction that we could by now call '*ordo corruptatis*' (order of corruption) in which the protagonist can envision an attack on her enemy (Roman Catholicism) "with its own weapons," of just the sort Ignatius of Loyola recommends to the exercitant when confronted with the Enemy. Once again, it is a matter of "[striving] with all possible effort to come over to the opposite of that to which she is wrongly attached" (Loyola 125), that is, her originally religious education and mental configuration.

Marcel Hénaff sees the libertine evolution in Juliette as a process parallel to that of ascetic beings, that is, similar to what we observe in the Jesuit *Spiritual Exercises*:

> [Juliette] often reproduces, almost verbatim, the prescriptions given in Saint Ignatius of Loyola's *Spiritual Exercices*. The libertine ascetic (if we may presume to combine these two words), like an Ignatian spiritual exercitant, forces himself to produce the optimal state of desire and sexual pleasure. (. . .) The exercitant retreats from speech, but he does so in order to make signs speak, so that another voice can answer his call: for Ignatius, this is the voice of God; for Sade, the voice of desire. What is noteworthy on the part of both Jesuit saint and libertine writer is that imagination is required to be the medium and instrument of this procedure (90–91).

In her travels and through her encounters with libertine masters, Juliette will learn how to become this ascetic who can only subvert the belief system she opposes through the imitation of its mechanisms and the discipline of exercises (the orgies). As a matter of fact, Juliette is herself the author of a method, which she will deliver to her companion Mme de Donis, a few days before killing her. Josué Harari calls this passage "the famous 'Discours de la méthode' that Juliette propounds to Madame de Donis" (1057); concerning this presentation of Juliette's discipline he adds that, "for Ignatius as for Sade, it is thus the imagination that is called upon to be the medium and instrument of the spiritual/sexual operation" (1059). This method consists in complete isolation and separation from libertine practice for two weeks. After this time, the libertine needs to put his/her imagination to work and encourage it through acts of solitary pleasure, and leave everything to imagination:

> Soyez quinze jours entiers sans vous occuper de luxures, distrayez-vous, amusez-vous d'autres choses ; mais jusqu'au quinzième ne laissez pas même d'accès aux idées libertines. Cette époque venue, couchez-vous seule, dans le calme, dans le silence et dans l'obscurité la plus profonde ; rappelez-vous là tout ce que vous avez banni depuis cet intervalle, et livrez-vous mollement et avec nonchalance à cette pollution légère par laquelle personne ne sait s'irriter ou irriter les autres comme vous. Donnez ensuite à votre imagination la liberté de vous présenter, par gradation, différentes sortes d'égarements ; parcourez-les toutes en détail ; passez-les successivement en revue ; persuadez-vous bien que toute la terre est à vous . . . (39).

For Ignatius as for Sade, it is thus the imagination that is called upon to be the medium and instrument of the spiritual/sexual operation (Harari 1059). This method consists in complete isolation and separation from libertine practice during two weeks. Juliette has also inherited some principles of mental discipline. After this period of ascetic preparation, the libertine needs to put his/her imagination to work and encourage it through solitary acts of pleasure, leaving everything to imagination. Unlike Descartes' method, Sade proposes through Juliette an education that will only be validated through the guidance of libertine masters. Sade's characters parody the excessive guidance of Jesuit education in order to duplicate their dynamics and operate their 'melting down.' Her asceticism is only validated by the guidance of *instituteurs*, or philosophical directors. Unlike Descartes, Sade is going to operate his deconstruction of the Roman Catholic faith through parodies of the system of spiritual guidance on which his work is based.

This parody needs Rome as its most significant theater, without a doubt. Once again, the city will play the role of "Guarantee of Meaning," but this time for the purpose of inversion. This is how the gigantic novel *Juliette* takes apart the Roman faith through a conservation of its mechanisms, while changing their functions. In the *Histoire de Juliette*, the protagonist chooses her sexual interactions with the clergy deliberately in the most sumptuous 'orders of corruption,' and 'brings herself to desire her very opposite.' But this construction of desire is first motivated by destructive acts. She remains in Rome five months before she obtains an audience with the Pope: it gives her the opportunity to get familiar with the multiple layers of the urban fabric and engage in destructive acts related to her inverted spirit of Christianity. She will realize most of these fantasies in the company of the Roman princess de Borghese; with her, Juliette first envisions becoming acquainted with the city through fire:

> –Écoute, me dit Borghese, j'ai sur cela un projet unique, je veux brûler à la fois, dans Rome ... le même jour ... à la même heure, tous les hôpitaux, tous les hospices, toutes les maisons de charité, toutes les écoles gratuites (818). Il y a (...) des hôpitaux situés dans des quartiers fort pauvres de Rome, et ces parties périront infailliblement (835).

Her desire to burn Rome is clearly oriented toward the Jesuit landmarks of the *Roma Ignaziana*, the epicenters of Jesuit activity, where they come in contact with corruption. In the second half of the eighteenth century, most of the Jesuits expelled from France and Spain had found shelter in the original missions of Ignatius in Rome (mostly hospitals and schools) and had gotten closer to the Pope. It is no coincidence that Juliette focuses on establishments such as hospitals and schools, and not on actual sacred spaces.

After five months in Rome, Juliette has acquired a certain reputation and has gotten familiar with the dynamics of the surrounding urban space. She can proceed to the Vatican—the sacred space *par excellence*—that she has been avoiding until then. Her well-deserved reputation awakens the interest of Pope Pius the

Sixth. She does not hesitate in calling the Holy Father by his family name Braschi. When she finally meets him, the two characters have already agreed to act in complete sincerity and transparency. Juliette has ordered him to put an end to Catholicism: "Prends donc ton parti, vieux despote, brise ta croix, brûle tes hosties, foule tes images et tes reliques aux pieds" (860). But soon the Pope convinces Juliette that there is an extremely philosophical and enlightened dimension in the conservation of religious imagination: "Je n'ajoute pas plus de foi que toi à toutes ces mômeries spirituelles, mon ange ; mais tu connais l'obligation où nous sommes d'en imposer aux faibles" (862).[38] Sade's suggestion through Juliette that behind the spiritual directors there are enlightened philosophers who understand exactly the manipulative nature of their direction could be seen as a rather harsh *clin d'oeil* to his former Jesuit teachers. Moreover, it goes along with Loyola's suggestion in the *Spiritual Exercises* that illusion must be adapted to the intellectual level of the exercitants, and that, if need be, the director should increase the artifice and do a "lighter version of the Exercises" (126–7). The Pope confirms to Juliette that only the directors need Enlightenment; the crowds should remain under their control.

But Juliette is the archetype of the rebellious student; she imposes more rules on the Pontiff and refuses to be an exercitant in this traditional meaning of the word. She is not only interested in sharing perverse moments with the Pope; she has come to tour the Vatican and to comment on the true nature of the sacred space; she requires a detailed visit of the entire structure: "charge un guide de toutes les clefs de ce palais, je veux tout voir.—Je sera ce guide moi-même, dit Braschi" (862). She gives orders to her own director and crosses at the same time the boundaries of spiritual contemplation. Consequently, her gaze inside the rooms of the Vatican systematically deconstructs the contemplative arrangments of the space. As Frappier-Mazur points out, "[Juliette's] main innovation is to replace esthetic distance with a high degree of closeness" (197). For instance, one of her first observations about the Vatican's interior deals with the Roman Catholic capacity to superimpose its greater narrative on pre-existing narrative forms: "Là tout se mêlait indistinctement. Près d'une Thérèse en extase se voyait Messaline enculée, et sous l'image du Christ était une Léda" (853). The Christian images are directly associated with Pagan figures associated with sexual lust. Bernini's famous sculpture of Teresa of Ávila appears in Saint Peter's in order to emphasize the Sadean connection between salvation and *jouissance*, a connection that reflects the nature of the interactions between Juliette and Pius VI.

In the same fashion, she comes to understand the superimposition of sacred spaces on previous sites of orgies and massacres; in order to excite her sexual appetite, the Pope tells her: "Cette superbe maison [Vatican] est bâtie sur l'emplacement de celle où Néron s'amusait à illuminer ses jardins avec les corps des premiers chrétiens" (862). We can see in this observation why Adorno and Horkheimer point to the pagan nature of Counter-Reformation Rome underlined in *Histoire de Juliette*: the most sacred place of Catholicism is directly connected to the extreme libertinage of Roman antiquity since it is its historical foundation. Also, Sade has observed in his travel notes from Rome that the Jesuits particularly enjoyed building their churches on the very sites of acts of past cruelty: "On y voit toujours les mêmes événements se répéter, les mêmes crimes, les mêmes vertus, la destruction des uns, l'élévation des autres" (244).

Her visit to Saint Peter's basilica turns into a *total inversion* of a baroque order of corruption. By her participation in the ritual conducted in the basilica, Juliette shows that transparency is possible even in the mystery of the liturgy. She succeeds in transforming it. Eric Boutoute translates Juliette's triumph over the Catholic ritual as a projection of Sade's own projection into the Baroque world; according to this principle, she cannot fail:

> Si Sade part bien en "guerre" contre le naturalisme canonique de son époque, c'est en prenant le chemin du baroque et du dionysiaque ... Chemin pour lui familier, naturel, où son être profond le guide infailliblement. Juliette faillit-elle jamais dans sa 'carrière libertine' en Italie ? (24)

In order to emphasize her inverted connection with Catholicism through paganism, Juliette receives communion from the Pope on the throne of Saint Peter through anal sex: "Sodomisée par le pape, le corps de Jésus-Christ dans le cul: Oh mes amis! quels délices! Il me semblait que je n'en avais jamais tant goûté de ma vie" (903). Again, the libertine surrenders to the Jesuit principle, participates in its practice, but eventually undermines it completely by emphasizing, for instance, what is common between communion and a total sensual experience that exchanges in a dinstinctly Rabelaisian fashion the traditional function of the mouth for that of the anus.

In order to receive the guidance and the direction of the Pontiff through this process, she has had to agree to obey the successor of Saint Peter unconditionally, as taking a Jesuit vow of total obedience to the Pope: "Ce que tu vas me dire fixera pour toujours ma façon de penser" (862). This pledge only marks the beginning of her initiation into the highly visual orgy that takes place in the middle of the basilica. During this very private mass, the Pope chooses a young man to be crucified upside down in order to incarnate Saint Peter himself before Juliette's eyes. The scene of extreme simulation goes beyond all the possible artifices used by the spiritual directors of the *Exercises*. However, it is not the only passage in the *His-*

toire de Juliette where such cruelty is performed in order to provide the exercitant with a simulation, as Frappier-Mazur reminds us: "Indeed, simulation is a favorite contrivance of the agents and governs numerous episodes, such as that of the insane asylum in *Juliette*, in which the inmates take themselves for God, Jesus and the Virgin Mary" (187). The orgy in Saint Peter's echoes this scene commented by Frappier-Mazur: it remains entirely liturgical, and images are created once again only for Juliette, as for any exercitant of the *Spiritual Exercises*. It is not a demonstration of church power for the crowds, but a revelation of the essence of that power through an inversion of the visual dynamics on which it is based. Sade uses one of the Church's favorite tools for conversion (visual simulation) in order to undermine the very essence of the faith. Once again, Sade proves to be an ex-student of the Jesuits who has learned the lessons of his former masters a little too well.

Juliette's tour of the Vatican happens in the middle of her long journey, just like Justine's tour of the convent in Burgundy that we analyzed earlier. These two episodes placed in corresponding novels have a lot in common since both sisters get to experience an architectural structure that guides exercitants through a compartmentalized act of contemplation. Nevertheless, these two episodes face each other almost like "negative prints:" while Justine is forced to follow every step of this long initiation into the inversion of Counter-Reformed visual dynamics, Juliette acquires a position of complete superiority over her *instituteur*: the Pope (a very close friend of *Justine*'s Severino, by the way) becomes her exercitant in a space that she will soon entirely control. Only by placing him in this position can she obtain from him a philosophical dissertation in which he acknowledges the eternity of Enlightenment philosophy that has been kept under lock and key in the Vatican library and behind the images created by Rome. For this reason, where Justine is forced to adore the image of the Virgin while being raped, Juliette proclaims the philosophical nature behind religious images. Their visions are, of course, complementary and also define the spectrum in which Enlightenment philosophy criticizes centuries of religious superstition.

Ultimately, Juliette's description of her stay at the Vatican goes beyond the limits of language:

> Pour éviter la monotonie des détails, je glisserai légèrement sur ceux des nouvelles orgies que nous y célébrâmes : la grande galerie fut le lieu de la scène ; plus de quatre cents sujets des deux sexes y parurent ; ce qu'on y célébra d'impuretés *ne peut se peindre* (905).

Beyond the deconstructive intentions of Juliette, there is no more room for describing the apotheosis of her stay in Rome. The orgies are not the purpose of her picaresque story-telling; they only support her philosophical dissertations. When she realizes how dependent on her discourse the Pope has become, she leaves Rome immediately and goes on to seduce more rulers in Naples: it confirms her once more in her position of philosophical director, always breaking with dependence.

Conclusion

The Sadean Enlightenment—that is, the Enlightenment that follows the Revolution—as a reaction against Loyolan imagination reaches its limits in this work of Sade. Juliette offers a repetitive yet comprehensive tour of Europe in which the tensions between the Enlightenment and the Counter-Reformation are exposed under Sade's microscope. In his capacity as an ex-student of the Jesuits, he possesses the power to envision this problematic in a deconstructive mode and to apply the vectors of Loyolan imagination to his own 'orders of corruption.' These *orders*—as we have seen in the preceding examples—have no connection whatsoever with divine salvation. On the contrary, they underline the immediate nature of salvation which does not exist outside of Nature itself. In other words, there is no salvation for the libertines outside of the immediacy of *jouissance*. Their confrontation with other European rules only confirms that power itself is based on the illusions of discourse, and that only the educated elites have access to the true salvation of *jouissance*, while the multitude must be fed with religious imagery. Two centuries prior to Foucault, Sade demonstrates through this long journey that truth and faith are just productions on which power is based and, also, that "we must produce truth as we must produce wealth" (Harpham 540). Juliette realizes this mechanism the day she leaves the convent and steps into the external world. Yet, just like Sade himself, she would not be able to understand the dynamics of power at work in the outside world if she had not received an education in the highly visual Catholic faith of the Counter-Reformation. Like Sade, her exile will lead her to the house of her Enemy, the Vatican.

But one question remains: why doesn't Juliette—or any of Sade's characters—pursue her journey in Spain, the very birth place of Ignatius? Sade's admiration for Spanish Golden Age authors—and particularly Cervantes—would have justified this episode. But Sade had never set foot on the Peninsula. Moreover, Spain is under the control of the Inquisition, though the cruelty of this institution's practices would not necessarily go *against* Juliette's cruelty ... As Geoffrey Galt Harpham points out, Spain reflects to Sade and the philosophers of the Enlightenment a "grisly spectacle of a nation degraded by fear of a secret and unaccountable institution that violated all the principles on which the Enlightenment was staked" (540). The increasing violence of Sade's texts dramatizes the appropriation of the Jesuit models, but the sense of Loyolan imagination never points to Spain. For a start, Loyola had to leave his own country because of problems with the Inquisition. Moreover, the Jesuits always kept their distance from the drastic methods of the Inquisition, and for this reason, had to develop outside Spain, as an educational structure with a mission. Because their methods were more flexible than those of the Spanish Inquisition and stood in contrast to them, they were recognized and respected in intellectual circles very rapidly. But this rapidly turned into intellectual dominion. Their ex-students often point out that the Jesuits are the motive force behind the Counter-Reformation. If the Society of Jesus had not been part of the picture, the Enlightenment might have happened earlier: the Inquisition was going to be an 'easy Enemy.' But the Jesuit teachers configured their students in such a way that they could only formulate their criticism within the principles of Loyolan imagination, as we have seen in the novels of Sade.

Beyond Cervantes' exaggerations, Gracián's distortions, Descartes' method, and Voltaire's attacks, Sade claims in this work that only a system that has the capacity to organize its own destruction can survive this destruction. From his point of view, the Revolution needs to work a lot harder in order to overcome two centuries of Jesuit intellectual dominion. He is aware that the main figures of the Enlightenment have been productive because of the familiarity they had of their enemy, and no other method works better than becoming this enemy. Yet the Revolution is another institution whose power rests on its capacity to feed the crowds with illusions.[31] Sade is the first to realize that this Revolution reproduces the mechanisms of the Enemy it has supposedly erased. Consequently he develops a certain nostalgia for his Catholic past:

> La fable chrétienne était absurde, soit, mais elle permettait des élans voluptueux. Que voit-on se former maintenant ? Des corps pincés, désaffectés, désinfectés, hygiéniques, régulièrement tronçonnés sans le moindre signe de lubricité apparente. Serais-je obligé demain d'aller me cacher dans les caves du Vatican, au milieu des collections obscènes des papes ? (Sollers 5).

Toward the end of his life, it is very probable that the *Etre Suprême* has convinced the aging marquis that the Roman faith had much more sensuality, now lost. It forces him perhaps to reconsider his career as a libertine writer who repeatedly attacked the baroqueness of Catholicism. In his *Idées sur les Romans*, the marquis de Sade will pay a paradoxical tribute to all of his fellow 'ex-students of the Jesuits,'especially Cervantes, Voltaire, and Diderot, whom he still admired above all. But the most interesting dimension of this restrospective look at his career as a writer and his participation in the development of the modern novel is the tribute he pays to his Jesuit teachers at Louis-le-Grand who encouraged him in the direction of literature. He recognizes in the *Idées sur les Romans* (1800) that they configured and formatted his imagination in a way that forces him to deny his authorship:

> Il faut avoir été leur victime pour savoir les apprécier; la main de l'infortune, en exaltant le caractère de celui qu'elle écrase, le met à la juste distance où il faut qu'il soit pour étudier les hommes ; ce n'est qu'en avançant qu'ils se perfectionnent ; ils n'arrivent au but que par essais. Sans doute il ne fallait pas aller aussi loin ... Qu'on ne m'attribue donc plus le roman de *Justine*: jamais je n'ai fait de tels ouvrages, et je n'en ferai sûrement jamais (31).

This surprisingly masochist confession of the marquis is a reflection on his own evolution as a writer. One needs to be placed in a position of confrontation relative to his/her Enemy (especially if this Enemy is oneself) in order to fully engage in an order of corruption. One needs to evolve in this process and master its art. Whether this art is fundamentally of a *good* or an *evil* nature does not truly matter. It is, rather, a question of the distance and position of the observer before the contemplated object. The old Sade admits that he might have gone a little too far in the process, and regrets the publication of his masterpiece. But he does not regret having engaged in this lifetime process in order to contemplate his career from this detached perspective. Paradoxically, the ability to have gone so far and to come back to a distanced understanding of his own actions as writer makes him one of the most successful students of the Jesuit system. His success in reproducing baroque orders of corruption in which his exercitants (readers) are forced to contemplate repetitions *tableaux* and accept liturgically that there is no salvation beyond the sensuality of illusion is an art that has not been mastered by many.

Afterword

Jorge Luis Borges once wrote that the baroque is "that style which deliberately exhausts (or tries to exhaust) all its possibilities and borders on its own parody ... the final stage [of any style] when that style only too obviously exhibits or overdoes its own tricks" (11). On the road from Ignatius of Loyola to Sade, we have established the continuity of these acts of simulation, defined as 'Baroque orders of corruption;' however, many links that deserved a detailed analysis have been left out, including fundamental philosophers of the Enlightenment, such as Descartes, Voltaire and Diderot. Nonetheless, they have been discarded because their road did not lead them to Rome.

The purpose of this project was to underline the connection between a father of the Counter-Reformation and a son of the Revolution, Loyola and Sade, two 'Barthean logothetes' linked by their visual projection into orders of corruption. Between them, the unarticulated sense of a 'greater narrative' increases in the arts coming out of Counter-Reformation Rome after the Reformation. The *Spiritual Exercises* participate in making the 'greater narrative' a priority over the Lutheran insistence on the direct personal studying of Scripture. *The Spiritual Exercises* force the exercitant to enter an "order of corruption" in which s/he is placed in contemplative states of tension and in simulated situations of contact with sin and physical decay. It all starts in the city of Rome, capital of Europe, where the *Spiritual Exercises* gave birth to the *Roma Ignaziana*, a physical application of the visual dynamics of the exercises on architectural structures, beyond the action of Loyola and the first generation of Jesuits. This method becomes successful outside its own practice and the "orders of corruption" turn into new (modern, according to Sade) aesthetic experiences recycled in secular arts and especially in literature. This transformation parallels the rise of the modern subject in the novel. Spanish authors related to or educated by the new order of the Jesuits will therefore be the first ones to adapt and transform the visual dynamics of Loyolan imagination in an attempt to improve this method and gradually place it in the service of Philosophy, Science, and Reason: Cervantes will exaggerate the importance placed on 'greater narratives;' Gracián will choose to challenge the linearity of this narrative and will invite his reader/exercitant to contemplate the eternal arts *beyond* the temporality of Christianity represented in the *Roma Ignaziana*. Matthew L. Jones argues that:

> [The] return to the *urbanité* of Rome's noninstitutionalized higher philosophy needed new forms of writing (49). Don Quixote's illusory windmills haunted the philosophical alternatives available to Descartes's contemporaries. Imitation and wonder made them unable to consider, to choose, and to rule themselves (58).

Yet, the *orders of corruption* were worth exploring from philosophical perspectives. The city of Rome reflected the epistemological anxieties of these writers as well as the atemporality of philosophical search. In this sense, Cervantes and Gracián prepare the way for the Enlightenment. However, when Spain returns to the dark ages of the Inquisitorial censorship, France opens the door to Cartesian Reason (paradoxically, another indirect outcome of the Jesuit imagination). This rise of Philosophy only begins with Descartes and will continue in the works of a generation educated in the tradition of the *Spiritual Exercises*. This is how the road ends with the Sadean inversions that I have commented on in the last chapters: they bring the aesthetics of the Counter-Reformation to a point of self-exhaustion through reversals. They also proclaim the death of the baroque, along with the Revolution.

Slavoj Žižek wrote in his provocative reading of the Christian narrative from a Lacanian perspective, *The Puppet and the Dwarf: the Perverse Core of Christianity* (2003), that such transgressive reversals are provoked by Christianity and that this perversion is at the core of the faith itself: "nowhere is [the] paradoxical reversal more evident than in the work of Sade, where the unconstrained assertion of sexuality deprived of the vestiges of *spiritual* transcendence turns sexuality itself into a mechanical *exercise* devoid of any authentic passion" (39). This is what has been shown in the last chapter of this dissertation. According to this principle, however, Sade would be one of the most faithful Catholics in history. Surely, Žižek envisions this problematic from the perspective of psychology; if we were to follow his general argument, we would conclude that the "order of corruption" is a simulation of the symbolic order in the imaginary of the subject, even if it seemed to be initially the opposite, that is, a pocket of imaginary within the symbolic order of a religious tradition. This approach would, of course, open up a whole new debate. His philosophical insights, on the other hand, are definitely grounded in literal connections with the texts we have studied here, and serve our needs better. Later on in the same essay, for instance, the Slovene philosopher evokes Hegel's notion of *Aufhebung* (sublation) and comes to the conclusion that the essence of Christianity rests on this early-nineteenth-century Hegelian notion:

> You must go through the lowest in order to once more reach the highest, the lost totality; you must lose immediate reality in the self-contradiction of the "night of the world" in order to regain it as "posited," mediated by the symbolic activity of the subject, you must renounce the immediate organic whole (82).

Although the critic does not mention Loyola's *Spiritual Exercises* in his analysis, the connection between his argument and this work is quite obvious: Loyola reinforces this characteristic of Christianity after the Reformation and insists on the sublation factor as no other saint from the period does.

Perhaps the following list of infinitive guidelines drawn from the *Spiritual Exercises* best recapitulates the 'Loyolan sublation' in correspondence with Hegel: "to know nothing about what is to be done, to become accustomed not merely to resist the enemy but even to defeat him" (124), "to bring oneself to desire the opposite" (125), "to order one's life through some disordered affection" (129), "to see in imagination and to consider my soul as imprisoned in this corruptible body and my whole compound self as an exile in this valley of tears among brute animals" (136), "to bring myself to greater shame and confusion" (137), "to look upon myself as a sore or abscess from which have issued such foul poison" (139), "to feel shame" (142). This is, as we have seen along our analytical trajectory, what defines Loyolan imagination. But it seems that the Loyolan sublation is another road that drew Sade to Rome. Perhaps Žižek is also right in this essay to add his own infinitive guideline: "to become a true dialectical materialist, one should go through the Christian experience" (6). Wasn't it the whole point of Sade's escape to Rome? Marcel Hénaff had already argued that, from this specific perspective, "Sade may be something of a Hegelian" (68). For this reason we should close this project with a brief review of Sade's itinerary in Rome.

In this *Voyage d'Italie*, a voyage of initiation to materialism, the young marquis makes a point of visiting and commenting on all the churches of Rome for an epistolary recipient named 'Madame la comtesse,' who has remained in France. In total, Sade gives a detailed description of sixty-four churches (from the outside and the inside) he visits in Rome. It is particularly interesting indeed to envision this early writing of the marquis as a *map* in this particular sense: the contemporary reader can follow his modern exploration of the urban space in innovative ways, since Sade follows the instincts of a *flâneur*.[1] No wonder that he will return to this detailed study of the city later on in his life when he is in the process of writing the *Histoire de Juliette* and will use it again as a map for the movement of his protagonist. In this travel account, the young writer does not show any interest in the contemporary Roman society and culture. He only does for structures.

Ironically, his observations are a pure review of Roman baroque architecture done in a quite Barthean structuralist mode, which is based on the pleasure in the interpretation. As we have seen in the *Histoire de Juliette*, Sade particularly likes to emphasize the structural connections between these baroque churches and the Pagan ground on which they are built. Also, his eyes are extremely critical of the 'unbreathable' nature of baroque interiors. He argues that this aesthetical experience could be defined as "le moderne de Rome" (121). Although he does not use the word *moderne* as we would use it nowadays, it is interesting to think about this word choice and how he associates it with *plaisir* and *sensation*: "Mon goût et mon sentiment ne sont ceux que d'un amateur du second ordre: je n'ai pas d'autre prétention. Mais j'avoue que c'est le moderne de Rome qui m'a fait le plus de plaisir et qui m'a fait éprouver une sensation plus vive" (121). These words in the mouth of an innocent explorer could sound completely meaningless, but they acquire meaning when this young aristocrat in visual awe turns out to be the seed of the divine marquis.

In the second chapter of this abandoned project, he describes these buildings one by one in an ordered way so that his correspondent is able to follow his steps and the itinerary of his visit as if she had laid a map of the city next to his account. We can follow the author in his *Voyage* from his entrance through *Il Popolo* to his detailed description of the art collections of the Roman *palazzi* in the heart of the city, as well as his interpretations of Bernini's fountains in the middle of Rome's beautiful squares. Most of all, the marquis admires greatly all of Bernini's works and seeks to interpret his sculpture as a form of rebellion against the illusion of the Roman faith. His criticism of Bernini's fountains in the Piazza Navona—a project directed by the German Jesuit Kircher and Pope Innocent X—emphasizes the right and hidden criticism made by Bernini, or in other words, "la bonne critique que le Bernin fit" (134) of the extravagant dome of Saint Agnes, the church that it faces, as a representation of an institution in its fall. Sade also claims to be very familiar with the kind of divine love projected in Bernini's representation of the ecstasy of Santa Teresa (87). He ceases to be a mere observer when it comes to the works of this 'other' ex-student of the Jesuits and former exercitant of the Spiritual Exercises. He pursues his *flâneries* through the sanctuaries of Ignatius.

Sade also argues that Jesuit art is above all other forms defined by its "bon goût" (79) and recognizes its lustful nature in Pozzo's *trompe l'oeil* of San Ignazio (105). For instance, he makes the effort to remain as objective as possible in his description of Bernini's Sant'Andrea al Quirinale, but cannot help emphasizing the sensuality of the architecture. Sade freezes several times during his visit of Jesuit buildings, and particularly remains in awe before the marble statue of Ignatius' follower Stanislas in the *oratorio* attached to Sant'Andrea. Suddenly the scientific tone of his descriptions disappears and gives way to the emotion: "Il faut le voir!" (88). Another similar moment of linguistic interruption happens when Sade encounters an inscription below a statue in the church of San Ignazio and writes it down without really knowing why: "ALTER IGNATUM ARIS, ALTER ARAS IGNATIO."[2] In this moment of reverence, the voyage of initiation seems complete: Sade meets Loyola, and—through him—the Enlightenment meets the Reformation. Sade recognizes in Loyola the hero of the Counter-Reformation, a projection of himself who also had the capacity to hallucinate his referent,[3] maybe his true path to an upcoming materialist worldview, if we want to follow Žižek's argument . . . His passion for the highly visual qualities of buildings such as Il Gesù, Sant'Andrea al Quirinale, and San Ignazio is obvious in all of these passages, when language is not enough to describe the mystical intensity of the effect it has on his senses as an observer. The scientific method he seeks to apply fails in the face of the pleasure he receives from the illusion. In 1771, when Sade freezes in front of the inscription in the church of San Ignazio, we could speculate that he might be thinking "Alter Sadum Aris, Alter Aras Sado!" deep down in his Sadean imagination in-progress. He has not designed his own order of corruption yet, or in other anachronic words, his Hegelian sublation. But he begins to admire. Ironically, today's art historians associate San Ignazio with "Sade-ian libertines moisten[ing] each other underneath a 'floating' Baroque ceiling" (Klein 42).

Perhaps Hegel and the German Idealism developing in the decades following Sade's travels in Italy provide the continuity in which we should contemplate the philosophical deconstruction of Loyolan imagination. After all, if "Ignatius' *Exercicia spiritualia* are nothing but a Christian version of a Greco-Roman [philosophical] tradition" as Pierre Hadot claims without further indications (82), it is natural for the *Exercises* to return to Philosophy, like humans return to dust. Perhaps there is nothing Loyolan about imagination according to Hegel's universal conclusions. Perhaps we should rather look for connections with Gothic literature, or the encounters with the Sublime in Romantic writings, or even in the renewed fascination for the corruptible in Symbolist and Decadent poetry. Perhaps we should let Loyolan imagination die with the emotive images of the baroque and admit its non-existence outside of the temporal boundaries we have set. Perhaps we can see it evolving more in philosophy and science than in the religious institution itself.[4] We could therefore recognize once again that the Jesuits have invested too much in the scientific and philosophical comprehension of their "orders of corruption"[5] and for this reason participate in the Modern detachment from traditional religious system even more than their opponents. They finally contradict the very purpose of their existence as a Catholic Order. Perhaps, in this sense, the *Spiritual Exercises* have voluntarily betrayed Christianity and have transgressed its most fundamental boundaries. Perhaps Christianity invites the believer to transgress its boundaries. Perhaps betrayal is indeed the highest form of faith and fidelity.

Notes

Chapter I

1. Originally titled *De Servo Arbitrio*, it stands in opposition to Erasmus's 'De Libero Arbitrio.' In the 19th century it is translated as *On the Enslaved Will* by Henry Cole (1823). Nowadays, the essay is found under the title *The Bondage of the Will*.
2. Cervantes underlines from the first chapter the extreme meagerness and the lack of moisture in his hero's brain.
3. Since we cannot exclude the existence of a Protestant Baroque and non-religious forms of Baroque art, we need to define our object of study as Catholic Baroque.
4. I am talking particularly about the explosion of Natural History as a discipline taught throughout Western Europe.
5. For this reason we should understand the notion of *exercise* as the Latin equivalent to the Greek *askesis*. As Matthew L. Jones reminds us, there is a whole tradition of 'spiritual exercises' within and outside the Renaissance: "These conflicting spiritual exercises offered different modes and ideals for cultivating the self: Ignatius' *Spiritual Exercises* (and its various reformulations), Michel de Montaigne's *Essays*, the humanist ideal orator/citizen Charron's *Livre de la sagesse*, Jean Bodin's *Methodus ad facilem historiarum cognitionem*, the alchemical romances of Béroalde de Verville, Eustachius a Sancto Pablo's *Exercices Spirituelles*, Pierre Gassendi's Epicureanism, Justus Lipsius's Neostoicism, Cornelius Jansenius's Augustinianism, Seneca's *De vita beata*, Epictetus's *Manual*, to name but a few" (55). From the Spanish

tradition, we could add Miguel de Molinos's *Guia Espiritual* (1675).
6. Elizalde, Ignacio. *San Ignacio en la Literatura*. Madrid: Fundación Universitaria Española, 1983.

Chapter II

1. André Favre-Dorsaz writes in 1951 in *Calvin et Loyola* : « Le livret de Loyola n'entre dans aucune catégorie littéraire » (143), « Loyola n'a jamais eu la prétension de devenir un auteur célèbre, encore moins l'auteur unique et par excellence de son temps. Ses notations laconiques n'ont pas été écrites pour être lues ou étudiées, mais pour être vécues et pratiquées » (144).
2. Two of these four essays are dedicated to the marquis de Sade, which remains the main focus of his work.
3. Blanchot, Maurice. *Sade et Lautréamont*. Paris: Editions de Minuit, 1963 ; Klossowski, Pierre. *Sade mon prochain*. Paris : Seuil, 1947 ; Beauvoir, Simone de. "Faut-il brûler Sade?" *Privilèges*. Paris: Gallimard, 1955.
4. that is, *breathable*, an adjective much more used in French that in English.
5. *Le Plaisir du texte*. Paris: Seuil, 1973.
6. "chacune de ses études, quoique d'abord publiée (en partie) séparément, a été tout de suite conçue pour rejoindre ses voisines dans un même livre: le livre des Logothètes, des fondateurs des langues" Barthes, Roland. *Sade, Fourier, Loyola* (7).
7. Loyola explains this notion on the very first page by comparing it to physical workout. It is the meaning of *exercise* that he wants the reader to adopt.
8. Especially in the works of Rafael Alberti and Damaso Alonso. See Elizalde's comparative analysis in the second half of *San Ignacio en la literature*, chapter V.
9. There is of course direct influences of the Ignatian practice on the drama of Pedro Calderón or Pierre Corneille, but this is not a direction that we will pursue in this analysis. Rather, we will explore here how it affects other spheres of the arts and the humanities in its time. Concerning Spanish Golden Theater, I am referring to: González Gutiérrez, Cayo. *El Teatro Escolar de los Jesuitas, 1555–1640: su influencia en el teatro del Siglo de Oro*. Oviedo: Publicaciones de la Universidad, 1997. Concerning French 17th-century drama, I am referring to: Boysse, Ernest. *Le Théâtre des Jésuites*. Genève: Slatkine Reprints, 1970. I also recommend for its chapter titled "Le théâtre des jésuites" the reading of: Le Brun, Annie. *Petits et Grands Théâtres du marquis de Sade*. Paris: Art Center, 1989. Another more canonical study that helps understand the phenomenon in Germany is: Müller, Johannes, S.J. *Das Jesuitendrama in den Ländern deutscher Zunge vom Anfang (1555) bis zum Hochbarock (1665)*. Augsburg: B Filser, 1930. A more recent and comprehensive study is: Valentin, Jean-Marie. *Theatrum Catholicum: les jésuites et la scène en Allemagne au XVIè et au XVIIè siècles*. Nancy : Presses Universitaires, 1990. I also recommend Elizalde's close-reading analysis of Calderón and Lope de Vega in *San Ignacio en la literatura*.
10. Following the logic of the Trinity and of salvation through its division in three territories (Hell, Purgatory and Heaven).
11. A very useful source for this particular connection is: Wittkower, Rudolf. *Baroque Art: The Jesuit Contribution*. New York: Fordham University, 1972. A very recent study comes back to this question in a much more controversial way: Levy, Evonne. *Propaganda and the Jesuit Baroque*. Berkeley: University of California Press, 2004. This question will be developed in the second chapter.

12. I purposefully chose here to designate the type of imagination described as Loyolan, instead of using the common term 'Ignatian' which more commonly and theologically designates forms of spirituality derived from the founder of the Jesuit.
13. We shall come back to this question in more details in the closing part of this chapter.
14. Roman Jakobson represents this totality in the form of the tree and so do the first Jesuits long before him when contemplating the works of Loyola in the world (see end of chapter 2).
15. Don Quixote, however, will become the 'negative image' of the Humanist traveler that goes abroad in order to study, and Cervantes will consciously keep his hero within the borders. He becomes the errant metaphor of a country condemned to remain focused on its inside. The term 'negative image' is chosen by Michel Foucault in *Les mots et les choses* to describe Cervantes' hero. He explains that Don Quixote can be read as 'the negative image of the Renaissance' because it parodies in a pathetic way ideals that have been lost by the turn of the seventeenth century.
16. Ignatius of Loyola was named after Loiola, the Basque *aldea* in the province of Guipfizcoa where his family owned a medieval castle. Manfred Barthel comments that: "Between two tiny market towns called Azeoita and Azbeitia in a green mountain valley is the castle of Oñaz y Loyola, though actually the word 'castle' sounds a trifle pretentious for this sturdy farmhouse built around a courtyard, with a lower story of dressed stone and an upper story of wood. But even so, the family had their own coat of arms" (21).
17. Formerly known as 'Al-Andalus.'
18. Unfortunately, the *Spiritual Exercises* have often been envisioned from purely religious and spiritual perspectives. In "Loyola", Barthes discusses the structure and the various mechanisms in the text but does not re-contextualize the text in an era of literary experimentation such as Renaissance Spain. However, he recognizes in the *Degré Zéro de l'Ecriture* that literature before the seventeenth century is in a phase of experimentation and that it does not quite figure out the "problématique de la langue" (41).
19. Barthes uses the term 'imaginaire' in the original version. I use the term 'image reservoir' here according to the translation of the essay by Richard Miller (Baltimore: John Hopkins University Press, 1976).
20. "the fruit that brought these sacred exercises to the Christian Republic is now a proven and a manifest fact in the entire world and all its parts" (my translation).
21. We can add the prefix 'meta' if we consider that Ribadeneira imitates the style of traditional hagiographies and tells the story of a saint that has read them and has imitated them.
22. John O'Malley contrasts Loyola's *Exercises* in their literary quality with this humanist work: "the *Exercises* were never meant to be read, as somebody might read Luther's "Freedom of the Christian" or Erasmus's *Handbook of the Christian Soldier*" (37).
23. However, some contemporary critics like to recognize Spain as the place where Erasmus will find its true audience. Marcel Bataillon and Eugenio Asensio both come to the question: "¿Cómo llegó este cristianismo erasmiano a florecer en España *más brillantemente que en otras partes*?" (75). [Why did Erasmian Christianity flourish in Spain some much brighter than anywhere else? (my translation)]
24. "While following up the exercise of his studies, some pious and instructed men gave him the advice that, in order to learn Latin well, and at the same time to deal with spiritual matters of devotion, he read the book *De Milite Christiano* (meaning the Christian soldier), that was written by Erasmus Rotterdamus, which had in the time a great reputation of wise man with elegance in his speech. And among those who thought so was Ignatius' confessor. And therefore, following his advice, he started with all simplicity and care to read for

himself, and to pay attention to the sentences and the eloquence. But a very new and amazing thing happened, and it is that while holding this book from Erasmus in his hands (the one I said), and while starting to read in it, simultaneously his fervor was weakening, and his devotion *was getting cold*. And as he continued reading, this feeling intensified. When he eventually finished the lesson, he felt like all the fervor he had before was gone and *had frozen*, and that his heart was shut off and his spirit was turned off, and that he was not the same man after this reading as he was before. And as he noticed it several times, eventually he threw away the book from himself, and he started to develop for it as for other books from the same author such a disgust and bad feeling, that he never wanted to read any of them again, neither did he permit that these books could be read in our Society, except with great wisdom and prudence" (my translation).

25. "[Ignatius of Loyola] and the Jesuits expanded a great deal of the Humanist movement within and beyond the Counter-Reformation" (my translation).
26. In her *Vida de la Santa Madre Teresa de Jesus y algunas Mercedes que Dios le hizo, escrita por ella misma*.
27. Even though a manuscript from 1420 has been found, the first known edition of *Amadís* does not appear until 1508.
28. "Ignatius of Loyola read them (novels of chivalry) with pleasure in his youth as a knight" (my translation).
29. "In spite of the anathemas of the secular and ecclesiastical authorities, the Inquisition never prohibited them" (my translation).
30. Unlike Ribadeneira, Camâra is ordered to write down the account of Loyola's life by the saint himself when he is dying in bed. This is why the title of 'autobiography' has been granted to and accepted for this work.
31. Since *Don Quixote* will be quoted repeatedly, I have chosen the original English translation by Tobias Smollett (New York: The Modern Library, 2001): "The first that master Nicolas delivered into his hand, were the four volumes of Amadis of Gaul. "There is, said the good man, something mysterious in this circumstance; for, as I have heard, that was the first book of chivalry printed in Spain, from which all the rest have derived their origin and plan; and therefore, in my opinion, we ought to condemn him to the fire, without hesitation, as the law-giver of such a pernicious sect." "By no means cried the barber, for I have also heard, that this is the best book of the kind that was ever composed, and therefore ought to be pardoned, as an original and model in its way." "Right, said the curate, and for that reason, he shall be spared for the present." (76)
32. "If there ever was a representative man from my land, it would be Iñigo de Loyola, the Guipuzcoan hidalgo that founded the Society of Jesus, the knight errant of the Church: the son of patient tenacity" (my translation).
33. "In *Don Quixote* it is largely proven that not only did Cervantes read the account and the *Life*, but that he also technically knew them by heart" (my translation). Ortés's study, *Triunfo de Don Quijote: Cervantes y la Compañía de Jesús, un mensaje cifrado*, is a 700-page comparative close reading of Ribadeneira's *Vida de San Ignacio* and Cervantes' *Don Quixote* whose argument is very original at the beginning but rapidly becomes repetitive. Nonetheless, it is the most extensive study on the parallelism.
34. When capitalized and underlined, I refer to the text. Here I am referring to the practice of the exercises.
35. "We would agree to go to Moorish lands, invoking God for His love, so that over there they would cut our heads off" (my translation).
36. Translation of 'chrétien contemporain' such as it is described by Michel de Certeau above.

37. In the case of *Amadis*, one of the most famous passage where we see the hero confront the 'enemy' in a vision of horror is without a doubt the battle with the Endriago in the Island of the Devil. In this passage, Amadis voluntarily goes after the beast and proves his value to the people by killing it.
38. *Sensual* meaning in this discussion: 'devoted to or preoccupied with the senses' (Webster Dictionnary).
39. I have quoted earlier the first meditation on Hell, which in a more minimalist form, prepares the exercitant for this deeper second meditation involving images such as people, noises and colors.
40. That is, the practice of the exercices before the first official publication of its texts.
41. Ribadeau-Dumas explains that: « Loyola rédigea alors ses fameux *Exercises Spirituels*, composés de rites mystérieux, de voyances, de répétitions de mots, de chiffres, de gestes, de génuflexions, d'allongements sur le sol. Dans les phrases brûlantes de son *Journal Spirituel*, Loyola exposa ensuite ses illuminations, ses éblouissements, ses apparitions. L'inquisition l'enferma une deuxième fois. Elle le garda six semaines. Expulsé, il quitta Salamanque, banni d'Espagne. Il se rendit à Paris, où il retrouva parmi les étudiants de l'Université de Paris l'official de l'inquisition, qui l'accusa de magie » (214).
42. As José Antonio Maravall points out in the introduction and the third chapter of his *Cultura del Barroco* (Madrid: Ariel, 1975).
43. Camâra writes: "While reading the life of Our Lord and of the saints, he stopped to think, reasoning with himself, "What if I should do what St. Francis did, what St. Dominic did?" So he pondered over many things that he found to be good, always proposing to himself what was difficult and serious, and as he proposed them, they seemed to him easy to accomplish (. . .) At this point the desire to imitate the saints came to him (23-4). We will analyze Ribadeneira's account more in detail.
44. Interestingly enough, the hagiography is the only genre absent from Don Quixote's library.
45. "It was such an extreme thirst for them that, if I did not have another book to read, it seemed that I had lost satisfaction" (my translation).
46. "we could enter and read lives of saints, which was my favorite genre (. . .) and I wished I could die the same way, not for the love that I thought I contained, but in order to enjoy so rapidly the great joys that I read were happening in Heaven" (my translation).
47. "He was at this time very curious and friend of reading the profane novels of chivalry, and in order to pass the time that he felt long and annoying, because he was sick and bedridden, he asked if they could bring him a book of this vanity. God wanted that there wouldn't be any of them in the house, but instead other books of spirituality, that they gave to him. They brought him two books, one of the life of Christ our Lord, and another of lives of saints, that they commonly call *Flos Sanctorum*. He started to read in them, at the beginning (as I said) to pass the time, but after little by little for pleasure. Because this is the advantage of good things: the more you deal with them, the better they taste. And not only did he start to really like them, but they even changed his heart to the point that he wanted to imitate them and work according to what he was reading" (my translation).
48. "And simultaneously he was recovering strength and breath in order to struggle and truly fight, and in order to imitate the Good Jesus, our captain and Lord, and the other saints, because since they have imitated Him deserve to be imitated by us" (my translation).
49. I am referring here to the 'mediator' of desire such as it is defined by René Girard in his definition of Triangular Desire.
50. In chapter XI of the *Vida de San Ignacio de Loyola*, Ribadeneira briefly mentions that the

Franciscans fathers were afraid of the dangers in which Ignatius was putting himself, trying to walk in the steps of the Passion. Manfred Barthel comments that: "The Franciscans decided that he had seen enough of Jerusalem, and before long he found himself back on board another vessel, outward bound (. . .) This strange episode is usually given short shrift by Loyola biographers, which to my way of thinking is a mistake" (30). The truth is, there are no precise record of what truly happened in Jerusalem.

51. This phenomenon will be discussed more in details in the third chapter.
52. Barthes describes in the chapter dedicated to the 'multiple text' the four levels of the text in which Loyola takes a central position and imposes himself on the practice of his exercises.
53. Here I refer to Anthony Raspa's notions again. In *The Emotive Image*, right before the passage that I quote on page 26, Raspa describes "Ignatius' use of the residue of medieval psychology" and asserts that "he maintained the medieval gradation of the powers with the memory at the bottom, the understanding in the middle, and the will at the top, to which he was deeply attached. But he transformed their activity, meant originally to be outside in the world of nature as well as inside the mind of man, in a wholly inner world" (45–6). This concept of gradation comes from saint Thomas Aquinas.
54. Anthony Raspa argues that "The anagogic method allowed the searcher after truth to look for four levels of meanings in things rather than two and was in that sense more liberal than Protestant typology" (25).
55. According to Barthes, the logic behind the final week of the *Exercises* is the following: "Les méditations élaborées par Ignace à partir d'un découpage du grand récit évangélique, dont les épisodes sont donnés à la fin des *Exercices* sous le nom de *mystères*, possèdent ces caractères ; on peut les résumer (le résumé en est donné généralement dans l'un des préambules : c'est l'*histoire*, la *narratio* cicéronienne, l'exposé des faits, *rerum explicatio*, le premier dépliement de la chose) ; on peut aussi les augmenter, les dilater, comme Ignace l'indique expressément ; elles possèdent enfin l'attribut pathétique de la structure narrative : le suspense ; car si l'histoire du Christ est connue et ne comporte aucune surprise anecdotique, il est toujours possible de dramatiser son retentissement, en reproduisant en soi la forme du suspense, qui fait l'ombre tardive ou incertaine à se dissiper ; lorsqu'il récite la vie du Christ, l'exercitant ne doit pas se hâter, il doit en épuiser chaque station, faire chaque Exercice sans s'informer du suivant, ne pas laisser advenir trop tôt, hors de leur place,des mouvements en consolation, en un mot respecter le suspense des sentiments, sinon celui des faits. C'est en vertu de cette structure narrative, que les « mystères » découpés par Ignace dans le récit christique ont quelque chose de théâtral, qui les apparente aux mystères médiévaux : ce sont des « scènes », qu'il est demandé à l'exercitant de vivre, à la façon d'un psychodrame" (64).
56. Return here to my earlier reference to Barthes on page 16.
57. "The aspects that characterize Mysticism, at least such as we have it in Spain—in saint Teresa, in saint John of the Cross–, are clearly different from these of the Baroque; they are rather anti-Baroque, in spite of their common ground of scholastic philosophy found on either side. It is clear however that we do not consider saint Ignatius as a Mystic" (my translation).
58. In this comparative context only it would not be fair to use the adjective 'totalitarian' since it does not apply to the entirety of Baroque aesthetics.

Chapter III

1. Rome as the *caput mundi*.

2. *Alumbrado* is a rather generic term, a category of spiritually enlightened mystics wandering around Spain during the Renaissance. They were usually associated with the Lutherans since they generally insisted on the central role of Scriptures in the life of the believer and its fundamental importance over the Church hierarchy.
3. Paris counts about 200,000 inhabitants in the 1550s, it is the most populated city of the Christian West. The several schools that composed the University count about 4,000 students, which is still an unusual number for the time.
4. "Ignatius had convinced a lot of his colleagues to abandon bad frequentations and friendships based more on sensual pleasure than on exercises of virtue, and that they should fill the holy days with holy works, through devoted confession and communion. Because they would commit to these devout exercises that Ignatius had advised them to perform, they begun to miss the literature classes that would still take place in Paris on holy days. When Ignatius's master saw his classes half empty, with his disciples missing, he took it very badly, and warned Ignatius to take care of himself instead of minding the sake of other lives, and that he would not stand in his way with the students if he didn't want him as an enemy" (my translation)
5. Rabelais' *Gargantua* offers a great criticism of the ongoing chaoses at the Sorbonne in the first half of the sixteenth century. He often underlines the intolerance of the great masters and the rapidity of condemnation for heresy.
6. All Spaniards (Francisco Javier, Diego Laínez, Alfonson Salmerón, Nicholás Bobadilla) for the exception of a Portuguese and a Savoyard (Simão Rodriguez and Pierre Favre).
7. It is particularly interesting to see how this oath is formulated in Câmara's more minimalist *Autobiography*, supposedly recorded from the dying Ignatius: " . . . at this time they had all decided, what they had to do, namely, to go to Venice and then to Jerusalem to spend their lives in the service of souls; and if they were not given permission to remain in Jerusalem, they would return to Rome" (80). Even though Ignatius is inclined to return to the Holy Land, where he had once failed to perform his mission and had been threatened of excommunication, he is also aware that the same risk still exists. This is why the oath is formulated with Rome as its 'second best' for the apostolic mission of the companions.
8. It is still a rather common association in the first half of the sixteenth century, given the number of geographic maps and common beliefs that place both cities as competing centers of the earth.
9. Thomas Lucas establishes the comparison in terms of demographics in *Landmarking* (1997): "In many ways, the Rome Ignatius entered in 1537 resembled the Jerusalem Jesus entered 1500 years before. Rome and Jerusalem were sites of strategic importance and intense psychological resonance for their peoples, and both shared a tradition of theocratic leadership. Each was an important cultic capital whose history was bound in sacred traditions of theophany and epiphany. Finally, neither Rome nor Jerusalem had a population proportional to its cultural and socio-religious importance: Rome of 1537 A.D. and Jerusalem of 30 A.D. each numbered somewhere between 40,000 and 50,000 inhabitants" (39).
10. In *The Jesuits*, Barthel writes: "I found one source that suggested that Iñigo had actually fallen into disgrace [from court] because of an ulcerated nose (*ozena* is the medical term), which in those days was commonly supposed to be the result of secondary syphilitic necrosis. It seems likely enough that the dissolute young Squire Iñigo might have contracted syphilis (which had been epidemic throughout Europe for the past twenty years), and we might be tempted to conclude that Ignatius's early biographers [Câmara and Ribadeneyra] had conspired to suppress the disagreeable evidence of their subject's youthful folly"(22).
11. This inspiration echoes the Pauline inspiration we might find in Martin Luther's reforma-

tion project, and later on, in Calvin's. Nonetheless, the two Reformers insist more on the importance of Paul's epistles in the New Testament than on a mimetic behavior after the conversion experience of the Apostle. Paul remains for the Reform essentially a theologian.

12. This episode will remain one of the favorite objects of representation of Jesuit art in the following century. They are both deeply emphasized in Câmara's *Autobiography* and illustrated in Ribadeneira's *Vida* as essential highlights in the presented narrative.

13. Art Historian Gauvin Bailey recapitulates the narrative importance of this episode in Jesuit history and adds that: "Ignatius' vision at La Storta took place at a small wayside chapel on the northern outskirts of Rome: Ignatius was left with Christ's message "I shall be propitious to you in Rome" and with God the Father's declaration to Christ "I want you to take this man [i.e., Ignatius] for your servant." The vision was an important one, since it confirmed for Ignatius the name of the Society of Jesus, the name his companions had earlier chosen for their *compagnia*. It also confirmed Rome as the center of Jesuit activity" (62).

14. Rome is not only the Babylon the Great who has paid its numerous sins with the sack of 1527, it is also—as I will point out here with the instance of the *Lozana Andaluza*—the tower of Babel, a multicultural and multilingual urban center whose existence reflects the conflictive relations of the city with the rest of the European powers and also threatens the wished-for unity of the Counter-reformed Church. If there is something else Rome is lacking, it is the sense of cultural unity that once made Florence the capital of the Italian Renaissance and that is making Spain the most powerful Catholic nation of the sixteenth century. The population that the first Jesuits will encounter upon their arrival is among the most diverse in all of Europe. For this reason, the city has acquired a rather negative reputation in the rest of the European cities: in the sixteenth century, it is a place of great multiculturalism where one can hear several languages in the streets, and even several religious communities cohabitating. Surprisingly enough, it is still one of the most peaceful places in Europe at the time for a Jew to live, unlike Spain that is still undergoing the ethnic cleansing of the *pureza de sangre*. Outside of the walls of the Vatican, Rome has turned into a tolerating 'tower of Babel' in a sixteenth century agitated by religious conflicts.

15. I refer here to prostitutes, lepers, disease, starving crowds, bodies in state of physical corruption such as Lazarus's.

16. As we know, Rome has lost its status of 'capital of the world' many centuries before Loyola's arrival. As a matter of fact, the reputation of Rome and its 50,000 inhabitants was rather negative in most of mid-sixteenth-century Europe. Prior to the sack of 1527, it was already depicted as a place for perversion and corruption where power and lust were intermingled. Rome was often the reason why the Holy See was the object of so much criticism in the rest of Europe.

17. In Golden Age Spanish it designates the 'clothes washers.' These women were very often associated with prostitution, as they will throughout several centuries. In 19th-century French novels, the *blanchisseuses* are still a cover name for prostitution outside the brothel.

18. "For this reason the majority of Rome an open brothel, and they call it: Rome the Whore" (my translation).

19. "The famous excursion of Lozana and Rampín through the streets and different places of the Urbe was carefully pre-designed by the author, by taking the couple to the places whose spatial dynamics offered a *plurality of senses*, sometimes in Spanish, sometimes in Italian. Senses that turned out to be very reflective of the main theme of the whole dialogistic novel: sex and its business" (my translation).

20. Term used in the *Arcades Project* when describing the movement of what Baudelaire had

previously called *flâneur*.
21. In spite of this negative reputation, the young Ignatius of Loyola had chosen Rome in 1523 as his first destination for pilgrimage, in sudden contrast with the austerity of the cave in Manresa where he had written the first exercises. When Ignatius was asked that same year by a young lady in Barcelona why he desired to travel to Rome, the saint had difficulties justifying his choice: "When he begged from a lady, she asked where he wanted to go. He hesitated a bit whether he would tell her, but at last he resolved to say no more than that he was going to Italy and to Rome. Surprised, she said, "Do you want to go to Rome? Well, I don't know how those who go there come back. (By this she meant that in Rome they profited little from the things of the spirit.)" (Câmara 42). Câmara the 'autobiographer' feels compelled to supplement the words of the mysterious young lady. However, this passage emphasizes the general feeling that has been cultivated about Rome for several centuries in most of Europe Late-medieval authors from the peninsula give us accounts of the second fall of Rome, the fall into corruption and abuses.
22. Announced by Martin Luther in his essays.
23. I am making particular reference here to conclusions made by Jacques Derrida on the topic of ruins:
"The ruin is not in front of us; it is neither a spectacle nor a love object. It is experience itself: neither the abandoned yet still monumental fragment of a totality, nor, as Benjamin thought, simply a theme of baroque culture. It is precisely not a theme, for it ruins the theme, the position, the presentation or representation of anything and everything. Ruin is, rather, this memory open like an eye, or like the hole in a bone socket that lets you see without showing you anything at all, anything of the all. This, for showing you nothing at all, nothing of the all. 'For' means here both because the ruin shows nothing at all and with a view to showing nothing of the all." (*The Rune of the Ruinous Ruin*)
24. In works such as *The Arcades Project* and according to his notion of *Trauerspiel* such as it is analyzed by Buci-Glucksmann.
25. One of the most obvious instances of this phenomenon in Rome is probably the Basilica of San Clemente whose ground floor stands on top of three underground floors each representing a different stage in the development of Christianity. In the very bottom of this architectural superimposition one can find one of the few surviving temple of the cult of the god Mithra.
26. Famous manual of artistic guidelines for sacred interiors published by Louis Richeôme, one of the first Jesuit art historians, in 1611. The models exposed in this work, such as Greuter's, will be imitated in the decorating of Jesuit churches and seminaries throughout the world.
27. Although the ruins are not such an allegorical motif here, given the fact that Rome was sacked in 1527 and still has a lot of buildings in decay by the time Ignatius of Loyola returns to Rome.
28. As Eamon Duffy reminds us, "it would take a decade for the city to recover from the trauma of the Sack. The population had halved, the artists had fled, building had stopped, house-prices plummeted. The golden bubble of the Renaissance had been punctured" (207). Let us not forget that the Rome of the late Middle-Ages and early Renaissance had an economy based on pilgrimages to the city: artists of all kinds, hotels, transporters, soldiers coming back from the Holy Land, inns, prostitutes and clergy were all beneficiating financially from the cult of the image and the pilgrim's obsession for its veneration.
29. *The Catholic Encyclopedia* (any edition) in the entry 'Clement VII'.
30. Thomas Lucas suggests that this 'scar on her history' is also at the origins of the Church counterattack in which Rome will engage in the second half of the sixteenth century. The

presence of the future pope Paul III explains the upcoming need to overcome the trauma occasioned by the act of aggression on the Church: "A half-century-long dream of an imperial papacy collapsed in the night of the Hapsburg sack of Rome in 1527. The pontiff and his court, including Alessandro Cardinal Farnese (later Paul III), barely escaped across the *passetto* to Castel S. Angelo. From the battlements they watched impotently as Lutheran troops paraded by in looted papal vestments and played ball with the heads of Sts Peter and Paul" (78). Such an image of the Church reduced to extreme humiliation could only affect the decisions made later on by Paul III, the pope that will approve the Society of Jesus and spend the rest of his reign financing the Jesuit architectural projects.

31. Generally speaking, the city of Rome in 1540 no longer participates in the general artistic enthusiasm of the Renaissance in the same fashion Florence, Pisa and Venice still do. However Rome attracts more artists from these Northern cities than Southern cities like Naples do. In a way, the city of Rome is, by 1550, in a state of limbo since it is still recognized for its history but not necessarily as a place of artistic development. Rome is no longer the strong capital of the Holy Empire it had once been, and has lost much control on neighboring kingdoms. Charles V is coming to end of his reign and his final decision to tolerate the practice of Protestantism weakens the political ambitions of Rome. Pope Clement VII (1523–1534), born as Giulio de Medici and cousin of former Medici pope Leo X, does not impose himself as a strong figure on the throne of Peter. He is too preoccupied by the maintenance of his relations with both Charles the Fifth and his enemy François the First, the king of France married to Catarina de Medici. After the reign of Leo X, the Medici family does not invest anymore in the artistic development of this city.

32. "Once he had entered Rome, Ignatius started to move his eyes around and to consider carefully the greatness of the *business* that he wanted to *undertake*, and to get prepared, through prayer and confidence in God, for the encounters and artifices of the cruel Enemy; because he knew and predicted that a great tempest of *works* would *unload* on them" (my translation).

33. Their success is due to the financial intervention of an influent character at the court of Paul III: "Some wealthy Spaniards soon provided for them and arranged lodging at the Hospital of San Giacomo. Armed with letters from Ignatius, they sought out Dr. Pedro Ortiz, who was Charles V's proctor in Rome (. . .). Ortiz, who had known Ignatius in Paris, gave them a cordial welcome and arranged an audience with the Pope Paul III, who requested that they hold a theological discussion he and his other guests could listen to during dinner. The Iñiguists, as they were called, must have impressed him with their learning, for he responded by blessing their pilgrimage and presenting them with a gift of thirty-three gold crowns" (Meissner 173). Although the story is once again presented here, as it is in Ribadeneira's *Vida*, as a mere coincidence, we can still wonder why Ignatius was not present at an event so important that it should determine the future of the Society. For hagiographic purposes, it is understandable that stressing the coincidences gives to the creation of the order a more miraculous dimension.

34. Such as Cardinal Caraffa, the future Paul IV (1555–9) who was a strong opponent of the Jesuits in 1537. Later on, his position toward the Society changed, especially after Loyola's death in 1556. Jean-Claude Guy writes in his introduction to the Seuil edition of the *Exercices Spirituels* (1982): "L'année 1553 fut marquée en Espagne par une véritable 'tempête contre les Exercices'" (18).

35. Still without a name, this group received in 1540 from Pope Paul III the official approbation as a religious order with the name of Company of Jesus. The Jesuit hagiography has always underline the importance of the "vision at La Storta" (1538) as a key moment in

Ignatius' realization who, about to enter Rome, would have seen the Lord inviting him to serve Him: from this comes also the name's choice of Company of Jesus. Gathered in the capital, Ignatius and his followers immediately received signs of benevolence from the pope who granted them some charges: Ignatius gave the *Spiritual Exercises* to Dr. Ortiz, known in the times of Salamanca and now in Rome as representative of Charles V, to Lattanzio Tolomei (relative of cardinal Ghinucci) and to the Venetian cardinal Gasparo Contarini; Fabre and Laínez taught instead at the Sapienza University, respectively Holy Scripture and Theology. They met also Rodolfo Pio di Carpi who became—the only one in the history of the order—protector cardinal of the Company. (my translation)

36. We cannot ignore the importance that Ortiz plays in this promotion process since he represented the Emperor Charles V who favored the Spanish religious presence in Rome; his words were always to be taken rather seriously by the institution and its hierarchy: "Dr. Ortiz retired with Ignatius to make the Spiritual Exercises and emerged from the month-long retreat a transformed man; if age and position had not prevented him, he would very likely have joined the group of Iñiguists" (Meissner 176). Ortiz's experience set the example for the community. A network of influential cardinals started to build itself around the newborn Society of Jesus, in imitation of Ortiz, as if they were a need for their 'doctrine.'
37. In complement, the story around the writing process of the *Exercises* would eventually be given an explanation that would fit the greater Christian narrative, first of all by Loyola's biographers, and later on by Father De Sanctis, professor of theology at the Colegio Romano. He will claim that the book of Exercises is a revelation equal at least to that of the Bible.
38. Martin Luther writes in *The Bondage of Will*: "On the same account I have thus far hounded the Pope, in whose kingdom nothing is more commonly said or more widely accepted than this dictum: 'the Scriptures are obscure and equivocal; we must seek the interpreting Spirit from the apostolic see of Rome!' No more disastrous words could be spoken; for by this means ungodly men have exalted themselves above the Scriptures and done what they liked, till the Scriptures were completely trodden down and we could believe and teach nothing but maniacs' dreams" (124).
39. Jean-Claude Guy writes: "Ce livre, en premier lieu, est publié 'hors commerce'. Personne ne pourra se le procurer, sinon de la main d'Ignace. Et sa correspondance nous le montre très hésitant à l'envoyer à d'autres qu'à des jésuites : ainsi, en juillet 1549, refuse-t-il à un prêtre de Gérone, Jean Gesti, l'exemplaire que celui-ci souhaitait recevoir (Lettre 806)" (Loyola, *Exercices*, 11).
40. That is, deprived of all images, without hierarchical separation, and whose only center is the Scriptures.
41. Barthes sees in it a theatrical process: "C'est en vertu de cette structure narrative, que les "mystères" découpés par Ignace dans le récit christique ont quelque chose de théâtral, qui les apparente aux mystères médiévaux : ce sont des « scènes », qu'il est demandé à l'exercitant de vivre, à la façon d'un psychodrame" (64).
42. The verticality is already an essential component of the Gothic aesthetics. So once again, Loyola recycles a 'narrative form' (if one accepts to treat the Gothic as such) already existing in the greater narrative of Christianity.
43. First chapter of: Raspa, Anthony. *The Emotive Image*. Fort Worth, TX: TCU Press, 1983.
44. In his *Spiritual Journal*, the reader will discover a more intimate version of Loyola. In this diary, the founder of the Jesuits presents himself as an extremely modest and sensitive person, constantly tortured by dilemmas (often related to money) and extremely indecisive and modest. It contrasts drastically with the 'totalitarian' parameters of the *Exercises*.
45. In mid-sixteenth-century Rome, these areas were precisely the eastern margins of the city,

the neighborhoods close to the Piazza Venezia and the Fori Romani, as well as these expanding from the Quirinale to Santa Maria Maggiore.

46. The site of the Madonna della Strada was extremely central in 1537 since the Papal court was living in the Palazzo Venezia (San Marco), two blocks north of this church. Next to it was the government of the city at the Campidoglio. The streets leaving the Strada to the south formed the Jewish neighborhood. Many princes and other wealthy aristocrats had their *palazzo* in the streets right on the northwest of the church. The poor and the prostitutes were everywhere to be found around the site chosen by the Society, and mostly west of it. The chapel and the house occupied a strategic angle also during processions, and these were numerous in the second half of the sixteenth century. All in all, the position was strategic since the future church of Il Gesù would be elevated high in order to dominate these many layers of the early-Modern Rome.

47. Until 1556, Ignatius lived with the ambition of constructing a magnificent church on the site of the chapel that he was occupying with his companions, but his financial resources and the neighboring population were in complete opposition with this wish. He initialized the project but never got to see its first wall. But the seeds of his efforts had been planted, and the dynamics of the exercises passed along to his followers. It is precisely between 1556 and the turn of the century that most Jesuit buildings are going to be built in Rome, as well as in other major cities in the rest of the world.

48. Originally, Michelangelo Buonarotti had designed a new Saint Peter's with its actual central dome, but four entrances for each cardinal point, in the form of the Greek cross (Duffy 213). Bernini's project was more appealing since it represented more the spirit of the Counter-Reformation.

49. Some of the late-15th-century popes, such as Nicholas V (1447–1455) followed by Sixtus IV (1471–1484) and Innocent VIII (1484–1492), had tried to make Rome the capital of Humanism and Renaissance ideals, but this direction is drastically interrupted by the Medici interest for political power and the abuses of the relative they had placed on the throne of Peter at thirty seven years old, Pope Leo X.

50. For instance, they have worked with and published Evonne Levy's research when Thomas Lucas, S.J., was preparing the catalog on his exhibit "Saint, Site and Sacred Tragedy: Ignatius, Rome and Jesuit Urbanism" in 1990 at the Biblioteca Apostolica Vaticana. In 2004, Evonne Levy publishes *Propaganda and the Jesuit Baroque*, where she implies several times that the Jesuits had a direct influence on the Nazis.

51. Notion developed by Italian scholar Carlo Galassi Paluzzi in his survey scholarly work *Storia segreta dello stile dei Gesuiti* (1951) in which the author tries to determine whether or not the notion of 'Jesuit style' is acceptable.

52. Sacred Mountain in Italian Piedmont that underwent about four centuries of construction.

53. Interestingly enough, that same year, Borromeo is working on his *Instrucciones*.

54. Originally Borja, but Italianized earlier on.

55. For instance, the directives of the Council of Trent, largely dominated by the Jesuits, are very much in favor of a revolution in church architecture. This council was going on while Ignatius of Loyola was dying, and ended on December 4th, 1563. By then, the type of architecture envisioned by Loyola was not only approved, it was suddenly highly recommended. The architecture that appears after Ignatius's death is going to use an architectural syntax and a vocabulary in reaction against the Renaissance who had done the same thing with the Gothic. Obviously its intentions are to give a form to the ideology behind the Counter-Reformation, and the representing of the creation formulated in the exercises is to be con-

sidered as an essential parameter in the designing process of these churches. We will not explore any further the effects of the Council of Trent in the development of Roman Baroque architecture. As Anthony Blunt once concluded, in his referential work on the origins of these new forms, Rome needed to mark its religious difference toward Protestantism in the North and Islam in the South, and the Council of Trent granted the necessary artistic freedom to do so (23). But the Jesuits at Trent already proved to be pioneers in a discipline that their founder had not mastered.

56. Rudolf Wittkower, Thomas Lucas, Evonne Levy in earlier works with Lucas, Gauvin Alexander Bailey, John O'Malley.
57. In an article published originally as "Le Pli Baroque" and later on translated as "The Fold."
58. Charles Borromeo underlines in his *Instructiones Fabricae et Supellectilis Ecclesiasticae* (1577) that: "the architect should see that in ths religious decoration of the façade, according to the proportion of the ecclesiastical structure and the size of the edifice, not only that nothing profane be seen, but also that only that which is suitable to the sanctity of the place be represented in as splendid a manner as the means at his disposal will afford. However, there is one feature above all that should be observed in the façade of every church, especially a parochial church. In the upper part of the chief doorway on the outside, there should be a painted or carved, with all decorum and devotion, the image of the most Blessed Virgin Mary, holding her son in her arms; on the right-hand side there should be an effigy of the saint to whom the church is dedicated, while on the left-hand side there should be made in the same manner the effigy of another saint to whom the people of that parish are particularly devoted" (63–4).
59. In this sense, it echoes the notion of "infinity" that Wölfflin associates with verticality and lines in his investigation.
60. Unlike the Protestants who insist on the inutility of images and their sacrilegious character and would, on the contrary, increase the presence of transparent windows in the temple.
61. In order from bottom to top: Satan, his demons, the souls of Purgatory, the living souls on earth, the exercitant, the spiritual directors, the Pope and his clergy, the blessed, the saints (several categories within this category), the angels, the Holy Virgin, Christ, the Holy Spirit and eventually the Father.
62. Although the original project was to 'fill' the center of the Gesú with a vertical altar connecting with the dome. Financially, however, it was impossible to realize. This altar, as seen on drawings, was in turn void of a center.
63. "The external façade directly affects the form of the altar, crowned by a broken tympanum, and similarly to the elements decorating the tympanum of the external part of the portal, also shelters the figure of St. Andrew in ecstasy, a work by Antonio Raggi. The heavily decorated interior, made of several tonalities of marble, is bordered by a splint. It creates an effect of unity in the space increased by an almost pulsate rhythm, due to the contrast of the chapel openings and the volume of the walls" (my translation).
64. Thomas Lucas sums up the situation: "It is in May 1955, and Ignatius, as usual, is trapped for cash. His archenemy Gian Petro Carafa has recently been elected pope, and large gifts promised to the floundering Collegio Romano have dried up. In a few months, the Theatine Pontiff, rabidly anti-Spanish, will order the Casa Professa searched for Spanish arms" (*Landmarking*, 169).
65. The construction of San Ignazio also proves that the Jesuits did not have the technical space to increase the quantity of narrative elements in Il Gesù.
66. I reiterate here the distinction I originally made in the precedent chapter between 'Ignatian'

and 'Loyolan.'
67. The pope's family name, Farnese, is engraved on the façade and his image is reproduced next to the vertical altar of St. Ignatius.
68. The project of reconstruction of Saint Peter's originated during the Renaissance, and was eventually placed under the control of Michelangelo Buonarotti in 1547 by Paul III. Naturally, it had to be modified and re-conceptualized after the sack of Rome and the aggressive communication between Protestants and Catholics at the Council of Trent. Indeed, a Renaissance reflection of Catholicism through its most holy temple could have been encountered in Michelangelo's original project of a basilica with four main entrances, in the form of the Greek cross, and facing the cardinal points. Such a project mirrored the ideals of Humanism and the image of a universal Church with multiple outreaches. With the Counter-Reformation however, such as we have seen it in the development of post-1550 Roman churches, the idea of a Humanist Saint Peter's basilica was no longer so appealing. It had to be transformed so that the sacred space could reflect the infallibility and intransigence of the Catholic doctrine. Michelangelo did not live to see much of his projects realized, and the dome was not completed until 1590.

Chapter IV

1. The anxiety I am referring to here is above all the political circumstances around the wars of religion in Europe, and Spain's choice to lock itself away from the Protestant threat. This anxiety is often reflected in Sancho Panza's apparently innocent comments, when he condemns Spain's attitude of isolationism toward the rest of Europe and its growing fear of being invaded by Protestant ideas: "¿está cerrada acaso España?"
2. Cervantes, who has found much inspiration in the story of Loyola, is very aware of the contradiction around novels of Chivalry and gives us an excellent bit of literary criticism in *Don Quixote*. He illustrates very well in his masterpiece the complexity of the status of these works in the sixteenth century in the episode when the curate and the barber decide to burn the books of Don Quixote in order to save his soul: "The first that master Nicolas delivered into his hand, were the four volumes of Amadis of Gaul. "There is, said the good man, something mysterious in this circumstance; for, as I have heard, that was the first book of chivalry printed in Spain, from which all the rest have derived their origin and plan; and therefore, in my opinion, we ought to condemn him to the fire, without hesitation, as the law-giver of such a pernicious sect." "By no means cried the barber, for I have also heard, that this is the best book of the kind that was ever composed, and therefore ought to be pardoned, as an original and model in its way." "Right, said the curate, and for that reason, he shall be spared for the present" (76). In this passage, it is interesting to see that the curate and the barber present the same argument to condemn the book to the fire and, at the same time, to save it from it. As is well known, the novels of Chivalry are clearly disignated as the origin of Don Quixote's madness. They are the fiction in which he wishes to transform his reality. Nonetheless, the values they contain turn him away from the Christian salvation of the soul.
3. Concepts pointed out by Hayden White and Louis Montrose in their respectively celebrated essays "The Historical Text as a Literary Artefact" and "Professing the Renaissance: The Poetics and Politics of Culture."
4. As I have pointed out in the previous chapter, Rome is a haven for Spanish clergy, nobility and artists, and they largely dominate all of its influential spheres. The upper levels of the

Spanish society frequently come to the Holy City or they at least receive frequent news from it, and the life of Ignatius somehow becomes a popular tale of national pride.
5. Title chosen by Thomas James Dandelet for his recent study (2001) of the 200-year period in which Spain develops a political and religious control of Rome: 1500–1700.
6. Ribera's first name changed from José to Giuseppe, and ended up in the interesting linguistic combination of Jusepe; it symbolizes the merging of two cultures and two languages in one.
7. William Byron writes: "The cultivated young churchman is popularly seen as conceiving a spontaneous sympathy for the exiled young poet; literary conversations are heard at monsignore's table. Cervantes' duties are thought of as combining those of secretary, major-domo, confidant, arranging his lord's correspondence, receiving his guests" (Byron 88). Even though Byron's vision here might be a bit romanticized in order to keep each episode of Cervantes' life in a perspective of national pride, we cannot ignore the definition of a chamberlain's description.
8. We know for sure that it is at least Cervantes' second encounter with the Jesuit fathers, since he had been partially educated by them in Seville earlier on.
9. "He visited his shrines, worshipped its relics, and admired its grandeur. Just as one recognizes the size and ferocity of a lion by its claws, so Tómas measured Rome's greatness by its marble ruins, its damaged and intact statues, its fallen arches, the remains of its baths, its magnificent porticoes and amphitheatres, and its famous and holy river, which always fills its banks with water and blesses them with countless relics from the bodies of martyrs buried there. He also measured it by its bridges, which seem to be watching one another, and by its thoroughfares, the very names of which make them superior to all other streets in any other city anywhere in the world (. . .). He also observed the authority of the College of Cardinals, the majesty of the Supreme Pontiff, and the crowds and variety of people and nationalities. When he had made a tour of the seven churches, confessed to a penitentiary, kissed the foot of His Holiness, and provisioned himself with an ample stock of *agnus deis* and rosary beads, he decided to go to Naples" (translation by Lesley Lipson, 1998, Oxford World's Classics).
10. Interestingly enough, the lion is also the symbol of the 'other' city of the peninsula, Venice.
11. Siciliano confirms: "Cervantes studied *gramática* with the Jesuits in Sevilla; he attended lectures given by Father Acevedo in the Colegio of Santa Catalina. It is the contention of Astrana Marín (and others) that the glowing tribute paid to the Jesuits in the *Coloquio de los Perros* is based on Cervantes' first relations with the Society in Sevilla. Incidentally, the Jesuits were teaching "algo de filosofía y casos de conciencia" (14).
12. 'He then moved on to the college recently founded by the Company of Jesus, where he must have studied two classes of Grammar. Cervantes wrote great praises of this Jesuit fathers, and he did it with a lot of affection, years after, in the *Colloquy of Dogs*" (my translation).
13. "I don't know what it is about virtue, since I've had little or no contact with it, but it delighted me to witness the loving care, dedication, and attention with which those blessed fathers and teachers taught those boys, training the tender shoots of their youth to stand erect and not become twisted or stray from the path of virtue, which they were taught along with their letters. I reflected on how they scolded them gently, punished them compassionately, inspired them with examples, encouraged them with rewards and gently and tolerantly bore with them. Finally, they *depicted the ugliness and horror of vice and portrayed the beauty of virtue*, so that, hating the one and loving the other, they would attain the end for which

they were created" (translation by Lesley Lipson, 1998, Oxford World's Classics)
14. "Because I have heard it said of these blessed people that there are no other citizens of the world as wise as them, and as directors and guides on the path to Heaven, no one can beat them. They are mirrors where honesty, the Catholic doctrine, the singular wisdom, and finally the profound humility are all reflected. This is the base for the entire enterprise of seeing and possessing God in the afterlife" (my translation).
15. "that Cervantes would know, read and admire [Loyola's] *Spiritual Exercises*, as it appears in fact in the *Colloquy*" (my translation).
16. This is precisely where one can compare Don Quixote to Tomás of *El Licienciado Vidriera*.
17. In this respect, Steven Hutchinson argues in *Cervantine Journeys* that: "Accordingly he has only disdain for courtly knights, who "travel throughout the world looking at a map" (II.6.80) without suffering hunger or foul weather, unlike true knight-errant. Nothing could be more antithetic to Don Quixote's style of travel than reading a map" (138).
18. There is in fact a crisis in the narrative course of the novel toward the beginning. Don Quixote's first sally happens without Sancho Panza. Panza has not been mentioned by the narrative voice. In this first sally, Don Quixote's solitude limits drastically the dialogic mode: "caminando nuestro flamante aventurero iba *hablando consigo mesmo*" / ["as he was walking, our shining adventurer was *talking to himself*]. At the end of the first sally, Don Quixote returns to his hacienda and goes directly to bed. It symbolizes the death of the solitary hidalgo unable to establish a dialogic connection with the world.
19. I am alluding here to the *code interprétatif* as described by Jean Starobinski earlier on in this chapter.
20. "Thou art not much in the wrong, replied Don Quixote; but, before it comes to that issue, a knight must travel up and down the world as a probationer, in quest of adventures, until, by his repeated achievements, he shall have acquired a sufficient stock of fame; so that when he arrives at the court of some mighty monarch, he may be immediately known by his works; in that case, as soon as he shall be seen to enter the gates of the city, all the boys will surround and follow him, shouting and crying, behold the knight of the Sun" (translation by Tobias Smollett, 202).
21. For instance, the story told to George by his brother in Steinbeck's *Of Mice and Men* shares the same function: it inscribes the two errant characters in a narrative and makes reality part of this narrative.
22. "He is Christian, yet he has not totally converted to Christianity. This conviction remains at the very core of his decision to become the center of the philosophical reflection. We are dealing with a new stage in the movement of 'return to the subject'" (my translation).
23. This is the object of a very extensive and meticulous study done by Federico Ortés: *El triunfo de Don Quijote: Cervantes y la Compañía de Jesús, un mensaje cifrado* (2002). In this convincing work, Ortés concentrates more on the *Vida de San Ignacio* by Pedro Ribadeneira and the obvious influences it had on the writing process of *Don Quixote de la Mancha*.
24. "Is it possible, that after all thy travelling in my company, thou art not convinced that every thing belonging to knight-errants, appears chimera, folly and distraction, being metamorphosed into the reverse of what it is, by the power of a tribe of inchanters who attend us, changing, converting and restoring each particular, according to their pleasure; and the inclination they have, to favor or annoy us: for which reason, what seems a barber's bason to thee, I can easily discern to be the helmet of Mambrino, and perhaps to a third, it will assume a quite different appearance" (translation by Tobias Smollett 246).
25. See particularly Ortes's *Triunfo de Don Quixote* and Elizalde's *San Ignacio en la literatura*. Julio Baena underlined recently in *Discordancias Cervantinas* (2003) that: "Nunca se insi-

stirá lo suficiente en el obvio paralelismo entre la narración de la conversión de Loyola y la del enloquecimiento de don Quijote. Cambia, tal vez, el género literario que les 'seca el cerebro' a ambos héroes, pero es idéntica la *determinación vital mimética* (salir a emular a otros caballeros/santos), la obsesión y concentración de energías . . ." (69). ["One will never insist enough on the obvious parallelism between the narration of Loyola's conversion and the *enloquecimiento* in Don Quixote. Maybe the literary genre that 'dries up the brain' to both heroes changes, but the mimetic vital determination is identical (to go out and emulate knights/saints), and so is the obsession and the concentration of energies . . ."] (my translation).

26. Five centuries of criticism have proven the narrative function of Don Quixote's psychological condition.
27. For instance, in the first part, there is a very odd chapter division:
    Fue a llamar a su amigo el barbero maese Nicolas, con el cual se vino a casa de don Quijote,
    [CAPÍTULO VI: *Del donoso y grande escrutinio que el cura y el barbero hicieron en la librería de nuestro ingenioso hidalgo*]
    el cual aún todavía dormía. Pidió las las llaves, a la sobrina del aposento donde estaban los libros autores del daño, y ella se las dio de muy buena gana. Entraron dentro todos (. . .) (109).
    Later on, the narrator interrupts the 'Aventura del Vizcaíno' with an anecdote about the discovery of Benengeli manuscript. This interruption happens with a chapter and part separation (*Don Quixote I*, between Chapter 8 and Chapter 9).
28. "I would your worship would take notice, replied Sancho, that those you see yonder are no giants, but wind-mills; and what seem arms to you, are sails; which being turned with the wind, make the mill-stone work. It seems very plain, said the knight, that you are but a novice in adventures: these I affirm to be giants, and if thou art afraid, get out of the reach of danger, and put up thy prayers for me, while I join with them in fierce and unequal combat" (Smollet's translation).
29. This akward confrontation underlines the difference between Quixote's worldview and the technological reality of 1605.
30. For Marthe Robert, in her *Roman des origines et Origines du roman* (1972), the double gaze and the *interpretative code* is a consequence of historico-political circumstances: "Sans doute au temps de l'Inquisition la dissimulation dans les ouvrages de l'esprit était-elle simplement mesure de prudence, les idées devaient ruser, et mieux valaient pour elles avoir l'art de le faire" (212).
31. "Even though I look like his father, I am his step-father"/ "This second part of *Don Quixote* that I am presenting to you is made of the same artifact and cloth I used for the first, and in it I give you a blown-up picture of Don Quixote, and eventually dead and buried, so that no one dares to have him returns for more"/ "Only for me was Don Quixote born, and I was born for him: he knew how to act and I knew how to write" (my translations).
32. Since God has abandoned the world, according to Georg Lukacs.
33. "He proposed to himself to get knighted by the first man he would encounter on his path, in imitation of many others who had done the same thing" (my translation).
34. Such as discussed in Barthes' *Loyola* and in the first chapter: "mettre en place une *machine capable de s'entretenir toute seule*" (73).
35. In the same fashion as we have it in the preceding quote from *Don Quijote*: "el primero que topase."

36. "Is Spain by fortune open, in such a way that it is necessary to close it, or what is this ceremony?" (my translation).
37. The space in most novels of Chivalry is fundamentally transnational and works after Cervantes, such as Mateo Aleman's *Guzman de Alfarache* or Baltasar Gracián's *Criticón* will also insist on the importance of crossing national borders.
38. "I am just upon the brink of darting, plunging and ingulphing myself into the profound abyss that opens wide before me" (Smollett 715) / "[you have] withdrawn me from the most delightful prospect and agreeable life that ever mortal saw or enjoyed" (Smollett 716). One can notice here the difficulty for the translator with the insistence on *vista* in Spanish. Smollett does not reproduce very faithfully the idea of *vida* and *vista* as intertwined concepts.
39. "This is my friend Durandarte, flower and mirror of all the brave knights in love of his time. He is, like me and many others, under the spell of Merlin, this French wizard supposedly son of the Devil" (my translation).
40. I say 'virtually' because Don Quixote renounces to be a knight-errant at the end of the second part and denies the salvation process in which he has been engaging since the beginning of the story. Maybe this is due to the fact that he has been excommunicated.
41. See Julio Baena, *El Círculo y la Flecha: Principio y Fin, Triunfo y Fracaso del Persiles* (Chapel Hill: University of North Carolina Press, 1996).
42. It is the central argument of Ruth El Saffar in *Novel to Romance: a study of the Novelas Ejemplares* (1974). Although her study focuses on the *Novelas Ejemplares*, the argument can be partially applied to the *Trabajos de Persiles y Sigismunda*.
43. "Spaniard, be gone, and go search your adventure somewhere else, if you don't want to die torn into pieces by our claws and teeth; and do not ask who is giving you this advice, but thank Heaven *you have found piety amongst the beast*" (my translation).
44. "There is no better asylum than the one found in the house of the Enemy" (my translation).
45. "You may give, good man, infinite thanks to Heaven for liberating you from the power of these malicious spells, which are everywhere to be found in the Northern lands. They say that some turn into wolves, male or female, because good and evil can come out of each gender. How it happens, I ignore it, and as a Christian who is Catholic, I do not believe it. But experience shows the opposite. All I can understand is that all these transformations are illusions of the Devil, with God's permission to punish this wicked kind of people for their abominable sins" (my translation).
46. "Maybe the laws of the human taste are stronger than those of religion" (my translation).
47. "With this different story, they admired the tellers, and it woke up thousands of praises for them, and thousands of good hopes that were announced to them, especially Auristela, who remained extremely fond of the two Barbarian women, mother and daughter" (my translation).
48. "I will tell you, discreet Barbarian, that the persecution performed by those called inquisitors in Spain tore me apart from my country; when they force you to leave it, you can call that 'tearing apart,' and not 'leaving.' I came to this island in odd circumstances, after infinite dangers, always thinking they were behind my back if I turned my head, thinking those dogs were biting my skirt; and even here I am afraid" (my translation).
49. "I left my house with the intention to go to Rome this year, since the Holy Father has opened up the arches of the Church's treasure and we are aware of the infinite graces that one can obtain from Him. I was taking it easy, more as a poor pilgrim than a rich knight. I came to this village (. . .) and as I was trying to save other lives, I lost mine in the process"

(my translation).
50. "Oh great, oh powerful, oh most holy, / spiritual city of Roma! Before you I take a bow / Devout, new pilgrim in humility / and admire so much beauty. / Thy sight, who supersedes thy reputation, / stops the genius, even the divine one, / from there that came to see thee and adore thee / with tender affection and bare feet. / The dirt of thy ground, that I contemplate, / mixed with the blood of martyrs, / is the universal relic of the earth. / There is no part of Thee that do not serve as example / of holiness, modeled as thee are / on the great model of the City of God" (my translation).
51. In his theory, the 'Guarantee of Meaning' stands as the visual proof of an ideology. In the case of Catholicism, Rome (as many other places) stands as the visual *axis mundi* that gives meaning to the faith.
52. "He went to seek the Jewish woman to ask her to lower the effect of the spells that were killing Auristela, or to just get rid of them entirely. (. . .) The Jewish woman did it like that, as if she had in her hands the distant health and sickness, or as if all bad things did not depend on God's will, just like the bad things that derive from guilt" (my translation).
53. "They showed her the death of Christ, the works of His life, from the manger to the Cross. They exaggerated the force and efficiency of the sacraments, and pointed their finger to the second table of our fall, that is, penitence, without which one cannot open the door of Heaven, a door that sin usually shuts. They showed her in the same fashion the ever living God Jesus Christ, seated at the right of the Father, being as alive and whole as in Heaven, made sacrament on Earth, whose most holy presence cannot be divided by any absence, because one of the attributes of God, among many other equal, is to be in all places, by power, by essence and by presence. They guaranteed her infallibly the Coming of this Lord to judge the world from the clouds of Heaven, and in the same fashion the stability and strength of his Church, against which the doors—I mean the forces—of Hell cannot do much. They talked about the power of the Holy Father, viceroy of God on Earth and holder of the keys to Heaven. Finally they were not left with anything else to say they thought could be given to Auristela and Periandro in meditation" (my translation).
54. "What we have here *given* are precisely those discourses, that is, the explanations of human existence given by the Catholic Church. (. . .) Cervantes has got the 'signified;' he is missing the signifier, and has to make it" (my translation).
55. "As you know well and as they have taught me here, our souls are always in a continuous movement and cannot stop but in God as its center. In this life, desires are infinite, and are chained one to another, and they work together, and they form a chain that probably gets to Heaven, and in the same fashion finishes in Hell on the other end. If you think, Brother, that this language is not mine, and goes far beyond the education I have been receiving during the few years of my life in those remote parts, I warn you that experience has painted and written greater things in the *tabula rasa* of my soul" (my translation).

Chapter V

1. In this respect, we cannot isolate Spanish literature from French literature in any ways since there was always an exchange.
2. I use the possessive adjective 'his' here and not 'her' because Gracián was writing for an exclusively male audience in 1657.
3. In opposition to animals, human are for Baltasar Gracián a very complex creature that never turns up twice with the same configuration: "Todos los tigres son crueles, las palomas

sencillas, y cada hombre *de su naturaleza diferente*" / "All the tigers are cruel, all the doves are gentle, and all men are different from one another by nature" (my translation). Therefore casuistry is essential from his point of view.

4. I already developed this argument in the first chapter, so I will avoid repeating it here. This aphorism deals with Gracian's notion of *mediodezir*.
5. This is not a translation; Foucault said this in English at a conference in Berkeley, California.
6. For instance, this 'rule' by Ignatius seems to denounce the illusions in reality in a Gracián-like fashion: "It is characteristic of the evil angel, who takes on the *appearance* of an angel of light, to enter by going along with the devout soul and then to come out by his own way with success for himself" (206).
7. That is, the salvation of the individual within the mortal parameters of social existence.
8. When Gracián is writing *El Criticón*, France and Spain are fighting for acquisition of territories around the Pyrenees, just like they were a century earlier, when Loyola was writing the *Spiritual Exercises*. In 1653, Spain loses the battle against France in Rocroi. It partially explains the many references that Gracián makes about the French being the cosmological opposites of the Spaniards.
9. The verb *enseñar* in Spanish would better translate the idea since it means *to teach* and *to show* at the same time.
10. "There is no thing that does not have its contrary to engage in a battle, for victory or for defeat; everything does and undoes: every action is followed by a reaction. The elements, that remain on the frontline, start battles amongst themselves; they follow the mixes, and take turn in destroying each other; the bad things dry up the good ones, and so does bad luck with chance" (my translation).
11. In works such as *Robinson Crusoe, Candide, Supplément au voyage de Bougainvillé*, etc.
12. Alexandre Cioranescu attempts to explain this notion in the following fashion: « Presque toute la production littéraire qui dépend d'une façon ou d'une autre des modes espagnoles, se caractérise par une préoccupation fondamentale, plus ou moins transparente, plus ou moins clairement expliquée : la conscience d'un monde trompeur, des fausses apparences dont nous sommes les victimes, de l'*engaño*, ou faculté de tromper, du monde réel et de notre imagination, avec, comme contre-partie, la conscience du *desengaño*, fruit de l'expérience qui représente la vie » (235).
13. "All come in as you both saw it, singing, and later come out crying, except for the jealous ones who do the opposite. The remedy to avoid this failure is to come down from the clouds from the beginning" (my translation).
14. "You are right indeed to complain about the chaos of the world, but you should not ask who ordered it this way; it is not about who organized it this way, but rather about who disordered it. Because you need to know that this Supreme Artifice was designed on purpose to appear as such today, and the *falsified nature of things* was placed right at the threshold of the world, and the true nature of things was thrown far away where it was never seen nor heard, where human beings would never found it" (my translation).
15. As it is simultaneously *affect* and *state* of the world. This is why this word only exists in Spanish; it has been impossible to translate it in another language since it is a junction of several meanings.
16. "What kind of art of yours is this? What capacity can see above one hundred eyes, and can hear with one hundred ears, and can work with one hundred hands? And process all of it with two gazes, doubling the attention in guessing how much need to be seen in order to decipher the entire world?" (my translation)

17. In the first half of the seventeenth century, however, this economic power turns into an illusion since Spain is not able to keep the wealth driven from Central and South America within its borders.
18. I associate *Don Quixote* to this tradition for the episode of "Montesinos' Cave" in which the hidalgo falls asleep but he dreams a whole adventure comparable to that of Ulysses or Dante. All these heroes are exposed to the underworld at some point in their epic journey.
19. German critic Krauss adds that these literary references all served "Gracián's purpose of putting on a "collective display of the intellectual and moral world through the developmental tendencies of the novel" as "no one had dared to attempt with such scope since Dante" (24). "For Gracián, all artistic representation served only to make *visible* the anatomy of thought"(27)." (Spadaccini 313).
20. It was already occurring during the Renaissance. With the Baroque, we witness the exhaustion of the revival of classical models.
21. Gracián becomes friend of the Viceroy of Aragon, the duke of Nocera, who will become his benefactor and protector.
22. "Spiritual matters are painted in figures of material and visible things."/ "What cannot be seen is almost non-existant" (my translation).
23. The New World Order is a notion that is very well developed in the collection by Spadaccini and Talens. We know that the conquest of America will also result in many conflicts between the Society of Jesus and the political powers. It will also result in internal wars within the Society itself, between the Jesuits in charge of the administration and those that are missionaries on the new continent.
24. Menippean satires are conventionally chaotic in organization, and it is usually difficult (if not impossible) to pin down the specific targets of ridicule. Some good examples are Rabelais's *Gargantua and Pantagruel* and Laurence Sterne's *Tristram Shandy*. The Russian theorist Mikhail Bakhtin devotes a lot of his attention to Menippean satire in general and Rabelais in particular, drawing attention to what he calls their dialogism.
25. See the 'books of monsters:' a genre of the Renaissance, ancestor of the 'freak show,' these books would be entire catalogs of *abnormal* cases (conjoined twins, unclassified animals, hermaphrodites, deformed babies, etc.). One of the most famous 'book of monsters' is Ambroise Paré's *On Monsters and Marvels* published in 1573. The problem is much more complex than asserted here, however. I suggest here that the difference between Gracian's monsters and those we find in the Renaissance is that Gracian's monsters are only allegorical while the Renaissance seems to be fascinated by what we may call materially real monsters (the ones listed in Pare's book). There are, however, allegorical monsters in Renaissance texts. For example, I have mentioned Dante several times in this chapter and his poem is being reprinted and commented upon throughout the Renaissance (by scholars like Landino and Vellutello) and many of his monsters are being read allegorically. In the epic poems of Ariosto and Tasso, monsters appear with great frequency and are also read allegorically. In fact, one of the ways in which Ariosto entered the canon was through the addition of allegorical interpretations of his cantos which were seen to ennoble his poem.
26. Chiron appears in Dante's Inferno with the other Centaurs who are guardians of the circle of the violent, shooting arrows into the sinners who are in a river of blood. Machiavelli also cites Chiron in *The Prince* (a political work which discusses the difference between appearance and reality, you don't have to be good, just seem so), Chapter XVIII and instead of depicting him as the perfect monster, he praises him as the perfect mentor for princes because he embodies (and this is good for Machiavelli) the human and the bestial, that is, rationality and brute force (and here Machiavelli is dismantling classical visions of morality

espoused by Cicero).
27. "Realize, said Chiron, that you are awake and dreaming. Oh, Bosch was such a great painter, now I understand his caprice! You will see incredible things (. . .) You won't find the sense in things and in a world that has no feet and no head, and as mercy will be left headless" (my translation).
28. "And not all are men; there are some horrible monsters and even devils living in the gulfs of big populations" (my translation).
29. "[men] have their guts more evil than that of vipers, a breath that contains more venom than that of dragons, envious and evil eyes worst than the basilisk's, dog teeth and perfidy noses covered with their wrath, bigger than the elephant's trunk. In this way, only man gathers all the offensive weapons that were divided between the creatures, and that is why he is the most dangerous of all" / "There is no other jumping sphinx that oppresses more the *meat* (I mean, the *men*) than the ignorance of himself" (my translation). The description cited here from the chapter on the "Moral Anatomia del Hombre" recalls many descriptions of the materially real monstrous creatures that we find in books like Pare's. The unknown, disordered, category-escaping monster is actually an assembly of known elements. Da Vinci suggested that painters who wished to depict monsters build them from diverse animal parts (a fun fact). So again, that distinction between the allegorical and the materially monster seems blurred here.
30. Also a Renaissance notion is the idea that the monster is a sign waiting for interpretation. I am thinking here of the way in which Benedetto Varchi begins his discussion of monsters at the Florentine Academy (1548): he begins with an etymology which links monster to "mostrare", it is something that shows, signifies, means something else when it is a portent. It speaks of the sin of the parents, of impending doom, of God's wrath. Monster should be understood as "prodigio."
31. "What happens? What do you see? asked the old man.—What am I supposed to see! What I could never want to see or believe: I see a monster, the most horrible I saw in my entire life, because it does not have feet, it does not have a head. What a disproportionate thing! No part corresponds to anything; there is no sense in all of him. What fierce hands it has! And it is not a wild animal, nor is it a fish; it is a bit of both. Its mouth is like a wolf's, from where no truth ever came out!" (my translation).
32. For instance, in the episode of the Medusa.
33. "the women, in Gracián's historical stage, has turned into a monster who succeeded in undermining the masculine values of virtue and courage"/ "any entity that gathers characteristics that do not correspond to its true nature" (my translation).
34. Once again, one of Gracián's "collages" made of various traditional sources.
35. "This deceitful female. O Betrayer, O barbarian! O blasphemous woman! Fiercer than the wild animal, is it possible that you have ceased your caresses in this, when they were so careful and affectionate?" (my translation).
36. "Everything has its middle; don't you go to the extremes. Go through the middle and you will be safe. Fly through the middle!" (my translation).
37. It is the subject of an entire chapter that José Antonio Maravall dedicates to the anxieties around urban development in his celebrated *La Cultura del Barroco*. In this critical work, Maravall underlines also that: "las extensas ciudades son el ámbito de los suntuosos templos jesuitas y no sabemos de otros templos más representativamente barrocos" (230) / "the major cities are the environment for the sumptuous Jesuit temples and we do not know any temples that represent the Baroque so well (my translation).
38. "All of this universe is made of opposites, and finds its energy in their confrontation (. . .)

There is not one thing that does not have its opposite so that it can fight it (. . .) like the Spaniards with the French" (my translation.

39. "This one over there that seems to you close to the earth with her feet, it is Heaven, the crowned head of the World and Lady of all of It, the sacred and triumphant Rome, for her value, knowledge, grandeur, order and religion; court of persons, office of men, since she restitutes it to the whole world and all the other cities are its colonies of principles" (my translation).

40. "It is called the Louvre (and I don't follow your evil inclination) because there traps have been prepared for the rebel wolves with sheep fur, I mean, these awful Huguenot beasts" (my translation).

41. "What do you see when you look?"—I see, said [Andrenio], a royal mother for so many nations, a crown for two Worlds, a center for so many kingdoms, a jewel for all of the Indies, a nest for the Phoenix, and a sphere for the Catholic Sun crowned with ray articles and blazons in light.—Well I see, said Critilo, a Babylon of confusion, a Lutecia of horrors, a Rome of mutations, a Palermo of volcanoes, a Constantinople of fog, a London of pestilences, an Alger of captivity" (my translation).

42. "In the Babylon of Spain, in the new wonder of Europe, in the mother of nobility, in the garden of divine plans (. . .) Madrid, Babylon, mother, wonder, garden, archive, school, genitor, portrait and heaven" (my translation).

43. Again, this is why most of Spanish artists study in Rome for a number of years before they integrate the court and find a benefactor that will help them developing their art in the homeland.

44. "It is well-know that the Jesuits are the first that seek to assimilate the Modern consciousness of the urban man as human being dwelling in the big city. *El Criticón*, in contrast with *Don Quixote*, participates in this sensibility and its spaces, although allegorical, are essentially urban" (my translation).

45. "I promise you that in order to live a man must protect his body from head to toes not with little eyes but with big and awaken eyes: eyes on the ears, to reveal falseness and lies; eyes on the hands, to see what it gives and above all what it receives; eyes on the arms, in order not to embrace too much and press too little; eyes on the very tongue, to watch many times what it is supposed to say; eyes on the chest, to see what it has to have; eyes in the heart, to see where it goes and who pulls him; eyes in the very eyes to see how they are watching; eyes and more eyes, and more again, and becomes in that way the great seer-captain in such an advanced century" (my translation).

46. Buci-Glucksmann develops her argument in the following manner: « À concrétiser ainsi l'abstraction du voir, ces allégories « voyeuses » symbolisent un théâtre qui autorise la multiplication infinie du visible, son exploration scientifique et ses fantasmagories poétiques. Aussi, dans cette grande somme romanesque du baroque qu'est *El Criticón* (1667), le « grand théâtre du monde avec 'son' balcon du voir et du vivre » est-il spectacle et labyrinthe des « prodiges » et des « merveilles ». Andremio, cet ensauvagé humain, apprend le monde, sa réalité et ses illusions, par la « grande variété des couleurs ». Et de s'écrier, en louant « le plus noble des sens » : « Eus-je cent yeux et cent mains pour savoir satisfaire les curiosités de mon âme, que je ne le pourrais pas ! » Et de célébrer le voir, comme sens du pluriel, de la multitude infinie, de la profusion et des différences, de la beauté. Chaque objet est une « nouvelle merveille » et la vue, « le plus noble des sens », obéit au futur principe leibnizien des indiscernables. En dépit de la plus grande diversité, « aucune feuille d'aucune plante, aucune plume d'oiseau ne se confondent avec celles des espèces différentes ». Et pourtant, comme Critilo, l'homme du jugement, lui apprendra vite, ce voir de la jouissance est aussi

lieu du leurre et de l'illusion : « Tout dans l'univers se compose de contraires et de discordances concordantes ... tout est arme et guerre. Le voir est double et, à ne suivre que les apparences, des pygmées humains peuvent être des géants de superbe et des êtres corpulents, dénués de toute substance ... » (93).

47. "Already victorious, they tried to pursue their path toward triumph in the eternally majestuous Rome, heroic theater of immortal acts, crown of the world, queen of all cities, sphere of great minds, who made the royal eagles fly toward Her, in all centuries, even the greatest. Even the Spaniards became her sons (...) Throne of enlightenment, whatever shines in her inhabits in the world, phoenix of the ages, when other cities perish, she is born again and becomes eternal, emporium of all good, court of the whole world, and everything fits in her. The one who has seen Madrid has only seen Madrid, the one who has seen Paris has only seen Paris, the one who has seen Lisbon has only seen Lisbon, but the one who has seen Rome sees all of them together, and enjoys the entire world at once, end of the Earth and Catholic gate of Heaven" (my translation).

48. "They came to a square so spacious and spicy crowned with contrasting buildings; some of them had so much majesty and looked like castles, some others were very poor, like philosopher's houses. There were even military pavillons stuck between school buildings. Our pilgrims were admirative to see so much contrast and variety in the buildings" (my translation).

49. In designing buildings that project the power of Absolutist rulers (Versailles, El Escorial, etc.)

50. "They insert mute statues between heavy columns in order to decorate the ostensible façades" (my translation).

51. "Animated stones talking with tongues of inscriptions" (my translation). There was one famous "talking" statue in Rome: for instance, "Pasquino." He is a broken (corrupted!) statue sort of at one end of Piazza Navona. Throughout the Renaissance until today people have anonymously stuck written messages to him, which oftentimes protested political or religious situations.

52. *il visibile parlar* (visible language) This is such an interesting moment in the comedy because we find ourselves on the terrace of pride (the first and most difficult vice to overcome). At the literal level, Dante is humbled before God's creation—these statues depicting examples of great humility—yet at the same time they actually spring from his own imagination (Purgatory as a concept had not yet become a widely accepted doctrine of the Church and so it lacked a stable, official iconography ...). So perhaps the real marvel is what the poet himself has created, "moving pictures."

53. "un Augusto para cada Virgilio, un Mecenas para cada Horacio, un Nerva para cada Marcial y un Trajano para cada Plinio" (Gracián 670).

54. "Quite a misconception of mine, said Andrenio, and this is the reason why the princes get richer and pay also excellent painters, famous sculptors, and honor them, and reward them much more than any excellent historian, any divine poet, or any excellent writer. But we see that paintbrushes can only portray the *exterior*, but the pen portrays the *interior*, with the same advantage the soul has on the body. The first kind of artists only express proportion, disposition, delicacy and even cruelty; but the second kind portray the understanding, the value, the virtue, the capacity and the eternal actions. The first category can blow life into their subjects temporarily, as long as the canvas will last, unless it is bronze; but the second category will give them immortality, for all the centuries to come. The first group will introduce their subject only to those who come to see them, but the second group to everyone that will read them, from province to province, from language to language, from centuries

to centuries" (my translation).
55. "I invite you to see, not only Rome, but the whole world at once, from a particular viewpoint where you can see it all. You will see not only this century, our time, but all the centuries to come"(my translation).
56. "What happened two hundred years ago, it is happening right now" (my translation).
57. "The shocking factor is not that the Jesuit would write a book about communion, but that he would write it at the end of a life dedicated to the elaboration of an eminently profane corpus distanced from the works and concerns of the Society (xvi). The skeptical trend that goes through all of Gracián's pages until *El Criticón* seems so distanced from this work. In *El Comulgatorio*, on the contrary, there is no place for doubt but all is based on blind faith. The Eucharist does not imply any *crisis*, but on the contrary it stands on an accepted truth (xxxv)" (my translation).
58. See also the introduction by Alonso Santos in Gracián, Baltasar. *El Criticón*. (Madrid: Cátedra, 1993): 22. In this analysis, Alonso Santos does not confront the two works but see in their difference certain logic: "*El Criticón para la inmortalidad, El Comulgatorio para la vida cristiana*" (22). Obviously, this approach remains very superficial.
59. "Imagine, when you are receiving communion, that you come to the orchard and that you absorb His bloody sweet with the cloth of your heart, that you get closer to the column and you untie Him to embrace Him in your arms and heal His wounds, putting in each of them a piece of your heart; realize that you are pressing Him against your crowned breast, even though the thorns are piercing, and that you feel it in the throne of your chest; that you move Him away from the arms of the cross, from where He was hanging in so much pain, and bring Him inside your entrails where He can rest" (my translation).
60. The motif of blood and washing appears seven times in the meditations of the *Spiritual Exercises*, and the exercitant is forced to imagine the sweating of blood that his hand is in charge of washing.
61. "associated to saint Ignatius' *Spiritual Exercises*, with the weight they have had on this work and other works by Gracián, since they recreate and place the images in a *lugar*, point by point, with all powers and senses involved in the play" (my translation).
62. For centuries after the publication of Loyola's *Exercises*, many Catholic writers are going to follow his tradition and publish their own 'Spiritual Exercises." This is why I feel that it is justified to call it 'literary genre.'
63. "The Virgin Mother goes out to search her son, which she loved as much as she desired. She was not looking for him like a wife looks for her husband in bed (. . .) The Virgin enters the temple and finds the knowledge of the Father in the middle of the doctors; her satisfaction got rid of her anxiety (. . .) She was forever thankful as well as gracious; she would sing a new song to God, because He had returned her beloved Jesus (. . .) From now on, she would always look after her Son God, and would never lose sight of Him, making sure with thanks that she would not risk to lose him again" (my translation).
64. "They salt their works a lot so that they do not rot" (my translation).
65. "Gracián takes the union of the Eucharist and sacrifice to its very last extremes, consubstantial to the sacrament, converting the tragedy of death into salvation. Years later, *El Criticón* will discuss a quite different transit, in which man will have to find, without any other auxiliary than those of virtue and his works, in solitude and without any other help, the unknown location of the 'immortal gates.'" (my translation)

Chapter VI

1. According to the *Dictionnaire Historique de la Langue Française* (directed by Alan Rey), "c'est un emprunt du XVIe siècle au grec *atheos* 'qui ne croit pas aux dieux'. Rabelais emploit le mot en grec à propos de Jules Scaliger" (135)
2. Gassendi, for example, had been a priest. This explains his great knowledge of Christianity.
3. His disagreements with Descartes were wide-ranging; aside from a number of important issues in their scientific theories about the nature of the world, they differed deeply concerning the nature of philosophical and scientific method. Although Gassendi shared much with Descartes, including an opposition to the Aristotelianism of the time, he was best known as a champion of Epicurus, whose philosophy he developed in a way that attempted to bring it into line with Christian thought. At the centre of this position is a mechanistic, atomistic view of the world, though Gassendi added to it a belief in the immortality of a spiritual soul which lay outside the physical. Nevertheless, he rejected both Descartes' argument for dualism and his account of the relationship between mind and body.
4. For a detailed investigation of Descartes' years at this institution, refer to: Stohrer, Walter John. "Descartes and Ignatius Loyola: La Flèche and Manresa Revisited." *Journal of the History of Philosophy* 17 (Jan 1979): 11–27.
5. As demonstrated by Matthew L. Jones in his recent investigation "Descartes' Geometry as Spiritual Exercise."
6. For reference on this connection please refer to the following article: Hermans, Michel and Michel Klein. "Ces *Exercices Spirituels* que Descartes aurait pratiqués." *Archives de Philosophie* 59 (Jul-Sep 1996): 427–40.
7. Jonathan Israel analyzes in *Radical Enlightenment* (2002) the reaction of the Jesuits in relation to the development of Cartesian thought in the years following Descartes's death: "When Descartes' remains were transferred to the imposing church of Sainte Geneviève-du-Mont, in Paris, in 1667, it was forbidden for any funeral oration to be delivered (...) The Sorbonne repeatedly reaffirmed its condemnation of Descartes' doctrines, as was widely noted in Spain and Italy as well as France. The largest teaching order, the Jesuits, increasingly stifled those voices within their own ranks sympathetic to Cartesianism" (39)
8. On the basis of free will, the Jesuits believed that every man was given the means in the world to execute the commandments of God, and that at every moment a man could find around him a solution handed to him by the Creator. Through *pouvoir prochain*, the just would be able to recognize this solution.
9. This question is central to the debates ongoing during the Enlightenment, since the Jesuits will be in charge of censoring publications, under the reign of Louis XV. Also, they sponsor a great number of literary figures around the *Journal de Trévoux*, a literary publication for the Jesuits and their friends. This literary group will initiate the attacks against the *Encyclopédie* and tries to come up with a similar project in order to counter-attack Diderot and his group of contributors. Among the group of Trévoux, only one name will remain famous throughout the centuries: the Larousse brothers' original dictionary was launched by the Jesuits of Trévoux.
10. It is interesting to note that in sixteenth-century Italian theater the Spaniard was often an object of fun (and of course Italian theater was all the rage in France, with Italian acting troupes routinely performing in France). The comic aspect of the figure derived from something other than what I am discussing here for the Spaniard was often a sort of dandy in love who spouted Petrarchan verse to woo his lover but mangled the Italian language.

More of a sort of linguistic misfit unable to seduce than the Latin Lover described here.
11. Madame de La Fayette is the first recognized author of this period to write a *Histoire Espagnole*, where characters obey the laws of their desire. Lesage's *Gil Blas*, to a certain extent, participates in the mythology of a Spanish decadent morality in which its main character participates until he realizes the vanity of this lifestyle. Even Robinson Crusoe, on his island, entertains a certain fantasy for the immorality of the Spaniards; he is almost more afraid of the invasion of the 'Spanish Papists' on his virgin territory than of a possible encounter with the Cannibals. Spaniards, along with Italians, conserve such an image in the rest of Europe because they have resisted the Protestant Reformation by a reinforcement of Catholic principles which often contradict the evolution of their social codes. The image of Spanish Catholicism outside of Spain seems to reflect the problematic raised by Pascal's *Lettres*, that is, a tolerance for various forms of sinful gratification. In summary, 'Spanish' is associated with 'Jesuit,' and 'Jesuit' is morally associated with 'libertine,' then consequently 'libertine' is associated with 'Spanish' in a triangular logic. In the meantime, there is still no such thing as libertinage in Spain. In the absolutist France of Louis XV, on the contrary, it becomes a genre of the novel as much as a lifestyle in aristocracy.
12. Please refer to Dorothy McGee's investigation conducted in the 1930s: she found a significant number of Gracián's works in Voltaire's library and did a philological comparison of some of their texts in order to stress the influence of Gracián in Voltaire. No one has worked on the comparison ever since.
13. This argument has been developed in Manfred Barthel's *The Jesuits*. It is interesting to juxtapose this assumption to the defensive argument of French Jesuit Caveirac. He responds to Voltaire's attacks in a paradoxical way in his *Appel à la Raison* (1762):
À la haine des hérétiques a succédé celle de tous les ennemis de la Religion, libertins, mécreans, indociles; et il ne faut pas en être surpris ... *odiosum sane genus hominum officia exprobrantium*... Les enfants des anciens disciples de l'Université ont hérité de l'éloignement inspiré à leurs pères. (5) Nous combattons les préjugés du siècle. Il a donc fallu combattre avec leurs propres armes. Il a fallu à regret nous éloigner des vues de Saint Ignace pour nous rapprocher de celles des ennemis de la Société. (10)
14. This fear as of the novel and its depiction of corrupt clergy as a threat to moral order can also remind us of the impact of the novella tradition in sixteenth-century Italy. In this sense, perhaps the Boccaccian novella is a precursor to the novel. Boccaccio's anti-clerical stance and multiple depictions of clergy as sexual predators and manipulators who use the church and its teachings to obtain their own personal sexual satisfaction lead to the censorship of the *Decameron*. Boccaccio's tales are repeatedly denounced as threatening the moral education of good Catholics. Juan Luis Vives, a converso who wrote the influential *The Education of a Christian Woman* (1528) included Boccaccio in a list of works that women should not be allowed to read (also included were chivalric epics).
15. Novelists who are not necessarily libertines also participate in this movement of representation, such as Diderot in *La Religieuse*. In this novel, Diderot depicts the individual desires of nuns in contemporary convents, whether they lead them to violence or lust.
16. The *prêtres réfractaires* were the members of the Catholic clergy who refused to abide by the rules of the Republic after the Revolution and united to re-establish the Ancien Régime in order to regain the pre-revolutionary status of the Church.
17. This text is a transcript of Lacan's press conference during his trip to the city of Rome in 1974.
18. By 'deconstructive,' I mean it in the Derridean sense. It makes perfect sense when Jacques Derrida himself recognizes the argument of both Sade and Lacan regarding the atemporal

nature of Roman Catholicism and its supremacy over other forms of spirituality in "Foi et Savoir": « Nous ne sommes pas loin de Rome, mais nous ne sommes plus à Rome. Penser "religion", c'est penser le "romain". Cela ne se fera ni dans Rome, ni trop loin de Rome. Chance ou nécessité pour se rappeler à l'histoire de quelquechose comme la « religion » : tout ce qui se fait et se dit en son nom devrait garder la mémoire critique de cette appelation » (12).

19. The double-faced masked figures discussed here seem to be the offspring/descendents of sixteenth-century court culture in which one always had to hide one's efforts with art (Castiglione's idea of sprezztura). The other model of dissimulation that seems to loom large here is Machiavelli who reveals that those in charge must be the most perverse (or he would probably say must abandon Christian virtue). The important thing for Machiavelli is not to be good but to seem good, an idea that connects perfectly with what the Pope says to Juliette in regard to the fact that the religious morality is needed to control the masses but the enlightened elite dwells beyond these rules/conventions, as we will see later on in this chapter.

20. Annie Le Brun has based the argument of her book *Petits et Grands Théâtres du Marquis de Sade* (1989) on this assumption. Le Brun is the first scholar to make a direct connection between Sade's education at Louis-le-Grand with the Jesuits and the abundance of baroque motifs in his works.

21. Again it seems that we are hearing the voice of Loyola disserting on the importance of hearing *historias* during the practice of the Exercises. The exact quote from which I have derived this series of directions in the art of creating mental visual scenes comes from the preliminary directions given to spiritual directors by Loyola: "The person who gives to another the method should accurately narrate the *story* (. . .). [The director should be] going over the points with only a brief or summary explanation (. . .). By taking this *story* as the authentic foundation, [the exercitant] can thus discover something that will bring better understanding or a more personalized concept of story" (121). I emphasize here that the translation for *historias* is not *history*, as it has been sometimes accepted in various translations of the *Spiritual Exercises*.

22. If we consider the parodic dimension of this work and admit that Sade imitates here the logothetic nature of Counter-Reformation spirituality, then Barthes' argument is no longer valid.

23. It appears obvious that Sade was familiar with the Spanish Golden Age novel *La Pícara Justina* written by Francisco López de Úbeda in 1605.

24. "Ultimate concern" is the definition of *faith* given by German theologian Paul Tillich

25. This also proves that Sade is not always working in the 'logothetic' mode that Barthes attributes to him.

26. In his recent investigation, John D. Lyons comes to a similar conclusion about François de Sales: "François de Sales is probably closer to Sade than is Loyola because, for one thing, he has more to say about the temptations of sexuality, and for another, the progression François de Sales describes in such detail in his two major works parallels the development Harari locates in Sade's method (. . .) The comparison that Harari and Barthes make between Sade and the meditative imagination seems highly persuasive. Sade's erotic imagination is a plausible adaptation (perhaps parodic, perhaps not) of François de Sales's work" (88). Although this is an extremely interesting parallel, it is another instance of 'suggestion without further discussion' already encountered in other scholarly works.

27. I have already developed this argument in a previous publication in *Congrès Sade* (2004), so I will not reiterate here my comparison between Don Quixote and Juliette. Nonetheless,

Foucault's assumption is based on the following argument: « le grand récit de la vie de Juliette déploie, tout au long des desires, des violences, des sauvageries et de la mort, le tableau scintillant de la représentation. Mais ce tableau est si mince, si transparent à toutes les figures du désir qui inlassablement s'accumulent en lui et se multiplient par la seule force de leur combinatoire qu'il est aussi déraisonnable que celui de Don Quichotte, quand de similitude en similitude, il croyait avancer à travers les chemins mixtes du monde et des livres, mais s'enfonçait dans le labyrinthe de ses propres représentations. Juliette exténue cette épaisseur du représenté pour qu'y affleure sans le moindre défaut, la moindre réticence, le moindre voile, toutes les possibilités du désir » (223).
28. In the *Voyage d'Italie*, Sade describes the chiesa delle Religiose as « peinte et ornée avec tant de goût qu'on la prendrait plutôt pour *une décoration d'opéra* que pour un temple de la divinité » (125–6).
29. The *ordo salutis* is the theological doctrine that deals with the logical sequencing of the benefits of Salvation worked by Christ which are applied to the believer by the Holy Spirit.
30. Pope Pius confirms here one of Juliette's fundamental belief, which she has previously declared at the beginning of her journey: "Voilà d'où vient que les puissances de l'Europe vivent toujours en bonne intelligence avec Rome; nous autres grands de la terre méprisons et bravons ces foudres fabuleuses du méprisable Vatican. Mais faisons les craindre à nos esclaves" (458).
31. Philippe Sollers developed this problematic in *Sade contre l'Etre Suprême* in 1996.

Afterword

1. He justifies his method to the comtesse in the following terms: « Pardon, madame la comtesse, si ma description ne se suit pas avec autant de méthode que celle de M. Richard. J'ai cru que, pourvu que l'indication fût juste, l'*itinéraire à suivre* était à peu près égal. J'indique les choses comme je les ai vues. C'est au voyageur qui *me suivra* à rédiger ensuite, comme il lui conviendra, chacun des objets qu'il voudra suivre. Quant à moi, j'écris à mesure que je vois et par conséquent, il ne faut pas s'attendre à un arrangement bien exact dans le détail. Encore un coup, je me suis attaché à la vérité et nullement à la symétrie » (84).
2. "J'ai cru devoir la retranscrire par sa singularité" (106). It means : "one gave Ignatius to the altars, the other gave the altars to Ignatius."
3. Marcel Hénaff wrote that "for Sade as for Ignatius, the imaginative concentration is nothing less than *hallucinating the referent*" (93).
4. For reference on this aspect of Jesuit history, see: O'Malley, John W., SJ and Gauvin Bailey, eds. *The Jesuits: Culture, Science and the Arts: 1540–1773*. Toronto: University of Toronto Press, 1999. Now followed by a second volume, *The Jesuits II* (2006).
5. Michel de Certeau writes in *La fable mystique* that the Jesuits were perceived to be "trop enclins à exceller dans les sciences et préoccupés davantage par les travaux intellectuels que la pratique des vertus" (336).

Works Cited

Adorno, Theodor W. and Max Horkheimer. *Dialectic of Enlightenment*. Trans. Edmund Jephcott. Stanford, CA: Stanford University Press, 2002.
Alighieri, Dante. *The Divine Comedy: Purgatory*. Trans. Henry Wadsworth Longfellow. New York: Barnes and Noble Classics, 2005.
Amadis de Gaula. Ed. Ángel Rosenblat. Buenos Aires: Editorial Losada, 1940.
Armas, Frederick de. *Quixotic Frescoes: Cervantes and Italian Renaissance Art*. Toronto: University of Toronto Press, 2007.
Auerbach, Eric. *Mimesis: the Representation of Reality in Western Literature*. Princeton, NJ: Princeton University Press, 1954.
Avalle-Arce, Juan Bautista. *Don Quijote como forma de vida*. Madrid: Fundación Juan March, 1976.
Avila, Teresa de. *Libro de su Vida*. México: Editorial Porrúa, 1992.
Avilés, Luis F. *Lenguaje y crisis: las alegorías del Criticón*. Madrid: Editorial Fundamentos, 1998.
Baena, Julio. *El Círculo y la Flecha: Principio y Fin, Triunfo y Fracaso del Persiles*. Chapel Hill, NC: University of North Carolina Press, 1996.
———. *Discordancias Cervantinas*. Newark, DE: Juan de la Cuesta, 2003.
Bailey, Gauvin Alexander. *Between Renaissance and Baroque: Jesuit Art in Rome, 1565–1610*. Toronto: University of Toronto Press, 2003.
Barthel, Manfred. *The Jesuits: History and Legend of the Society of Jesus*. Trans. Mark Howson. New York: W. Morrow, 1984.
Barthes, Roland. *Sade, Fourier, Loyola*. Paris: Seuil, 1971.

Bataille, Georges. *L'expérience intérieure.* Paris: Gallimard, 1954.
Blunt, Anthony. *Roman Baroque.* London: Pallas Athene, 2001.
Bocaccio, Giovanni. *The Decameron.* Trans. Mark Musa and Peter Bondanella. New York: Penguin Books, 1982.
Borges, Jorge Luis. *A Universal History of Infamy.* Trans. Norman Thomas di Giovanni. New York: Dutton, 1972.
Borromeo, Charles. *Instructiones Fabricae et Supellectilis Ecclesiasticae.* Trans.Evelyn Carol Voelker. Diss. Syracuse University, 1977.
Boutoute, Eric. *Sade et les figures du Baroque.* Paris: l'Harmattan, 1999.
Braider, Christopher. *Refiguring the Real.* Princeton, NJ: Princeton University Press, 1993.
Buci-Glucksman, Christine. *La folie du voir : une esthétique du virtuel.* Paris: Galilée, 2002.
Bussagli, Marco. *Roma: Arte y Arquitectura.* Königswinter: Könemann, 2004.
Byron, William. *Cervantes, a Biography.* Woodstock, NY: Beekman Publishers, 1979.
Câmara, Luis Gonçalves de. *The Autobiography of Saint Ignatius Loyola* Trans.Joseph F. O'Callaghan. New York: Harper Torchbooks, 1974.
Carrette, Jeremy, ed. *Religion and Culture: Michel Foucault.* New York: Routledge, 1999.
Castillo, David R. *(A)wry views: Anamorphosis, Cervantes and the early Picaresque.* West Lafayette, IN: Purdue University Press, 2001.
Caveirac, Abbé de. *Appel à la Raison des Écrits et Libelles publiés par la Passion Contre les Jésuites de France.* Bruxelles: Vandenberghen, 1762.
Certeau, Michel de. *La Fable Mystique 1 : XVIe et XVIIe siècles.* Paris: Gallimard, 1982.
Cervantes, Miguel de. *Don Quijote de la Mancha.* Madrid: Alfaguara, 2005.
———. *Don Quixote.* Trans. Tobias Smollett. New York: Modern Library, 2001.
———. *Novelas Ejemplares I and II.* Ed. Harry Sieber. Madrid: Cátedra, 2000.
———. *Los Trabajos de Persiles y Sigismunda.* Ed. Juan Bautista Avalle-Arce. Madrid: Clásicos Castalia, 1969.
Cioranescu, Alexandre. *Le masque et le visage: du Baroque Espagnol au Classicisme Français.* Genève: Librairie Droz, 1983.
Culler, Jonathan. *Literary Theory: a very short introduction.* Oxford: Oxford University Press, 1997.
Cyrano de Bergerac, Savinien de. *Voyage dans la lune.* Paris: Garnier Flammarion, 1970.
Dandelet, Thomas James. *Spanish Rome: 1500–1700.* New Haven, CT: Yale University Press, 2001.
Deleuze, Gilles. *Présentation de Sacher-Masoch : le Froid et le Cruel.* Paris: Editions de Minuit, 1967.
———. *Différence et Répétition.* Paris: Presses Universitaires de France, 1968.
———. "The Fold" *Yale French Studies* 80 (1991): 227–247.
Deleuze, Gilles and Félix Guattari. *Capitalisme et Schizophrénie: 1. L'anti- Oedipe.* Paris: Editions de Minuits, 1980.
Delicado, Francisco. *Retrato de la Lozana Andaluza.* Madrid: Renacimiento, 1916.
De Man, Paul. "Roland Barthes and the Limits of Structuralism." *Yale French Studies* 77 (1990): 177–190.
Derrida, Jacques and Gianni Vattimo, eds. *La religion.* Paris: Seuil, 1996.
Descartes, René. *Discours de la Méthode.* Paris: Hachette, 1937.
———. *Méditations Métaphysiques.* Paris: Classiques Larousse, 1950.
———. *Principes de la Philosophie.* Rouen: Jean-Baptiste Besongne, 1698.
Dostoevsky, Fyodor. *The Grand Inquisitor.* New York: Continuum, 1995.

Duffy, Eamon. *Saints and Sinners: a History of the Popes.* New Haven, CT: Yale University Press, 2002.
Elizalde, Ignacio. *San Ignacio en la Literatura.* Madrid: Fundación Universitaria Española, 1983.
El Saffar, Ruth. *Novel to Romance: a study of the Novelas Ejemplares.* Baltimore: John Hopkins University Press, 1974.
El Saffar, Ruth and Diana de Armas Wilson, eds. *Quixotic Desire: Psychoanalytic Perspectives on Cervantes.* Ithaca, NY: Cornell University Press, 1993.
Favre-Dorsaz, André. *Calvin et Loyola : Deux Réformes.* Paris: Editions Universitaires, 1951.
Forcione, Alban. *Cervantes' Christian Romance: a study of Persiles y Sigismunda.* Princeton, NJ: Princeton University Press, 1972.
Foucault, Michel. *Les mots et les choses.* Paris: Gallimard, 1966.
Frappier-Mazur, Lucienne. "Sadean Libertinage and the Esthetics of Violence." *Yale French Studies* 94 (1998): 184–198.
Fumaroli, Marc. *L'âge de l'éloquence.* Paris: Champion, 1980.
García Gilbert, Javier. "En torno al género de *El Criticón* (y otros apuntes sobre la Alegoría)." *Documentos A: Genealogía Científica de la Cultura* 5 (1993): 104–115.
Girard, René. *Le bouc émissaire.* Paris: Grasset, 1982.
———. "Triangular Desire." *Literary Theory: an Anthology.* Eds Julie Rikvin and Michael Ryan. Oxford: Blackwell Publishers, 1998.
Gracián, Baltasar. *Oráculo Manual y Arte de Prudencia.* Madrid: Bibliotecas Cervantes, 1932.
———. *El Criticón.* Madrid: Cátedra, 1993.
———. *El Comulgatorio.* Ed. Aurora Egido. Zaragoza: Larumbe Clásicos Aragoneses, 2003.
Gregg, Ryan. "The Sacro Monte of Varallo as Physical Manifestation of the *Spiritual Exercises*." Online Posting. Spring 2004. *Athanor* 22. <http://www.fsu.edu/~arh/events/athanor/athxxii/ATHANOR% 20XXII_Gregg.pdf>
Hadot, Pierre. *Philosophy as a Way of Life: Spiritual Exercises from Socrates to Foucault.* Trans. Michael Chase. Oxford: Oxford University Press, 1995.
Hanrahan, Thomas. "Cervantes and the Moralists." *Hispania* 74. (December 1990): 906–920.
Harari, Josue. "Sade's Discourse on the Method: Rudiments for a Theory of Fantasy." *Comparative Literature* 36 (Dec 1984):1057–1071.
Harpham, Geoffrey Galt. "So . . . what is Enlightenment? An Inquisition into Modernity." *Critical Inquiry* 20 (Spring 1994): 524–556.
Hauser, Arnold. *The Social History of Art II: Renaissance, Mannerism, Baroque.* New York: Vintage Books, 1985.
Hénaff, Marcel. *Sade: the Invention of the Libertine Body.* Trans. Xavier Callahan. Minneapolis: University of Minnesota Press, 1999.
Hermans, Michel and Michel Klein. "Ces *Exercices Spirituels* que Descartes aurait pratiqués." *Archives de Philosophie* 59 (Jul-Sep 1996): 427–40.
Hook, Judith. *The Sack of Rome: 1527.* New York: Palgrave Macmillan, 2004.
Houle, Martha M. "What the Libertine and Jesuit have in Common, and the Posing of Literary Problem." *Libertinage and the Art of Writing* 2 (1992): 43–58.
Hutchinson, Steven. *Cervantine Journeys.* Madison, WI: University of Wisconsin Press, 1992.
Imperiale, Louis. *La Roma clandestina de Francisco Delicado y Pietro Aretino.* New York: Meter Lang, 1997.
Israel, Jonathan I. *Radical Enlightenment: Philosophy and the Making of Modernity 1650–1750.* Oxford: Oxford University Press, 2002.
Jones, Matthew L. "Descartes' Geometry as Spiritual Exercise." *Critical Inquiry* 28 (2001): 40–71.

Kallendorf, Hilaire. "Depicting Demons: Counter-Reformation Restraints and Baroque Representations." *The Center and Clark Newsletter* 37 (2001): 5–6.
Kasier, Theodore L. *The Truth Disguised: Allegorical Structure and Technique in Gracián's Criticón.* London: Tamesis, 1976.
Klein, Norman M. *The Vatican to Vegas: a History of Special Effects.* New York: The New Press, 2004.
Lacan, Jacques. *Le triomphe de la religion.* Paris: Seuil, 2005.
Le Brun, Annie. *Petits et Grands Théâtres du marquis de Sade.* Paris: Art Center, 1989.
Levy, Evonne A. *Propaganda and the Jesuit Baroque.* Berkeley: University of California Press, 2004.
Loyola, Ignatius. *Spiritual Exercises and Selected Works.* New York: Pauline Press, 1991.
Loyola, Ignace de. *Exercises Spirituels: Texte définitif.* Ed. Jean-Claude Guy. Paris: Seuil, 1982.
Lovett, A.W. *Early Hapsburg Spain:1517–1598.* Oxford: Oxford University Press, 1986.
Lucas, Thomas M. *Landmarking: City, Church and Jesuit Urban Strategy.* Chicago: Loyola Press, 1997.
Lupton, Julia Reinhard. *Afterlives of the Saints: Hagiography, Typology and Renaissance Literature.* Stanford, Calif.: Stanford University Press, 1996.
Luther, Martin. *The Bondage of the Will.* Grand Rapids, Michigan: Fleming H. Revell, 1995.
Lyons, John D. *Before Imagination: Embodied Thought from Montaigne to Rousseau.* Stanford, CA: Stanford University Press, 2005.
Maravall, José Antonio. *La cultura del barroco.* Madrid: Ariel, 1975.
———. *Utopia and counterutopia in the Quixote.* Detroit: Wayne State University Press, 1991.
Mazzara, Richard A. "The Philosophical-Religious Evolution of Théophile de Viau." *The French Review* 41 (1969): 618–628.
McGee, Dorothy. "Voltaire's *Candide* and Gracián's *El Criticón.*" *PMLA* (1937): 778–784.
Meissner, W.W. *Ignatius of Loyola: the Psychology of a Saint.* New Haven: Yale University Press, 1992.
Minor, Vernon. *Baroque and Rococo: Art and Culture.* London: Laurence King, 1999.
———. *Art History's History.* Upper Saddle River, NJ: Prentice Hall, 2000.
———. *The Death of the Baroque and the Rhetoric of Good Taste.* New York: Cambridge University Press, 2006.
Mitterand, Henri. *Littérature XVIIè siècle.* Paris: Hachette, 1992.
O'Malley, John. W., SJ. *The First Jesuits.* Cambridge, Mass: Harvard University Press, 1993.
O'Malley, John W., SJ and Gauvin Bailey, eds. *The Jesuits: Culture, Science and the Arts: 1540–1773.* Toronto: University of Toronto Press, 1999.
Ortes, Federico. *Triunfo de Don Quijote: Cervantes y la Compañía de Jesús, un mensaje cifrado.* Brenes (Sevilla): Muñoz Moya, 2002.
Paré, Ambroise. *On Monsters and Marvels.* Trans. Janis L. Pallister. Chicago: University of Chicago Press, 1982.
Pavone, Sabina. *I gesuiti dale origini alla soppressione.* Rome: Editori Laterza, 2004.
Pérez Valera, José Eduardo. *Una nueva lectura del Quijote.* México, DF: Universidad Iberoamericana, 1994.
Perugini, Francesca. *Images de la femme en Espagne au XVIè et XVIIè siècles.* Paris: Presses de la Sorbonne Nouvelle, 1994.
Raspa, Anthony. *The Emotive Image: Jesuit Poetics in English Renaissance.* Fort Worth: Texas Christian University Press, 1983.
Rey, Alain. *Dictionnaire Historique de la langue Française.* Paris: Robert, 1999.
Rico, Francisco, ed. *Historia y Crítica de la Literatura Española: Siglos de Oro: Renacimiento.* Ed.

Francisco López Estrada. Barcelona: Crítica, 1980.
Ribadeau-Dumas, François. *Dossiers Secrets de la Sorcellerie et de la Magie Noire*. Paris: Pierre Belfond, 1971.
Ribadeneira, Pedro de. *Vida de San Ignacio de Loyola*. Barcelona: Cortezo, 1888.
Ricoeur, Paul. *Figuring the Sacred: Religion, Narrative and Imagination*. Minneapolis: Fortress Press, 1995.
Riley, E.C. *Cervantes' Theory of the Novel*. Newark, DE: Juan de la Cuesta, 1992.
Robert, Marthe. *Roman des origines et origines du roman*. Paris: Grasset, 1972
Rubridge, Bradley. "Descartes's Meditations and Devotional Meditations." *Journal of the History of Ideas* 51 (1990): 27–49.
Sade, D.A.F. de. *Voyage d'Italie ou Dissertations critiques sur les villes de Florence, Rome, Naples, Lorette*. Paris: Fayard, 1995.
———. *Œuvres III : La Philosophie dans le Boudoir, Histoire de Juliette*. Paris: La Pléiade, 1998.
———. *Justine ou les infortunes de la vertu*. Paris: Libraire Générale Française, 1973.
———. *Les Cent Vingt Journées de Sodome*. Paris: Editions 10/18, 1975.
———. *Idées sur les Romans et sur le mode de la sanction des Lois*. Paris: Editions Mille et Une Nuits, 2003.
Siciliano, Ernest A. *The Jesuits in Don Quixote and other Essays*. Barcelona: Hisapam, 1974.
Sollers, Philippe. *Sade contre l'Être Suprême*. Paris: Gallimard, 1996.
Starobinski, Jean. *L'oeil vivant*. Paris: Gallimard, 1961.
Stohrer, Walter John. "Descartes and Ignatius Loyola: La Flèche and Manresa Revisited." *Journal of the History of Philosophy* 17 (Jan 1979): 11–27.
Spadaccini, Nicholas and Jenaro Talens, eds. *Rhetorics and Politics: Baltasar Gracián and the New World Order*. Minneapolis: University of Minnesota Press, 1997.
Stinglhamber, L. "Gracián et la Compagnie de Jésus." *Hispanic Review* 22 (1954): 195–207.
Thomson, Arthur. "Ignace de Loyola et Descartes: L'influence des Exercises Spirituels sur les œuvres philosophiques de Descartes." *Archives de Philosophie* (1972) : 61–85.
Trapiello, Andres. *Las vidas de Miguel de Cervantes*. Barcelona: Planeta, 1993.
Trousson, Raymond, ed. *Romans Libertins du XVIIIè siècle*. Paris: Robert Laffont, 1993.
Unamuno, Miguel de. "Alma Vasca." *Alma Española*. (Madrid, Jan 1904): 3–5.
Voltaire. *Candide ou l'optimisme*. Paris: Librio, 2002.
Wittkower, Rudolph, and Irma B. Jaffe, eds. *Baroque Art: the Jesuit Contribution*. New York: Fordham University Press, 1972.
Zayas, Maria de. *Desengaños Amorosos*. Madrid: Cátedra, 1983.
Ziolkowski, Eric. *The Sanctification of Don Quixote: from Hidalgo to Priest*. University Park, PA: Pennsylvania State University Press, 1991.
Žižek, Slavoj. *The Puppet and the Dwarf: the Perverse Core of Christianity*. Cambridge, Mass: MIT Press, 2003.

Index

A

Absolutism 3–4, 133–135, 157, 167
Acquaviva, Claudio 78, 99
Ackerman, James 76
Adorno, Theodore and Max Horkheimer 200, 204
Alberti, Rafael 216
Alcalá de Henares 10, 31, 55
Alighieri, Dante 36, 38, 62, 108, 134, 142, 147, 158–159, 235
Alonso, Damaso 216
Alumbrados 55
Amadis de Gaula 27, 33–34, 46, 107, 218–219, 228
Avilés, Luis viii, 147–149
Auerbach, Erich 120
Augustine of Hippo 2, 19, 42, 57, 70
Avalle-Arce, Juan Bautista 118

B

Baena, Julio 123, 130, 230, 232
Bachelard, Gaston 23
Bailey, Gauvin Alexander 7, 11, 73–74, 81, 87, 222, 227, 243
Bakthin, Mikhail 144
Barthel, Manfred 16, 40, 46, 48, 57, 135–138, 184, 217, 220, 241
Barthes, Roland 9–10, 14–39, 45–51, 72, 81, 89, 114–115, 145, 157, 173, 187–192, 198, 216–225, 231, 242
Bataille, Georges 15, 20–21, 49–50
Beauvoir, Simone de 17, 216
Benjamin, Walter 63–64, 223
Bergerac, Cyrano de 8, 168
Bernini, Gianlorenzo 11, 86, 203, 212–213, 226
Bildungsroman 198

Blanchot, Maurice 17, 216
Blunt, Anthony 81, 89, 227
Boccaccio, Giovanni 40, 62, 111, 241
Borromeo, Charles 11, 76–77, 89, 226–227
Boutoute, Eric 187, 199, 204
Braider, Christopher 44, 114
Brothers Kamarazov 50
Buci-Glucksman, Christine 25, 108, 155, 223, 237, 245
Bussagli, Marco 85

C

Calderón de la Barca, Pedro 92, 133–135, 216
Calvin, Jean 27, 55, 216, 222
Calvinist theology 51, 151, 177, 200
Câmara 34, 37–40, 58, 218–219, 221–223, 245
Candide 142, 181–183, 234,
Casuistry 103, 111–112, 134–136, 177–180, 234
Caravaggio 11, 105
Carrette, Jeremy 136
Cascardi, Anthony J. 43
Castillo, David 121–123, 126–129, 140
Caveirac (Abbé) 170, 241
Cervantes, Miguel de viii-ix, 5, 8–14, 30, 34–35, 40–42, 46, 94–132, 134–137, 139–145, 156, 165–171, 186, 199, 206–207, 210, 215, 217, 228–233
Certeau, Michel de—*La Fable Mystique* viii, 7, 18–21, 25, 37, 50, 64, 218, 243,
Charles V 12, 29, 224–225
Checa, Jorge 138, 160
Chivalry (novels of) 10, 27, 30, 33–42, 49, 106–107, 113–119, 189–191, 218–219, 228, 232
Cioranescu, Alexandre 167, 180, 234
Clement VII (Pope) 63, 66, 223–224
Colegio Romano 78, 89, 225

Comulgatorio 161–165, 239
Confessions 42
Corneille, Pierre 92, 216
Crébillon (Fils) 169, 181
Culler, Jonathan 19

D

Dandelet, Thomas James 44, 97–98, 156–157, 229
Da Vinci, Leonardo 236
De Armas, Frederick 99, 101
Deleuze, Gilles 18, 25, 79, 81, 188
Delicado, Francisco 63–64
Delon, Michel 199
DeMan, Paul 10
Descartes, René 13, 168–169, 173–181, 188, 202, 207–210, 240
Diderot, Denis 9, 133, 143, 169, 180, 207, 209, 240–241
Don Quixote 5, 12, 33–35, 42, 46, 94–123, 131, 140–142, 149–154, 165–166, 189, 210, 217–219, 228, 230–235, 240–242
Dostoevsky, Fyodor 15, 50

E

Egido, Aurora 162–165
Erasmus 3, 30–33, 55, 112, 215–218
Être Suprême (Sade) 193, 207, 243

F

Favre-Dorsaz, André 216
Felipe II (Philip II) 12
Flos Sanctorum 42, 44, 219
Forcione, Alban 126, 140, 143, 153
Foucault, Michel—*Les mots et les choses* 5, 18, 104–108, 116, 136, 171, 176, 199, 206, 217, 234, 243

Francis Borgia 43, 77
Francis of Assisi—*Franciscans* 2, 43–44, 50, 55, 219–220
Francis Xavier (Francisco Javier) 43, 48, 89, 158, 221
François I 29–30, 224
François de Sales 242
Frappier-Mazur, Lucienne 199, 203–205
French Revolution 2, 4, 14, 169, 171
Frye, Northorp 144

G

Galassi Paluzzi, Carlo 226
Galt Harpham, Geoffrey 206
Gargantua 111, 221, 235
Gassendi, Pierre 173–174, 215, 240
Gesú (Church) 60, 69, 74–91, 158, 187, 213, 226–227
grâce efficace 177
grâce suffisante 177
Gracián, Baltasar ix, x, 9–13, 123, 133–176, 181, 207, 210, 232–247
Guy, Jean-Claude 224–225

H

Habsburg (dynasty) 29
Hanrahan, Thomas 102–103
Hatzfeld, Helmut 105–106
Hauser, Arnold 19, 27, 49
Hegel, Friedrich 108, 211–214
Hénaff, Marcel 192, 196, 201, 211, 243
Henri IV 4
Hume, David 181
Homer (*Odyssey*) 38, 117
Hook, Judith 67
Houle, Martha 177–180
Huchinson, Steven 117–119, 122, 230

I

Idées sur les Romans (Sade) 207–208
Israel, Jonathan 240

J

Jakobson, Roman 25, 217
Jansenists 177–179, 183
Jansenius, Cornelius 177, 215
Jarry, Alfred 54
Jerusalem 11, 44, 49, 56–65, 89–93, 109, 152, 163, 220–221
Jesuitenstil 8, 75
John Francis Regis 43
Jones, Matthew L. 210, 215, 240

K

Kallendorf, Hilaire 144
Kassier, Theodore 153
Klossowski, Pierre 17, 216
Krauss, Werner 151, 158, 165, 235

L

Lacan, Jacques 23, 147, 185–186, 210, 241
Laclos, Choderlos de 186
La cultura del Barroco 52, 219, 236
La Fayette (Madame de) 241
La Flèche (collège) 174, 240
La Rochefoucauld 142
Leo X (Pope) 224, 226
Lesage 241
Lettres Provinciales (Pascal) 177–180
Levy, Evonne 8, 43, 58, 75–83, 216, 226–227
Lives of the Saints 27, 40–41, 49, 87
Locke, John 173
Louis XIII 172

Louis XIV 172
Louis XV 240–241
Louis-le-Grand (Lycée) 169–170, 181, 187, 199, 208, 242
Louvre (Palace) 152, 237
Lozana Andaluza 63–64, 222
Lucas, Thomas 69, 74, 81, 91, 221, 223, 226–227
Lukács, Georg 94–95, 108, 165, 231
Luther, Martin 2–4, 7, 25–32, 55, 63–71, 75, 93, 112, 151, 217, 221, 223, 225
Lyons, John D. 179, 242

M

Madonna della Strada 74, 226
Madrid 99, 143, 151–156, 182, 216, 237–239
Magisterium 1, 5, 70
Manresa (Spain) 15, 37, 57, 95, 223, 240, 249
Maravall, José Antonio 52, 112, 219, 236
Mazarin (Cardinal) 172
Mazzara, Richard 176
McGee, Dorothy 241
Meditations (Descartes) 174–175
Meissner, W.W. 57, 224–225
Michelangelo 226, 228
Mimesis 43, 46, 120
Minor, Vernon 86, 113, 166
Mithra (god) 223
Molière 180
Montesinos (Cave) 117–119, 235

O

Oath of Montmartre 56
O'Malley, John W. 16, 32, 35, 217, 227, 243
Ortes, Frederico 35, 46, 218, 230

P

Pacheco, Francisco 144
Paré, Ambroise 235
Paris (France) 10, 29, 31, 55–56, 62, 69, 151–157, 169, 177, 181, 192, 195, 219, 221, 238, 241
Parker, Alexander 31
Pavone, Sabine 69
Pascal, Blaise 13, 177–180, 241
Paul, Apostle 11, 57–60, 70, 221–222
Paul III (Pope) 68, 70, 88, 91, 224, 228
Paul IV (Pope) 88, 224
Pérez Valera, José Eduardo 109
Persiles 96, 121–132, 156, 232
Perugini, Francesca 148
Peter, Apostle 2, 11, 56–57, 61, 65, 91, 101, 224
Philip IV 143
Pozzo, Andrea 83, 213
Prévost (Abbé) 169, 181
Principes (Descartes) 176

R

Rabelais, François 111, 171, 204, 221, 235, 240
Racine, Jean 180
Raspa, Anthony 22, 45, 72, 220, 225
Read, Malcom K. 136
Reformation 2–5, 9, 13, 16, 22–32, 40–45, 53, 55, 58, 66–70, 75, 88, 92, 96, 104, 209, 211, 213, 241
Reinhard Lupton, Julia 27, 40
Ribadeau-Dumas, Francois 39, 219
Ribadeneira, Pedro 1, 30–33, 41–43, 55–60, 67–69, 77, 89–90, 106, 217–224, 230
Ricoeur, Paul 96, 166
Rikvin, Julie 59
Riley, E.C. 106, 117–118, 121, 132
Rojas, Fernando de 28
Roma Ignaziana 88–92, 129, 151, 156,

160, 199–202, 210
Rubidge, Bradley 175

S

Sade, D.A.F. marquis de 14, 17–19, 143, 157–159, 168–209
Saint Barthélemy (massacre) 4
Saint Peter's Basilica 65, 73, 75, 90–91, 97, 203–205, 224, 228
Sant'Andrea al Quirinale 73, 77–78, 84–87, 213, 226
Savonarola, Girolamo 63
Smollett, Tobias 110, 218, 230, 232
Sollers, Philippe 207, 243
Sorbonne (Université) 29, 31, 44, 55–56, 169, 221, 240
Spadaccini, Nicholas 135–136, 140, 144, 149, 151, 153, 159–160, 165, 235
Spazierengehen 63
Starobinski, Jean 95, 112, 230
Stinglhamber, L. 137

T

Teresa of Avila 19–20, 27, 33, 37, 43, 203
Thomson, Arthur 175
Trapiello, Andres 102, 104
Trent (Council) 25, 66, 77, 88, 107, 144, 226–228
Trévoux (Journal de) 240
Trousson, Raymond 172, 184

U

Unamuno, Miguel de 12, 35, 105
Utopia 18–19, 112, 153, 183, 248

U

Valdés, Alfonso de 63–64
Valmont (vicomte) 186
Varallo (Monte) 76, 247
Vatican 4, 57, 65, 68, 91, 202–207, 222, 226 243, 247
Vidriera, (Licienciado) 100–102, 128–129, 230
Virgil 108, 142, 150, 158–159, 238
Voltaire 13, 142–143, 168–169, 180–184, 207–209, 241, 248

W

Wittkower, Rudolf 8, 75–76, 81, 216, 227
Wöfflin, Heinrich 6

Z

Zayas, María de 153
Ziolkowski, Eric 106–107
Žižek, Slavoj 129, 183, 210–213